Mischa Elman
and the
Romantic Style

ALLAN KOZINN

Mischa Elman
and the
Romantic Style

 harwood academic publishers
Chur • London • Paris • New York • Melbourne

© 1990 by Harwood Academic Publishers GmbH, Poststrasse 22, 7000 Chur, Switzerland.   All rights reserved.

Harwood Academic Publishers

Post Office Box 197
London WC2E 9PX
England

58, rue Lhomond
75005 Paris
France

Post Office Box 786
Cooper Station
New York, New York 10276
United States of America

Private Bag 8
Camberwell, Victoria 3124
Australia

Library of Congress Cataloging-in-Publication Data

Kozinn, Allan.
    Mischa Elman and the romantic style / Allan Kozinn.
        p.   cm.
    Bibliography: p.
    Includes index.
    ISBN 3-7186-0497-3. — ISBN 3-7186-0491-4 (pbk.)
    1. Elman. Mischa. 1891–1967. 2. Violinists—Biography
I. Title.
ML418.E48K7 1990
787.1'092'4—dc19
[B]   89-30876
                                                          CIP
                                                          MN

Contents

Acknowledgments

This book could not have been written without the help of Mischa Elman's family and friends, whose reminiscences of the violinist gave me a feeling for the dimensions of his personality and the strength of his beliefs and passions that I would not have gleaned from the public record alone. Mrs. Helen Elman, in particular, discussed her husband freely, lovingly, and at considerable length in a series of interviews that began in 1983; and she generously provided a variety of essential materials, ranging from musical manuscripts to tapes and typescripts of her husband's lectures. Josef Elman, the violinist's son, also provided some insights into his father's views. And the violinist's youngest sister, Esther Elman, provided a great deal of invaluable information about her brother's early career in America.

Among the violinist's friends, I owe a special debt of gratitude to Mr. and Mrs. Edgard Feder for the unique memories they conveyed; to Jacques Francais, for the technical perspective he provided; and to Shirley Thomson, not only for her recollections, but for her enthusiastic support of this project and for her behind-the-scenes efforts on its behalf.

Most of all, I must thank Joseph Seiger, Elman's accompanist from 1952 though 1967, for spending countless hours recalling discussions he and Elman had during their daily practice sessions and their travels together; for explaining Elman's musicianship in a way that only a colleague and collaborator could; for playing me a number of unreleased recordings (as well as many that were long out-of-print and which predated his own involvement with Elman) that expanded my view of the violinist's art immeasurably; for lending a hand in some of the less immediately rewarding phases of fact-gathering and research; and not least, for being consistently available to answer my questions as they came up during the writing of the book.

I am also indebted to the Mugar Memorial Library at Boston University, the Lincoln Center Library of the Performing Arts, and the Manhattan School of Music, whose collections yielded a great deal of important and unique material; and the archives of the *New York Times*. James R. Oestreich, the editor of *Opus*, provided an array of stylistic and editorial insights that helped enormously in the preparation of the manuscript. Tim Page, of *Newsday*, provided many important out-of-print recordings and books from his comprehensive library, and his grasp of (and enthusiasm for) the Romantic style helped me clarify my own ideas on the subject. Dennis D. Rooney spent countless hours researching the discography. And thanks, finally, to my friends and colleagues who listened patiently to tales of Elman, and who provided insights of their own, as the project took shape.

Preface

Mischa Elman's career straddled a radical shift in interpretive styles and audience tastes—one of the broadest shifts of its kind to occur since the emergence of the virtuoso concert soloist early in the 19th century. By the time of his death, in 1967, he was regarded by many as something of an antiquarian novelty act, a violinist from a vanished era who, to the end of his days, championed the style that had prevailed in his turn-of-the-century youth, but which had been out of fashion for decades.

Born in a small, backwards Russian town in 1891 and trained in Odessa and St. Petersburg, Elman inherited a tradition that stressed personality, individualism, and above all, the urge to communicate, as the central components of an interpreter's art. It was a style that exalted subjectivity, and within its framework, sheer tonal beauty and bravura display were held to be virtues rather than excesses. It was a style rooted in the grandeur of the late 19th century, when Romanticism was at its zenith—not only as a musical, literary and artistic style, but as an outlook on life—and when the great performers were fueled by the same impulses that drove Mahler, Bruckner and Tchaikovsky to pour their hearts and souls into their works. And it was a style that stressed the dominance of the interpreter as a necessary and vital intermediary between the composer and the listener.

This was confessional musicmaking, in the sense that both the compositions and performances of the era thrived on pure emotion, crystalized into sound and conveyed to listeners in a forthright, unequivocal, thoroughly committed way. Elman absorbed this approach during his student years, not only from his teachers, Alexander Fiedelmann and Leopold Auer, but from violinists like Sarasate and Ysaÿe, singers like Caruso and Melba, and pianists like Godowsky and Moiseiwitsch, all of whom he knew during the first decades of his life,

when his tastes were forming and his own career was getting underway.

What he learned from these great performers became the basis of
his own interpretive language. Supporting that language was a bag of
technical tricks and gestures—his own idiomatic expressions, in a
sense—which, when applied in the right way, could transform both
great works and trivial ones into statements that communicated
warmth and emotional depth. Or, as Elman liked to put it, humanity.

Like all fashions, musical and otherwise, this intensely personalized
approach was transitory, a phenomenon of its age. As the 20th century unfolded, Romanticism receded quickly. That was inevitable, for
the ways of the world that dawned at the start of the 20th century were,
almost by definition, anti-Romantic. The world was shrinking, and its
pulse was quickening; and by the time the century was scarcely two
decades old, technologies had emerged that made it virtually impossible for those brought up in the 20th century to regard the world in
the same terms that their 19th century parents had. Electricity worked
a special kind of magic. The internal combustion engine made horse-
less carriages and flying machines possible. Warfare grew more
savage as technology took some of the legwork out of devastation; but
in times of peace, the new manufacturing methods made life easier in
ways that multiplied by the year. And through the new communication devices—radio, the phonograph, and later talking pictures and
television—various forms of entertainment and culture could reach
people by the thousands and even millions, thereby changing audiences from local to global ones.

Naturally, the spirit of this modern, scientific world was reflected
in its arts. In music, it meant a retreat from, and even a repudiation of,
the values of the Romantic era, a stance that affected both composition
and performance. Performers began to strive for a level of technical
perfection that mirrored the precision of the mechanized age. As a
result, performance standards improved astonishingly, although
there were many—Elman among them—who feared that this high-
gloss technical wizardry was gained at a cost in expressivity. Expressivity remained a crucial part of the art, of course; and while the new
style posed as a kind of rational objectivity (the logical antithesis of the
overt emotionalism of the Romantics) it really wasn't, for thoroughly
rational objectivity would have been the death of the art. Rather, it was
merely a new kind of expressivity, more subtle perhaps, but at its best,

it remained charged with the emotions that have always made music a vivid, relevant force.

There was a change, though, in the public's notion of what was to be expressed. To those who rejected Romantic subjectivity in favor of modern objectivity, music was entirely the composer's show, and his thoughts and intentions were to be explored and conveyed as directly as possible—i.e., with the minimum of interpretive interference from the performer. For those who took this view to its extreme, the performer was no longer a kind of mystical collaborator with the composer (as the Romanticists allowed him to be), but simply a transmitter of the composer's ideas, as enshrined in the written scores.

In this shuffle of old and new styles, the musical luminaries of the century's early years came to be regarded as out of fashion by much of the younger audience, which greatly preferred players who purveyed the more modern approach.

For Mischa Elman, a man who had been pronounced one of the world's greatest violinists before he was out of puberty, this swing in the public's taste was a source of considerable frustration. The idea of modernizing his style merely to fall into step with his colleagues would not have occurred to him, for while he did not perceive his approach as old-fashioned, he recognized and cherished its singularity.

Elman's story is a fascinating one, on a human level as well as on a musical one, but its essence lies in his art—and in his faith that its communicativeness would prevail. In a way, it did. As the pendulum reached the other end of the spectrum, both critics and audiences began to wonder whether expressivity *was* dying. Music schools were pouring forth streams of brilliant but faceless young technicians, players who could dazzle with speed, accuracy and attention to detail, but who seemed afraid to take the risks one must take to make the music say something. In recent years, a growing number of critics have written wistfully of the days when great personal stylists held the stage. And as the best of the younger players have come to understand that there's more to musicmaking than fidelity to the printed note, they have begun to assert themselves more daringly.

At that, a complete return to the style Elman championed is not in the cards; but of course, Elman's performances—preserved on the hundreds of discs he made between 1905 and 1966—can be appreciated on their own terms, as emissaries from a lost world of expansive gestures, unbridled emotion, and unabashed charm. His views of some of the standard violin works are out of step with those more common today, but the best of his performances show those works in an unusual and intriguing light.

One must approach them, however, with the understanding that all performance styles are, ultimately, fleeting and flexible, and that every style that has attained some currency in the course of musical history has something to tell us, something we can learn from. After all, a performance—the naive notions of the objective/literalists notwithstanding—cannot reflect the aesthetic of a composer's time without reference to the performer's, for the notes of the score must inevitably mingle with the player's own sensibilities, which are shaped by the age he lives in. In our time, with its emphasis on the quest for authenticity, it is not particularly fashionable to admit this. But Elman and the Romantics had no problem with it: they were expressing themselves through the music, and expressing the music through themselves.

One of Elman's colleagues, the violinist Joseph Szigeti, explained this rather succinctly in one of his books, *Szigeti on the Violin*: "Whenever I let colleagues or pupils listen to the recordings of [the great violinists of the early 20th century], I warn them not to judge these by the standards prevalent today and to take into account certain idiosyncrasies rooted in the *Zeitgeist*."

The *Zeitgeist*—the spirit of the time: that's the key to understanding Elman's work, and his life as well. At the start, his playing was fully in tune with this spirit; later, when the *Zeitgeist* ran in a different direction, he waged a quixotic battle against it. In tracing the thread of Elman's life—from his childhood in Russia, through the European and American triumphs of his youth, to the managerial squabbles and intense artistic rivalries of his middle years, and finally, through his years as the sole practitioner of the style he had absorbed as a child from the great violinists of the 19th century—I have tried to keep Elman's relationship to the *Zeitgeist* in perspective.

Elman was a man who evoked strong reactions. To those who understood and admired him, he was a giant. To others, he could seem difficult and egotistical. He was a collection of paradoxes—extraordinarily generous in certain circumstances, demanding and even petty in others; outgoing and jovial some of the time, but also critical of the musical world to the point of bitterness. But through it all, what he cared most about was stirring the souls of his listeners with the sound of his violin. Of course, the Romantic violin style Elman championed is nearly as vivid a character in this drama as Elman himself; and since, by its very nature, it was a style that had more sides than one man's performances could encompass, I have tried to give it a perspective of its own. Thus, in the early part of the book, which covers the period when Romantic interpretation still thrived, I have departed occasionally from Elman's story to examine the art of his predecessors and colleagues. I have also explored the transition to the modern style, to a degree; but that's a huge field that, ultimately, stretches beyond the scope of this book. As the paths diverged, therefore, the focus of my discussion centers more exclusively on Elman's own style, as well as the changes that accrued to it—and the critical and popular perception of it—over the decades.

Allan Kozinn

A concertgoer went backstage after a Mischa Elman recital, and, after speaking enthusiastically about the performance, asked:

"How does it feel to be Mischa Elman?"

"You know," Elman replied, "sometimes I think it's all a dream."

CHAPTER ONE:

The Bright Horizon, the Bleak Backdrop

It was a Thursday evening, the tenth of December 1908, at a few minutes past 9 o'clock, and a feeling of anticipation and electricity could be felt everywhere in Carnegie Hall, from the parquet seats to the upper balconies. Three quarters of an hour earlier, the Russian Symphony Society of New York opened the second subscription concert of its sixth season with *Finlandia,* Jean Sibelius's blaze of national spirit, plus an unusual new Russian work, Alexander Scriabin's *Poem of Ecstasy.* As the players shuffled the parts on their music stands, replacing the Scriabin with the Tchaikovsky Violin Concerto, Mischa Elman, a 17-year old violinist from a remote Russian village, stood backstage, as eager to make his American debut as the audience was to hear him.

Earlier in the week, large posters bearing a hazy, almost sultry profile photo of the curly-haired youth and his violin had been plastered on billboards all over town, and the local newspapers carried large advertisements announcing the concert. It was, by the standards of those pre-electronic days, a media event. Thus, by noon on the day of the concert, the lines at Carnegie Hall's ticket windows stretched out of the hall and down 57th Street, and by early afternoon, every seat was sold, even the few dozen added to the stage, alongside the orchestra. Still, at concert time several hundred music lovers milled outside the hall, hoping to secure a seat.

New York concertgoers, then as now, were inured to debuts—even debuts trumpeted with the lavish poster and publicity fanfare that Elman's new American manager, Henry Wolfsohn, had orchestrated. Yet, young Elman had captured the imagination of the city's musical

1

public. Even before the concert publicity hit full swing, the violinist's name carried a certain mystique, born of reports from abroad that proclaimed him a musical wonder. By his early teens, he had won the hearts of tough audiences and tougher critics in Berlin, Vienna, Paris and London, and he numbered European and Russian royalty among his admirers. Indeed, as a rising star, Elman rated the New York press's full celebrity treatment. When his entourage docked in New York, two days before the debut, the reporters turned out in force; and the portrait their articles painted was of a genial, sensitive young man, possessed of a quick sense of humor and, most crucially, a serious dedication to his instrument and its literature.

But European reviews and New York personality features were not all Elman had going for him—there was also word of mouth, and some powerful words had been spoken by some powerful mouths on Elman's behalf. American travelers in Europe who happened to catch his early performances there confirmed the musical press's tales of this *wunderkind*'s virtuosity and interpretive ingenuity; indeed, several of Carnegie Hall's first tier boxes were filled with listeners who were already staunch supporters.

One was the opera impresario Oscar Hammerstein, a savvy promoter whose Manhattan Opera House was then challenging the primacy of the Metropolitan Opera. Hammerstein's battle raged until 1910, when he sold his company to the Met for more than a million dollars. But while it lasted, his venture was considered the more enlightened and adventurous, and his first discussions with Elman were typical of his flair for artistic experimentation. After hearing the violinist at a London charity gala, earlier in 1908, Hammerstein was so convinced that Elman would be a success in New York that he offered him not only a string of Sunday recitals at the opera house, but an unusual cameo role: for $1,000, Elman would play the "Méditation" from Massenet's *Thaïs*, from the orchestra pit, during a Manhattan Opera House production of the work starring Mary Garden. It was agreed, however, that Elman's first performances in the New World should feature him as a concerto soloist. And so Hammerstein sat back in his Carnegie Hall box to take in the concert as a mere spectator—almost.

Backstage, Elman clasped his violin[1] in his left hand, and with a confident smile he signaled his readiness to Modest Altschuler, the orchestra's conductor. If he was nervous, he didn't show it. He was, after all, a seasoned performer, and the idea of facing a large audience

filled him with excitement, not fear. Even so, he couldn't help thinking of this concert as a turning point, not only professionally, but personally. Until now, he was presented as a child virtuoso. Beginning
with this concert, though, he would be presenting himself as a mature,
adult artist. Aware that the American public and critics were suspi-
cious of the charms of juvenile talent, Saul Elman—the violinist's
father and the overseer of his training and career from the start—
decided that the time was right for a metamorphosis. Gone forever
were the navy and white sailor suits Elman had performed in across
the ocean: tonight he donned full evening dress, and he felt suitably
dashing and self-assured—enough so to jokingly demand a raise in
his allowance, to cover the wardrobe and entertainment costs an adult
career would necessitate.

If Mischa Elman himself felt ready to be judged as a fully formed
musician, Saul Elman quietly fretted about the perils of failure in New
York; and as he took his seat in the hall, he apprehensively surveyed
the sea of faces around him. He needn't have worried. As Elman strode
onto the stage, with Altschuler two paces behind him, the audience,
which had not yet heard him put bow to string, poured forth a torrent
of applause that lasted for several minutes. The violinist bowed a few
times, and tentatively ran his thumb across the strings of his instrument, checking its tuning one last time amid the tumult.

Finally, the applause died, and the orchestra's strings, followed by
the winds, embarked on the stately dialogue that introduces the
Tchaikovsky Concerto. Elman, buoyed by the warmth of the
audience's greeting and seized with an urge towards the dramatic,
swung his instrument to his chin in a grand, theatrical gesture, and set
his bow on the G string. The work seemed custom-tailored for him[2].
In the first notes of the slowly unfolding solo violin line, he drew forth
the rich, molasses-like tone that would soon become his trademark,
but as the first movement unfolded, he met the challenges of
Tchaikovsky's quick, fiery passage work with an astounding blend of
speed and precision. And so on for the rest of the score: the golden
tone returned for the lyrical middle movement, and was again
counterbalanced with virtuosic zest and fire in the finale.

"He felt," Saul Elman wrote, some 25 years after the auspicious
debut,[3] "as though he knew this public, as though he had played for
them for years.... His playing apparently surpassed all their expectations, and the listeners sat perfectly still without a move or a whisper,
with eyes fixed on the boy. As I watched their expressions, I could

plainly see that they were making a strenuous effort to coordinate their sense of sight with that of hearing, finding it difficult to believe that the heavenly tone ringing in their ears came from a violin played by the pale-faced boy in front of them—the manly dress did not for a moment conceal Mischa's youth, as he looked more like a schoolboy than an artist.

"Greatly inspired by the tremendous ovation," the elder Elman continues, "he summoned to his aid all the power of his virile temperament, and never before had his tone breathed greater vigor, nor been more subtle, radiating a gentle pleasing warmth that charmed the senses. The boy himself was in ecstasy. Never before had he poured out his soul so fully as he did on that memorable evening. He tore at his violin with a vigor and passion that gripped the heart. I first realized the full depth of his inspiration when I looked at him while he was waiting for the accompaniment. He posed for a moment. It was not a pose of rest. He was all impatience. His eyes flashed fire. His hands gripped the violin and bow, ready to strike anew at the given moment."

Saul Elman's recollections may have been colored by paternal enthusiasm, but the music critics in the audience documented the performance with prose nearly as flowery. The *New York Herald*'s reviewer noted the beauty of Elman's sonority and the flawlessness of his intonation, and waxed rhapsodic about his technique. "His trills, double stopping, runs and harmonics will impress every violinist as little short of extraordinary," the critic wrote, adding that "in brilliant cadenzas the music comes in dazzling scintillations." The critic from the *New York Times* noted "the exuberance of youth" in Elman's playing, while the representative from the *New York Tribune* wrote of the "flexibility, smoothness and energy [that] marked all he did in the Tchaikovsky Concerto," thereafter reciting the litany of techniques in both slow and fast passages that young Elman had mastered to "a lofty standard of perfection."

The critic for the *World* was more reserved, and was alone in suggesting that the performance was not blemish free, but he too was enthusiastic: "If there were a few slips of intonation, due to the tensity of excitement of the moment," he wrote, "if the sentiment of the *Canzonetta* seemed a little restrained and shallow at times, these were incidents at which it would be hypercritical to cavil in the face of an art so commanding and so magnetic." And finally, when the next edition of *Musical America* hit the stands, on December 19, the praise was even more effusive:

"Full of fire and Slavic passion," that journal's critic wrote, "he prosecutes his task with a dramatic intensity, a swing and dash, that completely subordinate the absolute technical mastery of his instrument which, while constantly impressing his hearers, is never obtrusive—never emphasized at the sacrifice of the glowing temperament that throbs through every strain from his bow. His tone is full and vibrant, the lower notes losing nothing in resonance and tonal charm. His cantabile is beautifully expressive and in the lighter lyrical passages he makes his violin sing and sob. In the cadenzas he shows resources little short of extraordinary."

The Tchaikovsky Concerto ends with a quickly ascending exclamation from the solo violin, and a few bars of hearty orchestral punctuation; and that December evening in 1908, a wave of frenzied applause filled Carnegie Hall as soon as the last orchestral chord was struck. The audience was on its feet when Elman returned to the stage for his first curtain call, and he came out several more times, eventually having to be shepherded away by Wolfsohn, who signalled to the audience that the young virtuoso was in need of rest. The debut, actually, was by no means over for him. After the intermission, the orchestra's strings played Tchaikovsky's sweet *Andante cantabile* from the String Quartet, Op.11 (a work Elman would later record himself, both in a violin and piano arrangement, and with the Elman String Quartet). Then Elman returned to play Wieniawski's *Souvenir de Moscow*, an unabashedly splashy display piece calculated to dazzle—and in Elman's hands, every bit as explosive as the work Altschuler used to close the concert, Tchaikovsky's *1812 Overture*. Again, Elman's performance was greeted thunderously, and this time, after several curtain calls, he offered an encore, the Gossec *Gavotte*.

On leaving the hall with a small entourage that included his managerial triumvirate—his father, Henry Wolfsohn, and his British agent, Daniel Mayer—plus Waldemar Liachowsky, his German-born accompanist, general secretary and friend, Elman found the sidewalk outside Carnegie Hall's 56th Street stage door lined with well-wishers, who applauded as he made his way out of the hall. He had come through this trial by fire triumphantly. But of course, his work was now only beginning. Before returning to London, the following April, he would play the Tchaikovsky again with the Boston Symphony, and he would give recitals as far south as New Orleans, as far west as Denver, and as far north as Montreal, with stops in Washington, Chicago, Cleveland and a handful of other cities. Already on his mind, though, was his next New York concert—his first solo recital in the United States, and a performance that was in many ways as crucial as this evening's orchestral debut. With Liachowsky accompanying him, he planned to open with a violin and piano reduction of Lalo's *Symphonie Espagnole*, followed with sonatas by Bach and Handel, the Sinding Suite, and a handful of popular arrangements that included Joachim's recasting of the Brahms *Hungarian Dance* No.4, August Wilhelmj's gorgeous transcription of Schubert's *Ave Maria*, and the expanded version of Paganini's twenty-fourth *Caprice* concocted by Elman's teacher in St. Petersburg, Leopold Auer.

Elman couldn't help but think about old Auer during the cab ride back to the Knickerbocker Hotel. And looking around him at New York's lights, tall buildings, and broad roads filled with automobiles, trolley cars and elevated railways, he couldn't help reflecting on the long and winding road he had traveled. At 17, he looked back at a path that took him from a feudal, scarcely civilized town in Russia, to the capitals of Europe, where elegance reigned, to this, the city of the future.

❖ ❖ ❖ ❖ ❖

Carnegie Hall opened on May 5, 1891, with a program that included several works by Tchaikovsky, conducted by the composer. Three and a half months earlier, on January 20, Saul and Yetta Elman of Talnoye, a small village in the Ukraine, near Uman and Kiev, celebrated the birth of a son who they named Mikhail, but who would thereafter be addressed in the diminutive form, Mischa.[4] The idea of such a place as Carnegie Hall, or of New York for that matter, was beyond the imagination of the Elmans and their neighbors; indeed, from the perspective of Talnoye, New York might as well have been another planet. The distance between the two places, at the turn of the century, was one that a mere measurement in miles could not convey.

Imagine the world Elman was born into. The concept of divine right was alive and well throughout Europe. Russia was ruled by Tsar Alexander III, whose son, Nicholas II, would be deposed in the revolution of 1917. In Germany, the headstrong Kaiser Wilhelm II was devising ways to win his country a place in the sun; while in England, Queen Victoria ruled an Empire on which the sun never set. In the United States, Benjamin Harrison sat in the White House, and Henry

Ford's first automobile wouldn't hit the road for another five years. The airplane, too, was still a science fiction dream. Travel over land was accomplished either by pure horse power, or by locomotive, and travel by sea was a time-consuming occupation—but, in its way, an elegant one that Elman would eventually find quite enjoyable.

It was a time, too, when many of the great composers still walked the earth. Brahms was alive, and so were Dvořák, Grieg, Rimsky-Korsakov, Gounod, Saint-Saëns, Puccini, Mahler and Bruckner. Debussy was not yet 30, and Ravel was about to turn 15. Stravinsky, Bartók, Berg and Webern were children. Movies and their stars were not yet born, but through the flourishing newspapers and illustrated magazines of the time, people spent their leisure hours keeping tabs on the stage actors, opera singers and musicians whose glittering reputations had captured their imaginations. Not that news of these stars travelled quickly to distant outposts like Talnoye. In fact, at the time of Mischa Elman's birth, the only truly world-class musical figure his father had heard of was the virtuoso violinist Nicolo Paganini— who had died 51 years earlier.

The society the Elmans lived in was isolated and insulated from this world. For them, even the Tsar was a distant figure, more myth than reality. Sitting in St. Petersburg, some 350 miles to the north, he ruled his vast nation by proxy, through a feudalistic system of local landowners who wielded complete power. Talnoye was situated on the property of a Count Scuvalov, and within its complex class system, the Elmans were not high on the ladder. During the early years of his marriage, Saul Elman sold hay by the bushel. But he was also a Talmudic scholar, like his father, and he supplemented his marketing income by giving Hebrew lessons.

The Jewish community in Talnoye, as in all Russia, was set apart— as Saul Elman puts it at the start of his *Memoirs of Mischa Elman's Father*, "We Elmans are children of the Ghetto." That ghetto, however, was a tightly knit community with a structure and, most crucially, a cultural tradition of its own. And the Elman family was deeply involved in that cultural side.

Saul Elman's *Memoirs* trace the family back to his grandfather, "a man of learning and local distinction," he tells us, who lived in Berdichev, about 40 miles southwest of Kiev and nearly 65 miles northwest of Talnoye. This first Elman was a *tallis*-maker—a weaver of prayer shawls—and a devoutly religious man who immersed himself in Talmudic wisdom. But he had also cultivated a sideline skill: he had taught himself to play the violin. In his last years, when failing sight made it impossible to continue weaving and studying, he turned this intuitive violin playing into a livelihood by becoming a *badchen*.

Part musician, part jester, the *badchen* played at various rites of passage—weddings, *bar mitzvahs*, funerals. His repertoire consisted of traditional songs with melodic outlines related to those of Hebrew prayer. It was, like the music of the black slaves in the southern United States, a genre tinged with the bitter sadness of oppression, although (again, like the Negro spiritual literature), it also contained songs of joy and hope. A hint of this musical accent can be heard today in Orthodox Jewish synagogues, largely because the music favored this most traditionalist branch of Judaism is based predominantly on a blend of ancient chant and Eastern European melody, both in prayer and in the non-sacred folk songs sung during holiday celebrations.

To modern Western musical ears, much of this music's expressivity comes from what might seem an overriding use of the minor mode. Yet, it's more complicated than major or minor. Rather, it is a musical language that bears the traces of the long, slow migration from the Middle East, through Asia minor, to the northern climes of Eastern Europe. There is certainly something Russian-sounding about it—the weeping character of some of its tunes are not far removed from the opening violin lines of Tchaikovsky's *Sérenade mélancolique*. By comparison though, much of the sad-tinged Russian folk music that we now hear channeled through the works of Borodin, Mussorgsky, Prokofiev and Shostakovich sounds somewhat squarer and simpler than the Hebraic folk-songs of the *badchen*, for this music's Middle Eastern roots give it far greater melodic flexibility. Beyond the whole and half steps of the Western scale, this music allows for an expressive meandering around and between what we would think of as the principal notes of the melodies.

It is, after all, primarily vocal music, and its singers were expected to apply whatever vocal "tears" and other tonal shadings the words required. In the instrumental realm, this tradition transferred most easily to the violin. Besides being portable and comparatively inexpensive, the instrument's unfretted neck allowed for a flexible intonation that let players manipulate notes with as much nuance as singers could; and the earliest *badchen* came to understand that by exploiting this quality, they could heighten the mood of the occasion for which they were playing. A good *badchen*, it was said, could draw tears of joy at weddings, and tears of grief at funerals, through the quality of his tone.

To this day, many listeners look back with a sense of wonder at the stream of Jewish violinists who poured forth from Russia at the turn of the century, bringing a uniquely emotional and individualistic brand of interpretation to European and American concert stages; and the flow continues still, with the generation of Israeli-born fiddlers, whose parents or grandparents came to Israel from Russia. The thread is an almost constant one, starting with Elman and continuing with Jascha Heifetz and the other Auer disciples, and later followed by Isaac Stern, Pinchas Zukerman, Itzhak Perlman and Shlomo Mintz. But there should be no mystery about the origin of this special expressivity: the tradition of the *badchen* is the inner light from which the 20th century Jewish violin style was kindled, and its resonance can also be felt in the work of Jan Peerce, Richard Tucker and other Jewish opera singers.

Mischa Elman's great-grandfather, the *badchen* of Berdichev, had an advantage over many of his colleagues. In Russian Jewish society, the musician was appreciated as an artisan of sorts, yet he occupied a low place in the social order. As a scholar and a *tallis*-maker, though, this particular *badchen* had a social advantage, and during his pre-musician years, he fraternized with other scholars and, most importantly from a musical standpoint, with the best of the town's cantors. Through the cantors, he learned the subtleties of the Hebrew musical culture; and his own background provided the connecting link between the techniques of this kind of musicianship and the spirituality that informed it. His son, Mischa Elman's grandfather, was named Josef, and he too was attracted to the violin. Accompanying his father to weddings and parties, and listening closely to the way he made his instrument evoke the spirit of the occasion, he taught himself to play, and devoted himself entirely to musicianship. It was a decision he later regretted. His father had become a *badchen* only in his years of "retirement," and had managed to maintain the social station he had enjoyed until then. Josef, a musician from the start, was part of the artisan class.

When he was still quite young, Josef Elman left Berdichev to become a professional musician in Uman, a town about 45 miles to the southeast, and quite close to Talnoye. There, and in neighboring towns, he rose to considerable local renown. Saul Elman testifies that his father was frequently "invited by Russian landowners to play at banquets—a singular honor for a Jewish musician.... A wedding without him was regarded as a failure, and bore even more resemblance than usual to a funeral. His playing of folk songs unlocked the treasures of their emotions, and Russians love to weep as much as to laugh." His strong point was said to be the quality of his tone; and townspeople who eventually heard his famous grandson perform conveyed their belief that Mischa Elman's tone was inherited from his grandfather. Yet, in spite of all that, Josele Umaner, as he was popularly known, was ostracized socially. "Yesterday," he would complain to his son, "people applauded my playing. But today, they meet me on the street and ignore me."

Consequently, Josef Elman saw to it that his son Saul stayed clear of music, and that he devoted himself to a course of religious study that would restore the family's status to what it was in his father's time. Saul loved music, but heeded his father's advice—at least, until he married and moved to Talnoye. His bride, the former Yetta Fingerhood, also came from a family tainted by professional musicians, and she enjoyed music as much as Saul did. So, on the pretext of having found a customer for one of Josef's extra violins, Saul wrote to his father asking him to send the instrument to Talnoye. He knew enough about the instrument to tune it and pick out a few melodies, preferring to pluck the strings rather than bowing them. Saul never nursed professional hopes: For him, his guitar-like violin was a pleasant pastime.

At the time of Mischa's birth, the Elmans lived in a three-room hut, with a roof of thatched straw and a dirt floor. Although he lived there for only two years, the memory of the place stayed with Mischa Elman throughout his life. "There was a living room and a bedroom," he recalled much later in life, "then you went into the kitchen where they had a big oven. It seemed to be made of dirt. It heated the whole house. I was impressed by the fact that when it was very cold, there were steps on the outside of the oven, and there was enough room behind it to warm yourself.... The toilet was in the yard. There was no bath: People went to the public bath, in the town."[5]

Mischa was the second son born to Yetta and Saul. The first died in infancy before Mischa was born, as did a third. A fourth son lived to the age of five, and died of injuries sustained in a fall. Elman's three sisters—Mina (born 1893), Liza (born 1902) and Esther (born in London, in 1905) lived to see their brother's success, and Liza and Esther survived him.

In 1893, soon after Josef Elman died, and after the birth of Mina, Saul ascertained that both the hay selling business and the market for Hebrew lessons would be greater in Shpola, a larger town about 15 miles to the northeast, situated on lands owned by the Countess Urusova. The family moved there, settling in a grey stucco house somewhat larger than the one in Talnoye, located near the wheat fields where the peasants worked. Times were not bright. "We were so poor," the violinist later recalled, "that the idea of having flowers in the house—I don't think my father or mother ever thought of them. We never observed birthdays. People couldn't think of things like that, because it would mean spending money." It was in this bleak setting, though, that Elman's interest in music was sparked. On winter evenings, the family would sit near the stove after dinner, and Saul would pick out folk tunes on his violin. He also, by then, had a guitar, on which he accompanied himself and his family during their evening sing-alongs. When Mischa was three years old, Saul noticed that the child took more interest in the violin than in his toys, and that he had learned to sing his father's folk tunes. His singing, accompanied by Saul's plucking, soon became a form of family entertainment, and as Saul writes in his *Memoirs*, Mischa "quickly learned to exploit the rest of us, and realizing how the demand for his [vocal] solos grew, he began to use them to get himself out of scrapes. Whenever he did something wrong and was detected he would immediately offer to sing! This was usually sufficient atonement."

The idea that his son might be exceptionally talented had not yet occurred to Saul Elman, whose deeply ingrained distaste for the professional musician's lot led him to insist that the violin be kept out of his son's way. By the time Mischa was five, though, he had discovered where his father hid the instrument, and began trying to play it in secret. Unaware that the instrument was normally played with a bow, he emulated his father and plucked the strings with his thumb— quietly, so that his mother, working in the kitchen, would not hear him. Apparently a patient child, he worked quietly by himself for several months; but the size of the instrument defeated him, and he failed to discover how his father managed to draw recognizable tunes from the tightly strung wooden box.

But he grew obsessed with the problem, and as it became clear to him that his efforts were yielding little, he became depressed, and confessed his secret desire to play the violin. Saul saw resonances of his own suppressed musicianship in his son, and decided to ignore his father's warnings and allow the child to play. A few days later, he brought home a miniature violin, and showed Mischa how the bow worked. Not yet in school, Mischa devoted considerable his time to this new toy; and within a few weeks, he had mastered a waltz called *Daisy*. His accomplishments were, perforce, elementary and intuitive; but Saul was impressed with the accuracy of the child's pitch, and as a proud father, he naturally couldn't help wondering whether his son's explorations revealed a special talent that should be nurtured.

Shpola had a little *ad hoc* orchestra that gave concerts in the parks and performed at weddings, led by a conservatory-trained conductor who was a local celebrity. It was obvious to Saul that this was the man to judge Mischa's talent, so one day he turned up at an orchestra rehearsal, Mischa and his miniature fiddle in tow, and approached the conductor. As Saul recalled that encounter in his *Memoirs*, the musician was uninterested in hearing the child, and he told Saul that the ability to play a couple of easy tunes didn't necessarily signify a great talent. The true test of talent and musicality, he said, was an ability to play with accompaniment; whereupon Saul suggested that the orchestra might accompany his son in a short selection to complete the audition. Saul does not tell us what the orchestra and Mischa played—possibly *Daisy* again—but he reports the conductor was impressed with the child's ability to keep up with the ensemble, unflustered by the circumstances. "Gentlemen," he told his players, "I must admit this boy is a wonder." For the next month or so, he took the child under his wing and taught him the rudiments of notation—harshly, it seems, for Elman later recalled that failure to recognize the notes resulted in a spanking.

Word of his orchestral trial, meanwhile, spread quickly around Shpola, and the family found itself in the limelight, both among their Jewish neighbors and in the town at large. Eventually, those at the higher end of the social order heard about the talented child, and Countess Urusova arranged for a command performance. Obviously, the Elmans were honored by the nobility's interest, but it had a bitter undercurrent for them, too. Not long before the Countess's interest was piqued, the Jews of Shpola had endured the ravages of a fierce, anti-Semitic pogrom. Interestingly, Saul Elman described this particular horror with cinematic but entirely impersonal detail. The Countess's request to hear Mischa play came "after Easter," he wrote, "shortly following the Massacre of Shpola. The town's wounds were not yet healed; the pillaged homes still remained in their wrecked state; the ugly gaps in the walls, shattered windows and doors served as reminders of days of horror. Still fresh in our minds were the images of the blood-stained lifeless forms of our martyrs as they lay butchered in the streets. The atmosphere was stifling."

Mischa was not too young to be deeply impressed with the terror of the incident, and although he rarely discussed it in interviews, his memories were quite detailed—if, in some respects, at odds with his father's dramatic portrayal. He did recount the incident for one interviewer, providing the details of the family's experience that Saul left out of his *Memoirs*: "I remember it was a wintry day, in the afternoon. My father used to go to pupils' houses, so he wasn't home. All of a sudden, we heard screams and the sound of stones on windows and doors. And I remember my mother saying, 'I hope father will manage to come home.' My father did get home, and when he came in, they locked the doors. They darkened the house with curtains, put out the kerosene lamps, and we went into the cellar. We stayed there for four days. I suppose we had something to eat. Why did it happen? When the peasants got drunk, they said, 'let's beat the Jews,' and the police did not control them. I'm not so sure anyone got killed. They damaged houses."[6]

The peasants rampaged with relative impunity, their punishment being nothing more than a brief detention period. Countess Urusova was in Paris at the time, and upon receiving news of the pogrom, she returned to Shpola and instituted an investigation; but as far as Shpola's Jews were concerned, the findings were an unsatisfactory whitewash, perpetrated by her estate manager who, they believed, was one of the instigators. The town's Jews formed a committee and put together their own report, but the Countess refused to hear it, and her underlings put about the rumor that the trouble was actually started by the Jews themselves, as a form of self-chastisement. It was against this scenario that Shpola at large began to take interest in young Mischa, and Saul had mixed feelings about this interest. Various local dignitaries—the town druggist and the town judge, for instance, two comparatively powerful forces in Shpola society—turned up at the Elman house to hear the child play *Daisy*, and reported to the Countess that the child was indeed worth hearing. Saul Elman's first inclination was to refuse to let Mischa play for her; but his friends argued that such a refusal would only fuel the pervasive current of anti-Semitism. Saul accepted, and a carriage was sent to collect him and Mischa.

The audition was a strange one: Mischa spoke no Russian, only Yiddish, so Saul stood in as interpreter as the Countess sat the little violinist on her knee and asked him questions. After thus setting him at ease, she asked him to play, and then made a radical proposal: she wanted to *buy* the boy from Saul, and to raise him not only as a Christian, but as one to whom the privileges of class would accrue. Saul grew livid as the interview continued, and when he declined the Countess's offer, she summoned a young priest, who suggested that cultivating young Mischa's talent required this ultimate parental sacrifice. The seething father, afraid to allow his anger free reign, remained silent, took his son's hand and started to leave.

The Countess had an alternate plan, though, one Saul could accept—namely, the offer of her own son's private music teacher. Even at that, Saul insisted that he be present at all of Mischa's lessons, lest the Countess try to tempt the child with the trappings of a palatial life so vividly distinct from his family's. Alas, the teacher was not as entranced with young Mischa as Saul would have liked, and as Saul saw it, if Mischa's playing was improving, it was by dint of his own hard work and a healthy amount of paternal guidance, not because of his fancy new music master. At the same time, Mischa began learning Russian and other elementary subjects, also through teachers provided by the Countess; and he became friendly with the Countess's son.

Eventually, the Countess decided it was time to show off the product of her benevolence, so she arranged a public concert—a debut for her six-year old protege, with the proceeds of the ticket sales going to the Elman family. Saul Elman's *Memoirs* don't tell us what was on the program; his concern, rather, was with the darker side of what should have been a thoroughly joyful day. On the morning of the concert, he learned that by order of the Countess, Jews were to be barred from the hall. In any case, all the tickets had been sold, and there were dignitaries coming from other towns to hear little Elman—so there was little Saul could do. "Now I was compelled to be a party to this shame," he wrote. "My child was to amuse those who in their blind passion had forgotten even the most elementary principles of human justice and who were going to hear and admire a poor Jewish boy, and make this an occasion for expressing their abhorrence of his people. The very thought was maddening."

At the concert, Saul sat at the back of the hall, hoping to leave with Mischa the second the performance was over. That was impossible, of course: the upscale audience wanted to fawn over the prodigy, and the Countess wanted to show him off. Walking up to the stage, she picked the child up and carried him up the aisle, stopping to let her friends offer words of encouragement. Saul trailed behind, silently but with a bearing that made it clear that he, a common Jew, was the child's father.

But if the humiliation of this debut seemed a dark cloud, the time, it had a silver lining. Saul felt it would be impossible to continue to accept the Countess's patronage after her barring of the Jews from Mischa's concert, and he spent the night of the event pondering this dilemma. By morning, a plan had emerged. He would take Mischa south to Odessa, a thriving metropolis compared with Shpola, and a city where Mischa could no doubt receive a far better musical education than the Countess could provide.

On the day of their departure, Saul and Mischa visited the Countess, who urged them to wait, but to no avail. Their parting was cordial, however, and the Countess supplied them with letters of introduction (which, it turned out, were of little use). Leaving Yetta and Mina in Shpola, Saul and Mischa set off on the three day wagon journey to Odessa, with the hope that Mischa would be accepted at the city's Imperial Academy of Music.

CHAPTER TWO:

Formal Studies,
and a Taste of Touring

Saul and Mischa Elman arrived in Odessa towards the end of summer 1897, and rented a dingy room behind a junk dealer's shop in one of the town's shabbier districts. Saul's immediate aim was to enroll his son at the Imperial Academy of Music, and he quickly established contacts with those who might help, including the widow of a wealthy arts patron named Puritz. After her husband's death, Mrs. Puritz had established a small music school for talented but poor children, in her home. Prevailing upon her connections in the musical world, she secured the services of a music teacher; and she donated her own services as general schoolmistress, teaching her charges mathematics, history and science between music lessons.

The teacher Mrs. Puritz had engaged for these classes was a young violinist, Alexander Fiedelmann. Fiedelmann listened to Mischa play, and gave him an elementary ear-training test before volunteering to teach him privately. Saul immediately proposed that Mischa be brought to the Academy, but Fiedelmann insisted that the boy was too young, and should study privately first. Saul was never convinced of the wisdom of this, and it was the first of many clashes Fiedelmann and the elder Elman would have. At the time, Saul did not feel sufficiently secure about the ways of music education to challenge the teacher, but as the months passed, the two came to be almost constantly at loggerheads over aspects of Mischa's education and early performance career. Indeed, Saul ended up disliking Fiedelmann so intensely that he refused to use his real name in his *Memoirs*, let alone credit him with the crucial part he played in Elman's early musical training.[1] Instead, he noted that "our troubles indeed began with this man's entry into our lives."

Whatever the personality clashes between teacher and father, Mischa Elman had much fonder recollections of Fiedelmann. He described him as a young man, pleasant looking and given to a few artistic affectations; and they were apparently on intimate enough terms for Mischa to call his teacher by the diminutive form of his name, Sascha. Later in his life, Elman insisted on giving Fiedelmann full credit for laying the foundation of his playing. "He was an excellent talent," Elman once told an interviewer, adding that "he wasn't a good teacher from a pedagogical point of view. He didn't give me the right foundation, technically. He gave me something more than that."[2] What he gave him, actually, was a series of goals. As Mischa took up each new piece, Fiedelmann would play it for him, giving a polished reading that not only conveyed the work's contours to the boy, but gave him an idea of what could be done with it once the notes were mastered.

Saul Elman's restlessness soon got the better of him. He was in a strange town, with a young boy who needed his attention—and with no immediate source of income. He had, just before leaving for Odessa, sold his house in Talnoye and left much of the proceeds with his wife; but those funds, as well as the money he brought with him to Odessa, would soon run out. He decided, therefore, to campaign for the reversal of Fiedelmann's decision that Mischa was too young to enter the Academy. His strategy involved a direct appeal to the Academy's director, a Professor Klimov. Fiedelmann, possibly getting wind of Saul Elman's efforts to bring Mischa to Klimov's attention, mentioned the child to the director himself, and an audition was arranged. As a result, Mischa was accepted as the school's youngest student. His tuition was waived, and the family was given a living allowance of eight rubles a month.

With their immediate goal accomplished, Saul and Mischa returned to Shpola to retrieve the rest of the family. Back in Odessa, they took another bleak, windowless apartment, and as Mischa entered the Academy, Saul found a few Hebrew students, and began looking for a more profitable endeavor. At one point, he came close to buying a tobacco shop; but backed out (losing what was, for him, a sizeable deposit) when he realized that he was buying the store only, with no stock. He continued to give Hebrew lessons, but also kept close watch on Mischa's development. Once again, trouble flared up between Saul

Elman and Fiedelmann—this time because Saul suspected, as he later wrote, a "determination to keep the boy back."

Why Fiedelmann would have wanted to thwart one of his prize pupils is hard to say, but Saul heartily disapproved of his teaching methods. "A selection, no matter how well learned," Saul wrote, "would be gone over *ad nauseam*, until Mischa could play it blindfolded. And yet the teacher would obstinately refrain from giving him new work." Mischa was six years old at the time, with no technical foundation to speak of. Indeed, he was progressing quickly, and his later memories of his lessons with Fiedelmann hardly seem colored by any idea of suppression. Saul, on the other hand, wanted to see his son's talent blossom instantly, and he was apt to see sabotage where there was none. Fiedelmann, no doubt, was simply being methodical.

Nevertheless, Saul wrote to Klimov, who responded, as one might expect, that the child must not be pushed, and that the Academy's judgement and experience should be trusted. Assuming that the father's complaints were founded in the family's financial problems, Klimov offered to increase the stipend—an offer that only raised Saul's suspicions further. It was his belief, by the end of Mischa's first term, that Klimov and his faculty knew the extent of the boy's talent, and were holding him back in order to keep him associated with their school longer. His solution was surprising. "There was only one course open to me," he wrote, "and I took it. I resolved personally to instruct my boy in advanced work; and with this object in view, I took pains to learn from the older pupils of Mischa's class the various methods used, as well as the curriculum of the year."

Convinced that Mischa was at last getting the proper training, Saul let his son's education settle into a routine. The Academy's program included non-musical subjects as well as musical ones, and in these it seems that Mischa's greatest aptitude was in mathematics. He was, generally, a well-behaved child, partly because, as he later recalled, his father was a strict disciplinarian. He brought him to school and retrieved him; and he rarely let him play games with other children. Given the combination of this regimen and his youth, there must have been times when a kind of childish frustration came to the surface. Elman himself could remember only one such incident, which took place when he was ten years old, around one of the examination periods.

"In my class there was a boy who wasn't too bright, especially in mathematics," Elman remembered. "And he had an uncle who taught Russian literature. Evidently this teacher did something unethical. He appeared at the examination when this boy was being tested in mathematics. Each pupil had to solve certain problems. I knew my subject, and I answered well. But this other boy did not, and he answered with difficulty. Yet, when the marks were posted, my report card had a 4 in mathematics, which was considered good; but his had a 5 which was better. I was not what you would call a mischievous boy. But I started to cry and I lost my temper. And I remember exactly what I did. We had inkstands on our desks, and I took every bottle and spilled the ink all over the floor, with the teacher there. They couldn't understand what had happened. So I told them, 'I don't object to getting 4, but I do object that he got 5.'"[3]

Mischa had other personal problems during that same examination period, in December 1901. He had been selected to play a concerto, with the school orchestra, at the Academy's end-of-term concert, and the school had presented him with a new violin for the occasion. During the first rehearsal, though, one of the students tripped him as he made his way towards the podium, and in falling flat on his face, he smashed his new instrument. Another instrument was provided; but the Academy's students had another practical joke in store. On the day of the concert, several of them began taunting Elman, telling him that he was too young to play a concerto, and that his appearance would put the school to shame. To escape this, he went into a closet and closed the door. Unfortunately, it was one that could be locked from the outside, and one of the students had a key. Mischa, locked in, simply sat down and practiced, assuming that Klimov, Fiedelmann or his father would eventually find him—which is what happened, but since no-one knew he was missing until curtain time, the concert was delayed considerably.

❖ ❖ ❖ ❖ ❖

More crucially, the winter of 1901–2 brought Mischa Elman's first contact with some of the established stars of the European and Russian violin worlds—namely, Leopold Auer, Adolph Brodsky, and Pablo de Sarasate. Auer, the director of the St. Petersburg Conservatory, Russia's pre-eminent music school, seems to have been in Odessa on something of a pedagogical inspection visit, rather than on a concert tour. A special program was arranged, the first work being a piano trio, with Elman, a few months shy of 11 years old, as one of the players.

According to Saul Elman, Auer was "astonished at Mischa's extreme youth and at his art of delivery. He embraced the child at the close of the selection, and holding the little boy up to the audience, said, 'Look at this tiny atom! Inside it is the most extraordinary force. At his age, had I played as he does, I should now be ten Auers, not one.'"

Saul Elman was not present at the performance, and he says he heard about Auer's comments third hand, from Mrs. Puritz, who may have exaggerated them somewhat. After all, Auer, born in Hungary in 1845, was also a child prodigy. When he was Mischa's age, he had already put in two years as a student at the Budapest Conservatory, and had just moved on to Vienna, where he studied with—and, in fact, lived in the home of—Jacques Dont.

Of course, what makes Auer's comment, as reported, especially odd is that despite the esteem in which he was held, it may have been that "ten Auers" wouldn't have amounted to all that much. Although he held an important teaching post, and had duties at the Russian court and at the Imperial Ballet, he did not enjoy the sterling virtuoso reputation that many of his European colleagues had; indeed, he was barely known beyond Russia's borders until Elman, Zimbalist, Heifetz and Milstein burst upon the scene, whereupon he was able to bask in reflected glory. Thus he was able, late in life, to enjoy the status of a violin legend, and to have the inadequacies of his last concert performances ascribed to age.

Auer had his share of technical problems, not the least of them being a pair of small hands that were, by Auer's own description, so weak and poorly formed for violin playing[4] that he had to practice constantly to keep in trim. When Auer was 13, his father tried to launch him on a career as a concertizing prodigy; but he failed to impress audiences, and eventually returned to his studies, this time with Joseph Joachim, in Hanover. Auer spent two years with Joachim, a period he considered pivotal in his development, despite the irregularity of Joachim's lessons. And it was through Joachim that he met the young Brahms (who had written a concerto for Joachim several years later) and Ferdinand David, the violinist for whom Mendelssohn's concerto was composed. It was a milieu that may well have fired young Auer to greater heights as a player, for he met somewhat greater success upon his return to the concert stage, in 1864. Still, he was no superstar.

He became concertmaster of an orchestra in Düsseldorf, and in 1866 he moved to a similar post in Hamburg. Two years later, he was invited to take over the violin department at the St. Petersburg Conservatory. During his first years in the post, Auer was plagued by comparisons with his more facile and flashy predecessor, Henri Wieniawski. Nevertheless, he stayed on at St. Petersburg for 49 years, and it took the Russian Revolution to displace him. Eventually, criticism of his playing diminished, and several prominent composers—including Tchaikovsky, Glazunov and Taneyev—admired his playing sufficiently that they dedicated works to him.

How did Auer play? In one of his books, Joseph Szigeti includes an unflattering account of a December 1913 St. Petersburg performance of the Beethoven Violin Concerto, conducted by Willem Mengelberg. It was a performance Auer himself was proud of: After it, he wrote to one of his students that "people did find I never have done it so well—think in my age!" Szigeti, however, had heard and admired Elman, Zimbalist and Heifetz by then, and he expected their teacher's performance to be a revelation—as he says, "to outdo them all, not only in the indefinable qualities of wisdom, style and format, but also in tone, technical perfection and elan. This juvenile anticipation was of course absurd," he adds, noting that "the robustness of Mengelberg's orchestral frame only emphasized the thinness and carefulness of the obviously nervous old master's playing."[5]

We can also get an idea of Auer's sound from a handful of recordings he made towards the end of his career[6.] The recording technology of those distant days stands as a scrim between Auer and today's listener, yet, a good deal can be learned. One is a recording of the Brahms-Joachim *Hungarian Dance No.1* (recorded in 1920, when Auer was 75), and it reveals a low-register tone coloring that is quite rich. In the higher-lying sections, though—and particularly the sections played in harmonics—Auer's intonation is less centered and secure. Interestingly, Joachim's own recording of the same piece (from 1903, when he was 72) shows traits that were very much the opposite. In the low-lying passages that open the arrangement, his tone is comparatively scrawny and uncentered; yet in the higher-lying, quicker sections, his playing is fleet and in tune, and a good deal more precise than Auer's.

Also notable is the difference in the two violinists' handling of the double stop rendering of the main theme, towards the end. Auer glosses over it quickly, while Joachim lingers, drawing out the harmonies.

In that respect, many of Elman's interpretations almost seem closer to Joachim's than to Auer's. Both of the older violinists, moreover, used a touch of expressive *portamento* in their playing, a stylistic sweetener Elman inherited. In fact, in Elman's early recording (1914) of the Brahms-Joachim *Hungarian Dance No.7*, some of his slides are quite audacious, as are his tempo manipulations. In terms of subjective personal style, this recording goes a great deal farther than those of his teacher and his teacher's teacher. It's a pity Elman never recorded the first of the *Dances* (or that Auer and Joachim didn't recorded the two Elman did set down, Nos. 7 and 17), for a direct comparison would be fascinating.

Whatever Auer actually said upon first hearing Elman, he was certainly impressed, and the next time Elman and Auer met, Auer made him an offer that would link their destinies. Meanwhile, Auer's visit was soon followed by that of another celebrity, Adolph Brodsky. Brodsky lived in England, and was director of the Royal Manchester College of Music. He was, however, Russian-born, and Jewish; and his ties to Russia and its musical life remained strong. It was Brodsky who, in 1881, gave the belated premiere of the Tchaikovsky Concerto, after it had lain idle on Auer's music stand for four years. Brodsky had also spent some time in New York City as the concertmaster of the New York Symphony Orchestra, under Walter Damrosch; and in 1895, he was invited to become the concertmaster of Manchester's Halle Orchestra, and to teach at the conservatory there.

Alexander Fiedelmann was a student of Brodsky's, and he was anxious to hear what Brodsky had to say about young Elman, particularly after Auer's visit. Brodsky was as impressed as Auer, but to Saul Elman's annoyance, Fiedelmann neglected to pass on Brodsky's comments, just as he had declined to report Auer's—a lapse Saul took to be part of a plot to keep his son in Odessa when better prospects beckoned. Believing Fiedelmann would prevent him from approaching Brodsky himself, Saul persuaded a musical friend to serve as go-between. After ascertaining that Brodsky had indeed heard and been taken with the child, Saul's friend delicately inquired about Mischa's further studies—and whether Brodsky would be interested in supervising them. Brodsky explained that he couldn't think of stealing his own former student's prize pupil, and added that he considered Fiedelmann a promising teacher who deserved the opportunity of working with an exceptionally talented student.

The Spanish virtuoso Pablo de Sarasate, on the other hand, did not stand on ceremony when he first heard Mischa Elman. Rather, he insisted that the prodigy abandon Odessa for one of the cultural centers—St. Petersburg, Paris, or Berlin—before it was too late. Sarasate had come to Odessa for a concert early in 1902, and on the day of his arrival, Saul Elman turned up at his hotel with Mischa. Undeterred by the desk clerk's insistence that the 58-year old violinist was tired after a long journey, Saul took a roundabout route, approaching Sarasate's accompanist. Both Sarasate and his pianist were used to the routine of proud parents parading in their prodigies, and the pianist acted as a screen, beyond which only the exceptionally talented could pass. It took only one short piece to enlist the accompanist's aid, and within a few moments, Saul and Mischa were led into Sarasate's room.

According to Saul Elman's *Memoirs*, Sarasate's examination of his son was thorough. First, he listened at a distance as the child played. Then he asked Mischa to repeat the work, this time circling him and looking closely at his bowhold, his stance and his fingerwork. Since Sarasate didn't speak Russian, and the Elmans didn't speak Spanish, Saul and the violinist settled on German. "Komm," Sarasate said gently to the child, "gib mir deine Hand." As he looked closely at Elman's hands and fingers, examined his bowhold, and then placed the boy on his lap, he asked Saul why they were staying in Odessa, where the child's talent would wilt. Saul explained that they lacked both the funds and influence to make a major move, let alone to get into an important urban conservatory; but in the hope of working toward that end, he solicited a testimonial from Sarasate.

"I heard Mischa Elman play," Sarasate wrote. "I am in a position to testify that he is the possessor of a great talent. If he succeeds in taking up his musical studies in either Paris, Berlin or St. Petersburg, he will, within a few years, be the pride of Europe."[7]

The letter was an artistic passport for the young violinist. Consider Sarasate's position at that time. At 58, he had but six more years to live, and virtually all his triumphs were behind him. He was, as the violin historian Boris Schwarz writes, "the last of the great 19th century virtuosos—suave, elegant, brilliant in a very personal way, idolized by the public in both hemispheres. He did not teach, and he left no school, because his art was too subjective."[8] Much the same can be said of Elman; indeed there are several parallels both in the outlines of their careers and in their performing styles.

Born in Pamplona, Sarasate began playing the violin at five, and performed publicly at eight. By the time he was ten, he had won a scholarship to the Madrid Conservatory, and the Queen of Spain had given him a Stradivarius violin. In 1856, when he was 12, Sarasate attended the Paris Conservatoire, where he studied harmony and theory for three years. Thereafter, he embarked on an concert career that took him through Europe, the Orient, and the Americas. But the period of his greatest success began in the 1870s.

Sarasate's playing inspired the creation of several of today's repertoire standards, among them the Bruch Concerto No.2, the Saint-Saëns Concertos Nos. 1 and 3, plus the *Introduction and Rondo capriccioso*, Lalo's *Symphonie Espagnole*, and Wieniawski's Concerto No.2; and of course, several of his own compositions have remained violinistic showpieces to this day. Elman recorded three of his works, the *Caprice Basque* (with Percy Kahn, in 1910), the *Romanza Andaluza* (with Walter H. Golde, in 1916), and of course, the lexicon of virtuosic display, *Zigeunerweisen* (with Carroll Hollister in 1931, and again with Joseph Seiger in 1958). He also recorded Sarasate's arrangement of the Chopin *Nocturne in E-flat}*, Op.9, No.2—itself a fabulous example of Romanticized free adaptation—three times.

At age 11, Elman may have been unaware of Sarasate's biographical details, but he knew some of his music, and he knew enough about him to regard him as a role model. More than Auer and Brodsky, after all, Sarasate was truly an international celebrity—a globe-trotting star who, with his deep, dark eyes, his thick moustache, his long hair and his virtuosic manner, struck the impoverished Russian youth as appealingly exotic and successful. At the end of the interview, Sarasate gave Mischa a cash gift and a pair of tickets to his recital. And the performance Elman attended that evening was so different from anything he had hitherto seen that it led him to think long and hard about every aspect of violin playing, from interpretation to showmanship.

We can glean something of what Elman heard that night from a series of recordings Sarasate made in 1904,[9] two years after his Odessa visit. They are startling period pieces that bring the Romantic virtuosic style to life. The *Prelude* from Bach's E major Partita, for instance, is converted by Sarasate into a devilishly speedy perpetual motion piece. There is no mitigation of the tempo he establishes in the opening bars; yet the agility with which he maintains the independence of line is astounding. Tempo aside, Sarasate's approach is surprisingly literal—although at the clip he takes, there was hardly time for embellishment. Perhaps his reading of the Chopin *Nocturne* is more telling, for in this sweet, elegant work, he turns the score to the service of the violin, and embroiders Chopin's melody with a rhapsodic ornamental latticework that, regardless of its infidelity to Chopin's text, is a treat to hear. Most intriguing, of course, is Sarasate's handling of his own music, upon which he lavishes all manner of color and effect. Even through the limited fidelity those ancient discs afford, one can hear what can only have been a finely-calibrated approach to shading. From the lower strings, he would draw a warm, rich timbre some of time; but its sequel would be cast in a coarse, brusque tone. Higher up, his tone was pure and precise, although he was not averse to some quick sliding, or to offering runs of descending or ascending trilled figures, *pianissimo*, when such effects promised to add some dazzle to the performance.

Elman, in his earliest recordings, revels in the same spirit of unabashed timbral splendor as Sarasate; and his youthful exuberance, combined with his own technical facility, led him to emphasize his instrument and the variety of gorgeous sounds he could draw from it even more than the old Spanish master. If Sarasate influenced him, that influence was filtered through Elman's own personality—something that becomes clear when you compare Elman's recordings with Sarasate's, work for work. In Sarasate's Chopin arrangement, Elman is even more ornamental than the transcriber—more so in his recording from the 1950s, in fact, than in his earlier renderings. Interestingly, in his first recordings he dropped the opening phrases an octave, to take advantage of what was already considered his loveliest range. In the Sarasate originals, Elman was inclined to ease up on the tempos of individual sections within the works, setting forth the music soberly but poetically, without sacrificing any of its innate fire or display value.

The Elmans, naturally, were ecstatic with their Sarasate letter, and although prudence told them to keep it a secret for awhile, Saul couldn't help letting word of the visit, and the endorsement, get back to Fiedelmann. The Imperial Academy's administration found this intensely annoying, and regarded it as an attempt on Saul's part to undermine their authority over his son—which it was. From the Academy's point of view, Saul was a chronic malcontent. His son was being schooled free of charge, and his family had been given a monthly stipend; yet his attempts to oversee his son's education, mixed with his complaints about the course that education was taking, continued unabated.

Saul held fast to the view that the school was deliberately holding Mischa back, and when the 1902 term ended, the conflict between the father and the schoolmasters came to a dramatic head. For the first time, Mischa failed his end-term performance examination, and his scholarship to the Imperial Academy was withdrawn. In his *Memoirs*, Saul insisted that this failure was due to Fiedelmann's maliciously withholding Mischa's examination piece until it was too late for him to learn it properly. The school, however, placed the blame with Saul, citing his meddling in Mischa's studies, and taking him to task for giving Mischa extracurricular pieces which, added to his regular course work, placed too great a strain on him. Most of Odessa's musical community believed the school's version, and Saul was ostracized as an interfering father.

There were, he reasoned, two courses open to him: he could beg the Academy to take Mischa back, and promise to leave teaching to the teachers. Or, he could find a way to raise the money it would take to place Mischa in a better school, in a larger city. That seemed an enormous prospect, for his income from Hebrew lessons was scarcely enough to support a family that now included himself and Yetta, 11-year old Mischa, nine year old Mina, and a newborn daughter, Liza. If Mischa was to study in a large city, money would have to be raised, and quickly. The obvious thing to do was to take Mischa on a concert tour; but having just been marked as an aggressive stage father, Saul had no wish to be labeled a child exploiter. The family discussed the idea of a tour at length. And in the end, it was Mischa himself who was most eager to undertake the venture.

They began with a tryout in Nicholaev, a town less than 40 miles northeast of Odessa, and the only town of any size they could reach on the three rubles in their budget. Mischa's reputation as a talented charge of the Academy had preceded him to Nicholaev, and upon their arrival, Saul and Mischa visited the local music school, which helped arrange their concert. It was a success: they netted 400 rubles, and returned to Odessa to map out a tour of the province they had left when they moved to Odessa. After a two week stay, they left Yetta and the girls once again, with Kiev as the first destination. Recitals in Berditchev, Chudnov and Elizabethgrad followed, all of them profitable—yet, in all, hardly profitable enough to make a trip to Paris

or Berlin possible. By then, Saul ruled out St. Petersburg as a possibility, having heard rumors to the affect that Leopold Auer, a Jew
who had converted to Russian Orthodoxy, often persuaded his Jewish
students to follow the same course.

Word of Mischa's tour, meanwhile, got back to Odessa considerably exaggerated: Reports had it that the child had performed in St.
Petersburg, Berlin, Paris and London—and that Saul had been living
lavishly on the earnings. By the time they returned to Odessa, at the
end of the summer, the tour had become a *cause célèbre*, and the local
newspapers vilified Saul as a tyrannical exploiter of his own child.
"Everybody who thought he had anything to say on the subject was
given an opportunity to unburden himself," Saul wrote in his *Memoirs*,
"the only exception being me."

Back in Odessa, Saul hired a private teacher for Mischa,
Fiedelmann's chief local rival. This brought Fiedelmann to Saul, and
the teacher persuaded Saul to bring Mischa back to the Academy.
Upon arriving at the school, Saul was told that his son would be accepted again only if Saul agreed, in writing, not to remove Mischa from
the Academy for five years, and not to take him on tours during school
vacations. Saul declined. But although he realized that his options
were eroding, coincidence again came to his aid. On his way home, he
noticed a newspaper advertisement for a Leopold Auer concert in
Elizabethgrad. A few hours later, father and son were on a train bound
for that city.

Their first attempt to see Auer, that afternoon, was rebuffed by one
of Auer's students who found fault with Mischa's fingering and
bowhold, and refused to let Auer see him. They had better luck that
evening: Auer's concert was in the same hall Mischa had played in a
few weeks earlier, and the house manager offered to introduce them
to Auer during the intermission. Auer remembered Mischa from his
visit to Odessa, nearly a year earlier, and hearing Saul's account of
their predicament, he extended his stay in Elizabethgrad an extra day
in order to hear Mischa again and offer his advice. The next day, the
three met, and although Mischa was too nervous to play at first, he
eventually settled down and gave a brief program for Auer that included the Paganini *Caprice* No.24, and the Wieniawski Concerto No.2.

In the discussion that followed, Auer disabused Saul of his religious
fears, and told him that the doors of the St. Petersburg Conservatory
would be open to Mischa—indeed, that attending the Conservatory
would be the only safeguard against squandering the talent he had

nurtured these last six years. He also provided a letter to St. Petersburg's Police Commissioner, requesting that the Elmans be granted the special permission required for Jews to live in the city. The two returned to Odessa, relieved, overjoyed, and brimming with hope. A few weeks later, at the end of 1902, they set off on the long northward journey to St. Petersburg.

CHAPTER THREE:

Studies in St. Petersburg

Saul and Mischa Elman arrived in St. Petersburg in January 1903, and after an evening's recovery from their long journey, they went to the Conservatory. For Mischa, the St. Petersburg Conservatory was a dazzling place—huge, ornate, and swarming with music students whose fresh uniforms made him acutely conscious of his own tattered clothes. Talking with some of the students in the large foyer, the Elmans learned that word of Mischa's brief tour in the Kiev region had made its way to St. Petersburg; and naturally, the other violin students wanted to hear the youngster play—as did some of the faculty, who had been told of the child's presence. Within half an hour of their arrival at the school, an impromptu recital was arranged in one of the classrooms. Among the works Mischa played was Wieniawski's Second Concerto, certainly an adequate display piece with which to win over his skeptical new colleagues.

After a few selections, Auer arrived and took charge of Mischa, sending him to the Conservatory's office to properly register. There was, as Auer explained to Saul, little he or the school could do in the way of providing money for the family; and Saul responded that his major concern was seeing that his son's education was properly administered. This time, in fact, he resolved to leave the matters of Mischa's studies and repertoire entirely in Auer's hands, and to limit his involvement in Mischa's education to walking him to the Conservatory in the morning and collecting him in the afternoon.

Auer elected to take Mischa into his own class—a decision that surprised some of the faculty, since Auer, as head of the department, usually took only the most advanced students. What he must have seen in Mischa, though, was a violinist who was already far beyond the basics, but who, at age 12, was still malleable. Not that the boy was

31

a *tabula rasa*: between the music Fiedelmann had given him, and the works his father put on his stand between lessons, he had played through a lot of music, and found his preferences. Plus, he had seen Sarasate and other touring violinists; and having performed himself, he had developed some impressions about the way certain interpretive touches appealed to audiences.

When Auer quizzed the boy on the more purely technical part of his repertoire, he found that Mischa's early training had been deficient in elementary bowing and fingering etudes, but he opted not to make Elman play these at this late date. We may assume, therefore, that Auer found Elman's technique sufficient for his stage of development, for he would otherwise certainly have asked him to devote some time to the primary etudes—which, after all, can be used as corrective as well as formative studies. Instead, Auer concentrated on repertoire and interpretation during the next year and a half.

In these matters, Auer was authoritative but by no means dictatorial. That he did not impose his own style on his students is borne out by the fact that each player who emerged from Auer's studio had a unique interpretive approach. Auer saw himself as a guide, as someone who could help the young player avoid technical and interpretive pitfalls, while giving him the best literature. He let his students follow their intuition; but he made them think hard about intuitive gestures. In short, what Auer conveyed was a sense of probing musicality. His students' interpretations invariably differed from his own, but he left it to them to justify their approaches in performance. If the interpretations worked, Auer supported them; if not, his questions and criticisms led the student to continue exploring until he came upon a more solid, supportable approach.

Beyond that, he stressed a number of interpretive points in his lessons with his most advanced students.[1] One of them was the importance of nuance—something in which he felt young players needed a good deal of guidance. "If you wish to make a really favorable impression as a performer on the violin," he wrote in *Violin Playing As I Teach It*, "you must avoid monotony and lack of color.... Monotony is the death of music. Nuance is the antidote for monotony." Auer went on to explain that nuance is a function of three elements over which the violinist had to exercise complete control: dynamics (which he described as a variation of both loudness and intensity), timbral manipulation, and finally, tempo gradations, each of which affects the way the ear perceives the shape of a musical phrase.

Auer did not, however, want his students to manipulate these elements merely for the sake of effect: he wanted them to emulate the impulses of nature. "Take Nature for a model," he wrote, "that is my advice to every player." Moreover, this application of nuance had to embody some subtlety. "Individuality in nuance," he prescribed, "should never degenerate into bizarre affectation. There is always a borderline, easily recognizable, where the temperamental oversteps the aesthetic bounds of propriety, and turns into caricature."

In addition to his precepts on nuance, though, Auer conveyed to his students more general information about style; and on this topic, his views were set in an interesting historical and philosophical perspective:

> There is no one definitely established way of playing a given work by a master, for there is no absolute standard of beauty by which the presentation of a violinistic art-work can be judged. A type of playing extravagantly admired and cultivated in one age may be altogether rejected in another. The general aesthetic sense and sensibility of the period in which we ourselves live...is the only standard of judgement to which we can refer the artist's interpretation. If the violinist satisfies this aesthetic taste of ours...and if he moves us, if he convinces us, if he makes us feel that he is revealing to us beauty's true soul—then his interpretation is justified, his style is faultless.[2]

He goes on, in fact, to warn against tradition, arguing that an adherence to stylistic dictates prevalent at specific times in history can only lead to stagnation in art. As he put it, "Tradition in reality weighs down the living spirit of the present with the dead formalism of the past." This approach clearly impressed young Elman, for he argued similarly to the end of his days, decrying musicological attempts to rediscover and re-establish the styles that prevailed during the lifetimes of the great composers.

The other side of this argument, of course, is that a composer's expressive impulses are inevitably bound up in the performance practices of his time, and that the music he writes is conceived within the dictates of what is to him a familiar stylistic language, with assumptions concerning tempos, phrasing habits, nuance and coloration, and local quirks and conventions that notation itself does not always capture (and which performers and musicologists of later eras must therefore surmise, based on descriptive writings of the time).

The battle between those who take this view and those who believe, as Auer and Elman did, that the performer's reading of a work's spirit must prevail, is one of those perennial differences of opinion that keep music a vibrant and varied art. The strength of Auer's influence in this matter is clear when you compare comments each of them made in their discussions of stylistic appropriateness. Auer put it this way in *Violin Playing as I Teach It*, in 1921:

> Are we to deny the beauty of [an interpretation] by which we are moved because someone who has never heard Spohr himself play the same work, but who has carefully collected statistical evidence to establish his 'traditional' rendering, explains that Spohr's interpretation must be considered the only vital one, being "traditional"?[3]

Elman, some four decades later, conveyed a similar sentiment through a pair of anecdotes, which he included in his articles and speeches, and told many an interviewer. The first involves an encounter with a musicologist:

> In the course of our conversation, he said he had not agreed with my interpretation [of a Mozart concerto], that in his opinion, it had not been in the "composer's spirit." I replied I was sorry he hadn't enjoyed it, but that, much as I respected his learning and erudition, I felt no artistic guilt at his failure to do so. At this debonair reaction to so grave a charge he raised his eyebrows and I added with a laugh, "Look here—aside from the notations Mozart made and which are merely indicative, I don't know how he wanted me to play that work. What makes you think *you* do?" After a moment, he laughed too.[4]

The second involved an encounter between Elman and a listener at a concert:

> Once, at a recital of a violinist colleague of mine, while I was still applauding his playing of the Bach *Chaconne*, a lady tapped me on the shoulder. Leaning forward, she murmured, "that was enjoyable, but it wasn't Bach, was it Mr. Elman?" To which I replied, "I'm sorry madame, but I never heard Bach play it." So don't say, "this is not Schumann," or "this is not Mendelssohn." There is no such thing as *right* and *wrong* interpretation when you deal with the higher echelon among *established artists*. Who can say what is

right or wrong if the listener is completely captivated by what is played?[5]

Another thing Auer stressed in Elman's lessons was the importance of developing a feeling of ease on the concert stage. He considered Elman ready to perform, and his policy was not only to allow public performance by his students, but to encourage it and even arrange opportunities for it. "Platform work makes the artist," Auer told Saul Elman. "The artist's soul responds fully to the fast-beating pulse of a sympathetic audience."[6] Within Mischa's first few weeks in St. Petersburg, in fact, Auer arranged for him to perform at a dinner party at the home of the Kreitzers, friends of Auer's who were arts patrons. Saul was invited to attend as well, and he reports that at the conclusion of Mischa's performance, he was handed 300 rubles. The performance was by no means a public event, but the setting was high-toned enough for there to be newspaper accounts of it the following morning. "Without a single exception," Saul Elman wrote, "the St. Petersburg critics agreed that Mischa was the greatest child marvel the world had ever known."[7]

That performance led to another within a week at a similar evening given by the Bersons, another wealthy family given to arts patronage; and the Bersons undertook to provide Saul with a monthly stipend for the support of Mischa and the rest of the family. Saul was also asked to suggest an appropriate gift for his son. That was easy: as Mischa's technique and repertoire developed, and as his blossoming career of salon performances grew, he was finding that his instrument was not as responsive as he would have liked. The idea of getting Mischa a new violin was on Saul's mind, and that's what he told his host. Saul was then asked what a new violin might cost, and Saul, not having studied the market, named a price he considered princely, 300 rubles. Handed the sum, he was directed to purchase a new instrument.

What he wanted was a violin by one of the great Italian makers, and he went to the shop of a violin maker he had met during his travels through the city, a Mr. Geiser. Geiser told him that Italian violins cannot be had for 300 rubles—but that it didn't matter, because Leopold Auer had been to his shop the previous day and had selected, for Mischa, an Amati, built in 1654, and valued at 3,000 rubles. Moreover, the instrument was paid for by a patron who, anonymous at first, turned out to be the Grand Duke Herzog Meklenburg-Sterlitz. A few days after Mischa received the violin, an invitation to play at a musicale in the Grand Duke's home arrived, via Auer.

By the time Mischa's first term ended, in May 1903, he had given quite a few of these performances which, though private, were no doubt strenuous, for his audiences were wealthy patrons and noblemen who could help him if they considered his talent worth cultivating, or thwart him if his playing struck them as commonplace. The term examinations were even more highly pressurized, for they were held in public, and attracted this same influential crowd. Saul Elman describes the audience as one unlike any he had yet laid eyes on—a "spectacle so dazzling, so overpowering in point of wealth and elegance that it suggested to me some great imperial pageant where the mighty of the land were gathered to greet their sovereign. As far as my eye could reach I saw ladies arrayed in silk and gold, their heads and necks bedecked with sparkling jewels; beside them sat men of high rank in brilliant uniforms of lace and gold, an occasional full dress suit here and there giving a touch of relief from the wealth of bright glowing colors."[8]

Mischa's test piece was the Mendelssohn Concerto, to piano accompaniment, and his performance was impressive enough to further his reputation both among his classmates and in St. Petersburg at large. This was a good thing, not only for Mischa's prospective career, but because the Elmans, as Jews, needed a special permit to live in St. Petersburg, and as the school term came to an end, so did the term of Mischa's and Saul's temporary papers. A measure of local renown couldn't hurt, although it didn't guarantee the permit renewal they sought.

The Conservatory's secretary had to apply directly to the Minister of the Interior, Vyacheslav Plehve; but Plehve, notorious for his violent anti-Semitism, was not a man given to displays of liberal open-mindedness, nor was he keen on approving exceptions to his decree that Jews be kept out of Russia's major cities. Appointed to his post in 1902, Plehve established a regime that was short-lived, yet hatefully authoritarian and damaging not only to the subjects of Tsar Nicholas II, but ultimately, to the Tsar himself. In July 1904, Plehve was assassinated.

As it turned out, the Conservatory was able to arrange for Mischa to stay in St. Petersburg for the duration of his studies, but Saul and the rest of the family—with which he intended to return after a summer in Odessa—had to petition for a new permit. Saul put that off until the start of the next term, and took Mischa home to Odessa where a group of local impresarios were anxious to present him in a string of performances. Saul steadfastly refused: although Auer had prescribed plenty of performing experience, Saul felt that Mischa had just finished a difficult term in which he had acquitted himself admirably, and that rest would be prudent. Saul did agree to let Mischa perform in one concert, a charity gala arranged by the Mayor of Odessa.

❖ ❖ ❖ ❖ ❖

Upon their return to St. Petersburg, Saul and Mischa lodged at a hotel run by a Jewish army veteran who, Saul had been told, had a sideline specialty in obtaining residency papers for Jews who wanted to settle in St. Petersburg. As it turned out, the hotelier was actually an extortionist, in whose interest it was to prevent those papers from arriving (an easy enough task), while threatening his waiting guests with betrayal if they failed to meet his cash demands. The Conservatory's application on Saul's behalf, filed during the previous term, had not yet been acted upon, but several of the wealthy arts patrons Saul had met during Mischa's first round of private concerts agreed to shield him from the police; and upon his decision to leave the hotel, one of the patrons allowed Saul to register as his butler, and found him a rat-infested basement room, which he had to share with a group of hard-drinking laborers.

There Saul remained for two months, and during the hours Mischa spent at the Conservatory, he made the rounds of various ministries, hoping to resolve his permit dilemma. The police chief, Lopuchin, was sympathetic, although his best suggestion was that Saul and his family convert to the Russian Orthodox faith. However, for Plehve, anti-Semitism was by this time also a political stance, for a pogrom the previous Easter had won a good deal of support for those in the Jewish community who were suggesting that their co-religionists no longer submit to this murderous harassment without fighting back. Articles accusing Plehve of responsibility for the massacre were privately printed and publicly circulated; and the matter became an international one when the *London Times* ran a lengthy story laying the blame for the pogrom at Plehve's door. This inflamed the Minister's determination to keep the Jews out of the cities, and Elman's petition was one of many that were summarily denied.

Saul took this news to Auer, who had considered the Conservatory's application a mere formality. Infuriated, Auer personally visited Plehve and argued the case, to no avail. Auer then suggested that Saul apply again on his own behalf, asking only that he be allowed to stay in town during Mischa's period of study, without the rest of the family. As a last resort, Auer told him, he could register as a student at the St. Petersburg Conservatory, and take up the violin (as Jascha Heifetz's father would do, some years hence). The sympathetic police chief, Lopuchin, approached the matter from a different angle. He arranged a musicale at which Plehve and the rest of the Tsar's cabinet were present, and invited Mischa to perform. Plehve hadn't made the connection between the prodigy and Saul Elman's petition, and when pressed for an opinion, he echoed the popular sentiment and claimed he'd never heard a finer violin recital.

The next morning, Saul Elman's petition was waiting for Plehve when he arrived at his office, along with a missive explaining that it concerned the father of the violinist he had heard the night before. Plehve relented, providing a permit for the entire family.

❖ ❖ ❖ ❖ ❖

For Auer, though, a new strategy was taking shape during the closing months of 1903. He and Mischa had, in their first year together, covered an enormous stretch of the standard violin repertoire, and as Auer saw it, it was time to prepare Mischa for the next step in his career—one that, if handled properly, would not only guarantee Mischa success, but would establish Auer's reputation throughout Europe as a master teacher. His plan was for Mischa to make his debut in Berlin, at that time the center of the musical world, and the home base of Auer's teacher, Joseph Joachim. Auer had not yet produced any students capable of seizing Berlin's attention without having first gained Joachim's imprimatur. Thus, as Auer knew, this debut was of key importance to both of them and would have to be carefully prepared.

Before a date could be set, Auer temporarily shelved his plan, for Joachim announced that he had discovered a sensational prodigy, a young Hungarian named Ferenc von Vecsey. Born in Budapest in 1893, von Vecsey began his studies under his father's instruction. In 1901, he was taken to Jeno Hubay, who was by then the central performer and teacher of the Hungarian school. Hubay, born in 1858, had studied with Joachim in Berlin between 1873 and 1876, and thereafter, with a recommendation from Franz Liszt, he took a post in Paris. There, he met Henri Vieuxtemps, with whom he undertook further studies. As the violin historian Boris Schwarz has noted,

"Vieuxtemps's decisive influence on Hubay is very significant: it brought a French orientation to his playing—elegance, brilliance, warmth of tone—which overshadows his earlier German training. It is this cross-fertilization between the approaches of Joachim and Vieuxtemps which lent Hubay and the Hungarian school a specific coloration."[9] After a brief spell on the faculty of the Brussels Conservatory, Hubay joined the faculty at the Academy in Budapest in 1886.

From a historical perspective, Ferenc von Vecsey can hardly be seen as Hubay's prize pupil. His students included Emil Telemanyi, Joseph Szigeti, Sandor Vegh, Eugene Ormandy and several others whose careers proved to be of more lasting importance. Von Vecsey was, however, Elman's first real rival. When the young Hungarian played in Berlin, in October 1903, he impressed both the local critics and Joseph Joachim, who proclaimed him the world's greatest child prodigy. Soon after this triumph—capped by a performance before Kaiser Wilhelm—von Vecsey and his father undertook a European tour that brought them to St. Petersburg with enormous fanfare. Moreover, von Vecsey's father bore a letter from Joachim to Auer, asking that Auer do whatever he could on the boy's behalf.

Auer did go out of his way to assure von Vecsey a good reception. In those days, particularly with child performers, it was common to give the critics a chance to hear the player before the public debut recital—thereby allowing for an advance review through which the musical public might be alerted to an event worth attending. This system was also a matter of sheer practicality for the performer, who would normally make his debut with a solo recital—which meant that he had to hire a hall and pay the allied presentation and publicity costs. Advance reviews hardly guaranteed an audience; but without them, a newcomer stood little chance of drawing a crowd or breaking even on the evening. Auer arranged such a preview for von Vecsey, and personally invited each of the St. Petersburg critics, conveying, in his letters of invitation, Joachim's enthusiastic comments about the young virtuoso.

But musical politics thrived, then as now. The von Vecseys were warned that Auer had a prodigy of his own, and that he would probably work behind the scenes to undermine the success of young Ferenc's preview. Thus, at the last moment, Auer received a telegram from the senior von Vecsey informing him that due to unforseen circumstances the child could not perform. It was a clever move, actually, for by the time they withdrew, Auer had conveyed Joachim's praise to the critics. Meanwhile, the von Vecseys and their supporters arranged for Ferenc to make a seemingly impromptu debut with the St. Petersburg Philharmonic, thereby providing both a public debut and a hearing by the critics, without having to shoulder the cost of presenting a recital.

The Elmans and Auer attended the Philharmonic, and were impressed with what they heard. Already a superb technician, von Vecsey produced a tone that, like Hubay's, leaned towards the deeper end of the spectrum. He used his vibrato lavishly, perhaps too much so—Joachim had only recently reproached him for relying to heavily on it; and his use of *portamento* was equally lavish[10.] After the concert, the Elmans and Auer went to the artists' room to offer their congratulations, and the two young violinists immediately struck up a friendship that lasted many years, despite the competitive roles in which the public quickly cast them.

Auer, though, considered Mischa clearly superior. What he saw in von Vecsey was a child who was technically secure and perhaps Mischa's equal on that count; but one whose tone showed little coloristic variety, and whose playing was still one-dimensional. As an interpreter, Elman struck Auer as by far the more interesting, and hearing von Vecsey strengthened Auer's resolve to prepare Mischa for a Berlin debut. The day von Vecsey left St. Petersburg, Auer redoubled his efforts to fortify Mischa, and he began to seek further public performance opportunities for him.

A prime one presented itself in January 1904, when it was announced that the French conductor Edouard Colonne would conduct an orchestral concert in Pavlovsk. Auer used his influence to persuade the concert committee there to allow Mischa to appear at that concert as soloist in a violin concerto; and in the weeks before Colonne's arrival, his scheduled appearance was given great play in the Russian newspapers—as, for that matter, were the opinions of those who felt that Auer's championship of Elman, who was just about to turn 13, was drawing his attention away from the rest of his students and was ill-advised.

Colonne was a problem too, at first. Not having been told that his soloist was a child, he met Mischa the afternoon of the first rehearsal and flew into a rage, shouting at the orchestra's manager that he hadn't come all the way from Paris to perform with a child, and that he considered the notion a grave insult. He announced that if Mischa played, he would not conduct. Auer insisted that Mischa not withdraw, leaving the orchestra management to straddle the line between heated argument and diplomatic discussion with both its esteemed guest and the well-connected violin professor. A compromise was reached, whereby Colonne would conduct the purely symphonic works, and Elman would play his concerto to piano accompaniment.

At the concert, Colonne led the opening symphony, then left the stage to Mischa and his pianist. The audience was a sympathetic one, and having read colorful accounts of the feud, the listeners signalled their support for the child (and its distaste for Colonne's unfeeling display of temperament) by giving him a long ovation. When the applause died, Mischa put his Amati to his chin, and after a page of the Mendelssohn Concerto, the conductor, watching from the wings, realized he had made a mistake. He came out on stage, and stood to the side, transfixed. For the audience, this was quite a spectacle—a dormant orchestra and a famous conductor watching as a teenage violinist made his way through the Mendelssohn to the accompaniment of a piano reduction.

At the concerto's conclusion, Colonne walked towards Mischa and threw his arms around him, while the audience responded more vocally. Later, Colonne apologized, promising to make up for his behavior by throwing his support behind Elman when he decided to make his debut in Paris. A year later, Mischa took him up on the offer, and appeared with the Colonne Orchestra. Meanwhile, reports of the evening's success spread quickly, and within a week, Mischa was invited to play at the French Club in St. Petersburg, and at a variety of other private musicales. He also performed at the city's Deutsche Lieder-tafel, a club at which Auer gave a concert annually. This time, Auer pleaded illness at the last moment, and turned up with Mischa, saying that he was too ill to play himself, but that his student would be able to stand in for him. That recital, too, was a success; in fact, the audience had him repeat the entire program.

As the 1904 term drew to an end, Auer decided the time was right for Mischa's trip to Germany. Since foreign touring was generally frowned upon the Conservatory's administration, Saul had to apply for a leave of absence on his son's behalf, due to illness. The leave was granted, and so far as the faculty and administration of the Conservatory knew, Mischa's doctors had ordered him to Germany to take a cure. A few weeks later, when newspaper accounts of Mischa's first German concerts found their way back to St. Petersburg, Auer innocently told the angry administrators that they should make the most of the situation. "After all," he said, "it's more useful to have one of our students causing a furor in Berlin than to have him be a source of income to Berlin doctors and druggists."

Auer and Saul did, however, have an agreement about the length of the tour. Realizing that success in Berlin would bring packs of promoters to the Elmans' door, Auer warned Saul that Mischa was still young, and that he should avoid the temptation to play too much. They agreed that the tour would last three months, and that Saul and Mischa would then return to St. Petersburg. They hired an agent, who they met through Auer—a singer and part-time impresario named Fiedler—and signed a three month management contract with him. Having heard Mischa play, and knowing Auer to be a trustworthy judge of talent, Fiedler invested virtually his entire savings in the enterprise of presenting Mischa's Berlin debut. He selected a date, October 14, 1904, and booked the Bechstein Hall.

At the end of September, Auer gave Mischa an especially long final lesson—a rather difficult one, as it turned out. Having Mischa perform before his entire class, he flew into a rage when Mischa misplaced an eighth note in one of his recital pieces. He expressed intense disappointment that Mischa would be going to Berlin unprepared, and that his sloppy playing would disgrace his teacher. Auer, it turned out, wasn't really all that upset with the performance: he was indulging in some not particularly good child psychology. He knew that a string of successes had given Mischa a feeling of security about performing, but he knew, too, that child players who felt too secure often let their talent deteriorate. He wanted to send Mischa off to Berlin with a touch of humility, something to keep him working hard. And he wanted Mischa to feel a sense of responsibility towards his teacher and friend, and to understand that both their reputations were at stake.

Mischa recalled that last lesson, and Auer's teaching in general, more than 30 years later: "Auer was a strict teacher, and was never lenient with the pupils he liked. Though generous and kind to a superfluous degree, he was easy to displease. I played three hours before his master class once. He interspersed my playing with innumerable bravos. I made one little slip of technique, and he put me out of the class. That was his discipline. But I've never regretted his severity because of the helpful and sincere purpose behind it. Auer's firm faith in me, his devotion and his readiness to make any sacrifice for me have had as much to do with my career as anything I have done."[11]

At the time, however, Mischa took Auer's criticism quite personally, and the following morning, when Saul suggested that they stop by
the Conservatory to bid Auer farewell on their way to the train station, Mischa's first response was that they shouldn't bother; but Saul
prevailed, partly because he wanted to ask Auer what the previous
day's incident had been about. He was also curious about German
programming tastes, and about whether Auer would provide a letter
of introduction to Joachim. As Saul recorded in his *Memoirs*, Auer's
advice was fatalistic. "It would not be possible to program anything
the Berlin audience hadn't already heard," he said. "The question is
not *what* Mischa plays, but *how* he plays." Similarly, he argued that a
letter of endorsement "would not help Mischa. He must be judged on
his merits."

At last it was time for father and son to make their way to the station. "Above all," Auer told them as they left, "do not lose courage."

CHAPTER FOUR:

The Conquest of Europe

The moment they arrived in Berlin, Saul bought all the local newspapers, anxious to see what sort of publicity Fiedler had arranged on Mischa's behalf. There was none: the most he could find was a tiny announcement reading "The 12-year old[1] Mischa Elman will appear on October 14 in Bechstein Hall," amid a long listing of the month's concerts. Fiedler, their agent, met them at the station, and they gathered from his glum demeanor that he had tried to interest the newspapers in the boy, to no avail. He had, however, arranged a private concert for the Berlin critics.

The critics' audition almost had to be cancelled, though. On the evening of their arrival, and with their prospects looking bleak, the Elmans settled into an inexpensive hotel with gas lighting—a system new to Saul Elman. In Shpola and Odessa, kerosene lamps provided light, and wood or coal stoves were used for heat and cooking. In St. Petersburg, they had electricity. Saul didn't realize that to turn off a gaslight, the valve had to be closed, so he merely extinguished the flame, thereby filling their room with lethal gas. When they awoke, both were weak and dizzy; in fact, as soon as they stepped out of bed, they each collapsed. Saul was able to cry for help, and a doctor was summoned as their room was aired. When Mischa came to consciousness, it was 9 o'clock. He was due to play for the critics at 1 o'clock, in four hours.

Fiedler was summoned, and he arrived in time to hear the doctors say that on no account was Mischa to be disturbed. Having gone to great lengths persuading the reviewers and Berlin music world dignitaries to agree to hear Mischa—and with his financial stability riding on the success of the public concert, a few days later—Fiedler was against cancelling the afternoon recital. But then, neither he nor Saul

45

had the heart to persuade Mischa to play it. They didn't have to, it turned out, for at 12:30, Mischa insisted on getting out of bed, getting dressed, and giving his performance.

It was a difficult task, though: They arrived late, and the audience, with its Teutonic admiration of punctuality, had grown restive. Saul recalled the scene vividly in his *Memoirs*:

> Mischa at last appeared. Perfect silence settled on the great hall....Violin in hand, he now stood before [his judges], hollow-eyed and pale, his frame shaking with weakness and fear, his head bent toward the left as though it were too heavy to hold upright. For half a minute he stood so, and to me it seemed a lifetime.
>
> Suddenly he made a hasty movement. He was tuning his violin. In a moment all was changed. The boy was transformed. His eyes flashed fire, his body became strong and elastic. He led his bow across the violin and the concert was underway....He played like one possessed. I think the reaction which set in must have worked for a time as a stimulus, and he stood there in his little white knee breeches and white sailor blouse, his eyes kindled with a sacred fire, firmly grasping his violin and swaying to and fro, utterly lost to his surroundings.[2]

Perhaps father Elman can be forgiven his mystical prose, for it was miraculous that Elman played at all that day, let alone a program that included the Tchaikovsky Concerto and the Bach *Chaconne*. He was supposed to play several other works as well, but by the end of the *Chaconne*, he had taxed his endurance to its limit, and during the applause he walked over to the piano, set down his violin, and collapsed. The audience had not been told about the gaslight incident until then, and while a recounting of the tale made colorful reading in the evening newspapers, the Elmans were more interested in the critical appraisals of the performance, which were unanimously glowing.

With this first hurdle behind them, Saul and Mischa realized that their work was only beginning; and Saul, in particular, wanted the reviewers' opinions fortified with an endorsement from Joachim. He wrote to the old professor and asked for an appointment, which was granted, although when they met, Joachim's initial questions struck Saul as rather cold and businesslike. After the opening pleasantries, Mischa asked Joachim what he would like to hear him play and Joachim suggested that he play some Tchaikovsky—a composer to whom Joachim was not partial. The examination, as Saul Elman describes it, was rather like the encounter with Sarasate, except that this one took place before Joachim's students. "Every time the child performed some remarkable feat of technique," Saul reports, "the professor would turn to the students and nod his head significantly, and from the ever-growing intensity of his expression, I saw that his interest in the performance was steadily growing.

"There was no applause," Saul continues. "No one dared to applaud until Joachim led the way. The students looked puzzled and stared at the professor, who remained sitting in his chair, meditating with bent head. I was in no hurry. I knew that he was comparing Mischa and von Vecsey. I was wise to accord him ample time for deliberation."

Joachim's assessment, however, struck Saul as annoyingly ambiguous. As Saul quotes him, Joachim said, simply, "I am now facing the second great wonder," leaving Saul unsure whether he meant the second prodigy to come to him recently, or that he considered Elman's talent second to von Vecsey's. To Mischa, however, he said only, "you play very well for your age," a comment the young violinist considered condescending, and which he remembered a year later when, after hearing Joachim perform with his string quartet, young Elman— by them somewhat more firmly established—went backstage to pay his respects. "You know Professor Joachim," Elman observed, "*you* play very well for *your* age." In fact, Elman was never one to let a good joke slip by without getting the most mileage out of it, and at the end of his career, he turned it on himself yet again. "When I was a prodigy," he told interviewers, "people said I play very well for my age. And now, I'm the oldest violinist still playing concerts, and people are still saying the same thing!"

The advance notices guaranteed that the Bechstein Hall would be full for Mischa's official debut the next Sunday, although in truth, there turned out to be comparatively few tickets left for the general public after those set aside for the critics, prominent local musicians and other celebrities had been given away. His program included the Paganini Concerto in D major, Wieniawski's *Fantasy on Airs from Faust*, Tchaikovsky's *Sérenade mélancolique*, Sarasate's *Zapateado*, and Beethoven's *Romance* in C major. For his encores, he played Sarasate's Chopin *Nocturne* arrangement, the *Serenades* by Drigo and Arensky, and a few other short works.

The reviews were again laudatory, and many made reference to von Vecsey—who, only a few days earlier, had played the Beethoven Concerto with the Berlin Philharmonic, under Joseph Joachim's baton. Most avoided making qualitative comparisons, and instead noted the excellence of both young players. Where comparisons were made, Elman was called the better of the two. "Somewhat older than the Hungarian wonder-child," wrote the critic of the *Berliner Borsen-Courier*, "this very intelligent Elman presents one, both in his bearing and in his playing, with a more mature, more self-possessed impression. It was as though an accomplished, fully matured master stood before one, so remarkable, so warm was the tone in the cantilena, so full of verve and emotion were the sounds which issued from Elman's violin." The critic of the *Vossiche Zeitung* assented: "If one compares Mischa Elman with the year-younger (sic) Ferenc von Vecsey, the scale sinks deep in favor of the former."[3]

Otherwise, the critics judged Elman as a mature artist, and their praise was lavish. The reviewer for the *Berliner Borsen-Zeitung* called the recital a "brilliant event," and noted that "of the sheer perfection of the artist's performance, one did not know what to admire first: the mature virtuosity of his technique, his great rounded tones so full of musical life; or his remarkable grasp of musical organization." The critic from the *Berliner Lokal-Anzeiger* wrote that "things upon which the finest talent must exercise the greatest diligence over long years of study are mastered by this boy as though they were trifles. And how his tone rings out!" This reviewer did find the program itself lacking in musical depth, adding that only the Chopin arrangement "gave the little virtuoso a chance to show that he is endowed with an amazing musical instinct and an admirable interpretative power."

Interestingly, the critics who compared him to other great violinists of the time unanimously settled on one name: Sarasate. "The world will soon be talking about Mischa Elman," wrote one reviewer, who went on to predict that, "a second Sarasate has arisen." The critic of the *Berlin Morgen Post* was more specific: "Mischa Elman is the ablest violinist since Sarasate," he wrote, "with whom he shares in remarkable technique, true musical execution, and the sweet, soothing tone so caressing to the ear."

❖ ❖ ❖ ❖ ❖

Even before the concert, Fiedler and the elder Elman prepared a plan of attack for the rest of Germany. As impresarios, they were both naive. Approaching the tour in much the same way Saul managed Mischa's earlier tour of Western Russia, they mapped out an itinerary, and upon arriving in each town, they hoped to engage a hall, advertise for a week in the local newspapers, and then give the concert. Their original idea was to begin with a recital in Dresden. Unfortunately, the death of a state figure (and a 30 day mourning period) intervened; so they set their sights on Hamburg instead, and arranged a concert through an agent there. Their Hamburg contact, however, also represented von Vecsey, and Mischa's rival had already scheduled two concerts in the same town that month.

Moreover, the promoter regarded von Vecsey as an established young star, and Elman as a newcomer; so Elman's concert was treated as any other inauspicious debut, and was so sparsely attended that the box office receipts failed to cover the costs. The reviews, however, were as favorable as those published in Berlin, and here too, Elman was favorably compared with von Vecsey. More importantly, the two critical successes brought Elman to the attention of several conductors—among them Max Fiedler, director of the Hamburg Philharmonic, and Oskar Nedbal, conductor of the Prague Philharmonic both of whom turned up at the violinist's hotel and offered him engagements with their ensembles. Add to these Colonne's promise of a Paris performance, and the prospects for the future helped Saul and Mischa overcome the financial disappointments of the Hamburg debut.

The Elmans remained in Hamburg, and Mischa played the Mendelssohn Concerto twice with Max Fiedler's orchestra before they left for Dresden, where Mischa again found himself playing opposite von Vecsey; and from Dresden they went to Leipzig, where, after a second recital, the conductor Artur Nikisch came backstage and offered Mischa an engagement with the Gewandhaus Orchestra. For the occasion, he played the work that would soon become a signature piece, the Tchaikovsky Concerto, and his account was such a success that the Leipzig orchestra's management was compelled to waive its long-standing rule against allowing soloists to play encores. From Leipzig, Saul and Mischa returned to Berlin for another recital there.

Joachim had been unable to attend the first recital (von Vecsey was playing the same day), but he came to this one. He did not, however, visit the artists' room after the concert, and Elman's supporters took this as an affront, or at least, as a mark of his preference for von Vecsey. Joachim did, however, send the Elmans an invitation to his home a few days later, requesting that Mischa bring his violin. When they arrived, Joachim was quite friendly; and after Mischa played, Joachim said he stood ready to help the young violinist in any way possible.

Only a few weeks had passed since the Berlin debut, but with a string of successes behind them, the Elmans were feeling satisfied and prosperous. Their next major hurdle was Vienna, and they planned to make their way through Germany's smaller towns before presenting a debut there in November. Word of Elman's playing had reached Vienna from Germany by the time of their arrival, so the Elmans had to do relatively little publicity of their own. Once more, the reviews dwelt on the impressiveness of his technique and his striking interpretive maturity.

For the rest of November and December, the Elmans made Vienna their headquarters, and made numerous forays back into Germany. During their stay, however, new players entered the game—professional managers and agents. Mischa's successes in Germany and Austria had left a trail of newspaper accounts that made his marketability an unambiguous issue to those in the concert trade. Several made appointments to see Saul and Mischa, in hopes of signing the boy to a management contract. Others cabled the Elmans with career advice combined with offers of their services, and when the Elmans sent no reply, several travelled to Vienna to present themselves and their services in person.

At first, Saul deflected these offers. He knew that he and Fiedler, as beginners in the management business, could not manage Mischa's concert career forever; but then, as Saul saw it, they hadn't done badly. Indeed, their first encounters with the business side of the music world left both Saul and Mischa with a strongly negative impression—one that stayed with the violinist for the rest of his life, and which undoubtedly served as the basis for his own mutually unsatisfactory relationships with a long string of managers. To the Elmans, these managers seemed greedy, superficial and exploitative. In his *Memoirs* Saul writes of their claims that their primary interest was in Mischa's artistry, and their displays of fondness and protectiveness. Saul, of course, had a deep-seated distrust of strangers intent on handling his son's career, and he saw these professionals as a personal threat.

Still, the managers did offer plenty of ready money, and Saul found this tempting. It seemed, too, that if Mischa's worldwide career was to be launched, it might to wise to strike while the iron is hot. On the other hand, he had promised Auer he would bring Mischa back to St. Petersburg in December. Indeed, Auer had warned him against just this sort of temptation. Unsure how to handle the situation, Saul wrote Auer a long letter detailing Mischa's triumphs, and discussing the managerial offers. Auer, in his response, was cautionary but practical:

> It seems good fortune follows in the footsteps of true talent. I admire your strength of character, as demonstrated by your ability to maintain your mental equilibrium in the face of their greatest temptation. As to your attitude toward agents and impresarios who, in view of Mischa's unparalleled success are bound to cross your path, my advice to you is not to ignore them altogether. Sooner or later you are bound to have to deal with these people in some way. They constitute an integral part of the profession, being inevitable in the career of every artist big or little. The wise thing to do is discover the ablest agent with the least capacity for dissimulation, but in view of the fact that the problem of choosing the right man is one of extreme difficulty, I advise you to exercise the utmost care lest you endanger the boy's career.[4]

The right man to launch Mischa's career arrived at their Vienna hotel as they were packing to leave for St. Petersburg. His name was Grossmann. Wearing diamond rings, a jeweled stickpin, and a gold chain, and virtually chain-smoking Havana cigars, he was the most ostentatious manager they had encountered yet, and he spoke with assurance about his prominence in European musical and managerial circles. His list of clients confirmed his boast, though, and one name in particular caught the Elmans' eye—Ferenc von Vecsey. At the end of their first meeting, Saul Elman declined Grossmann's offer. The manager, however, prevailed upon a mutual acquaintance who was a banker; and before the day was out, the banker persuaded Saul that a contract with Grossmann could only benefit Mischa. Saul engaged an attorney to negotiate the terms of the contract; and three days later, Mischa's career was put in Grossmann's hands. The relationship was not to start, however, for several months, and during that period it was to be kept secret, since the Elmans had not formally ended their managerial relationship with Fiedler, and Grossmann had agreed to terminate his relationship with von Vecsey.

With that arranged, the Elmans boarded the train for St. Petersburg, arriving early in 1905, in time for the family to be reunited for Mischa's fourteenth birthday. At the Conservatory, Auer conducted what was partly a lesson and partly an examination, the point of which was to see whether the rigors of the tour had taken a toll on the violinist's

technique, and whether the admiration of the public and critics led to
sloppy habits. Auer determined that his pupil survived the tour well—
that Mischa's technique was in good shape; that he was clearly not
neglecting his practicing; and that the maturity and sensitivity of his
playing had withstood the giddy temptations of public acclaim.

"You need no longer have any fears on Mischa's account," Auer
told Saul Elman. "He is no longer a pupil. He is today a finished artist. You can tour the entire world with him and there is not the slightest
doubt that his progress will continue."

Decades later, critics debated the wisdom of Auer's decision. "Thus
we find that at barely fourteen, Elman's days of formal training were
over," observed Henry Roth. "This undoubtedly had a serious effect
on Elman's future musical development. No 14-year old, even a talent
of genius proportions, should discontinue supervised study, particularly in the 20th century, with its proliferating musical and reper-
torial demands."[5]

Auer's decision to let Mischa leave the Conservatory with his bless-
ings seems to have been an academic point, for by signing with
Grossmann, Saul and Mischa had signalled their own intentions quite
clearly. So with Auer's benediction, Elman's formal training came to
and end. His professional career had already begun.

Saul wanted Mischa to rest a few months before undertaking his
next tour, but soon after their return to the Russian capital, Mischa
received a cable from an English manager named Lichtenstein, whom
Grossmann had contacted, and who offered a string of orchestral appearances in London. Mischa wanted to accept the offer, so father and
son set off by train once again. On the way, Mischa managed to break
a tea cup in his right hand, which suffered deep lacerations and had
to be suspended in a sling—a sight that alarmed Grossmann and Lichtenstein when they met the Elmans at the train in London, for the latter had arranged a musicale for the day after their arrival. Like the
performance for the Berlin critics, this London salon concert was an
event staged for the brokers of power and opinion in cultural circles.

Lichtenstein quickly took Mischa under his wing. As soon as they
were installed in their hotel, he summoned a pair of physicians to examine and bandage Mischa's hand. They advised that he might be able
to perform the following day if he rested sufficiently in the meantime.
The next morning, Lichtenstein arrived early, and brought Mischa a

new silk sailor's suit. He then set about teaching the child common English phrases, and gave him a quick lesson in British social niceties.

The musicale, presented by Lady Palmer, took place at the Salle Erard on Great Marlborough Street. Lichtenstein took Mischa there by automobile, but on the way stopped off to allow Mischa to play a brief, unannounced recital for a group of critics. The musicale itself took place at 5 o'clock, and was, Saul reports, astoundingly successful. It must have been: a week later, Lichtenstein arrived at the hotel with an invitation from Buckingham Palace, summoning Mischa to give a command performance for King Edward VII and King Alfonso of Spain.

In the meantime, he made his public debut, at Queen's Hall on March 21, 1905, with the Tchaikovsky Concerto, accompanied by an orchestra led by Charles Williams. The audience was so taken with the performance that after the first movement cadenza, full applause burst forth, drowning out the following orchestral passage—a rare occurrence in polite London. The critic for the British violin journal, *The Strad*, called Elman's London debut "a veritable triumph." He went on:

> From the moment he stepped onto the platform until he had played his last encore at 11:20 p.m. (and even then the public seemed to want some more) his success in this country was an assured thing. He tackled the terrific difficulties of Tchaikovsky's D major Concerto as though they were a mere bagatelle, and although Auer said it was almost unplayable, and Hanslick (who ought to have known better) called it all sorts of dirty names, this little fellow literally "waltzed round it," made light of its technical pitfalls, and gave a rendering of it so thoroughly in accord with the spirit in which it was written that the audience literally rose at him.[6]

The performance at Buckingham Palace was Elman's first before royalty, and sharing the program with him were the Australian soprano Nellie Melba, and the Italian tenor Enrico Caruso. Elman and Caruso began a long friendship that afternoon. In years to come, they would spend a great deal of time together in London and in New York. Recalling his first meeting with Caruso, Elman told interviewers that the beauty of Caruso's singing that evening at Buckingham Palace was enough to make him forget his own stagefright.

In the few weeks he'd been in London, Elman had decided that he liked this city better than any he had yet visited, and that he would like to settle there. A few months later, Saul brought Yetta and the girls from St. Petersburg, and by the summer of 1905, the Elman family was established in a large house in Hampstead. That November, the youngest of Mischa's sisters, Esther, was born.

Almost immediately after the March 21 debut concert, Mischa and Saul decided to cap their run of successes with a debut in Paris. Both Lichtenstein and Grossmann warned them that a Paris debut took time to arrange, and that the French public was capricious, so Saul decided to take the matter of the French debut into his own hands, arranging it as he had arranged the German tour. Of course, it was now a good deal easier for them to finance this sort of venture, even without firm plans. So, a few days after the London debut, they set sail for France, and on April 2, Mischa played a recital at the Salle des Agriculteurs. His program included works of Bach, Paganini and Saint-Saëns. It was not the great splash they had hoped it would be; but they were able to arrange for something more impressive by calling on Edouard Colonne.

When they arrived, Colonne was preparing for his orchestra's annual all-Wagner concert; but he had promised to present Mischa with his orchestra, and he opted to keep that promise in an odd way. Since the tradition of the Wagner concerts precluded having a soloist on the program, Colonne decided to schedule Mischa's concerto appearance during what would normally have been the intermission. Those who wanted to hear only Wagner could leave the hall, while those curious about the 14-year old violinist could hear him. When this plan was announced, Paris's Wagnerians wrote letters of protest to Colonne, and threatened to riot if the concert went on as planned. Colonne warned the Elmans about the strength of this sentiment, but added that "should they make good on their threat, it will only serve our purpose and add to Mischa's success. I want you to bear in mind that no great artist has ever appeared in Paris who was not booed at first. Do not vex yourself. Leave it to me."

Saul trusted Colonne's judgement, and he was heartened to find, on the evening of the concert, that the controversy surrounding Mischa's appearance helped fill the hall. At the intermission, when Mischa took the stage, there were no protests; nor were there any demonstrations of hostility as he made his way through the Mendelssohn Concerto. Rather, the audience was wildly enthusiastic, and called him back six times before Colonne invited him to return with his violin and play an encore—thereby breaking another house rule. This was too much: the protests from the heretofore patient Wagnerians were loud and direct, and so were the responses of those who wanted to hear the encore. Eventually, Colonne called a halt to the fracas with a brief speech about art being more important than the house rules. He asked those who didn't want to hear the encore to either be quiet or leave; and when the protests began anew, the police escorted some of the more vocal dissenters out of the hall. Mischa remained on stage to play a handful of encores before the Wagner concert continued.

Besides his concert successes, the Paris visit yielded more tangible fruit—Mischa Elman's first recordings. These were cylinders, and are now exceedingly rare, not have ever been transferred to LP. Among the works he recorded at his first sessions in the studios of the French Pathé label were an unaccompanied Bach work (the *Gavotte* from BWV 1006), the Drigo *Serenade*, a Schubert *Moment musicaux* (arranged by Auer), and Schumann's *Abendlied* (arranged by Joachim). Recording was a new and unusual experience for Mischa. It required, for one thing, that he set aside his Amati and use an aluminum violin that resonated in a way that, when captured by the recording horn, inscribed on a cylinder and then played back through the horn, sounded slightly more like a violin than a real violin did. This didn't bother Mischa, though. Walking through the streets of Paris, he had encountered some record shops where, for a franc or two, he could hear recordings of violinists and pianists whose names were magic to him. He wanted his own playing to be similarly available, and he began his recording career exuberantly. The following year, in London, he began making recordings for the Gramophone and Typewriter Company, a company later known as His Master's Voice.

Back in London, Mischa was again drawn into the social whirl he had been enjoying at the time he left for Paris. After the Buckingham Palace concert, he became a darling of London society, and was frequently invited to aristocratic dinner parties, with and without his violin. His London agent, Lichtenstein, usually tagged along; but after Mischa's initial successes, Lichtenstein persuaded Saul to stay home when Mischa went on these outings, partly on the grounds that he

hadn't cultivated the formal manners English of high society. Actually, Lichtenstein was probably used to the child prodigy and adoring
father combination, and from his point of view, it was always best to
keep the father at a distance—not, as Saul insisted, to deny him a
measure of joy in his son's success, but simply as a way of keeping
Mischa's blossoming career under professional control.

Saul agreed, at first, that it would be best to stay out of the picture
during Mischa's social visits, but eventually he grew curious about the
time Mischa was spending at these grand houses. He was particularly interested in meeting Baron Alfred Rothschild, who Mischa and
Lichtenstein visited weekly, and who had given Mischa a number of
lavish gifts, ranging from a gold watch inscribed "To the genius, Mischa Elman" to the use of an automobile and driver. On one occasion,
midway through 1906, Saul decided to take a stand, and insisted that
if Lichtenstein didn't take him along, Mischa would not attend either.
Lichtenstein claimed to use all his influence to obtain an invitation for
Saul. When they arrived at the Baron's home, though, the seemingly
well-connected Lichtenstein disappeared, and Mischa presented his
father to the Baron. It emerged that the Baron didn't know Lichtenstein
at all. That ended Lichtenstein's association with the Elmans, his
capable handling of the violinist's London career notwithstanding,
and it fortified the negative feelings about managers that Saul began
to develop in Vienna, and which he instilled in his son.

In the summer of 1905, the whole Elman family left London for a
vacation in Ostend, Belgium, where they were reunited with Leopold
Auer. They had, by then, acquired a secretary, a Mr. Geller, who came
into their lives after stopping Saul on the street and insisting that he
be taken to meet Mischa. Starting as a hanger-on, Geller quickly in-
gratiated himself to Mischa, if not entirely to Saul, who considered him
odd but harmless. Saul was hoping their vacation in Ostend would
put some distance between them and Geller; but the persistent fan followed them to the resort, and it was during this trip that he confided
to Saul that he was desperately low on funds, but that he would make
a diligent secretary. Reluctantly, Saul took him on, and he held the
position for three and a half years.

At Ostend, Mischa and Auer spent a good deal of time working on
repertoire together, particularly on the Brahms Concerto, which
Mischa planned to add to his active repertoire during the 1906 season.
Auer was to return to Russia at the end of the Ostend trip, but agreed
to visit London in 1906. To make the invitation as attractive as pos-

sible, Saul promised Auer there would be ample opportunity for public performance, and many eager pupils. His main object, though, was to bring Auer within shouting distance, for despite Mischa's unbroken string of successes, Saul was wondering about the firmness of the musical ground on which his teenage son was treading. Over the past few months, he saw Mischa coming under the influence of managers like Lichtenstein, social pillars like Rothschild, and hangers-on like Geller, all of whom diluted his own influence somewhat. He wanted someone around whose motives he trusted, and whose influence would pull Mischa homeward.

Auer did come to London in the middle of 1906, but not to stay. Rather, he established a studio and took a few pupils—an arrangement he maintained each summer until 1912, when he moved his studio to Dresden. He also, however, played a string of duo concerts with Mischa in England, their centerpiece being the Bach Double Concerto. At the end of the summer, Auer returned to Russia.

Elman, meanwhile, played a recital at Queens Hall in May, and in June he made his debut with the London Symphony, playing the Brahms Concerto. The orchestra's conductor, Hans Richter, told Mischa after the concert that "the best thing I can wish you is that you remain as pure and unspoiled in your art as you are now."[7] The Brahms became the centerpiece of his concerto repertoire for awhile. In October, he played it with Nikisch in Leipzig—a dreadful experience, he later recalled, for Nikisch apparently didn't like the Brahms, hadn't prepared it well, and refused to devote much rehearsal time to it. Throughout the winter, he played the work with other European orchestras under more satisfying circumstances.

In England, the Elmans settled into normal family life for the first time in a decade. Having quickly learned English, Mischa became an avid reader; and during his first years in England, he acquired a few other non-musical hobbies, among them a penchant for motoring around the countryside and a fondness for chess. By the end of 1906, he had also hit upon a comparatively comfortable approach to his concert schedule. In the winter, he would tour Holland, Germany, Austria-Hungary, Poland, Denmark, Norway and Sweden; and in the summer, he would mix concertizing with vacationing in England and France. In England, his system was particularly simple. Usually, he was able to arrange things so that he could have lunch with his family in London, catch a train for the city where he was to play that evening, and train back to London immediately after the performance.

By 1907, he had made his way around Europe several times, and was comfortably established with his family in London. But for Mischa Elman, at 16 years old, there were still worlds to be won. The Orient and Latin America were high on his list of exotic places he wanted to see. He was also anxious to tour the United States. But it would be another year before that particular dream was fulfilled.

CHAPTER FIVE:

A New World

Early in 1907, the prospect of playing for the American audience, let alone winning its heart, seemed distant indeed. Having dismissed Lichtenstein as their English manager, the Elmans hired a replacement, Daniel Mayer; and on their request, Mayer began testing the waters in New York and Boston. The responses he received were not heartening. Most American managers demanded guarantees against possible losses, and those who didn't insist on an indemnity flatly refused to take a chance on the violinist on the grounds that the American public did not care for prodigies. Von Vecsey, for instance, had made his New York debut in 1905, and despite his European acclaim, American response was lukewarm.

A ray of hope emerged at the end of 1907, after Mischa's appearance at a London charity gala arranged by Nellie Melba. The program was predominantly operatic, but Melba, who became acquainted with Mischa at his first Buckingham Palace performance, thought it might be nice to have him on the program as a collaborator, and invited him to play a violin *obbligato* to Gounod's *Ave Maria*. Saul insisted that his son's appearing on a program merely as an accompanist would damage his reputation as a soloist, and Melba agreed that an artist of Elman's drawing power did deserve to appear on the bill in his own right.

Because the program was a long one, there were to be no encores. But after Elman's rendering of Sarasate's *Zigeunerweisen*, the audience refused to stop applauding, and in the interest of getting on with the show, the management let him break the rule. He played five encores before finally retiring to the artists' room.

Oscar Hammerstein, the American opera impressario, was in the audience that night, and he was as impressed by the response of the audience as by Elman's playing. He visited the Elmans backstage, and told Saul that they must go to America, the sooner the better. Saul found Hammerstein puzzling, but amusing. "I did not quite understand all he said and meant," Saul wrote in his *Memoirs*. "Here was a stranger, a man I had never met before. In one minute he became as intimate with me as if he had known me since childhood. And then his way of talking; he spoke in three languages at the same time. Yiddish, English, and German were so blended that I simply could not help laughing."

At that, Saul didn't think Hammerstein—an operatic impresario, not a concert promoter—would be interested in promoting Mischa's career in America. Nevertheless, the next day Hammerstein arrived at Mayer's office and offered to present Mischa in a string of Sunday concerts at the Manhattan Opera House. Saul harbored doubts. He reasoned that the Manhattan Opera House would be a less auspicious venue for his son's debut than a Carnegie Hall concert with orchestra, so in agreeing to the opera house series, he insisted that an orchestral debut must come first. Hammerstein agreed, and while arranging for the orchestral debut was not his province, he embarked on a publicity campaign on Mischa's behalf immediately upon his return to New York. Soon American magazines and newspapers were carrying stories about the boy and his rise from poverty in Russia to success throughout Europe.

Hammerstein orchestrated this publicity brilliantly, without, at first, mentioning his own connection with Elman. In his first interviews, he concentrated on his impressions of Europe (a common focus for musical figures returning to America in those days), singling out Elman as an outstanding young star of the London concert scene. A few interviews later, he confirmed that he had persuaded young Elman to come to New York for a series of Sunday recitals.

All this press attention caught the interest of several orchestra managers and promoters, including the management of the Boston Symphony, which solicited the advice of its newly appointed conductor, Max Fiedler. Having by then conducted several of Elman's appearances with the Hamburg Philharmonic, Fiedler advised the orchestra to engage him. Thus, the Boston Symphony was the first American orchestra to offer Elman an engagement—although it turned out to be the second orchestra he actually performed with. Several agents cabled to offer their services; but one, Henry Wolfsohn, gained an advantage over his colleagues by attending one of Elman's

London recitals while there on business. He took Mischa onto his roster, and set the wheels in motion for an American tour, to commence in the winter of 1908.

For Elman, meanwhile, the business of giving recitals and playing concertos in England and on the continent continued apace. The recitals were frequent, but not all were the full solo recitals that are the norm today. Rather, many were split programs, in which two or three artists performed alternating sets. A particularly interesting example is a concert presented at London's Queen's Hall, on December 15, 1907, under the auspices of the Sunday League. Elman topped the bill: on the program his name is printed in large letters, preceded by the notation, "Special Engagement of The Great Violinist." Under his name, separated by a line and in smaller letters, were the names of three singers: Miss Caroline Hatchard, Miss Violet Elliott, and Mr. John F. MacCormack (sic)—the soon to be famous Irish tenor, then at the start of his career. McCormack had appeared on the same series earlier that season (with his name spelled correctly on the program), and he had shared concert bills with Elman before then. The concert began with a duet, Denza's *Nocturne*, sung by Hatchard and Elliott, followed by Elman's performance of the Mendelssohn Concerto, to piano accompaniment. Miss Elliott was then featured in an aria, Carey's *Break, Break, Break*, and McCormack sang Simpson's *The Awakening*. Elman then returned to the stage to play a Tartini sonata, followed by Caroline Hatchard singing David's *Thou Charming Bird*. Elman returned again to play Bach's *Air on the G String* and Senegaglia's *All' Anticha*. Next came a pair of songs from Elliott, Bischoff's *The Summer Wind* and Findon's *A Little Fleet of Cloud Boats*. John McCormack then contributed an old Irish air, *The Snowy-Breasted Pearl*, and Hatchard returned for *The Night and You* and *A Birthday Song* (both unattributed); and Elman took the stage for his final offering of the evening, a pair of showpieces—Zanelli's *Tempo di Minuetto*, and Sarasate's *Caprice Basque*. The concert closed with another duet between the two ladies, Glover's *I Heard a Voice in the Tranquil Night*.

Quaint as programs of this kind may seem today, they offered their listeners variety, and they were quite common. Elman performed in many such recitals during these early years, although he clearly preferred to play on his own. This mode of programming was also current in the United States, and although Elman participated in relatively few concerts of this type after his American debut, some of the American mixed recitals carried considerable prestige and tempting fees, and some paired him with performers of comparable stature. He participated in these until the 1920s.

Otherwise, his recitals tended to begin with one of the less titanic concertos, reduced for violin and piano—among those he favored as his opener around 1908 were Lalo's *Symphonie Espagnole*, the Bruch-G minor, the Saint-Saëns B minor, the Spohr D minor, and the Mendelssohn. From there, the program would continue with a large Baroque work—the Bach *Chaconne*, or a Handel sonata—and then a group of Romantic works and display pieces by Wieniawski, Tchaikovsky, Sarasate, Sinding, and sometimes even Hubay. Of these, Elman's clear favorites were Tchaikovsky's *Sérenade mélancolique*, Wieniawski's *Fantasy on Themes from Faust*, and Auer's arrangement of the Paganini *Caprice* No.24. Elman varied the blend from program to program, and by mid-1908, Elman was able to tell interviewers that his repertoire comprised more than 200 works.

By the middle of 1907, Elman also had his first steady accompanist, who doubled as secretary and general factotum, Waldemar Liachowsky[1.] Liachowsky, a young Russian Jew, had spent much of his life in Berlin, where he attended the university and subsequently took an accounting job at an artist management firm. The Elmans met him in Berlin on their first trip there, in 1904, and Saul was particularly taken with the young man's earnestness and sobriety. Liachowsky was not a professional musician, but a dilettante who devoted much of his leisure time to accompanying friends who were amateur singers and players. "He loved music deeply," Saul's *Memoirs* tell us. "The more I knew of him, and the more I learned of him, the better I realized that he was honesty itself; the finest expression of sincerity, a man of refined manners, a gentleman through and through."

Those qualities, Saul reasoned, made Liachowsky a suitable companion and confidante for Mischa, who, at age 17, had spent most of his life traveling with his father. Since Geller, their English secretary, was about to give up his post and move on to another job, Saul hit on the idea of offering Liachowsky the unusual position of secretary and accompanist. Mischa vetoed the idea at first. He didn't mind having Liachowsky handling his paperwork, but he wasn't keen on having an amateur pianist supporting his performances. On the other hand, Liachowsky's technique was sufficient, if not glowing, and he would certainly be easily guided by Elman, whose playing he admired unquestioningly. After some discussion, the violinist decided to give

Liachowsky a chance, and the next time the Elmans visited Berlin, they offered the pianist the combined post.

Liachowsky hardly needed prompting from Mischa to polish his side of the repertoire. As Saul describes him, the pianist had, in Berlin, acquired all the virtues of the conscientious Teutonic worker—compulsiveness, drive, and an impulse towards the methodical. These qualities did, however, have certain drawbacks when grafted onto the pattern of life the Elman family had established. "He tried," Saul writes, "to convert our house with its slip-shod Russian methods into an orderly, systematically functioning institution, a thing which we were, at first, inclined to take good-humoredly, because of our growing affection for this naive person.... The trouble was that we Russians, who had been from childhood accustomed to disorder and chaos, could not possibly get his point of view. Disorder, confusion exasperated him, [while, by contrast] System, especially according to German rules, seemed to me to be in opposition to everything natural and true."

Elman and Liachowsky were touring together by the end of 1907, and it was through Liachowsky that the violinist evolved the extensive system of requirements all of his later long-term accompanists would live up to. These were interesting business relationships wherein Elman, as the employer, contracted the accompanist's exclusive services on an annual basis rather than by the concert. The pianists were expected to work with him daily for several hours, usually from mid-morning to early afternoon. They could also expect to hear from him sometime later in the day, when he might call to invite them over for tea, a game of chess, or dinner, all of which inevitably led to more playing.

In most cases—or, at least, in the handful of cases where the relationship lasted several years—the accompanists didn't mind this extracurricular work, and most became close to Elman and his family, personally and socially. Naturally, there were times an accompanist rebelled. For instance, early in the violinist's career, a newly hired accompanist startled Elman at the end of a recital by refusing to play encores, on the grounds that his agreement covered only the printed program. That, of course, was an extreme case, and the pianist was looking for a new job the next day.

❖ ❖ ❖ ❖ ❖

Elman was on his way to a place among the ranks of the great virtuoso violinists by now, but he was still a relative newcomer to a concert world that was by no means lacking in great players.

In fact, speaking strictly in terms of the violin, these first years of
the 20th century were rich indeed. Joachim and Sarasate had died (in
1907 and 1908, respectively), but the Czech violinist Jan Kubelik was
well established in the firmament of the concert world, as was the Belgian virtuoso-composer Eugene Ysaÿe. The Polish violinist Bronislaw
Huberman was highly regarded on the continent, but was less successful in England and America. Fritz Kreisler's career was flourishing on both sides of the Atlantic, as was Jacques Thibaud's, although
Thibaud performed to somewhat less acclaim at first. There were also
other new contenders: Joseph Szigeti, a Hungarian a year younger
than Elman, was at the start of his international career, but although
he made a successful London debut in 1906, his first American concert
was not until 1925.

Each of these violinists had a loyal following. More to the point,
each had a unique set of stylistic characteristics, quirks and calling
cards that shine through the scratchy surfaces of their early recordings. Whatever their sonic flaws, these discs provide a surprisingly
good overview of this otherwise lost interpretive world.

That there are so many recordings from Golden Age of violin playing is a quirk of technology. The earliest recording machines, with
their primitive horns and etching styluses, did a rather poor job of capturing the sounds of orchestras and pianos; but the voice and the violin
could be captured and reproduced quite nicely, and many singers and
violinists were given the opportunity to make records. The two
violinists who topped the list in 1908 were, unquestionably, Eugene
Ysaÿe and Jan Kubelik.

Ysaÿe, born in 1858, was the son of an amateur violinist who was
also music director of Liege Cathedral. After early lessons with his
father, he entered Liege Conservatoire; but he was apparently a lazy
student, and his teachers found the technique his father had taught
him at odds with their own approaches. He was soon expelled. A few
years later, in 1873, Henri Vieuxtemps chanced to pass Ysaÿe's house,
where he heard the strains of his own Fourth Concerto. Vieuxtemps
arranged to have Ysaÿe accepted at the Conservatoire again. Later,
Vieuxtemps invited him to study in Brussels.

While a student, Ysaÿe performed as concertmaster and solo
violinist of the Kursaal Orchestra, at Ostend, and soon he took up a

similar post in Berlin. Meanwhile, he performed a good deal else-where—including recitals in 1879 with Clara Schumann as his sonata partner. In 1881 he left Berlin for Paris, where he became friendly with Franck, Chausson and Debussy, each of whom composed for him. In 1886, he returned to Brussels to teach at the Conservatoire; but he was also a touring virtuoso, and he didn't let his teaching post inhibit him. He made his London debut in 1891, and there incurred the displeasure of George Bernard Shaw, who regarded him as a dazzling showoff who placed display above musicality. In 1894, he paid his first visit to American concert halls, where he was a good deal more successful.

Ysaÿe made a handful of recordings[2] in 1912, late in his years of violinistic greatness, although he did continue playing for many years thereafter. In 1919 and 1920, he and Elman toured the United States jointly, and in 1920, the two appeared together in Belgium, before the violin-playing Queen Elizabeth; but it was widely conceded by then that Ysaÿe's abilities were diminished. Ysaÿe recognized this, and he had by then shifted his attention to conducting and, with greater ener-gy than ever, to composing. His 1912 recordings, however, reveal a rich, sensuous violin sound—one that was timbrally consistent rather than coloristically varied. Even on the high strings, Ysaÿe produced the kind of full, throaty sound one expects from the violin's lower range.

Yet, despite the consistency of his sound, his playing hardly seems monochromatic or limited. In Wilhelmj's arrangement of the "Prize Song" from Wagner's *Die Meistersinger*, he draws a breathtakingly pure *pianissimo* sound, and he was generous in his use of vibrato, which was neither wide nor wobbly. Ysaÿe was also fond of the the expressively deployed slide; but perhaps the most striking characteris-tic of his playing on these recordings—and, according to contem-porary published accounts, of his live performances as well—is his *rubato*. He manipulated the shapes of his phrases in the personalized way that was a hallmark of his era, yet even as the notes within those phrases were extended, stretched or shortened, the essential rhythmic integrity of the full phrases remain unmarred. In every case, Ysaÿe's thoughtful approach shows the music in a new and exciting light—a fine example being his dreamy, lilting rendering of Kreisler's *Caprice Viennois*.

Moreover, his technique seems nearly flawless on these discs. In the Kreisler, the double-stopped melody comes through with graceful as-surance, and in the Vieuxtemps *Rondino* and the finale of the Mendelssohn Concerto, his passage work is fleet and his intonation is firmly centered. The recordings aside, one can infer a great deal about Ysaÿe's technique and temperament from the music he wrote, particularly the exquisitely textured and delightfully virtuosic solo sonatas.

Like Ysaÿe, Jan Kubelik was in many ways the quintessence of the Romantic violinist; yet, his playing inhabits a very different world. Kubelik was highly regarded in the United States at the time of Elman's debut. In fact, one of the articles heralding Elman's arrival began: "The great popularity of Kubelik in this country will be challenged in the coming season by another youthful virtuoso on the violin." Yet, Kubelik's moments in the top ranks were numbered by then, just as Ysaÿe's were. By 1910, the shine on his technique was beginning to dull, and he retired from the stage between 1915 and 1921, returning to a limited career thereafter.

Eleven years older than Elman, Kubelik was born near Prague and studied at the Prague Conservatory with Otakar Sevcik, whose *School of Violin Technique* method books promote technical polish through a series of grueling exercises. In 1898, he made his Vienna debut, and was proclaimed an incarnation of Paganini. Two years later he played in London for the first time, and in 1902 he toured the United States and began recording for Victor. His first American tour was said to be so successful that he was able to purchase a $160,000 castle from the proceeds.[3] Curiously, the violinist's popularity in the United States seems not to have been mirrored in his reviews. In 1907, a critic from the *New York Times* admitted that "few have the power of so ravishing the senses with the sheer beauty of his tone, the charm of his cantilena, the elegance and ease with which he masters all the technical difficulties," but found "something aloof in him as he plays."

Kubelik's recordings are magical, though. He was among the first violinists to make discs; indeed, when the Gramophone and Typewriter Company published its first Red Label catalogue, in September 1902, Kubelik was the only instrumentalist offered, the rest of the list comprising singers.[4] Unlike Ysaÿe, Kubelik reveled in coloristic display. More often than not, he produced an uncommonly sweet, lilting tone, but where the music warranted it (in, say, Paganini's *Moto perpetuo*), he applied a sharp, bright edge to his playing, achieved through an aggressive bow attack. In some works (for instance, in his rendering of Wieniawski's *Mazurka*, Op.19, No.2), he moved seamlessly between these styles.

There is plenty in Kubelik's discography that shows the era's tendency towards sheer display, too, the most unusual item being an unaccompanied violin fantasy on a theme from Donizetti's *Lucia di Lammermoor*, a dazzler that sets a bowed, double-stopped melody against a *pizzicato* accompaniment at times, and includes an array of showy runs and filigree. Kubelik's thumbprint, however, is his unusual use of *portamento*. He applied the effect to everything—from Drdla and Sarasate to Handel and Mozart—but he appears to have developed a personal interpretive code governing the speed, type and amount of *glissando* each composer's music could bear, for he varied his application of the effect by according to the era and composer.

A particularly fascinating example is his recording of the second movement of the Tchaikovsky Concerto. Arriving at the trilled D that closes the solo line's first phrase, he lingers for an instant over the last D before the ornament; but instead of going up to an E-flat to execute the trill, he moves down to a C-sharp, slides quickly back to D, then begins the trill. Elsewhere, he uses this false-descent-and-glide trick where the music's ascending leaps are greater; and he uses it in descending passages as well, by overshooting the lowest note and then sliding up to it. For instance, in the second phrase of the same Tchaikovsky movement, the trill is replaced by a falling line, from the three repeated D's to C, B-flat and A. Here, Kubelik plays the three Ds, then executes a rapid slide from B-flat to C before continuing the phrase. Elman, in each of his recordings, played the phrase crisply, as written.

Also among the recordings in circulation during Elman's early years—and possibly among the discs he heard during his first trip to Paris—were Fritz Kreisler's earliest efforts, recorded in Berlin for the Gramophone and Typewriter Company in 1903 or 1904. These performances, considerably more vivacious and precise than the later Kreisler recordings that are most readily available today, show a predilection for fine coloristic shading. There is also a touch of Kubelik-style *portamento* in Kreisler's rich-toned reading of Bach's *Air on the G String*, although for the most part his slides are more straightforward, and he uses them more sparingly.[5]

Compared with the early recordings of Ysaÿe, Kubelik, Kreisler and Elman, though, the first discs by the young Jacques Thibaud and Joseph Szigeti hinted at the dawn of a new school. Particularly in Baroque music, they abandoned interpretive pretension and played nearly as if their renderings were literal accounts of the notes on the page, with very little added in the way of embellishment or subjective *rubato*. They were, in this sense, among the first of the modern violinists, and the forerunners of the interpretive approach that has prevailed through much of the 20th century. Thibaud, for example, recorded the *Gavotte* from Bach's solo Partita No.3, BWV 1006, in 1905. He did lean on the phrase endings a little, and he occasionally emphasized the climactic points with a touch of vibrato (particularly on double-stops). Yet, on the whole, the reading is remarkably straightforward.

In an age where the performer's will ruled, this made Thibaud's playing unpopular in some quarters. Nevertheless, he must have straddled the Romantic/Modernist line at times, in ways his early recordings don't convey; for in an account of his first American concerts, published in *The Etude*, in January 1904, the violinist's Bach is criticized for the "exaggerated *portamenti* [which] are highly displeasing to a sensitive musical ear."

That same review also gives us an impression of the American feeling (or, at least, one American reviewer's attitude) about the flood of young European violin stars, and may help explain the resistance the Elmans encountered upon making their first American inquiries, as well as their trepidation about putting Mischa's career on the line by going there:

> It is the custom, nowadays, for all European "celebrities" to visit our shores, and to acquaint us, long in advance of their coming, with their exceptional musical virtues. Each one of these is "managed" by some enthusiastic concert agent, who carefully and systematically prepares our minds for wonders, which, alas, are wonderful only in that they are so commonplace and disappointing. Year after year these clever agents successfully manipulate press reports, and by the time they have strewn cargos of their peculiar literature throughout the land, the majority of concertgoers are firmly convinced that they will have the privilege of listening to the greatest artist of all ages.[6]

Of course, the process described in the *Etude* column remains alive today, and some of the promised wonders turn out to be great artists indeed, while others are flashes in the pan. Today, a young European violinist about to embark on his first American tour can rely not only on advance press, but on the fruits of technology—concert broadcasts, commercial recordings and even videotapes, all of which convey something of his performing manner long before he sets foot on these shores. In 1908, the primitive gramophone gave listeners only the faintest glimmer of what was to come in this regard.

As a new business, the fledgling record industry was booming. There were, by then, record shops in every major city of the world, including one that opened in St. Petersburg in 1900, two years before Elman arrived there. By 1902, the Victor Company, in the United States, was selling enough discs to turn a million dollar profit, and in 1903, England's Gramophone and Typewriter Company was reporting earnings in the millions as well. By 1905, Victor's profits had increased twelvefold, and the future looked brighter each year. What's more, Victor and Gramophone & Typewriter had entered into an agreement whereby matrixes would be exchanged, so that each company could sell both labels' stars on its own side of the Atlantic. Thus, Elman's early British G&T recordings were available to Victor, although the American label did not take up the option until 1908, when his American appearances were imminent.

Yet, in the early 1900s, as now, the bulk of the record world's profits came from pop discs. And in the serious concert world, records were still looked upon as something of a novelty, for understandable reasons. First, the discs held only four minutes of music, so the recorded repertoire was, until the advent of the multi-disc album, limited to brief works or edited versions of longer pieces. When the companies began making orchestral recordings, the sound technology necessitated a certain amount of rescoring. Cellos, for instance, were replaced with bassoons, which recorded better. Leaving quality aside, the quantity in which these discs could be produced and distributed was a fraction of what it is today. And record reviewing, as an extension of concert criticism, had scarcely begun. Many musicians, from Ysaÿe to Nikisch, provided endorsements proclaiming that the recordings they had heard were lifelike. But mention in the press of recordings by even the most famous players was rare. In fact, although Elman had already made some cylinders in Paris and a handful of flat discs in London, the American newspaper and magazine accounts of his career don't mention them.

Elman's early recordings for G&T tell us a good deal about his technique and performing persona in the years approaching his first American visit. His first offered a pair of short, spirited works, played back to back in just less than three minutes—Schubert's third *Moment musicale* (subtitled *Air russe* and arranged for violin and piano by Leopold Auer) and a *Perpetuum mobile* by Joseph Böhm. The Schubert gave Elman an opportunity to show not only his facility, through its mostly double-stopped melody, but to display a vivacious and daring interpretive personality. He molds the music with an almost gypsy-like rhythmic abandon, using a very different brand of *rubato* than Ysaÿe, Kubelik, or Kreisler. Rather than adhering to the classic definition of the effect—that is, the lengthening of certain notes and the compensatory shortening of others within the same phrase—Elman reshaped each phrase as it suited him, transforming the salon piece into a lively folk dance. In the Böhm, by contrast, he made his violin spill forth the quickly bowed figuration with dazzling precision, and within strict metronomic constraints.

In his next few discs, he expanded on these traits, particularly those heard in the Schubert. One fascinating disc contained an excerpt from Wieniawski's *Fantasy on Themes from Faust* (specifically, the paraphrase of the garden scene). In this intentionally lugubrious account, Elman takes full advantage of every lilting, long-note passage, bathing the music in the glow of his tone. It's difficult not to admire young Elman's ability to make these lines sing through a combination of sensitive dynamic shaping, a narrow and thoughtfully applied vibrato, plus a generous and seemingly intuitive use of *portamento*. If the double-stopped passages of the Schubert went by too quickly to convey much beyond ebullience, those of the Wieniawski allow Elman to linger and to savor their effect.

Elman wasn't entirely pleased with the recording, though, for in order to first the performance on a single disc side, the recording director, Fred Gaisburg, suggested that the violinist truncate the work, and improvise a short finale. What Elman provided was essentially a bare cadential figure—an arpeggiated chord punctuated by a languid slide and some light, distant pianistic rumbling. At the end of the take, Elman turned to Gaisburg and said, "This will do, but it isn't *Faust*. It's *Faust* decomposed."

The next couple of discs were lively trifles—the *Swing Song*, by Ethel Barnes, and a *Gavotte* by Bohm. Elman's fifth G&T disc, however, brought together all the sides of his art suggested by his first selections. This was Drigo's *Serenade*, a short coloristic work drawn from a recent (1900) ballet *Les Millions d'Arlequin*, and set for violin and piano by Auer. After a brief introduction (piano roulades over an energetically strummed violin accompaniment), Elman plays a fast solo cadenza that takes him up and down the fingerboard, and into the work's innocent, sweet theme, and he literally slides through the tune without reservation, sometimes even using a Kubelik-style *portamento* to enhance the warm, sentimental effect he hoped to convey.

The discs that followed continued along similar lines. They were, perforce, encore pieces and excerpts, ranging from Haydn and Mozart dance movements, and the first of his five recordings of Schumann's *Träumerei*, to vignettes by Gossec and Grétry, and showpieces by Saint-Saëns and Wieniawski. In each, Elman's playing is assured and outgoing, and his interest, clearly, is in manipulating the strands of the works until they not only convey his private view of the music's spirit—and, not incidentally, so that they might serve as canvasses upon which he could paint with the full range of tonal color at his command.

These were glorious days for young Elman. His interpretations were free and thoroughly personalized, and everyone around him— his parents, his managers, his accompanists, his record producers, his audiences, his friends in London's high society, and even the critics— expressed only unbridled admiration. Six year earlier, he had been a pale, sickly and rather fragile child; and in another decade, his hairline would begin to recede, just as his newly found appreciation for fine food would begin to tell. At the moment, though, he was a successful, prosperous 17-year old, who cut a fine figure, and whose deep blue eyes, trim build and his bushy dark hair made it possible for personality columnists to treat him as a matinee idol. From this time until his marriage, in 1925, stories describing him as an eligible bachelor in search of a wife were published in embarrassing abundance. Elman had also picked up both the fundamentals and the subtleties of English quickly, and his ability to turn a humorous or ironic phrase made him a favorite of columnists, who knew he could always be counted upon for a witty comment about London, women, the music world, travel, food, or whatever their roundups of comments from celebrities required.

Elman enjoyed this side of his career, and for the rest of his life he savored his reputation as a raconteur. He also enjoyed playing practical jokes, and although he found a kindred spirit in Enrico Caruso in that regard, he had little problem concocting pranks of his own early on. He liked, for instance, to catch people off guard, and the earliest recorded example of this took place during his first visit to Leipzig, during his 1904 tour. Through a well-connected friend, he petitioned for a full scholarship to the conservatory there, at least partly in the hope of eliciting an unbiased opinion of his playing. But the deadline for scholarship petitions had passed, and the director was not only disinclined to audition Elman, but treated him harshly. Eventually, he agreed to consider the petition, but Elman would have to audition before the full faculty the next morning. Elman would have gone through with it; but as he was leaving, the director opened an appointment book and asked him his name. Instead of making one up, he told the truth. The director, who had just read the reviews of Elman's recital, was not amused.

This incognito gag was one Elman played frequently in the early years, when people knew him by name and reputation, but didn't always know what he looked like. Doubtless, he often hoped to be recognized, and when he wasn't, he turned the situation into a game that inevitably proved uncomfortable for all concerned. During an American tour in 1917, for example, he arrived in Buffalo and invited a friend who lived there to lunch. The friend arrived with a pair of young ladies, and introduced Elman as Joe Brown. Inevitably, the discussion turned to music, and when one of the girls said she was an avid concertgoer and record collector, Elman asked her which violinists she liked. "My favorites are Kreisler and Elman," she told him.

"I play the violin myself," he told her, "but I am unable to judge the difference between the two." He then brought out his violin, and asked her what she liked that Kreisler played. She was partial to *Caprice Viennois*, so Elman began playing it, only to be interrupted by his guest, who complained that his tone was too scratchy. "Young lady," he calmly replied, "if you had found fault with my interpretation, my intonation or anything else, I would not argue with you. But I must defend my tone: I consider it as good as Elman's." That, she contended, was an absurd claim. "Well, what do you particularly like from Mischa Elman's repertoire?" he asked. Her choice was his arrangement of Beethoven's *Minuet in G*. He took up the violin again, and played the miniature with all the panache he would have given it if were on one of his programs. But the girl was unmoved, and again criticized Elman's tone.

Elman put down his violin, a little perturbed by then. "Do you know," he said, "sometimes I am taken for Elman?" She doubted it, but her image of the violinist was based on a publicity photo of a slightly earlier vintage, plus a certain amount of fantasy. "Elman is tall," she said, "and you're short. Elman is slender, and you're stout. And Elman has bushy hair; you're getting bald." "And what if I were to tell you that I am Mischa Elman?" he asked. "In that case," she retorted, "I should bow very low and say, 'Oh, Mr. Elman, I am highly honored.'" Elman reached into his jacket and produced his calling card. Still, she was unimpressed, knowing that the friend who had escorted her to lunch knew Elman and assuming that this Joe Brown must have met him too. "No matter how well I might know Elman," the violinist said, "I feel certain he would not allow me carry this watch around with me," whereupon he handed her the gold watch that had been inscribed to him by Baron Rothschild. The young woman felt humiliated and began to cry, but Elman eventually set her at ease, and he took up his violin again and serenaded his guests with excerpts from the Brahms Concerto.[7]

In late summer, 1908, Wolfsohn wired that he had arranged an extensive tour of the United States for Elman. His Boston Symphony debut was to be towards the start, a month after his arrival; but the first two concerts, a concerto appearance and a recital, were to take place in New York, at Carnegie Hall. After discussing his programs with Liachowsky, Mayer and Saul Elman, the violinist decided to use the Tchaikovsky Concerto, which had brought him tremendous luck in Europe, as his introductory orchestral vehicle. At the end of November, Mischa and Saul Elman, Waldemar Liachowsky, and Daniel Mayer set sail for New York. According to news accounts published soon after their arrival, Mischa claimed that he didn't practice at all on the voyage. That's unlikely. Later in life, he even managed to practice on airplane trips, fingering the strings of his violin silently while flying from one concert to the next. He did, in fact, play one concert on shipboard—a recital for the benefit of a child whose mother died during the journey.

The party docked in New York on Tuesday, December 6, two days before the debut, and found that Wolfsohn had done his job well, for waiting on the pier was a swarm of reporters from the New York dailies. As soon as the Elmans passed through Customs, they found themselves giving an impromptu press conference, the questions covering mostly non-musical matters—whether Mischa liked sports, whether he had been involved in any shipboard romances, what he thought of the United States.

The Elmans took up residence at the Knickerbocker Hotel, then a headquarters for visiting musicians. On Wednesday, they went to Carnegie Hall for the first rehearsal with the Modest Altschuler and his Russian Symphony Orchestra. But upon their arrival, they found several dozen people in the hall—musicians, critics, and interested well-wishers who had the connections to gain entrance to what was supposed to be a closed rehearsal. Elman at first objected to the presence of the crowd, since this was to be a rehearsal, not a preview performance. Wolfsohn persuaded him, though, that it was in his best interests to proceed as if there were no-one listening. As it turned out, the audience proved beneficial, its enthusiasm helping to dispel Mischa's and Saul's few lingering doubts about their American prospects.

CHAPTER SIX:

Establishing New Roots

The morning after his Carnegie Hall debut, Mischa Elman was the toast of New York's musical world. A week later, the response to his first solo recital was similarly enthusiastic, but for a single reservation expressed by a critic from the *New York Times*, who wrote that young Elman "has in abundance what is known as 'temperament'; and his playing suffers from its lack of poise and restraint." Within a decade, other reviewers would amplify this criticism, which grew even more acute as performing fashions changed, and as "temperament" was gradually banished as a legitimate (or at least fashionable) expression of an interpreter.

But for the time being, Elman had good reason to feel jubilant, for his success in New York was repeated in Boston and throughout the country during his four month introductory tour. The programs Elman played during this visit typically began with a concerto (accompanied by Liachowsky at the keyboard)—either Lalo's *Symphonie Espagnole*, the Mendelssohn, or Spohr's Concerto No.9. Next came a Handel Sonata (he alternated between two of these on the tour), or sometimes the Ferdinand David arrangement of Corelli's *La Folia*. In his Boston recital, he followed the Corelli with the Saint-Saëns *Introduction and Rondo capriccioso*; but in most towns, he played a short group consisting of Beethoven's *Minuet in G*, Dittersdorf's *German Dance* and the Gossec *Gavotte*, or combinations of Schubert, Schumann, Sarasate and Paganini vignettes.

In April 1909, the Elmans returned to London, and Mischa again took up his performance commitments in England and Europe. He returned to the United States later in the year, and it was during this second visit that he fulfilled his obligation to Oscar Hammerstein by playing a string of Sunday recitals. He also gave one of his more un-

75

usual performances—a reading of the Méditation from Massenet's *Thaïs*, given during a Manhattan Opera performance of the work featuring Mary Garden. This engagement led to an altercation with the musicians' union. The concertmaster, feeling displaced, had lodged a complaint, and when Elman and Hammerstein arrived at the rehearsal, the orchestra players put down their instruments and walked out of the pit. Negotiations ensued, and it was decided that Elman could play the "Méditation," but that, as a non-union member, he could not take a seat with the orchestra.

Meanwhile, Elman had turned 18, and as a subject of the Tsar, he was required to enter the Russian army. This needn't have been much of a problem—he could simply have renounced his Russian citizenship and taken an English passport. He chose not to do this; but until his military status was seen to, touring Russia was out of the question, for he would have been arrested and inducted.

There was a way out. Having by then performed several times for the English royalty, he prevailed upon Queen Alexandra—the wife of England's King Edward VII, and sister of the dowager Princess Marie Fedorovna, Nicholas II's mother—to intercede on his behalf. She did, and Elman soon received an exemption from the Tsar, who declared the young violinist a national treasure. He was required, however, to return to Russia and give a string of concerts, presented under the Tsarina's patronage, in exchange for this exemption. While in Russia, he spent some time with Auer and gave a recital for the violinists who were then in Auer's class. As it turned out, these were Elman's last performances in the major cities of Russia (although he did make a brief excursion into Latvia in 1931). With the outbreak of the First World War, Elman stopped touring in Europe. By the time the war ended, Russia had endured its 1917 Revolution and was in dangerous disarray. Towards the end of his life, Elman considered touring the land of his birth once more, and with the help of David Oistrakh he embarked on negotiations that would have resulted in a Russian tour but for a number of insurmountable obstacles.

Back in England, in 1909, Elman continued making recordings for the Gramophone Company (the Typewriter having been dropped from the name after the company introduced an unusual line of dialed typewriters that proved a commercial disaster). Slowly, he built a substantial record catalogue, and now that he had made his name in America, his records were released on both sides of the Atlantic. By 1910, advertisements placed by the Victor Company in concert programs and popular magazines informed readers that there were 48 Elman discs available.

Among Elman's best sellers of the time were the Tchaikovsky *Melodie*; Op.42, a Burmeister arrangement of a Mendelssohn quartet movement, called *Capriccietto* in this guise; the Saint-Saëns *Rondo capriccioso*; and the first of his five recordings of the Dvořák *Humoresque*, an extremely popular item in Elman's hands. Unfortunately—but unavoidably, given the limits of recording technology—Elman found himself documenting the least musically significant selections in his sizeable repertoire. These were the crowd-pleasers he placed in the final groups on his programs, or used as encores. Recording full-length works was out of the question at the time; and when multi-disc sets for longer works came into fashion, the symphonic literature was given first crack. This didn't matter much to Elman at the time. His audience loved the small pieces—indeed, many sat patiently through Handel and Brahms sonatas just to hear them, and for some, the concert didn't begin in earnest until the encores. Elman appreciated the enthusiasm of this part of his public, and when interviewers commented that his audiences liked the encores best, he replied good-naturedly that "by the time I start to play the encores, I'm warmed up and ready to play."

Nor was it lost on either Victor or the Gramophone Company that the public for popular encore pieces was sizeable and should be continuously served. During his visits to America in the early years, and through the 1920s, Victor gave Elman *carte blanche* for recording time at its Camden studios. He had only to telephone the company and say he wanted to record, and Victor would send a limousine to bring him to the studio.

Among the most enduring of the recordings made during this period were the four sides Elman recorded with Enrico Caruso. Elman and Caruso had become friendly during the violinist's first visit to London, and they saw a good deal of each other as Elman devoted more time to touring the United States. Both were resident at the Knickerbocker; and since both were shining stars on the Victor roster, the idea of making recordings together was natural.

The first of the sessions took place on March 20, 1913, with Percy B. Kahn at the piano.

The first recording was, in fact, one of Kahn's own compositions—a charming *Ave Maria* in which the violin is heard in a brief introduction, then stays silent through Caruso's first few bars, taking up again at the end of the phrase. Elman is certainly in the background here, and in the intense climax, his high-lying accompaniment is entirely outshone by the intensity of Caruso's voice. Yet, through much of the piece, Kahn gives the violinist a series of appealing contrapuntal responses to the vocal melody, and he takes full advantage of the instrument's range. Elman, for his part, mirrors the melodrama Caruso brings the music, and despite his apparent distance from the recording horn, the sweet tone he produces here accounts for a good deal of the disc's charm.

Elman and Caruso also recorded Massenet's *Elegie* that day, in an arrangement that gives the solo violin a verse-long introduction and affords Elman the opportunity to foreshadow the power of Caruso's reading with remarkable freedom and subtlety. This is a reading in Elman's most Romantic style—rich-toned, the vibrato tightly controlled, the dynamics attentively manipulated, and with *glissandi* applied lavishly by both performers throughout the reading.

Elman recorded this piece again four decades later, with the soprano Rise Stevens, accompanied by Brooks Smith. This time, Elman removed most of the *glissandi* from his introduction, leaving only the slides he considered necessary in evoking the work's mournful atmosphere. Otherwise, his contribution here is somewhat more extensive than on the Caruso recording. Modern recording technology afforded him a more prominent place in the balance, and this time Elman provides a few amplifications between the verses—including a rather attractive few bars of double-stopped harmonization—not included on the Caruso disc.

The last two Elman-Caruso recordings were made nearly two years later, on February 6, 1915, with Gaetano Scognamiglio accompanying. The first work set down was Denza's *Si vous l'aviez compris!*, a work for violin and piano to which a text was later added. Elman here surrenders the melody to Caruso, and is left with comparatively little to do beyond the brief, simple introduction and a sweetly climbing melody, set behind the tenor's lead, beginning after the first verse. Of greater interest is the more outgoing Leoncavallo serenade, *Mon gentil Pierrot*, which begins with a quick burst of violin playing that returns later as a connecting link between verses. Rather than fading into the background, as it does in the Denza, Elman's violin continues energetically in tandem with Caruso's voice, and finishes the selection with a sprightly figure, played *sotto voce*.[1]

❖ ❖ ❖ ❖ ❖

By the time he made the second pair of recordings with Caruso, Elman had decided to make New York his home. The previous autumn he had arranged for his mother and sisters to join him in the United States, and upon their arrival, he took a sabbatical from performing—although he did make some exceptions, the session with Caruso being among them. The few seasons leading up to this vacation, however, had been extremely hectic and demanding for him. In the winter of 1912, he made an extensive tour of Europe, where he played a series of ambitious programs, with Percy Kahn accompanying. Typical of these was one that included a Beethoven sonata, the Bruch G minor Concerto and the Bach *Chaconne*, plus a dozen short favorites. The tour that followed was a series of concerto appearances, at which he played a program of three works—the Bruch G minor, the Beethoven, and Lalo's *Symphony Espagnole*.

One unusual high point took place in London, when he received an invitation from a Russian Grand Duke who was staying at the Savoy and wanted to meet him. When Elman arrived, he was greeted by Sergei Diaghilev, the Russian impresario who had commissioned Igor Stravinsky's *Firebird* two years earlier, and *Petroushka* the previous season. Diaghilev brought the violinist to the Duke's suite, where the nobleman had a special request. One of Russia's prima ballerinas (and a former mistress of Nicholas II) Mathilde Kshessinska, was performing in London, and the Grand Duke hoped Elman would play the violin solo in *Swan Lake*, as Auer traditionally did in St. Petersburg performances. Elman was agreeable; and to comply with the request, he rearranged a program he was playing the same evening at the Albert Hall, so that by means of a strategically placed intermission he could get from there to Covent Garden in time to play his solo, then back to his own concert.

At the start of the 1912–13 season, Elman was back in the United States, and by all accounts, the 21-year old violinist continued to enjoy the extraordinary popularity he had won with his first American concerts. In *Musical America*, one finds a fascinating account of a performance Elman gave in November, when he travelled to Boston with the New York Philharmonic and its conductor, Josef Stransky, to play the Brahms concerto. Some of Elman's fans were so enthusiastic about his performance that they disrupted the flow of the concert. "After his performance," notes a *Musical America* report, "there was a demonstration more flattering to Elman than to the majority of his audience. This consisted in applause which lasted for nearly fifteen minutes, long

after Mr. Elman had shown that he had nothing more to offer as a performer, and even after Mr. Stransky, who had finally been obliged to
mount his platform, had raised his baton for the following number. It
was not until the greater part of the audience had begun to hiss a small
and obstinately persisting contingent that it was finally possible for
the performance to proceed."

Elman, in an interview from this period, speculated about the
general public's strong reactions to musical performances, couching
his explanation in terms that show a decidedly Romanticist view of
the art, projected into a modern context. "I am sure," he said, "it is because music makes an intimate appeal through the most easily
aroused emotions. The average man or woman comes tired to an evening concert after a long day of business, of housework or shopping.
The mysterious charm that exists for all of us in even only one exquisitely turned musical phrase brings in a moment that relaxation,
change, recreation, which instantly relieves depression and puts the
soul once more in tune with itself. To hear a well-loved or well remembered piece is like having the warm sun flash out from behind the
clouds after a shower."[2]

The interviewer, using Elman's mention of well-loved pieces as a
springboard, jumped on to the subject of interpretative freedom,
noting that Elman played some of the standard repertoire "quite differently from some of the veterans of the violin." Elman's reply recalls
Auer's arguments against a reliance on tradition, and it puts into
perspective Elman's view of the performer's role, as opposed to the
composer's, in the creation and life of a piece of music:

"Tradition," he said, "does not exist. It is simply what the artist feels.
Is there any tradition about a composition when it is written? No. Absolutely no. There cannot be. The composer first learns the tradition
of his own work on hearing it played for the first time by some great
artist. Then along comes another great artist and plays the same work.
Perhaps the composer hears several new things in it, some new
developments of its possibilities of which he never dreamt and thus a
second 'tradition' is introduced, and so on and so on. Every great artist has the right to exercise his own taste and judgement and to make
a new 'tradition' for every work, so long as he can justify his interpretation.

"And," he added, "apropos of that, I am perfectly sure if we artists
could print upon the program or lecture in advance to explain and justify any new reading of the whole or part of a standard work which

we perform, intelligent music critics would at once see and praise us for what is oftentimes referred to as a violation of tradition."

As the discussion continued, it emerged that he considered himself a modernist, and he stressed his belief that any great composer would approve of his interpretive thrust.

"The introduction of what I may call modern feeling and expression into classical works," he explained, "is something which must come and has come of itself, in sympathy with our general attitude toward music. For instance, undoubtedly I, in common with all the other leading virtuosi, play the Beethoven concerto in quite a different style from the way in which it was played in his own day, but at the same time if he could hear it as played today, it is an absolute certainty that a composer of his immortal genius and catholicity would approve of any rational differences in the reading which may exist."

Around this time, Elman took up another field of endeavor. First for G. Schirmer, and later for Carl Fischer, he began editing short violin works for publication under his own imprint. Some of these were commonplace violin etudes—some of the Rode and Kreutzer studies—to which Elman added a piano accompaniment. Others were violin and piano arrangements of songs by Schubert and other composers, works Elman played as encores, and for which there was certainly a market among students and amateurs. Thus, by the end of 1912 Elman had a hand in all areas of the field open to him as a virtuoso performer—concert work, recordings, and publications. By the end of the decade, he would add composing to the list.

All this was netting the young superstar an income reported to be around $100,000 a year. As always, Saul Elman managed his son's money; but as the stakes grew higher, Saul found himself out of his depths. Unfortunately, he refused to admit as much, and although he was, by then, getting free and reliable advice from the Rothschilds, in London, he did not always act upon it. One such suggestion he rejected was an opportunity to buy ground floor stock in a new company the Rothschilds were involved in financing, the Netherlands-based oil company that became Royal Dutch Shell. Saul asked the Rothschilds to guarantee him a 5% annual yield on his investment, but the bankers were, of course, unable to make any firm guarantees. Instead, Saul chose to invest heavily in prewar German government bonds—an investment that was lost when the war broke out.

That was not the greatest of the family's worries, though. Mischa and Saul had embarked on their first journey below the equator in the summer of 1914, making what Saul describes in his *Memoirs* as a "meteoric flight through Australia" and scoring "dazzling triumphs." But when news that tensions in Europe had erupted into open warfare reached them, they cancelled the rest of the tour and returned to the United States, where they turned their efforts to bringing the rest of the family over from England.

In New York, Elman returned to the Knickerbocker, while Saul rented a first floor apartment in a building on Claremont Avenue, at 119th Street, near Columbia University. It was a far cry from what Yetta, Mina, Liza and Esther had grown used to in London, where they had a large house in Hampstead, with separate bedrooms, a nursery, and a sizeable garden that backed onto the tenor John McCormack's adjacent property. Their first New York residence, by contrast, was a small, thoroughly urban apartment in which the sisters shared a bedroom. But the living room, while far smaller than what they were accustomed to in London, was large enough to accommodate two pianos (an upright and a baby grand), and it was roomy enough for the Elmans to use for evenings of chamber music.

Yetta and the girls left the Hampstead house, and most of their possessions, and booked passage for New York with the intention of eventually returning. Theirs was to be a dangerous passage, and they knew it: German torpedo boats were already threatening merchant, commercial and travel vessels, and when they arrived at the docks, they found that their ship—the Lusitania—had been painted black for the voyage, a precaution against being sighted. The Elman family arrived in New York in October, 1914. Six months later, the Lusitania was torpedoed.

With the family safely established on Claremont Avenue, Elman might have returned to his normal schedule, but for one crucial hitch: he had designated 1914–15 as a season of European touring. Obviously that was out of the question now. It was too late to arrange anything of consequence for the American season already underway; in fact, the important American violin engagements were to be played that season by a countryman and fellow Auer student with whom Elman maintained a friendly rivalry in those early years, Efrem Zimbalist. If the feature accounts published in New York newspapers are to be believed, Elman and Zimbalist had worked out a plan of alternation whereby they kept out of each other's way: when one toured Europe, the other toured America.

Zimbalist was a year older than Elman, and began his studies in St. Petersburg a year earlier; yet, he remained there until 1907. The reason, apparently, is that Zimbalist was a willful and sometimes wayward student, one more inclined towards student politics than towards practicing. In 1905, for instance, his academic misdemeanors included picketing Auer's class, and arriving at the conservatory in a red shirt.[3] What made it possible for him to keep his place at the Conservatory in the face of these conflicts was his undeniable talent, and when he was finally graduated, he was awarded a Gold Medal and the Rubinstein Prize, among the highest honors the Conservatory could bestow.

Soon after completing his studies in St. Petersburg, Zimbalist took the path Elman had travelled a few years earlier—first to Berlin, where his debut with the Brahms Concerto was a great success, and a few months later, to London. In 1911, he made his American debut with Max Fiedler and the Boston Symphony, playing the Glazunov Concerto, then a comparatively fresh work, having been composed only six years earlier.

Zimbalist also signed with Victor, and his early discography shows a penchant for the unusual. Along with a few of the Wieniawski, Brahms-Joachim and Saint-Saëns standards, there are pieces by Hubay, Cui and Albert Spalding, and arrangements of works by Glinka, Drigo, Pierne and Chopin (not the *Nocturnes* many of his colleagues played, but the "Minute" Waltz).[4] There were also a handful of Zimbalist's own pieces—charmingly tuneful little works that seem deceptively simple, but which demand, in some cases, considerable speed and flexibility.

The biographical outline of Zimbalist's early life may lead one to expect a fierceness in his playing, but in fact, on disc his hallmark was an abidingly refined gentleness. His manipulations of timbre were limited. Rather than exploit the range of colors available to him, Zimbalist consistently produced a deep, rounded tone, which served him well in both outgoing and elegiac music. It was an attractive and admirably pure sound, embellished with a vibrato so subtle that Zimbalist seemed hardly to be using the effect at all. He did, in certain slow pieces, take advantage of his opportunities for judiciously placed *glissandi*, but all told, his playing was straightforward and unadorned for its time.

In this regard, Zimbalist's work is almost a precursor of the modern style, closer to the style with which Heifetz would soon make his name than to that of Elman and his predecessors. Considering Zimbalist in the context of his time, therefore, it is easy to see why some players of the old school (Carl Flesch, for one) found his playing short on personality. Elman, nevertheless, had only praise for Zimbalist, and he consistently singled him out when interviewers sought his opinion about other violinists.

During the 1914–15 season, Elman had ample opportunity to hear other violinists, plus a good many operas and symphony performances. Making the most of his cancelled European season, he announced a year's sabbatical, and said he planned to use the time to relax—to play chess, to catch up on his reading, to attend concerts and to spend time with his family.

For the first time in a decade—for the first time in his adult life—he was able to practice and to study music at leisure, and to reflect on music and musicmaking without the interruptions and pressures of travel and performance. He was able to observe the musical world around him, and to examine its changing stylistic currents, yet these observations did not lead to a change of direction. Rather, he returned to the concert stage with an even firmer resolve to continue on the path he had always taken.

Elman told the musical public what he was up to in an article he wrote for the May 9, 1915 issue of *The World Magazine*, "The Musical Making Over of Mischa Elman." Mainly, the article provides an overview of the music he had heard over the preceding seven months, and a hefty program it was. He praises an "inspired interpretation" of the Brahms Second Symphony by the Boston Symphony, and goes on to support Brahms against his detractors by arguing that he "can think of no composer who has Romantic feeling to a more marked extent." He had also come to terms with a work he hadn't previously regarded so highly—Beethoven's opera, *Fidelio*.

His thoughts on Wagner were mixed: "For me," he wrote, "of all operas [Wagner's] *Die Meistersinger* is nearest the perfect ideal. It is what I call 'healthy music.'" "But," he adds, "*Tristan and Isolde*, wonderful though it is, is apt to overstimulate the emotions." Still, the extraordinary sound world of Wagner struck Elman as worth exploring in greater detail than an evening in the opera house could afford, and during this year away from the stage he began buying Wagner scores and studying them at the piano. Elman never tired of this investigation: Joseph Seiger, Elman's accompanist in the 1950s and 1960s, has vivid recollections of arriving at the violinist's apartment for rehearsal, or for Sunday afternoon tea, and finding Elman at the piano reading through *Die Meistersinger*.

As for soloists, Elman wrote that he considered it a privilege to hear Kreisler, and that Zimbalist "is an excellent artist, who deserves the success he has won." His pianistic heroes were more plentiful. Josef Hofmann, he wrote, "has everything a pianist should have," He was equally impressed with Leopold Godowsky, both as a "wonderful intellect" and as "one of the greatest living pianists." Ossip Gabrilowitsch, he added, "convinced me, and musically helped me by his spontaneity and gifts of natural expressiveness." And finally, "the exquisite touch of Harold Bauer showed me tonal colors I shall never forget." Then there were singers. From Caruso, he says he "learned things I could learn from no other singing artist." But he also greatly admired Giovanni Martinelli and the soprano Melanie Kurt, both of whom he heard at the Metropolitan Opera.

Besides listing the concerts he felt inspired by, Elman made a few more generalized observations. Once again, he addressed the question of tradition, reiterating his belief that "every musical artist and every organization should be given abundant opportunity to express individuality." But this time he added a new clarification to his argument: "There is one thing, however, upon which I insist, and on which I believe the public unconsciously insists—and that is that the interpretation must not go outside the frame of the 'musical picture.'"

Concertgoing and private practice were by no means the extent of Elman's musical activities during his year off, though—he cherished the reaction of an audience too much to give it up fully. Thus, he began what became a lifelong tradition of weekly musicales. Every Friday evening, Saul Elman would borrow as many chairs as he could from the neighbors, who would be invited to the apartment to hear a private chamber music session involving Mischa and some of his friends. At first, the ensemble consisted of Elman, Modest Altschuler—the conductor of Elman's New York debut, who was also a cellist—and the pianist Clarence Adler, who had recently been signed on to teach Liza and Esther. Eventually, a second violinist and a violist joined the group, putting an array of music at the group's disposal, ranging from the literature for piano quartet and trio, through the string quartet and piano quintet repertoire.

Eventually, the Friday evening chamber music readings grew quite crowded, the extra guests consisting primarily of musicians Elman met and invited to come along. And since everyone hoped to do some playing, the sessions turned into games of musical chairs that lasted into the early hours of the morning. One of the original ensemble members, Clarence Adler, recalled the evenings fondly in his memoirs:

> I have never known such an indefatigable musician as Mischa. He abounds in love and energy for music, and is never too tired to play.... No matter how late I left his apartment, there was still music making. I remember one wintry night. It was after 2 A.M. when my wife and I were at the door bidding his parents goodnight. Mischa suddenly noticed that we were leaving. He called us back saying, "You can't go yet, it's too early. Besides, I want to play the Tchaikovsky Trio (a composition which requires nearly 50 minutes of strenuous playing) with you." Of course I stayed and played and it was a rewarding experience.[5]

CHAPTER SEVEN:

The First Dark Clouds

During Elman's sabbatical, his manager booked an itinerary of nearly 100 concerts for the 1915–16 season, a hefty schedule for those preairplane days. The season began with a 12 city tour as soloist with Walter Damrosch's New York Symphony, and a series of concerts with Leopold Stokowski and the Philadelphia Orchestra. Mixed in were a handful of recitals in the midwest, leading up to Elman's return to Carnegie Hall at the end of October. For his concerto appearances, he chose a work new to him, the Goldmark Concerto in A minor, and he played it, according to *Musical America* "with an earnestness and a loftiness of purpose that showed him to be a finer artist than ever."

A few days earlier, his Carnegie Hall recital won similar praise. His program was an unusual blend of favorites and novelties. On the familiar side, he offered the Wieniawski-Kreisler *Caprice*, an arrangement of Bach's *Air on the G String*, Sarasate's *Zigeunerweisen* and Dvořák's *Humoresque*; but along with these, he played a set of variations on a Mozart theme by Scolero, and a set of Elman's own transcriptions, that of a Weber *Country Dance* and of a piece called *Nuit de Mai*, by a composer named Michaels. Elman included two concertos this time, Ernst's in F-sharp minor, and a Vivaldi work in G minor. For the latter, his accompanist, Walter H. Golde, was supported by an organist, Frank L. Sealy.

Even more successful than the Carnegie Hall recital, though, was a similar concert the violinist gave at the Brooklyn Academy of Music in mid-November. According to a report carried in the November 25 *Musical Courier*, the full house was so enthusiastic that Elman played an encore after every work but the Vivaldi. "His extra numbers," the critic wrote "were almost as numerous as the compositions set down on the printed list and many persons, doubtless, would have been glad if the violinist had hired an assistant with big placards to display the names of the supplementary works after the manner of a Sousa concert."

This season also marked the start of a series called the Friday Morning Musicales, held bi-weekly at the Biltmore Hotel. Each concert featured a handful of prominent artists who performed groups of short selections for an audience of wealthy socialites, who then went on to the major business of the day, a fancy luncheon. Elman was the star attraction of the second of these, which took place the morning after his Brooklyn recital, and was packed despite the day's miserable weather. He played, according to one account, "ingratiating and masterfully finished performances of Saint-Saëns's *Rondo capriccioso* and shorter musical numbers, and was received with rapturous applause as usual." Joining him on the program were two singers, Louise Homer and Anna Fitziu, and a pianist, Clarence Bird. Kreisler and Giovanni Martinelli performed at the third event, and Elman returned several times.

He also played (as did Artur Rubinstein) at the Bagby Morning Musicales, a similar series offered at the Waldorf Astoria on Mondays. A description of one of the Bagby mornings ended thus: "Mr. Elman does not like to play when women are gabbling, and forgetting that these musicales are fashionable ones he stood patiently waiting for the audience to be still before beginning his concerto. How brave!"[1]

The most detailed assessment of Elman's post-sabbatical performances, though, was a lengthy review published in the *Boston Transcript* after his recital there in early December. Under the subtitle, "The Violinist Newly Ripened and Refined," the critic opined that Elman had played more interesting programs in the past (the Boston recital was essentially the same as his Carnegie Hall program), but that "seldom in recent visits has he seemed so poised and steadily pleasurable a violinist." In his amplification the reviewer took the opportunity to note certain interpretive traits of Elman's that had bothered him in the past: "By every sign of his two concerts here this autumn," he reported, the other concert being Elman's visit with the New York Symphony, "Mr. Elman's year of retirement was a year of self-discipline, self-ripening and self-purification, and in it he has purged himself of nearly all the errors of taste and errors of effect that a little while ago seemed to cloud his distinctions and imperil his future. There was not a suggestion of commonness in his playing, his program, or in himself yesterday; not once did he try merely to capture and impress his audience.... He sentimentalized not so much as one piece or one movement, though some of the music might easily have tempted him. He did not drag pace or exaggerate rhythm; he neither smeared nor slid; he made not an effect—in transition, in climax, in the return of a melody, in the molding of songful phrases—for the sake of effect."

Interestingly, the reviewer also noted a change in Elman's stage demeanor—something not often commented upon until now: "He no longer consults the ceiling; he has put aside what the tennis players call 'foot work,' and if he sways his body to the rhythm and contour of the music the motion seems spontaneous instinct in him." And so on, for 23 inches of small type. Within two years of this description, however, critics in New York were taking the violinist to task for some of the very excesses here claimed to be purged; and in his Vitaphone films, made 11 years after this Boston report, Elman does indeed sway to the music and glance skyward during his performances.

In the midst of his return to active concert life, Elman began reading of the devastation and strife described in reports from war-torn Europe, and the contrast between these descriptions and the peace and prosperity he was enjoying in America bothered him. Philanthropic organizations had started to raise funds to assist refugees, and Elman immediately began contacting them to offer his services, free of charge, to be used in fundraising. His first approach was to a Jewish relief organization, but to his consternation, his generosity was rebuffed on the grounds that people who should be making generous cash contributions might feel that their obligation was discharged simply by purchasing a concert ticket. Another New York organization accepted his offer, though, and soon after his Boston recital, he returned to Carnegie Hall to play a benefit concert that reportedly raised several thousand dollars.

❖ ❖ ❖ ❖ ❖

For the rest of the 1915 season, the 25-year old violinist could do no wrong. There were, of course, some who preferred Kreisler, Zimbalist and other violinists before the public at the time, but by and large, Elman was the acknowledged sovereign of the violin world. In the press, there were occasional objections to some of his more personalized interpretative turns, and to his stage stance, which bordered on the balletic when he felt particularly inspired. Yet, even these complaints seemed faint in the face of the overwhelming praise his concerts earned throughout the world. As one *Musical Courier* writer had observed a few years earlier, "the critics were generally in unqualified praise...since that was about the only thing possible under the circumstances."

At the start of the 1916 season, however, the critical perception of Elman began to change. On this tour, he and a new accompanist, Philip Gordon, were playing a Nardini sonata, the Spohr D minor Concerto, Chausson's *Poème*, Elmanized etudes by Rode and Wieniawski, an arrangement (by Leon Smatini) of a Chopin Impromptu, Sarasate's *Caprice Basque*, Ernst's *Elegie*, and intriguingly, waltzes by Godowsky and Rissland (the latter a violist with whom Elman had been playing chamber music, and who eventually joined the first Elman Quartet). Outside New York, things went quite well. In Chicago, for instance, the critic of the *Herald* was content to note that "it is not necessary at this stage of Mr. Elman's activities to reconsider the qualities of his performance," other than to cite the beauty of his tone and the emotional impact of his interpretations.

But scarcely two weeks after that performance, when Elman played his signature concerto—the Tchaikovsky—with Stransky and the New York Philharmonic, the critics did reconsider the qualities of his performance, and quite harshly. The reviewer for the *Christian Science Monitor* set the tone by wondering, at the top of his review, whether the mature Elman had fulfilled the promise of his youth. "As he proceeded from movement to movement of the well-worn concerto, which probably few have played more frequently than himself, it was impossible to avoid feelings of disappointment. The mere technique was as wonderful as ever, and the most intricate passages were those with which he dealt most easily. But it was when he came to interpreting the spirit of the music, notably in the *Canzonetta*, that he failed, if failure may be the word to apply to a performance which never lapsed in executive accomplishment."

The problem with the slow movement, the critic elaborated, was Elman had "infused [it] with an exaggerated sentimentality which was aggravating, and so dragged the tempo on more than one occasion as to give Mr. Stransky some trouble in following him." The critics from the *Times* and the *Herald* also cited the slow movement as particularly egregious, the former calling Elman's performance "mannered and erratic," later adding "lachrymose" to his description. Like his *Monitor* colleague, the *Times* critic felt forced to cringe on Stransky's behalf, so obvious was the gulf between conductor and soloist much of the time.

The *Globe*'s reviewer, meanwhile, pointed accusingly at Elman's "caprices" and "exaggerations," and the *Sun*'s objected to the violinist's twisting and turning during the more energetic passages— or, as the critic put it, his "Nijinskyizing."

Reading the papers the next morning, Elman must have been stunned, and when the usually supportive *Musical Courier* arrived a week later, he felt the sting of criticism yet again. "What is wrong with Mischa Elman?" the Courier's writer asked at the start of his report. "He played the Tchaikovsky violin concerto at the Philharmonic last week and gave a distressing exhibition musically, rhythmically, and one might almost say, technically." Elman didn't have much time to worry about this, though, for the next few months included another handful of New York concerts; and he decided that if the larger part of his audience felt as the critics did, he'd soon find that out. On November 19, ten days after the Philharmonic appearance, he had his answer. That night, he was the most prominent of three soloists performing at an orchestral concert at the Metropolitan Opera House (his colleagues were the contralto Sophie Braslau, and the baritone Arthur Middleton); and two hours before curtain time, according to a report in the next morning's *Telegraph*, the line of hopeful ticket buyers was stretched half way around the block. When the concert began, the Met was packed, and hundreds of music lovers had been turned away. That night, Elman played the Goldmark Concerto, the Wieniawski *Polonaise* and Wagner's *Albumblatt*. He was, the paper reported, "in perfect form."

Early in December, he left New York for a series of out-of-town performances, the last of them in Baltimore. He had to be back by mid-month, however, to play another run of concerts with Stransky and the Philharmonic. Saul went with him on this trip, and upon their return, they were heading by taxi from Pennsylvania Station to the Ansonia Hotel, where the family had recently taken a suite, when their cab collided with a trolley. Elman was thrown against the front seat, and was struck by flying glass. A doctor was summoned, and the violinist's head was bandaged. When he arrived at the Ansonia, though, his head was still bleeding, so Saul took him to a hospital, where doctors advised him to cancel his concerts for the next several weeks.

The newspapers announced that he would be out of commission for the immediate future, but Elman would have none of that. Even though the intervening Metropolitan Opera performance had been a success, he wanted to do battle once more at the scene of his recent critical defeat. To cancel the Philharmonic engagement under any circumstances, he reasoned, might seem as a bow to critical censure. He insisted on playing, and the day of his performance the papers carried the notice that he would appear. Thus, with a bandage on his right temple, and a physician waiting backstage, Elman played the Bruch Concerto in G minor to an audience that was vociferous in its appreciation, and to critics inclined to forgive his previous outing. "Whatever the cause," wrote the critic from the *World*, "there was none of the exaggerated sentimentality that has marred this gifted musician's work this season. His attack was clean instead of being slurred, and his tone was pure and steadier than in recent endeavors here. Rhythmically, Elman was beyond reproach and his technique [was] at its best."

If Elman's stage mannerisms tried the patience of New York's music critics, they soon drew comment from reviewers around the country too. After a January 1917 recital in Detroit, one reviewer drew a vivid description of the violinist. "With his eyes closed and seeming totally oblivious to everything about him....he appears to so lose himself in his rendition that he almost turns his back on his hearers." This, the writer continues, "shows [that Elman] has not reached full maturity," adding pointedly that "when he will be content to forget himself and offer only his music, appreciation of his work will be even greater." He then described Elman's interpretations in glowing terms.

On the other hand, in Louisville, a month later, the author of a lengthy assessment of Elman's recital thought he noticed "a new degree of freedom from sentimentalization of melody (although this characteristic is not entirely gone), a new restrained use of the luscious tone in which no violinist surpasses him, [and] an increase in the capacity to make the audience feel the form of the composition he is playing." But laudable as the critic found this, he wondered whether Elman's audiences would follow him on that path. "It is in numbers in which sheer beauty and variety of tone are the chief requirements, that Elman is at his best," he argued. "Notwithstanding all of the artist's new depth of sincerity, one still has more regard for him as a Romantic poet of the violin than as a comprehensive interpretive artist."

For the layman who knew what he liked, which is to say a rich tone and emotional performances, Elman and his playing remained a magical force. One music-loving layman who chanced to hear Elman during one of his jaunts through the midwest at this time was Carl Sandburg, a young poet composing and assembling the works that were to make up his first volume, the *Chicago Poems* of 1916. One of these—actually more a piece of symbolic prose reportage than a poem in the traditional sense—is called *"Bath,"* and concisely conveys something of Elman's power to brighten even the most depressed spirit with his playing:

A MAN saw the whole world as a grinning skull and cross-bones. The rose flesh of life shriveled from all faces. Nothing counts. Everything is a fake. Dust to dust and ashes to ashes and then an old darkness and a useless silence. So he saw it all. Then he went to a Mischa Elman concert. Two hours waves of sound beat on his eardrums. Music washed something or other inside him. Music broke down and rebuilt something or other in his head and heart. He joined in five encores for the young Russian Jew with the fiddle. When he got outside his heels hit the sidewalk in a new way. He was the same man in the same world as before. Only there was a singing fire and a climb of roses everlastingly over the world he looked on.[2]

In early 1917 Elman, as usual, alternated recitals with orchestral appearances, and this season, his orchestral repertoire revolved around two central works—the Brahms and Beethoven—plus a novelty the violinist found few conductors were adventurous enough to take, a three movement concerto by Max Vogrich, entitled *E pur si muove*— the astronomer Galileo's response when pressed to recant his theory that the earth revolves around the sun. The Vogrich never made it into the standard literature, but it was a piece Elman felt gave him a good deal to do within a mildly contemporary framework. He had also, by then, recorded one of Vogrich's violin and piano works, *Dans le Bois*, based on Paganini's sixth *Caprice*.

One conductor who took a chance on the Vogrich was the Philadelphia Orchestra's Leopold Stokowski, whose trust was rewarded in the strongly favorable reviews. In the *Philadelphia Press*, for instance, the reviewer described the Vogrich as "a modern work with modern embellishments of an old-fashioned idea in music." Elman, he added "has never played a better concert in this city." Even so, Elman and Stokowski knew that the violinist's audience demanded something more familiar, so as a sweetener, they also offered the Saint-Saëns *Introduction and Rondo capriccioso*.

Elman's renderings of the Brahms Concerto also drew favorable reviews in some parts of the country, but here again, his physical contortions invited less adulatory comment. When he played the Brahms and the Saint-Saëns in St. Louis, for instance, the *Democrat*'s critic described his interpretations as "truly thrilling," and he was clearly taken with Elman's energy and his desire to please, the latter made manifest by his return to the stage with Philip Gordon to play a Scarlatti encore. Amid his flowery praise of Elman's tone and his ability to play cleanly at great speed, though, the reviewer couldn't help pointing out that Elman's habit of twisting towards the conductor was getting in the way of the performance and should be conquered.

In New York, Elman's difficulties with the critics intensified. His Brahms, with Walter Damrosch and the New York Symphony, in March, was tersely reviewed as a "somewhat perfunctory" performance by the *New York Post*—one of the few papers that had refrained from attacking his Tchaikovsky the previous fall. His performance, further, was compared negatively with Kreisler's.

But worse still was the press's vehemently negative reaction to Elman's reading of the Beethoven Concerto, for which he had introduced his own first and last movement cadenzas, following in the tradition of Joachim, Auer, and most recently, Kreisler. Actually, his performances of the concerto proper drew laudatory reviews. After the February 10 New York Philharmonic performance, at which he unveiled his new cadenzas, one paper offered a kind of backhanded praise by noting that "it was one of [Elman's] better days, when his extraordinary powers celebrate the music rather than the executant." The reviewer quickly added, though, that the cadenzas were "in deplorable taste." The *Musical Courier* review was no kinder. After describing Elman as being in rare form in the concerto itself, the critic added that "criticism can fall alone upon the very inartistic, overelaborate and vastly too long cadenza in the first movement—his own—and one almost equally inartistic in the last."

Elman never understood the resistance to his cadenzas—not in 1917, and not in the ensuing decades, when he insistently played them. In truth, the first movement cadenza is rather lengthy. Although he undoubtedly played it more quickly in his younger years, when he recorded the work with Georg Solti, in the mid-1950s, the first movement cadenza clocked in at about four and a half minutes, nearly a fifth the running time of the full movement. At least one of his accompanists argued the point with the violinist, particularly in light of the criticism it was drawing; but Elman refused either to abandon or shorten it.

"Look," he told his pianist, taking up the violin to illustrate his point, "it all makes sense: I have four bars of one kind of figure, balanced by four bars of a contrasting one, and so on. If I cut something, I will ruin the balance. Besides," he added, "Kreisler's cadenza is only two bars longer than mine." Kreisler's is, however, of a different character. Both are inventive explorations of the fingerboard, certainly, and both explore some of Beethoven's themes. In Elman's, though, the themes are more obscured, and their entrances, at various places in the cadenza seem more sudden and capricious. There is also a good deal more sequential repetition in Elman's cadenza, a device that poses various technical challenges for the player, but leaves the listener with the impression of a somewhat shapeless solo. There are differences in tempo too; so while Elman's and Kreisler's cadenzas are of nearly equivalent lengths on paper[3,] their characters are very different.

Elman's championship of his cadenza did, however, result in some odd critical confrontations over the years. One of these involved Olin Downes, the senior critic of the *New York Times* through the mid-1950s. Downes, who was five years older than Elman, admired the violinist and maintained a cordial friendship with him through much of his life. Their earliest professional contact dates back to January 1909, when Downes was a critic for the *Boston Post*, and reviewed Elman's first Boston performance of the Tchaikovsky Concerto. Downes considered the debut a triumph, adding in his review that it was "the more gratifying in that it represented the appeal of sane, vital art, which, whether Mr. Elman had been eighteen or fifty, would have exerted the same effect upon the enthusiastic audience."

Four and a half decades later, in 1954, Downes reviewed another Elman performance of the same work, this time calling the violinist "a sovereign master of his instrument," and noting that his interpretation that "was that of a ripened artist whose heart and soul were in every note that he sounded."

Even so, in the December 31, 1937 edition of the *Times*, Downes reviewed a New York Philharmonic concert at which Elman was soloist in the Beethoven. "This listener," he wrote, "is frank to say that he considers the Elman cadenzas quite out of the frame of the concerto and not in the best taste. They are too long, they lead unduly to virtuosity, and they distract attention from the logic and the taste of Beethoven's symphonic developments."

Elman was not the only one upset by Downes's reaction. A correspondent in White Plains wrote to the critic a few days later, pointing out that on January 5, 1936, Downes had reviewed Elman's Beethoven cadenzas much more favorably. "Mr. Elman played his own cadenzas," the earlier review reads, "which were not too long and were substantially musical; possibly a trifle modern for the concerto's period, but on the whole solid contributions. The anticipation of the rondo in the free passages which connect the second and last movement was a slight extension of Beethoven's own ideas, and it felt perfectly in place, proportionate to the passage."

The correspondent then went on to comment: "I thought that change of mind was a woman's privilege, but I see that it must be extended also to musical critics." Downes, puzzled by his own inconsistency, sent the letter to Elman for comment, explaining that he never read his own previous reviews, because he did not wish to be bound by his former opinions. He wondered, however, whether the cadenzas he disliked in 1937 were substantially the same as those he had praised in 1936.

Elman replied in good humor, thanking Downes for passing the letter on to him, and adding the following ironic touch:

> For your information, I played the identical cadenzas in 1938 [sic] that I played in 1936, without cutting or adding anything to them; and, what is more, there was very little difference *in tempo* between the two performances. You have only yourself to blame for having had to undergo the torture of listening to the same cadenzas—for you know my admiration of you as a critic and who knows but that it was due to your encouraging critique that I stuck to the same cadenzas.

Besides his Beethoven cadenzas, Elman was, around 1917, doing a good deal of composing in his spare time, and whatever the criticism, he had no intention of giving it up. The best known of his pieces were, naturally, violin works which he included on his programs and took into the recording studio. The first of those he recorded was a charming, almost impressionistic piece with a gently-rocking piano accompaniment, *In a Gondola*. The second was not an original work, but an arrangement of a traditional Hebrew melody, *Eili, Eili*. Yet, Elman's setting is so personalized that perhaps the setting is best described as an impassioned fantasy on a folk theme. In it, Elman manipulates his instrument's voice brilliantly, beginning in the low register for one verse, shifting higher for the next, and later indulging in multiple stopping before flying off into an ecstatic cadenza. On the recording of the piece he made during this period, accompanied by Emanuel Balaban, Elman produces a tone with an almost vocal quality, shaded so sensitively that one can almost hear the Hebrew text being intoned.

The most widely-traveled of Elman's violin works, however, was his *Tango*. This is a fine gloss of the tango style, cast in the distinctive rhythm of the exotic dance. The rhythm is set forth steadily in the piano part, while the violin moves in and out of those syncopated contours. Elman gives the violin an inventive melody, and offers plenty of display-quality detail work; yet the piece is couched in an authentic-sounding accent. Taken together with his Debussian paraphrase, *In a Gondola*, this *Tango* indicates an ear that was sharply attuned to different styles, and which could synthesize short forms effectively. Elman played his *Tango* in concert as early as 1917, often with a companion piece he never recorded—a setting of the spiritual tune, *Deep River*.

As an adjunct to his violin works, Elman began composing songs around this time, probably because his sister Mina was developing into an accomplished singer, and hoped for a career as a recitalist. Of course, Elman's love for opera and for the voice had been flowering ever since he became friendly with Melba, Caruso, McCormack, Frances Alda, Marcella Sembrich, and Ernestine Schumann-Heink, among others. Several singers included a few of Elman's songs on their recital programs. Among those performed in 1916 and 1917 were "Key to the Heart," and "To My Mother."

As Elman's career hit its first stretch of rocky critical terrain, trouble was brewing in his homeland, and interviewers assigned to write about Elman inevitably asked him, as a Russian who still held his country's passport, what he thought about the political upheaval. Elman was of two minds about this. On one hand, he had generally been well-treated during his Russian years, and he was grateful to have been released from his obligation to serve in the Russian military. On the other hand, he knew that the kindness he received was due to the fact that he was not a common Russian, but a young celebrity. And he was aware that the violence, ill-will and discriminatory ordinances directed against Russia's Jews were sanctioned by the Tsar and his cabinet.

Elman's confused feelings about his country and its doomed ruler—and his naivete about the situation—come through clearly in the interviews he gave during Russia's revolutionary period. One of the earliest of these dates from March 13, 1916. Speaking to a reporter from *Des Moines Register*, he firmly declared himself "a loyal subject of Russia," and he described the Tsar in remarkably sympathetic terms.

"One should appreciate and understand the psychology of the Russian situation before they judge the Tsar of Russia," Elman asserted. "The Tsar of Russia is acting according to his knowledge and training. Despite all that he has done to the Jews in Russia, he was not so cruel in intent as mistaken. It must be remembered that his environment is a factor. He has no way of knowing the truth about his country or his people. There is graft, as there is in any country, of course. His advisors do not tell him the truth. He has been taught that his will was law and that he could do no wrong since he represented the church.

"If the Tsar of Russia was educated to know that if he did things which would be kindnesses to the people," he added, "he would be the most popular monarch in Europe today. He does not know, but some day he will know.... There will come an evolution sooner or later. I do not say how the evolution will come about, but I think the war [World War I] will make a great change."

A year to the day after Elman gave this "evolution" interview, the first wave of revolution swept through Russia and toppled its government. Of course, the worst of the revolutionary terror was yet to come, but on March 20, 1917, while on tour in Texas, Elman responded to questions about Russia's future quite differently than he had 53 weeks earlier. Ever the optimist, he told an interviewer for the *San Antonio Light* that the revolution was a good thing, and that it would no doubt result in "a liberal monarchy, such as that of England, set up with a king for a figurehead, a Congress of Parliament in control and the people having a vote. The republic will come later," he added, launching into a startlingly utopian interpretation: "After that, perhaps, something better and higher, with all national boundaries thrown down."

Elman's historical viewpoint had also changed considerably during the year. "The revolution had to come," he pronounced. "The Russian people have been suppressed too long. They have been starved physically and mentally. Over there, I don't believe I ever saw a peasant pick up a newspaper to read. Most of them did not know how to read, and those who did were not interested in anything. They were dull, apathetic. What was the use, they felt, in reading of things in which they had no share? They were prevented from reading of what the poor people of other lands were permitted to do and say and vote for. The revolution and what it stands for has put new heart into them. Now, they have something to think about—the future and what it will mean to them and their children, the liberties, the opportunities."

One thing Elman objected to in the "old" Russia, interestingly, was the system of patronage from which he benefitted early in his student years. "In Russia," he told his Texan interviewer, "a musician, a man or woman who excelled in any line, never has had a chance to work out his own destiny by the force and power of his own talent, his own individuality. With things as they were, it was necessary to have the patronage of some noble, some member of the royal family—influence of some kind, in order to get ahead. Now, I hope, all that will be changed."

Elman expanded on this theme at the start of the next season, in a statement he prepared for distribution by his manager in his 1917 publicity kit. A sweeping, optimistic assessment of Russia's situation, this was published by newspapers across the country, from Toledo, Ohio to Tacoma, Washington.

"It is a well-known fact," Elman began, "that great art can only prosper in an environment of social well-being. The artist seeks for himself the freest expression of his personality and flees from those countries where this impulse is continually being suppressed by an inflexible social system. The Russian autocracy has caused our best minds and spirits to seek their inspiration and to make their homes in other countries. Russia as a democracy may become a second France. For is not the Slav genius capable of the highest achievement? And has it not shown by its accomplishment in the past when it was downtrodden and repressed, how unquenchable is its essence and spirit? I look forward with the greatest hope to seeing this regenerated Russian people take its place beside France and the United States as the host of artists and the patron of art."

Meanwhile, Elman and other artists of a liberal bent set about showing their support for what they hoped would be a democratic regime by staging several large benefit concerts. Among the grandest of these was an all-star bash held on May 27, at New York's huge Hippodrome, on Sixth Avenue between 43rd and 44th Streets—a hall the impresario

Sol Hurok described as a "glittering, tinsel, rococo place of fantasy and farce, burlesque and beauty."[4] The concert was given under the auspices of two newspapers, the *New York Herald* and the *American Hebrew*, and its proceeds went into what was called the Russian Liberty Fund—a fund which, the *Musical Courier* explained (in a review dated May 31), would be put towards the creation of "a statue of Liberty which shall represent America's gift to the new Russian democracy." The article went on to note that the concert raised more than $10,000 for the fund; but more interesting was the listing of highlights published in the review's subhead:

> Frances Alda Sings the "Swanee River"—Mischa Elman Plays Several Things and Then Some More—Victoria Bosko Performs a Liszt Rhapsody—John Philip Sousa Conducts De Wolf Hopper's Favorite Number from "El Capitan" and De Wolf Hopper Sings It; While George Harris Chants the New Russian Anthem, Adding to the Success of a Nazimova Tableau

Noteworthy, too, is the paragraph devoted to Elman's appearance at the gala:

> When Fred Niblo, announcer of the evening, introduced Mischa Elman, the applause that sounded throughout the house showed clearly that he was not unknown to those who could not be classified as being among the usual concertgoers. He played three numbers, all of which were given in a manner bespeaking his superior art. *Ave Maria* (Schubert) seemed, however, to delight the most, perhaps because it was more familiar than the other numbers. Next came his own arrangement of Weber's *Country Dance*. Owing to the length of the program it was announced that no encores would be permitted. The audience in several cases insisted on breaking this rule and one of them was with Mr. Elman. After several unsuccessful attempts had been made on the part of the announcer to continue, the piano had to be brought back and the violinist reappeared with his instrument and played MacDowell's *Indian Lament*, much to the audience's pleasure.

Elman's disappointment in the Russian Revolution's aftermath was so intense that he renounced his Russian citizenship. He had already decided that he liked the United States best of all the countries he had lived in; now he needed a home, and America was the logical choice. In 1923, he became an American citizen.

CHAPTER EIGHT:

A Rival Arrives

At the beginning of 1917, the 26-year old Elman was comfortably enthroned at the pinnacle of the violin world, and while there were those who took issue with various aspects of his style, his popularity overwhelmed this criticism, and there was no-one on the concert scene to challenge his primacy. He had easily supplanted Kubelik, and he had displaced Kreisler in the public's affections. He was well-paid for his concert appearances, and sales of his recordings and sheet music editions added to his hefty income. He remained a favorite topic of leisure magazines, which continued to devote more ink to his status as an eligible bachelor than to descriptions of his performances, or discussions of his musical views.

But the period in which Elman was popularly deemed "the world's greatest violinist" was coming to an end; in fact, his eventual successor as the king of the fiddle—his first serious rival since the days of von Vecsey—arrived in New York to make his debut in the first weeks of the 1917–18 season. This was another brilliant young Russian prodigy, and yet another product of Leopold Auer's classroom. His name was Jascha Heifetz, and from his first moments on the American stage, he meant to usurp Elman's crown. Ultimately, he succeeded.

Heifetz was a decade younger than Elman, but there are some similarities in the outline of the two violinists' early lives. The son of an accomplished amateur violinist, Heifetz began to play the instrument at age three. He was soon enrolled at the local conservatory, where he studied with Ilya Malkin, a student of Auer. Like Elman, he gave his first public performances at age five, and he was taken to the St. Petersburg Conservatory when he was 10. Both Fritz Kreisler and Albert Spalding heard him during this period, and they reported that they were deeply impressed by his talent and facility. In 1911, he gave a series of recitals in Odessa, each reportedly attended by enormous crowds.[1]

Nevertheless, his first attempt to kick off his international career—in Berlin, where Elman, von Vecsey and so many others had started their own world conquests—proved unrewarding. After his Berlin debut, in 1912, one critic wrote that he rated more highly than von Vecsey, but that he was not yet Mischa Elman's equal.[2] His Berlin orchestral debut, with Nikisch and the Berlin Philharmonic in the Tchaikovsky Concerto, was even less successful: the critics found him possessed of a small tone and an indistinct personality; and some took the occasion to rail against prodigies. Chastened, Heifetz returned to St. Petersburg and resumed his studies with Auer until 1916.

By then, however, his list of successes was growing impressive—as were those of his classmate, Toscha Seidl. A year younger than Heifetz, Seidl joined Auer's class in 1912, the year of Heifetz's Berlin performances, and he left the Auer fold in 1915. Seidl's recordings for Victor, HMV and Columbia[3] show him to be an outgoing player with a bright sound and a somewhat more attractive tone than one hears on Heifetz's records from the same period. Like Heifetz, and Zimbalist before him, Seidl leaned in the direction of interpretive objectivity. Yet, his playing was by no means unadorned, and in slow works, he was capable of producing a beautifully lyrical sound. Thus, his rendering of Hubay's *Herje Kati*, on one hand, is a picture of speed, precision and sprightliness, while his performance of Elman's *Eili, Eili* arrangement is as soulful as Elman's own.

Seidl was highly regarded through the early 1920s, but he never attained star status as a soloist, and by the late 1930s he was making his living as a film studio violinist. He can be heard, for instance, playing quite sweetly on the soundtrack of *Intermezzo*, a classic love story starring Leslie Howard as a concert violinist and Ingrid Bergman (in her first English language role) as his romantic interest. Hearing his recordings today, one can only wonder why Seidl did not succeed, but the answer may lie partly in the timing of his career. Although he set forth on the touring life before Heifetz, he did not make his American debut until April 1918, six months after Heifetz's startling first appearance. When he did arrive, the tide of Heifetz's popularity was rising, and the market for young Russian virtuoso violinists may already have been taxed to capacity.

Heifetz's Carnegie Hall debut took place on October 27, 1917, and like Elman's nine years earlier, it was an event heralded by considerable advance publicity. New York's musical elite—star soloists, managers and other power brokers—turned out for the recital, and heard the young Russian play a program that included the Vitali *Chaconne*, Wieniawski's Concerto No.2, and several short dazzlers and transcriptions including the Auer arrangement of the Paganini *Caprice* No.24.

Besides kicking off Heifetz's American career, the concert was the source of a joke that Elman came to resent. Elman attended the concert in the company of the pianist Leopold Godowsky, and between two of the works on the program, he complained to Godowsky that it was an unusually warm evening. Godowsky's replied, wittily, "not for pianists." At the time, Elman was amused, but he found it irritating that Godowsky immediately reported the exchange to a newspaper columnist, and that the joke not only became frequently cited, but invariably used at Elman's expense. As Elman would later explain to his friends, "you know, it *was* a warm evening, for late October."[4]

Looking back, we sometimes compress history in a way that is not true to the flow of events at the time; and while many now assume that Heifetz swept away his competitors with this single concert, it actually took him several years to fully win the public's heart. Impressive though his playing must have been at this time, his first recordings for Victor, made on November 9, 1917, less than two weeks after the concert, lack the warmth, the fullness of tone, and the deftness of interpretive ingenuity one hears on Elman's from this period.

For these first discs, on which he was accompanied by André Benoist, Heifetz chose a nice variety of pieces—Schubert's *Ave Maria*, Drigo's *Valse bluette* and Beethoven's *Chorus of Dervishes* from *The Ruins of Athens* (both arranged by Auer), Elgar's *La Capricieuse*, and Wieniawski's *Scherzo-Tarantelle*. That these are performances by a young wizard with technique to burn is beyond argument: in the Wieniawski and Beethoven selections particularly, Heifetz's speed and precision is quite startling.

In the less overtly showy pieces—the Schubert for instance—he applied a comfortable but tightly focused vibrato to the music's flowing lines, along with some *portamento*, put to good effect. In fact, he was not at all averse to using slides as coloristic devices then, and although he later modernized his style and banished them to a great degree, his early recordings of slow movements are packed with them. Especially interesting in this regard is his 1920 recording of the *Canzonetta* from the Tchaikovsky concerto, in which his luxurious slides resemble those applied by Jan Kubelik a generation earlier.

Nevertheless, Heifetz's earliest recordings have an almost detached quality, one that his early detractors considered a sign of interpretive frigidity. It wasn't long before Heifetz overcame this. As he matured, his playing developed in an interesting way: the passion that was missed in his earliest recordings eventually found its way into his performances, yet at the same time he kept the brilliance of his technique in the limelight, and using that technical precision as a springboard, he responded to changes in musical taste around him, and remained on the edge of a new stylistic approach. This was a rational, objective school, a response to the emotional, subjective one from which Elman emerged. It became the predominant approach to violin playing, and to musical performance in general, for most of the 20th century.

Five days before Heifetz's debut, Elman had played his own Carnegie Hall recital, with works by Vivaldi (as arranged by Nachez, and accompanied, as lately had become Elman's preference, by both piano and organ—one playing the string parts, the other the continuo), Lalo's *Symphonie Espagnole*, a Handel Sonata, Paganini's *I Palpeti*, as well as his own arrangements of *Deep River* and an Albeniz *Tango*. The recital was attended, as the *Times* critic observed, by "a throng as large as Carnegie Hall could seat, with extra accommodations on the stage." And unlike so many of the violinist's recent concerts, this one drew no criticism, either of his interpretations or of his bearing. "Mr. Elman," wrote the critic, "was in his best form in respect of tone, purity of intonation, vigor of bowing, dazzling brilliancy of the left hand, finish of phrasing, and obvious sincerity of purpose. There was less forcing of the sentiment," he added, "less resort to sensational display to impress the unthinking among his listeners than has sometimes been the case."

The December issue of *Vogue* also published a glowing review of Elman's recital—and its music columnist's comments are particularly interesting, given the proximity of Heifetz's legendary debut. "Of all the concerts that have come within the ken thus early in the season, that of Mischa Elman has been the most applauded. In the past, we have dared the wrath of Mr. Elman's myriad devotees by suggesting that he had become somewhat careless of the exactions of good taste, that he had played too much to the facile plaudits of sentimental enthusiasm, that he had neglected the ceaseless cultivation of his notable talents and surprising technique in order to follow the trail of easy popularity." But this time, reports the critic, Elman played "with notable dignity" and "with great purity of tone and accuracy of intonation." Also noted were "the uncannily mysterious *legato* tone" which was compared to "a voice from the tomb in one of Poe's tales."

After his recital, Elman made a quick trip to the midwest, but was back in New York in time to scout out the latest of the vaunted competitors; and after the Heifetz concert, he returned to the recital trail. There was a repeat of the Carnegie Hall program in Boston early in November—a recital that also drew both an enthusiastic audience response and critical recognition of his communicative powers (and of the fact that "he sways less to the rhythm of his music than has been his custom"). The following week, he played the Wieniawski D minor Concerto in Philadelphia, with Stokowski, and this time the lately hostile *Musical Courier* had only praise for his performance. The Philadelphia audience, however, was so vehement in its approval that the conclusion of the concert was delayed, to the critic's consternation.

"A storm of applause broke forth that fairly raised the house," he reported in the November 22 issue. "After the usual three or four recalls some temperate individuals thought there had been enough congratulatory noise, but others decided to the contrary, so the ovation degenerated into a riotous bout of ridiculous hand clapping that continued for many minutes.... Meantime, Elman got tired of doing the marathon between the wings and stage center, so he decided to remain out of sight after the sixth appearance. Stokowski, who had stepped down from the platform, stood with his back to the audience throughout the bombardment, and thought terrible things."

Elman still occasionally played split concerts with other artists—a form of programming that was quickly going out of fashion, yet which persisted in New York and in a few cities around the country. The Metropolitan Opera House concerts were a special case, being a popular series that allowed patrons to hear a handful of artists each time. Elman was a favorite at these, and on November 18, the day after the last of his Philadelphia concerts, he played the Wieniawski at the Met. The same issue of the *Musical Courier* that covered his Philadelphia appearance ran a review of this concert, reporting that Elman "played like one inspired," and that he was recalled to play six encores.

One of Elman's most intriguing dates of this part of the season, however, was a joint recital with the soprano Frances Alda, before an audience of 4,300 in Detroit. Elman and Alda had recently made a handful of recordings for Victor—Rabey's *Tes Yeux*, Hollman's *Chanson d'amour*, Gounod's *Ave Maria*, and Braga's *Angel's Serenade*. In the tradition of the old fashioned musicale, however, the artists performed separate groups of works, with their own accompanists, collaborating on only one selection, the Gounod.

At the end of December, Elman returned to New York for a second Carnegie Hall concert, this one featuring another Handel sonata, Nardini and Ernst concertos, and groups of smaller works, all prefaced by the violinist's own arrangement of *The Star-Spangled Banner*—a concession, perhaps, to the spirit of nationalistic zeal occasioned by America's entry into World War I the previous April. In the reviews, this arrangement was criticized as "presumptuous," but the program itself was reviewed in strongly supportive terms. So were the performances he gave with the New York Symphony on tour in early January, and his Beethoven Concerto performances with the New York Philharmonic, at Carnegie Hall in February.

The enthusiastic tenor of this series of reviews from late 1917 gives an interesting historical perspective on Elman's place in the violin world at this time. Nowhere is he compared negatively with Heifetz; and in fact, the reviews published during the season after Heifetz's New York triumph paint a much kinder picture of Elman's playing than those published in the year before Heifetz's arrival.

Elman was, clearly, Heifetz's main competitor at the time of his debut, with Zimbalist also high on the list of popular violinists. Soon however, both Heifetz and Elman would have to contend with Fritz Kreisler's return to the American concert stage—a return that, ultimately, had more serious consequences for Elman than for Heifetz, for in a musical world that was already beginning to debate the merits of the rationality over emotionalism, Heifetz had the former category virtually to himself, while Elman and Kreisler were left to battle for dominance of the latter.

Kreisler was born in Vienna in 1875, and entered the Vienna Conservatory at age seven. Three years later, he completed his studies there, and graduated with the conservatory's first prize in violin. He went to Paris, where he spent the next two years at the Conservatoire, and again won the top prize for his instrument upon his graduation at age 12. The following year, 1888, he traveled to the United States with the pianist Moriz Rosenthal, serving as an assisting artist at the pianist's concerts, but also giving a few performances of his own. These were not particularly successful, and in 1889, the 14-year old Kreisler set his violin aside and returned to school to complete a general course of education. A short stint in the Austrian army followed, but in 1896, he was performing again, and in 1900 he returned to the United States to do battle with Jan Kubelik.

Kubelik and Kreisler vied for dominance of the violin world through the first decade of the century, and as Kubelik's career began to fade, Kreisler became the more popular performer. Eventually, though, both were overshadowed by the stream of young Russians sent forth by Leopold Auer, starting with Elman. Kreisler and Elman admired each other enormously in those early days, and they struck up a friendship that lasted until Kreisler's death, in 1962. One of Kreisler's short works, in fact, the *Rondino on a Theme of Beethoven*, was dedicated to Elman. "I happened to be with Elman and Godowsky just after I had blocked out the *Rondino*," Kreisler said, "but of course it was only in sketch form. Elman took it and began to play it. Then Godowsky chimed in on the piano, and the two did a clowning act of stamping with their feet and caricaturing my composition. So I punished Mischa by dedicating it to him."[5]

Elman was annoyed when Kreisler admitted to having faked the stream supposed "transcriptions" of works by old masters—not only because he felt they were fine enough works to stand on their own merits, but also (and perhaps primarily), because he had not been let in on Kreisler's private stunt. When Kreisler disclosed, in 1935, that he was in fact the author of a purported Vivaldi Concerto, as well as more than a dozen other works said to be by Couperin, Martini, Cartier, Popora, Pugnani, Stamitz and Francouer, Elman told a *New York Times* reporter that "it is indeed a surprise that one who stands so high for all that is beautiful, pure and true in art as Kreisler should have resorted to such means in these so-called arrangements, which would take a high place of themselves, without his having to attribute his compositions to older sources, when these composers are unable to enjoy the plaudits or endure the criticisms which these compositions may or may not evoke."

Still, there were no serious disagreements between them. When Kreisler lived in Berlin, during the 1930s, Elman visited him there whenever he was on tour, and on these visits he would play piano accompaniments for Kreisler as the violinist-composer tried out his latest works. Apparently, Elman had little opportunity to play his own instrument for Kreisler during these visits: whenever he took up his violin on these occasions, Kreisler's wife would invariably curtail the performance by standing at the bottom of the stairs, calling to Kreisler that it was time to leave his studio and join his other guests.

When Kreisler died, in 1962, Elman marked the occasion at a Carnegie Hall recital, a few days later, by announcing that he wished to "pay homage to my great colleague and friend," and giving a serene reading of Kreisler's *Preghiera in the Style of Martini* before continuing with his printed program. Interestingly, Elman still thought of the piece in its older transcription guise, and described the work as being "by Martini-Kreisler." Elman also devoted one of his last LPs to works by Kreisler, including, naturally, the *Rondino* that had been dedicated to him.

Kreisler's early American career continued apace until 1914, when he was called to active military service in Austria. By the end of the year he was released on medical grounds (although some dispute whether he was actually wounded, as is often claimed), and he returned to the United States, which had not yet entered the war. For the next three years, he performed, often to great acclaim; and he continued making records. These days, his later recordings (those of the late 1930s, consisting primarily of his own works) are the most frequently reissued and the best known. In this early period, though, he recorded a good deal of standard literature, the highlight of this wartime period being a fascinating 1915 account of the Bach Double Concerto, BWV 1043, with Efrem Zimbalist as the second violinist, and a string quartet serving as the orchestra.[6]

When the United States entered the war in Europe, Kreisler cancelled his American engagements and stayed out of sight. A few anti-German groups had already staged demonstrations against him outside his concerts, and although he was married to an American, he had served in the Austrian army and he felt it would be unwise to fight the tide of public sentiment. His instincts were good, as the unfortunate case of the conductor Karl Muck proved soon enough. Muck, the director of the Boston Symphony, was known to be a German nationalist, and rumors soon circulated that he was an enemy agent, involved in anti-American terrorist activities. The orchestra's founder, Major Henry Lee Higginson, dismissed this as sheer insanity, and refused to fire Muck. But the conductor was arrested in March 1918, and although charges were never officially filed against him, he was detained until 1919 and then deported to his homeland.

Kreisler stayed off the stage for two years. He then made a two-pronged comeback. First, in early October 1919, he unveiled a Broadway musical, entitled *Apple Blossoms*. Composed to a book by Victor Jacobi, the play starred Fred and Adele Astaire and was quite successful. Then, on October 27—two years to the day after Jascha Heifetz made his debut—Kreisler returned to the concert stage, playing at a benefit concert for the Vienna Children's Milk Relief fund.

Kreisler's return came at a time when tastes were shifting and when the roles of performers and composers were being closely examined. The most vehement debates concerned central questions of interpretation: was the composer best served by direct, unadorned readings of their scores? Or were they better served by performances infused with the personalities of the players, even if these personalities found their expression through alterations of the composer's texts? Were performers, in other words, merely servants of the composers? Or was it their right, as creative artists in a different realm, to mold a composers' works to suit their own temperaments and messages?

To a degree, these questions have never been, and can never be, fully resolved: not only are the stylistic latitudes acceptable to the public and the musical press in a state of perpetual flux, but persuasive arguments have been set forth on each side. After all, even listeners with the most literalist sympathies find little to admire in performances that are metronomically correct, and which bear no signs of interpretive insight. Yet, how many music lovers, even among those inclined towards the Romanticists, would support the contention that the composer's wishes, as conveyed through his writing, may be deemed inadequate by a performer? Moreover, the breadth of interpretive latitude some composers were known to have tolerated (or even encouraged) makes it difficult for performers and listeners to know where to draw the line between a performer's interpretive mandate, and the need for a composer's specific intentions to be conveyed.

Recordings have given us a number of examples that would seem to lend weight to the argument that performers should take an active and even aggressive hand in bringing a work to life. One of the most provocative is the case of the Mahler Fourth Symphony, as conducted by Willem Mengelberg. Mahler's scoring is careful, detailed, and packed with specific performing directions, many of which Mengelberg contravenes in his recording, a monument to the art of recomposing a work in performance. Rhythms are stretched and distended far beyond the bounds of what we would think of as acceptable today. Yet, in his letters, Mahler wrote glowingly of Mengelberg's way with his music.

What do we make of Mahler's endorsement? Indeed, what do make of Mahler's own conducting? Accounts of his New York Philharmonic performances of the Beethoven symphonies describe Mahler's approach as astonishingly freewheeling in terms of tempo and even orchestration. For that matter, what can we glean from the fact that Rachmaninoff admired Vladimir Horowitz's interpretations of his music, even though Horowitz's early Rachmaninoff recordings are quite different from Rachmaninoff's own? Clearly these composers did not see their works as being immune to interpretive variety, and allowed a great deal more of it than listeners and performers allow today.

Whatever the arguments in favor of performer input, the brand of grand Romantic interpretation in vogue at the turn of the century was falling from favor by the start of the 1920s, and this trend would continue inexorably over the next five decades. Why did this change in taste occur? By the late 1970s, when the trend towards supposed musical objectivity had reached its peak, critics lamenting the lack of personalization in performances tended to blame the jet plane (for its role in shrinking the globe and replacing regional musical accents with a homogenous global style) and recordings (for granting a spurious "definitiveness" to certain performances, which unduly influenced the developing interpretations of younger players).

But the roots of this change in style can be traced back farther, to the *Zeitgeist* of the early 20th century. This was a crucial moment in the history of civilization: the industrial revolution had kicked into a new phase, and was by this time truly global. Mass production was becoming the norm, and as the items people used in their day to day lives came to be consistent and uniform, expectations of this sort of uniformity overflowed to areas of life where uniformity traditionally had no place—the arts, for one, and music in particular. At the same time, the war in Europe was showing the darker side of the newly mechanized world. For the first time, warfare reached to (and from) the skies, and a battery of newly efficient weapons, including poisonous gas, made war's inevitable carnage greater, more widespread, and more frightening than ever.

For composers, poets and painters, the arts were an outlet for their feelings about this too rapidly changing world. Meanwhile, trends towards providing theater and concerts at "popular" prices meant that for a broadening public, the arts could offer moments of solace and escape. Those who had always attended performances no doubt continued to cherish the variety of styles the world of the arts (and, it must have increasingly seemed, *only* the world of the arts) still offered. But a new kind of listener was filling the concert halls, many of whom were coming to classical music without previous experience of it, while others had firmer cultural backgrounds, but were part of a younger generation inured to the ways of the modern world.

What they had in common, if for different reasons, was the not unreasonable belief that musical performances should adhere to the blueprints the composers provided in their scores. But one difference between these listeners and their elders was that where older listeners regarded that blueprint as reasonably elastic, the younger ones saw it in more plastic terms—more akin to the mold from which mass produced glassware might be made than to a design idea from which a potter might make similar but varied pieces.

This new kind of listener reasoned that if there was a great variance between two readings of a classic work, then one of the players was taking liberties that could not be justified in the score. Taken a step further, if two performers worked from the same musical blueprint, but turned out radically different readings, one of their performances was probably closer to the composer's notion, than the other, and therefore superior. Only within this broader context can a finger be pointed at the growing world of recordings. As a larger public bought phonographs and discs, perceptions and expectations of these artifacts began to change. People had come to think of recordings not as an artist's calling card, presented via a piece of music, but as the piece of music itself. The medium, as Marshall McLuhan was later to observe, was becoming the message. Moreover, as the recording industry matured as a business, the catalogues grew fat with competing versions of favorite works; and one side effect of recordings was that they made invidious comparisons between great artists not only possible, but for the collector with limited financial means, necessary. The press and public had always debated the merits of performers, and to an extent, this kind of either/or situations existed as performers fought for recognition as the most popular and exalted in their fields. Records, however, allowed a microscopic examination of a performer's art that was often unfair or beside the point—or at least, beside what had traditionally been the point of live performances.

Thus, if the concert world already tended towards the hierarchical, recordings added further weight to the assumption that great performers can be ranked. This turn of history had unfortunate consequences for Mischa Elman, and in later years, he frequently lamented the prevalence of this notion, both privately and publicly.

In the early 1920s, however, the situation was still rather fluid; in fact, any final reckoning of the pecking order among the great violinists, pianists and conductors would have to wait until the larger stylistic issue was settled. When the smoke cleared, the strict and streamlined approach of Arturo Toscanini displaced the more freely breathing and manipulative styles of Mengelberg and Furtwangler, among conductors; and among pianists, Artur Schnabel's aristocratic approach displaced the personalized renderings of Elman's friends Leopold Godowsky and Josef Hofmann—although Vladimir Horowitz, a grand Romantic by any standard, did not begin his American career until 1928. But Horowitz's Romanticism, like Heifetz's, differed from the subjective interpretation that had come before. It was personal and individual; but it was also glitzy, highly polished and modern. For the moment, the two styles would co-exist, if not entirely peacefully.

CHAPTER NINE:

Touring with Ysaÿe, and the Return to Europe

The need to compete with other violinists did not sit well with Elman, who had spent nearly the first three decades of his life as the violin world's focus of attention. Now he found his position challenged by both older and younger violinists; and what he found especially upsetting was that there wasn't much he could do to prevent his public from straying. Critical attacks were easier to handle: when, in 1916, he drew a stream of scathing reviews, he addressed the problem by rethinking his approach and modifying his stage demeanor. Having accomplished this, were the public and press now going to desert him for Heifetz and Kreisler? Elman was not inclined to speak out against his rivals in the press: When asked about them by interviewers, he deflected the questions by discussing the need for interpretive variety. "There is no single *right* way to play a work," he would often say. "There is no *best* interpretation. There are simply different points of view, and every great artist has his own." If pressed, Elman would praise those violinists he liked as worthy artists and colleagues, but he no longer went out of his way to single them out for particular recommendation, as he had done in Kreisler's and Zimbalist's cases a few years earlier.

Yet, it would hardly be fair to paint Elman as ungenerous towards the colleagues he most admired. During the 1919–20 season, he undertook an extensive duet tour with Eugene Ysaÿe in the hope of helping the older Belgian master reclaim some of the public he had lost over the preceding decade. He also continued to include Kreisler's music in his programs, and he did so long after these vignettes fell out of fashion. And in the 1930s, he paid homage of sorts to Heifetz by

113

recording his younger colleague's arrangement of Dinicu's *Hora staccato*, one of Heifetz's most popular showpieces.

Privately, though, Elman found the matter thoroughly frustrating, and because his frustration never abated, many who knew him only casually—and particularly those who knew him only through the channels of the music business—came to regard him as cantankerous and bitter. An early description of the way Elman was apt to express this bitterness is cited in a 1940 memoir by a manager who represented Elman during the 1930s, Charles L. Wagner. Wagner seemed to truly admire Elman's artistry, and in his book, he describes Elman as "one of the world's finest virtuosi." He added, however, that the violinist was prone to "making enemies right and left through an inordinate jealousy of other violinists and a disagreeable manner of showing it." He gives one example:

> My office was the scene of such a tempest when Mischa met the authoress of a book about artists, containing an excellently written page on himself, but with a picture of Kreisler on the cover carrying the caption "King of Violinists." In a raging temper Elman shouted, "If Kreisler is king, I am the emperor!" The authoress fled and for years denounced him everywhere, for which I could hardly blame her.[1]

Others who knew Elman recall that his puzzlement over the immensity of Heifetz's popularity was almost obsessive. "It was an amazing thing," one of the violinist's friends explained, "but at his own dinner parties, he would always, without fail, turn to the person next to him and ask, 'Can you tell me why Heifetz has such success?' He thought Heifetz was a great violinist, and never said à word against him; but he was mystified by the fact that Heifetz was considered the personification of the violin."

This line of questioning occasionally extended to other violinists, and when Elman raised this question outside his circle of friends, the results could be disastrous. A few months before he died, Elman played a concerto performance in Florida, after which he was feted at a dinner attended by about a dozen of the orchestra's patrons. Towards the end of the dinner, he stood up and inquired of the assembled guests, "Tell me, what is it about Isaac Stern's playing that makes his name a household word?" One guest, an elderly philanthropist, took the intent of the question too literally.

"Mr. Elman," he responded, "I don't know anything about music. But I heard Isaac Stern play at the White House last week, and I have a tape of the concert. If you'd like to borrow it, I'd be happy to lend it to you." Elman was visibly rankled, and curtly declined, whereupon another guest tried to save the situation. "What I love about your playing, Mr. Elman," she offered, "is that your tone is so *schmaltzy*." That, of course, went over poorly as well: "He *hated* when people said his playing was *schmaltzy*," another friend confirmed. "He used to say, 'I don't understand this—what does *schmaltz* have to do with music?'"

❖ ❖ ❖ ❖ ❖

Unfortunately, competition with his colleagues was not the only problem of public life that plagued Elman. A number of more personally distressing experiences had occurred from the time his career began, and during his years at the top, they intensified. The most common dilemma was a predictable one: he became the object of various con artists. The most frequent and troublesome were the "long lost relatives," who turned up at his hotel rooms when he was on tour. Often, they had researched his family structure, but claimed to be members of branches he'd never heard of; and invariably, they were low on funds. The first time one of these fraudulent relatives approached him, he was amused; soon enough, the gambit wore thin, and he began to find the intrusions irritating.

Some intrusions were more sinister. During one of the violinist's first American tours, his mother, in London, received a telegram with the news that Saul had taken ill and died during the trip, and that Mischa was stranded and penniless. The message urged her to wire funds to Mischa, care of the message's sender. After an initial moment of panic, Mrs. Elman decided that the claim must be false, if only because Mischa certainly had the means to acquire funds at his disposal. She checked his itinerary and wired Saul, who responded that he was very much alive and that Mischa was in no danger.

One of the oddest and most disturbing of these intrusions, was a case in which Elman's life was put in jeopardy. In the early months of 1920, Elman began receiving telephone calls regularly during his morning practice sessions with his new accompanist, Joseph Bonime. At first the calls seemed normal enough: they were from a man said he was a violinist, and he began by asking Elman questions about repertoire. As the conversations continued, the caller grew increasingly agitated, and charged that Elman was the only impediment standing between him and his own destiny as the world's greatest violinist. If he could kill Elman, he said, the world would be his.

Elman dismissed the calls at first, but after several, Bonime suggested having them traced. They came from a public telephone in a drug store in the Bronx. Bonime went to the drug store, and asked if the owner could give them a description of a man who used the store's telephone almost every day at just before noon. The druggist did better than that: he was gave Bonime the man's name and address. Bonime decided to have a chat with the caller, but when he arrived at the address, he found only the threatening caller's father, who said that his son used to play the violin, and had been quite good; but that he had returned from the war shell-shocked. He assured Bonime that his son was harmless, and begged him not to bring the police into the matter.

After Bonime's visit, the calls ceased. One morning, though, the caller turned up at 404 Riverside Drive—Saul Elman's apartment at 113 Street, where Elman was staying. When the maid answered the door, the agitated visitor asked to see Elman; but she wisely judged that Elman would not want to see him, so she said the violinist was out. Elman was practicing in a room at the back of the apartment, though, and the man could hear him. "He's here," the visitor insisted. "That's him playing the violin." "I'm sorry sir," the maid replied, "that's one of Mr. Elman's students, who arrived early for a lesson, and is using the time to warm up. Mr. Elman should be here in half an hour, if you'd like to come back." The man left, and the maid informed Elman and Bonime. This time they called the police, who found a crowd gathering on Riverside Drive when they arrived a few minutes later. Unable to kill Elman, the caller had killed himself.

These occurrences intensified into the 1920s. Some were petty, some were potentially dangerous. Some were merely financial (although the attempted swindles were sometimes elaborate and involved large sums), and some involved personal threats. At the same time, professional challenges began to weigh heavily on Elman too—not only those posed by other violinists, but those that arose from Elman's increasingly rocky relationships with those he selected as his managers. All this had an effect on Elman's public persona. As a child prodigy, and as a young man touring through Europe and America, he had been open and outgoing, and he engaged visitors in lively, enthusiastic, friendly conversations. He enjoyed meeting people and socializing, and when he was the center of attention, he would freely discuss whatever came to mind. To a great degree, these characteristics remained with him, but his brighter edge—the outgoing, almost bouncy personality that journalists described in their accounts of his early interviews—was wearing down, and as the outside world made unwelcome incursions into the serenity of his private life, he began to erect an outer shell and a wariness about those who were not part of his trusted circle.

"There were two sides," the pianist Joseph Seiger recalls, "almost two Mischa Elmans. One was the private man—the family man, who was extremely warm and generous to those he knew. I knew of many cases in which he helped needy musicians, usually secretly, because he didn't want it known who he was helping or how much he gave them. And then there was the other side—the hard-working, dedicated musician, who put a screen between himself and the public. When I got to know him well, I realized that this was a form of self-protection that he had evolved after having been hurt. Early in his career, he took quite a few beatings—not artistically, but financially. He really learned a lot the hard way, and in order to avoid these things, he had to somehow separate himself from everyone else. As a result, a certain image of Mischa Elman got around. People thought of him as an egomaniac, but that wasn't really the case.

"Of course, the other thing that added to the egotistical image," Seiger adds, "was that he could be outspoken. In that way he was very much the opposite of Heifetz, who was a more reticent man. When people asked him his opinions, Heifetz would say as little as possible, and avoid making lengthy statements. With Elman, if the subject was one that he cared deeply about, his temper would rise and he would just let it out. In this way, he put himself on the spot many times."

❖ ❖ ❖ ❖ ❖

One professional association that did not end as happily as it might have was that between Elman and the theatrical impresario Florenz Ziegfeld. By 1920, there were indications that Broadway musicals by classical musicians would come into vogue. Kreisler's *Apple Blossoms* had been a hit in 1919, and Zimbalist also did nicely with his musical, *Honeydew*. Zimbalist's work was not really an attempt to emulate Kreisler: at a dinner party in the summer of 1918, Kreisler and Zimbalist embarked on a discussion of the theater, and one of them suggested that they each write a musical. Obviously, the idea appealed to them both, for they went their separate ways, composed their works, and offered them to the public in close succession.

Elman would probably not have entered the lists here if not for Ziegfeld's commission. From Ziegfeld's point of view, the violinist was an ideal choice for the project. Not only was he a renowned soloist who was very much in the public eye but, in recent years, he had emerged as a composer of charming, short pieces, some of them light songs. Ziegfeld set about acquiring the rights to Richard Harding Davis's *Soldiers of Fortune*; and he hired Augustus Thomas and Gene Buck to prepare the libretto and the song lyrics. Elman's input was to be limited to the composition of the music, but it was on that last element that this light theater piece would sink or swim. "I want a blockbuster," Ziegfeld told Elman. "Don't let me down."

The violinist found the prospect of composing a musical appealing, although he had his doubts about the health of Broadway, doubts he had expressed candidly in one of the interviews he gave during his sabbatical year, 1915. That season, Elman attended virtually everything Broadway had to offer, and he was decidedly unimpressed. "I do not think the public is treated as it should be by the theaters here," he observed, adding in his still idiosyncratic English that "the great majority of entertainments at present are superficial. There seems to be very little provided for the people who are willing to have a little brains mixed with their amusement. The musical pieces seem the worst in this respect. In most of them, the music does not amount to anything, and the *libretti* are without any real cleverness.

"There does not seem to be much improvement in the more serious pieces," he continued. "Some of the plays which are devoted to displaying the stars are really stupid from beginning to end. The public is the victim.... It is a shame to treat the public of New York that way, because it is ready for something good. If they cannot get good plays why do they not revive standard plays of people like Oscar Wilde or Bernard Shaw? You can disagree with either of these authors, but at least when you are done with them they have given you something to discuss. It is hard to see how, with the present style of plays, the public taste will not be spoiled."[2]

Elman's contract with Ziegfeld specified the number of musical pieces the score was to include, and set forth a schedule by which the creative team was to work. In essence, the contract, signed in mid-April 1920, specified that all the lyrics had to be delivered to Elman by August 1, and that Elman was to deliver the completed work to Ziegfeld by the beginning of February 1921. For this work, Elman received a $10,000 bonus in advance, and he was promised 3% of the box office receipts. When August arrived, Buck supplied lyrics to all but three of the required songs; but Elman felt he could work on his settings without them, so long as they arrived in sufficient time for him to meet the February deadline. The effort Elman went to was impressive in many ways. All told, he completed 14 numbers,[3] two of which are nicely flowing instrumental interludes. These are entitled "Melodrame" and "Tango." The latter was an astute piece of coloristic writing: it suited the work itself, which was set in a fictional land (Olancho) where Spanish was spoken; and it recalled Elman's own popular violin work, expressed this time through a larger orchestral canvas.

The other selections are songs and choral numbers, and in truth, Elman was not given a lot to work with, for some of Buck's couplets are truly dreadful, even by the standard of contemporary Broadway musicals: "Some men aspire to paint or write, and some love high finance," begin the three mercenaries in their title song, "but we desire to warn and fight through life, and take a chance." There are lovelorn plaints by pining ladies, and a love song, sung by one of the soldiers to his cigarette—a touch Freud might have loved, although it no doubt irked Elman, who strongly disapproved of smoking.

Given that, Elman's settings have a certain charm. There are, in truth, times when his melodies are rhythmically square and a bit constricted, and on occasion he chooses an unlikely word to stress with a high note or a strong beat. But these flaws could have been fixed in a light revision. At any rate, once the he finished fitting out the lyrics with his own tunes, Elman set about orchestrating them and he did so ambitiously, setting each piece for flute, oboe, two clarinets, bassoon, two horns, two cornets, trombone, various percussion instruments, harp, two violins, viola, cello and double bass. On occasion, he replaced (or doubled) the flute with a piccolo; and in one instance he even added a section of mandolins for color. Among the dozen vocal numbers, there are parts for nine solo voices, plus sections for men's and women's chorus.

By February, Buck had still not supplied the three missing lyrics, but Elman was unconcerned. But he was in for a shock when he arrived at Ziegfeld's office with the score, only to find that the producer had lost interest in the project and meant to use the missing numbers as a pretext for cancelling the agreement. He made no judgement on the score itself at that time; in fact, he refused to accept it, taking the position that it was an incomplete work and therefore did not meet the terms of the commission. He demanded that Elman return the advance.

Elman was outraged. He had worked hard on *Soldiers of Fortune*, and cut down on his touring in order to complete it. He regarded the lack of three songs—a failing that could not, at any rate, be laid at his door—as insufficient reason for the project to be cancelled at this late date. Besides, the commission had been announced in the press, and Elman felt that his public was awaiting the play's production. If it were not to be produced, it might appear that Elman was either incapable of composing an extended theater piece, or that his work wasn't good enough for Ziegfeld.

From Ziegfield's office, he went directly to the suite of Phillips, Jaffe and Jaffe, attorneys-at-law. Elman hoped to force Ziegfeld to hold up his end of the contract and produce the work. Failing that, he felt that he should be allowed to keep the advance, having met his own obligations; and he wanted Ziegfeld to publicly acknowledge that it was his own unwillingness to produce the play, rather than Elman's failure to complete it, that stood in the way of a public performance. To this end, he sued Ziegfeld for breach of contract, seeking damages to the tune of $100,000.

Later in life, Elman turned the incident into a light-spirited anecdote, one he repeated frequently in his public speaking engagements. Here is his view of the Ziegfeld affair, conveyed during a speech at the Lamb's Club exactly 40 years after the legal battle was joined:

> The late and legendary Florenz Ziegfeld, not to be outdone [by Charles Dillingham, who produced Kreisler's *Apple Blossoms*], commissioned me to write the score for a work to be called *Soldiers of Fortune*, in collaboration with Gene Buck and Augustus Thomas. To bind the bargain, it was Mr. Ziegfeld's suggestion that he pay me a certain sum as a bonus on the signing of the agreement, over and above the royalties I would eventually receive. When the work was completed Mr. Ziegfeld declared that though he personally loved the score, he thought it "too good" for Broadway, and asked me to return the bonus. I hope you won't think any the less of me that I declined to do so, feeling that I was entitled to at least that for the time and effort I had expended. And though I was disappointed at losing this opportunity to enter the exciting world of Broadway, what made me adamant in my refusal was my convic-

tion that there is *nothing* that's "too good" for Broadway, providing it's good! Mr. Ziegfeld said he would be obliged to sue me, and
I replied that in that case I would take my violin to court, play the
melodies for the jurors and let them decide if they were "too good"
for Broadway. Mr. Ziegfeld gave me a long, level look. "In that
case, you win," he said coldly.[4]

That's not quite how it happened: It was Elman, not Ziegfeld, who
initiated the lawsuit, in June 1921. Ziegfeld, predictably, countersued,
asking for the return of the advance plus $10,000 damages. In fact,
having refused to accept the score, the producer could not have
pronounced the work either "too good" or "not good enough" for
Broadway. Ziegfeld's attorneys saw his refusal to accept Elman's
manuscript as a tactical error, and as late as 1926, both sides in the dispute were still in court wrangling over a sub-issue—namely, whether
Ziegfeld had the right to make a photostatic copy of the score, in order
to submit it to a panel of experts capable of pronouncing upon its fit-
ness for the stage. Eventually, the Appellate Division decided that
Elman should not be required to furnish Ziegfeld with a copy of the
score.

It wasn't until June 1929 that the matter was settled, the outcome
being that Elman could keep the advance, and that all rights to the
work revert to him. There was a complication, though. It turns out that
a quarter of the advance had been furnished, through Ziegfeld, by the
music publishing firm of T.B. Harms, which considered that it still
owned the publishing rights. According to the settlement between
Elman and Ziegfeld, it became the producer's obligation to obtain a
release from Harms. By the middle of the following April, exactly 10
years after the work was commissioned, Ziegfeld had not yet obtained
the necessary release, and was about to take up an extensive project
in Hollywood.

This was academic, really. By then, Elman had no intention of
taking his decade old musical to another firm, and he had lost interest
in seeing the work produced. But the lack of a release from the
publisher was a loose end, and Elman hated loose ends. So in April
1930, Elman sued Ziegfield yet again. And so it went.

❖ ❖ ❖ ❖ ❖

During this period, Elman was playing more than 100 concerts a
year, a goodly amount in those days of rail and sea travel. They were

often grand affairs, too. At the end of 1918, he played a series of Sunday concerts at the Hippodrome, and attracted crowds that filled the hall's 5,000 seats, plus another 1,000 seats on the immense stage. A year later, he opened his 1919 season at the same hall, and drew the same size crowd, which was as enthusiastic as it was large. On the latter occasion, he played a challenging program that included the Bach *Chaconne*, a Handel sonata, an Ernst Concerto, plus two sets of short paraphrases and dazzlers, and half a dozen encores.

Two months later, he drew 6,000 listeners to the Hippodrome yet again, this time for a duo recital with Eugene Ysaÿe. At 61, Ysaÿe's powers as a violinist had been waning for some time, and in 1918, he had accepted a full time conducting post, the podium of the Cincinnati Orchestra. He had also decided to focus more of his attention on his composing, and besides his many well known violin works, he composed an opera, to a text in Walloon. Ironically, if his technical powers were leaving him, his imagination continued to explore the violin's possibilities, for it was not until 1924 that he completed his greatest contribution to the violin's literature, the set of six solo sonatas.

Elman admired Ysaÿe enormously. As a student of Wieniawski and Vieuxtemps, he represented a link to a world already gone. He must also have reminded Elman of Sarasate, for although the two were entirely dissimilar physically and as interpreters, there was a majestic assurance to Ysaÿe's playing that Elman had not seen since that Sarasate recital in Odessa so many years earlier. How it happened that the two decided to play together will remain a mystery, but whoever suggested the duo saw his instinct considerably rewarded, for their concerts were invariably sold-out.

Ysaÿe apparently made an amusing traveling companion, for Elman returned from each trip with a new store of anecdotes. In fact, they must have made a comic pair, in many ways, for they were polar opposites in virtually every respect. Ysaÿe, a huge man, dwarfed Elman, who was still comparatively thin, youthful, and much shorter. Elman was balding, while Ysaÿe's full head of long hair led many a writer to describe him as "leonine." And while Elman had certainly developed a hearty appreciation of food by then, his appetite was nothing compared with Ysaÿe's. When they embarked on their journeys, Elman would stop at his parents' house and pick up a box of knishes, made for them by an aunt, who, in the best Jewish tradition, wanted to be sure the violinists didn't go hungry during their journey.

Ysaÿe made his way through these so quickly, though, that after a few trips, Elman began asking for larger boxes and more knishes. Meanwhile, Ysaÿe would leave the train at virtually every station, Elman reported, and he would return with a pie or some other delicacy.

When Ysaÿe wasn't eating, he was smoking one of the pipes in the large collection he brought with him. Elman was amused by Ysaÿe's penchant for naming his pipes after women. After their first journey together, Elman told his family about a time when, in the middle of the night, Ysaÿe asked, "Where's my Josephine—have you seen her?" Elman didn't know what he was talking about at first, but of course, he soon caught on.

The friction between them was slight and, predictably, it centered on their stage presentation. One particular disagreement was about the relatively trivial matter of music stand placement—something that can be blown out of proportion when two artistic egos are involved. They had agreed to share a music stand, rather than to clutter the stage with two; but Elman noticed that Ysaÿe stood off to the side and behind Elman when they were playing. Since Ysaÿe was taller, he could look over Elman, but soon the younger violinist began to feel that this made it seem as if only Ysaÿe had committed the music to memory. Elman complained, and Ysaÿe agreed to play at a distance from the stand equal to Elman's.

For the tour, they had only worked up two or three full programs. Of course, the repeatability of programming is another thing that has changed in the nearly seven decades since these concerts took place. While it would be unheard of for a soloist to play the same piece twice in a season in a given city today, back then the practice was not all that uncommon. Elman frequently played the same program in Brooklyn as he would give in Manhattan a week later; and even in Manhattan, where he was at that time playing as many as ten times a season, he could repeat a work or two with impunity. With Ysaÿe, for instance, he played the Molique *Concertante* at the Hippodrome in November 1919, and again at their concert in the same hall in April 1920. Both concerts also featured a Mozart *Concertante*, which one report describes as an arrangement from a piano concerto.

Otherwise, the duo's joint repertoire included the Bach Double Concerto, the Moszkowski Suite, Op.71, a Handel sonata and a set of six duets by Godard, as well as a Paganini encore. All these works, even the concertos, were accompanied by Bonime. Elman undoubtedly tried to persuade Ysaÿe to join him in the recording studio during their journeys together; but Ysaÿe's lack of interest in the recording horn and its medium-fidelity products is evident from the fact that he called a halt to his recording career after those few 1912 discs. What a pity, though, that this collaboration was not preserved.

The April 1920 duet concert was Ysaÿe's and Elman's last joint outing in New York; barely a month later, Elman sold out the Hippodrome once again for a solo appearance. This was a gala concert, for it was to be not only Elman's last New York appearance of the season but, it was announced, his last for the next few years. Elman's plan was to return to Europe that summer, and to reintroduce himself to an audience he had not played for since 1914. For this concert, Elman was accompanied by a string orchestra, which he conducted, in the Bach E major Concerto, the Paganini Concerto in D, and, as an encore, Bach's *Air on the G String*. The concert also included a group of five short pieces, in which he was accompanied on the piano by Frank Scaley, and a performance of Beethoven's "Kreutzer" Sonata, in which he was accompanied by his sister Liza, who was 18 years old. Liza Elman had studied with Benno Moiseiwitsch in London and at the Curtis Institute. Elman's youngest sister, Esther, was a pianist too, and studied with both Josef and Rosina Lhevinne, at Juilliard; but she never accompanied him in concert.

"With Liza," Esther Elman recalled, "my brother only played the major sonatas, not full programs, because to tell you the truth, he never liked the idea of having a woman as an accompanist. He was very conservative, in many ways, and of course, he was brought up to feel that if he were walking out on stage, the woman should walk out first. Of course, if he were the soloist, *he* would have to go out first, so that posed a problem of etiquette for him. With my sister, it was different, because they were playing sonatas. In a sonata, both parts are equal. It's not a question of a soloist and an accompanist, so it was acceptable for her to walk out first."

In preparation for Mischa's return to Europe, meanwhile, Saul Elman had gone to London late in 1919. He was shocked at what he found. The genteel country he had left five years earlier was now chaotic, and the British class system was beginning to disintegrate. When he arrived at his house in Hampstead, he found that the couple he had engaged to oversee it had left, and that the place had not been cleaned in the recent past. Nor could he find domestics to replace them. In the end, he decided to sell the house and the furnishings. He was even more shocked, though to run into Waldemar Liachowsky, the young Germanized Russian who had been Elman's first regular accompanist. Liachowsky had settled in London, but had not been able to make a living as an accompanist. When Saul Elman found him, he was working as a dancer in a cabaret act.

"London looks like a graveyard," Elman told an interviewer after receiving a detailed letter about conditions there from his father. "The people all show signs of the intense suffering that has been their lot." He added, however, that he expected the situation to return to normal, at least so far as concert life was concerned, by the following year. Besides, he said, "I must keep up my reputation there as well as here. While I regret keenly that the 1919-20 season will be my last [in America] for some time to come, you may rest assured that if the American people want me back again, I will certainly come back! I love America, and when I go, I leave some of my best friends behind."[5]

One of those friends was an interesting character named Fred J. Erion, an amateur violinist who lived in Buffalo, New York, and who had met Elman after a recital in Saratoga, in 1917. Erion was eight years older than Elman, and as a young man, he was a talented enough fiddler to travel to Prague for a course with Jan Kubelik's teacher, Otakar Sevcik. It was, in fact, during his student years in Prague, in 1905, that he first saw Elman perform. Eventually, Erion gave up the violin and went into business. But he retained his fondness for the instrument, and for music in general, and Elman saw in him a kindred spirit of sorts. With Erion, he could engage in musical and technical discussions, a luxury he had previously enjoyed mainly in the company of colleagues and competitors, and rarely with an enthusiastic admirer.

The two soon became the best of friends, and Erion traveled with Elman on several of his tours, including his return to Europe in 1920. At one point, Elman made Erion his "personal secretary," unofficially, and suggested that Erion have cards printed to that effect, which he could use to secure introductions to other artists he wanted to meet. The results were not always felicitous. On one occasion, Erion sent one of his cards backstage to Josef Hofmann. Hofmann knew Elman well, and not only did not believe that he had a personal secretary, but knew that Elman was, at the time, touring South Africa. He refused to see Erion, but sent the card to Saul Elman with the suggestion that legal action be taken against the fraudulent secretary. "We artists," Hofmann wrote, "have to protect ourselves against such impostors."[6]

In a way, Erion did act as Elman's personal secretary, for when arrangements went awry, during their travels, it was Erion who set them right. Erion also proposed writing a chronicle of his journeys with Elman, and Elman agreed to allow this, calling Erion "my Boswell." Erion took that role seriously, and throughout his life, he wrote frequently to Elman, filling his letters with detailed reminiscences of incidents that occurred on their tours of the United States (1918), Europe (1920) and Japan (1936-7). Eventually, in around 1951, Erion collected most of these stories in a short unpublished memoir entitled *Fiddling Around*.

Elman's managers had arranged an extensive season for him, a 125 concert year that included performances in Germany, France and England, as well as his first tour of the Orient, starting with a six concert run at the Imperial Theater in Tokyo. The tour began, however, in Veviers, Belgium, where Ysaÿe was directing a festival in honor of the centenary of his teacher, Henri Vieuxtemps. He engaged Elman to play the Vieuxtemps Fifth Concerto at a gala attended by the King and Queen of Belgium.

Ysaÿe met Elman and his entourage at the Veviers train station the afternoon of the concert, but Elman's trunk had been detained at a customs stop at the French border, and although he had his violin (which never left his sight during his travels), he lacked a full dress suit—an important component in a concert to be played before royalty. In lieu of a rehearsal, therefore, Ysaÿe, Elman and company toured the Veviers clothing stores in search of an appropriate suit, but were unable to find one in Elman's size.

This occasioned a special announcement by Ysaÿe, who mounted the podium, turned to the audience and began, "Your Highness, ladies and gentlemen; because Mr. Elman's trunk has been lost, he will be obliged to appear in his street clothes this evening. But I assure you that after you hear him play, it won't matter to you whether he had any clothes on at all."

Elman walked out in a three-piece suit and gave a performance that held the audience spellbound. At its conclusion, the King and Queen arose, and the audience and orchestra followed their example. For a full 20 minutes, Erion writes, there was pandemonium in the hall: "The violinists kept on rapping at the backs of their fiddles with their bows, while the wind instruments sent forth their notes of acclaim. Men in the audience threw their hats in the air, and Ysaÿe, who was a tall man and powerful, kept lifting Elman shoulder high. It was electrifying!"[7]

After the performance, Elman was introduced to Queen Elizabeth, who said, "Mr. Elman, I am overwhelmed," and presented him with a medal. The next evening, the performance was repeated. Elman and Erion stayed several days in Veviers, where they frequently visited Ysaÿe, and on one occasion went to a Bohemian cafe with Ysaÿe's sons. "The place was well filled with men and women, and the entertainment was furnished by a trio of men well along in years, who perhaps in bygone days had been good musicians" Erion recorded. "After dinner, one of the Ysaÿe boys suggested that Elman, he, and his brother, take over the trio and play a number. Elman agreed. The younger Ysaÿe played the piano, his brother the cello, and Elman the violin. The composition they chose was by Godard. Noise and chatter gave way to silence and attention, while they listened to that beautiful music. Elman's playing on the old musician's fiddle made it sound like a Strad. When the music stopped, there was a rising vote of thanks, a shouting of bravos, and a long round of applause."[8]

Before leaving Veviers, Elman was invited to the Palace once more, where he and Ysaÿe played a private recital for the Queen; and in return, the Queen brought out her own violin and serenaded the two musicians. Elman, used to royalty by then, was impressed. "She's a woman of considerable talent," he later commented to Erion.

From Veviers, Elman went to Berlin. The day of his recital, however, he received a letter from someone claiming to have known him in Russia, and who suggested that if he did not pay a considerable sum of money, he would do well to cancel his concert. The letter was signed, simply, "Communist." Elman took it to the police, who told him not to worry about it, but assigned him extra protection. The concert, which took place in a hall so tightly packed that extra seats were placed in the aisles, went on without incident.

In Berlin that September, Elman was reunited with Liachowsky, and during the first part of this European season, Liachowsky served as his accompanist. His main program was, as usual, a rather athletic one. It began with Vivaldi's G minor Concerto, accompanied on the organ where possible, and continued with the Vieuxtemps Fifth. Next came the Bach *Chaconne*, and then two groups of short works—among them Wilhelmj's paraphrase from *Siegfried*, a Paganini Etude, Elman's own transcriptions of light pieces by Grieg, Beethoven and Fauré, and to close the program, Sarasate's *Caprice Basque*.

From Berlin, Elman went to London, via Brussels. On the way, his trunk was misdirected once again, and Erion ended up retracing their steps through Holland and Germany, while Elman went ahead to England. At Dover, he boarded a train for London, and was joined in his compartment by a Spaniard, who spoke no English, but recognized the violinist. It turned out that he was a musician as well—he showed Elman a brochure on which he was pictured on the podium of a Madrid orchestra. He had also seen Elman perform several times as a child, so far as Elman could make out, and had always admired him. Since they couldn't converse, other than through a complicated and tiring pantomime, Elman took out his violin and played to the Spaniard from Dover to London.

CHAPTER TEN:

The Romance of the Road

These had been artistically turbulent years for Elman, who had grown from an adolescent performer into a mature, polished artist during his first decade in America. He had seen his art was admired for its individuality; yet, he also learned that artistic subjectivity was not necessarily an unlimited mandate. At that, he had shown considerable flexibility in meeting the criticism directed at him, and after quickly retrenching, he managed to cut his losses and continue on his successful path. As the decade ended, he faced serious competition from a newcomer, Heifetz, and a returning king, Kreisler; but he met their challenges head on, and won the most enthusiastic reviews of his career to that point. Even the Ziegfeld affair had been an interesting sideshow, for disappointing as its outcome was, Elman had enjoyed the process of composing the piece.

So was his collaboration with Ysaÿe, a resounding success for both artists. And if he had any doubts about his reception in Europe after so long an absence, these were dispelled immediately. So were any concerns he might have had about his ability to conquer entirely new territory. In Japan and China, he found that his legend had preceded him, and when he performed there, he played to packed halls.

As he moved into the 1920s, therefore, Elman stood on a solid foundation. As the decade began, he was touring on his own in Europe, revisiting places he had not seen since he was a child under his father's supervision. This was a voyage of discovery for Elman, but he was hardly a carouser. If he enjoyed the place in European social life that his position as an artist opened to him, he seemed immune to many a temptation. He did not drink, and what romance there was in his life was kept discreetly out of public view, even though the press was beginning to speculate about the various actresses and singers he had been seen escorting to concerts, the theater and parties.

What was of greater concern to Elman at this stage of his life—his thirties—was his place in the world, and his future, not only musically, but personally. He observed Europe and its people closely, and he felt comfortable there. Yet, New York had become his home, and he had found his greatest fortunes in America. He resolved to solidify his relationship with his new country by seeking citizenship, a process he began in middle of 1919. Eventually, Elman grew extremely patriotic, and in the 1940s, he went so far as to suggest to one of his longtime accompanists, another Russian, that he either take American citizenship or find another job.

In 1919, though, citizenship was also a matter of convenience, for the Russian passport he carried was of quickly diminishing value, and was causing problems in his travels. To Elman, who set his occupation down as "violin artist" on his citizenship application, a musician should be a free spirit, able to tour the world at will, unfettered by the nuisance of global politics. He was still toying with the idea of establishing a household in London, a city he had loved nearly as much as New York, and which would make a logical base of operations for his European touring. And he was looking, or so he told the British press, for an English bride to maintain that household for him.

The newspapers loved it: as a touring virtuoso and recording star in his early thirties, and with an income between $75,000 and $100,000 a year, he was an ideal catch, and the news that he was in the market for a wife served to intensify the already steady flow of interviews in which the questions posed to him concerned his views about women, love and marriage, rather than the violin and music. Some of the resulting stories were exquisitely silly. One London publication, for instance, put out the word that Elman was in England wife-hunting:

"Twenty years wandering around the world in search of the ideal wife has brought Mischa Elman, famous musician, to London," the report began, "and on Wednesday, at Queen's Hall, he will select an English woman for his bride." The article went on to say that the violinist was taking applications, and that he "has agreed to interview prospective brides at any time at his hotel."

Immediately thereafter, another paper reported that Elman "was besieged by sixty-eight blonde young English misses who...offered to marry him instantly."

Elman soon abandoned the notion of a home in London, but resolved to tour Europe annually. In September 1922, at the start of his first American tour in two years, he filed his final naturalization papers; and eight months later, on May 17, 1923, he took his oath of citizenship in New York, an act naturally accompanied by a good deal of press coverage. In New York too, the press speculated on Elman's marriage plans. When pressed to describe his ideal woman, Elman first concentrated on looks. He wanted her to look exactly like the woman who appeared in so many of the paintings by the French artist Jean Baptiste Greuze (actually the painter's wife). When the questioning went beyond looks, though, the intensity of Elman's conservatism could be astounding. Today, feminists might consider his frank comments to a *New York World* reporter positively inflammatory:

"It is true that the modern woman, with her cigarettes and her make-up is rather distasteful to me," the violinist said. "I am not used to that, that's all. I was brought up to admire the delicate and incompetent woman of the '90s. Today's woman is independent, able to take care of herself, but less attractive to the strong, protective longing of the male. Why deny this? It is inevitable. Man wishes to be the superior. He wishes to dominate." "If he marries an emancipated woman," he added, "he must constantly struggle against her will. There is conflict, no peace. Moreover, it is especially hard for an artist to make a success of marriage. How is he to be equally devoted to his family and his art? Inevitably, one or the other must suffer."[1]

Elman eventually modified some of these opinions (at least the last one); but he clearly wanted to defer the question for some time to come.

Interestingly, the conservatism of his social viewpoint was not reflected in his musical tastes. Later in the same interview, he reported with clear enthusiasm that "jazz has simply taken Europe by storm. One hears it everywhere. To me, it has vast and exciting possibilities. Out of its wonderful rhythms will grow new ideas. It will become known as the American classical music." He went on to propose that an American national conservatory be founded (in Washington, preferably) and that jazz and the classics be taught side by side.

This is a point on which Elman's views remained firm over the years, even though it was, for many decades, a view not widely held by classical musicians. As jazz emerged from its southern, black roots to become the pop music rage of not only the northern American urban centers, but of European cities too, many a conductor and concert artist rose to decry it, sometimes in terms with openly racist overtones. Some two decades after this interview appeared, for instance, the New York Philharmonic conductor, Artur Rodzinski, cited jazz as "a direct cause of child delinquency" in a published interview, and Elman, still a devoted jazz fan, came to the genre's defense with an eloquent and perceptive response.

"To protest today against swing and jazz," he told a *New York Times* reporter, "is as silly as it was for our grandfathers to protest against the waltz. Swing is just a social expression of our city youth and is a good outlet for their emotions. It is no more to be deplored than the breakdown dances, let's say, in the country. As for the element of jazz itself, it is the one remaining free improvisatory factor in the whole of music, and as such, as every good musician knows, holds untold possibilities for the creative music of the future."

❖ ❖ ❖ ❖ ❖

Just as the press was growing so curious about Elman's private life, he met the woman he would eventually marry, Helen Frances Katten. Both were passengers on a ship heading for London from New York, in 1921, and they met when the violinist's sister, Liza, and Helen's mother confined themselves to deck chairs because they were both prone to seasickness.

"I wasn't smitten with Mischa at all," Helen Elman recalled many years later. "I thought it was funny that he asked me to dance, even though he seemed not to know how. He was very sweet to me, but there was no big romance, then." The day they arrived in London, they went their separate ways, Elman to the Ritz and the Kattens to the Savoy. That evening, though, Elman had arranged to meet a group of friends for a midnight snack at the Savoy, and when he arrived, he telephoned the Kattens and invited Helen to join them. Among the crowd were Benno Moiseiwitsch and a handful of other musical celebrities, certainly heady company for a young girl from San Francisco.

The daughter of a German immigrant who had settled in California and had recently retired from his successful wholesale business, Helen Katten was an independent-minded but cultured girl, who numbered several professional musicians among her relatives. Her own musical interests, however, were those of a devoted amateur: she played the piano, but apparently only modestly. "Once, when I knew

Mischa was coming to visit, I played a piece of Chopin," she says, "and when he came in, he said, 'stop that.' I never played for him again." She did, however, attend concerts regularly, and she had seen several of Elman's San Francisco recitals.

The Kattens and Elman ran into each other a few months later, in Paris. "I wrote home to a friend that I was having a wonderful time, and that Mischa Elman was being very attentive to me, which really wasn't so," she explained. "He took me out a couple of times, and that was it. It didn't mean anything to me, except that I was with a celebrity, which was a new experience. And I wanted to brag to my friends at home, as a young girl would." Elman asked, however, that the Kattens contact his parents when they arrived in New York, and tell them that both he and Liza were well. He had, in the meantime, written to his parents that the Kattens would be staying at the Plaza, and would call on them with word of his progress in Europe. At 8:30 in the morning, the day after the Kattens arrived in New York, Saul Elman was at their door, inquiring anxiously about Mischa and Liza.

It was only by chance that Helen and Mischa met again, a few years later, in San Francisco. In the meantime, Elman had fallen in love with a 22-year old New Yorker named Mildred Stone. They had met in the summer of 1922, at Lake Placid, New York, where Elman was visiting Mildred's brother-in-law, a violinist named Rudolf Polk. By October, their summer romance had blossomed into an engagement, which the Stones officially announced on October 16 (two days after the newspapers carried an unconfirmed report that the violinist had at last "found the 'ideal girl' he had been searching for.") The engagement was short-lived. Although it was announced in November that Mischa and Mildred would marry on Christmas Eve, rather than waiting until the summer, as originally planned, by mid-December the papers carried word that the wedding was off, for reasons neither the Stones nor the Elmans cared to discuss. "They mutually agreed," Liza Elman told the *American*, "that they had made a mistake."

Towards the end of the following season, Elman's touring took him to the West Coast. In San Francisco, his local manager, Selby Oppenheimer, invited Elman to dinner, and decided to invite a young lady to round out the table. Since he was friendly with the Kattens, and knew that they had met Elman in Europe, he asked if Helen would like to come along.

"And that did it," Helen says, "although in a way, it got off to a bad start, because at one point someone offered me a cigarette. I wasn't a smoker, particularly, but I did smoke occasionally, and somehow I thought it would make an impression. It did, but not the impression I wanted it to make. When I took the cigarette, Mischa looked at me and said, 'don't tell me, Miss Katten, that you're smoking too.' So I put it down. Mischa was very particular about that."

Elman had a date the following evening with another girl, who lived on the same street as the Kattens, but he resolved to cancel it. "What are you doing tomorrow," he asked Helen, who also had a date that she decided to break when he asked the question. "Nothing," she replied. "Well, stay home," he told her, "because I'm visiting someone on your street, and I can tell them that I have to leave early because I have a concert coming up, and I have to practice." That evening, he turned up at the Kattens' home, and as Helen explains, "we really fell in love right away." Accompanied by the Oppenheimers, she attended most of his concerts in the area, "and after that," she says, "I saw him all the time."

Their courtship was not quite the whirlwind that his romance with Mildred Stone had been; no doubt that experience had taught him the wisdom of taking these things more slowly. For their part, the Kattens admired Elman as a violinist, and as a seemingly nice young man. But they worried about their daughter becoming romantically involved with a performer. "A musician," Helen's father warned, "is like a sailor. He travels the world, and he has a wife in every port. I don't want you to suffer." Elman understood his concern, and in fact, he too suggested caution. "You have to think about this very seriously," he told her when they began discussing marriage, in December 1924. "You have to understand that I travel a great deal, and that I always will. I don't want you to be upset about that. I don't want you to be jealous when I'm away. Think it over."

When Elman left for New York, he and Helen were not engaged, much to Helen's chagrin, for he wanted her to spend some time considering the problems facing an artist's wife, as well as the prospect of moving to New York, a few thousand miles from her family. He also felt it would be proper to discuss his prospective marriage plans with his family before actually getting engaged again. After five days passed, Helen had not heard from her beau, and finding it depressing waiting at home for a letter or a telephone call, she visited a friend.

While she was away, a telegram from Elman arrived. Her parents, who were celebrating their anniversary that day, had also received several telegrams, and mistakenly opened the one from Elman as well.

When Helen returned home, she was greeted by her aunt, who called to her as she approached the house, "oh, darling, hurry up, you're engaged!" Inside, Helen's mother handed her the telegram, which read, simply, "If marriage is a mistake, may I commit this error with you?" She wired back, "Yes, Mischa. All my love."

On May 6, 1925, in San Francisco, Mischa Elman and Helen Katten were married in a private ceremony, attended only by family members. They traveled to New York a few days later, and from there they went to Europe for their honeymoon.

During their European tour, Elman went violin shopping, and Helen resolved that when he found the instrument of his dreams, she would buy it for him as her wedding gift. Their search ended on the Rue de Madrid, in Paris, at the lutherie of Caressa and Francais. Two years earlier, Elman had bought a 1735 Stradivarius from the firm, and although he had not been fully satisfied with that instrument, he knew that the firm kept a fine stock of valuable instruments, and he hoped for better luck.

This time, Albert Caressa brought out a 1717 instrument, the Stradivarius that had once belonged to Madame Jean Francoise Recamier, an intimate of Napoleon's whose name had become the instrument's identifying sobriquet. Madame Recamier sold the instrument to Count Molitor, an officer who had distinguished himself in the Napoleonic wars, and it had remained in the Molitor family since then. Elman thought it was one of the most exquisite instruments he had ever played.

Unfortunately, there was another customer in the shop at the same time, an American collector named Posner, who was also interested in this particular Strad. Caressa put the two men in different rooms, and brought the violin from one to the other. Elman played it, Posner examined it, and as each bid for it, the other outbid him. Finally, when the price reached $50,000, Elman grew restless, and a bit suspicious about whether there was really another bidder in the shop, and he called his end of the bidding to a halt. "Look," he told Caressa, "I love the violin, but this is as much as I'm going to pay for it. I don't care who you have next door, but I'm an artist, and I will put this violin to good use on the stage. If you want to sell it to me, fine. If you want to sell it to someone else for more money, that's fine too."

Caressa did not go back to Posner's room for his bid. "You're right," he told Elman. "You have the violin." Elman continued to wonder whether there had really been a second bidder, but soon after he acquired the violin, he was introduced at a party to Posner, who told him that he had been the competitor, and that he, like Caressa, was just as happy to let the violin go to an artist of Elman's stature. This confirmation that Caressa had not only dealt honestly with him, but that he had sacrificed a potentially greater profit so that Elman could have the instrument deeply impressed the violinist, and served as the basis of a friendship that lasted several generations: Caressa's daughter and Francais's son eventually married and moved to New York, where they maintained the family business. Their son, Jacques Francais, continues to uphold the firm's tradition; and Elman patronized the family's New York shop until the end of his life, not only bringing his instruments there for repair, but spending his afternoons in the shop, listening to young players and discussing recent concerts.

In his concert life, Elman was finding the sailing smoother than ever in the early 1920s. He derived both energy and satisfaction from the realization that there remained worlds to conquer, and the success of his collaborations with Ysaÿe had given him a yen to pursue further partnerships with his peers. In Europe, his managers arranged for engagements with major orchestras, in which Elman was not simply a guest for one of the great concertos (or two shorter ones), but rather, the focal point of the entire program. His Berlin Philharmonic appearance of February 1922 is an example. Directed by Willy Hess, the concert began with the Vivaldi Concerto in G minor. In the central position was the Brahms Concerto; and Lalo's *Symphonie Espagnole* served as the finale.

His return to the United States had been as successful as his European seasons. During the 1922–23 season, he played 107 concerts in 29 weeks, including six in New York (four of them at the Hippodrome). Between the New York concerts, he traveled across the continent, giving three recitals each in Chicago and Boston, and two each in Philadelphia, Montreal, Los Angeles and San Francisco. Josef Bonime remained his accompanist, but in his New York concerts, he continued to play a sonata or two with Liza, and occasionally with a more celebrated partner.

In March, 1923, for instance, he appeared at a recital arranged by New York's Beethoven Association, at Aeolian Hall, where he performed a pair of Beethoven sonatas, with Josef Hofmann at the piano.

Olin Downes, in the *New York Times*, found the two artists remarkably well-matched. He felt, in fact that they had not only worked hard to create that impression, but that they had taken into account the current trend towards objectivity in working out their interpretations. "The performances of the Beethoven sonatas," Downes wrote, "were almost flawless in the technical sense, of crystalline clarity and of perfect classic proportion. Each of the players had resources of technique and tone which he never dreamed of employing, [and each adopted] a scale of dynamics and sonorities much more modest than they would have consented to if the work had been a modern sonata or concerto with orchestra. Their careful blending of tone qualities gave the final unity to the interpretations....There was careful abstention from an overemotional or a hyper-romantic style....The performances were in every sense a joy and a lesson in the interpretation of classic music."

Another of Elman's collaborations that year must have been even more fascinating. On May 20, 1923, at Carnegie Hall, he gave a concert with Auer on the podium. Auer had taken a circuitous route to the United States. During Elman's London years, Auer had established a teaching studio there, but in 1912, he moved the venue of his non-Russian teaching to a small town in Germany, near Dresden. War broke out while Auer and his pupils were there, and as had happened to the conductor Karl Muck in Boston, their status as enemy aliens caused them some problems. After a few months of house arrest, Auer and his charges were permitted to return to St. Petersburg.[2] The following summer, he taught in Christiania (later renamed Oslo), Norway, and he continued to hold his course there until 1917. But the political situation in Russia was too volatile for Auer's comfort, and early in 1918 he set sail for the United States, where, at age 73, he again established himself as a teacher.

By then, of course, his reputation had spread far and wide, thanks to Elman and his other illustrious students. Years later, the flood of Russian violinists who had their start in Auer's studio was commemorated in *Mischa, Jascha, Toscha, Sacha*, a song by George and Ira Gershwin, writing under the name of Arthur Francis.

For their joint Carnegie Hall appearance, Auer conducted Elman in a program even grander than the three-concerto concerts he had played in Europe the previous year. The Vivaldi was again the opener, but this time the Beethoven Concerto followed, and the Tchaikovsky Concerto closed the program with a string of encores Elman offered (with Bonime) as a parting gesture. All told, the concert ran nearly three hours. Elman once again played his own cadenzas in the Beethoven, which were admired this time by the *Times* and the *Globe* reviewers, but criticized in the *Herald*, whose reviewer wrote that Auer's cadenzas for the concerto were more dignified.

The most interesting aspect of the concert, from a historical perspective, was the performance of the Tchaikovsky Concerto, a work with which both performers were closely associated—Elman as one of the earliest to win it acclaim instead of derision, and Auer as its original dedicatee. According to the only account that discussed the performance of this work in any depth, it was an unusual reading. "Those who remembered Professor Auer's relation to the early history of this concerto," wrote Pitts Sanborn in the *New York Globe*, "must have observed with interest that under his direction the slow movement was less slow than fiddlers usually make it, and that parts of the finale, per contra, hit a pace that would have been fatal to any technique a whit less impeccable than Mr. Elman's."

Elman and Auer remained close through the rest of Auer's life; and after Auer's death, his widow remained in touch with the Elmans, occasionally sharing a Carnegie Hall box with Helen Elman when Mischa performed. The next time they shared the headlines, though, Elman was the center of a dispute centering around a concert in Auer's honor. Early in 1925, a committee headed by Mrs. Charles Guggenheimer arranged to commemorate Auer's eightieth birthday with a gala event at which Auer was to be feted in a Carnegie Hall concert by the students he set on the path toward greatness. The greatest of the Auer disciples were invited—chief among them, Elman, Heifetz and Zimbalist. Josef Hofmann, Sergei Rachmaninoff and Ossip Gabrilowitsch agreed to appear on the program as well.

The concert was scheduled for April 28, although Auer's actual birthday was June 7. This posed a problem for Elman and his manager, Max Endicoff, for they had already scheduled Elman's Carnegie Hall recital for April 26. Since Elman's recital had been scheduled first, and since there was more than a month between the proposed Auer concert and Auer's birthday, Elman and Endicoff considered the timing of the gala was unfair, and they wondered in whether the inconsiderate scheduling had been done purposely, as a way of drawing attention away from Elman's own recital. In any case, this put Elman in an uncomfortable situation. He could play in the Auer concert, although as he perceived it, his appearance there put his own recital at risk; or he could refuse and risk offending Auer. Assuming Auer would understand, Elman chose the latter course.

In declining the invitation, though, Elman at first gave no reason, and the committee organizing the event wasted no time in conveying its shock to the press. Word quickly spread that Elman had refused to perform in a fit of pique when he learned that Jascha Heifetz would also be on the program. The newspapers gave that theory play in the headlines of their stories on this odd little tempest, and Elman and Endicoff emphatically denied it. Privately, they suspected that the theory had been planted by a partisan in the Heifetz camp. It was, in any case, one of the first public assertions that the competition between Heifetz and Elman had grown into a full-fledged, heated rivalry. When the stories first appeared in the New York newspapers, Elman was in the midst of a tour; and what free time he had was devoted to Helen Katten, and to the plans for their wedding in early May. So it was left for Endicoff to do the explaining, and he handled the situation awkwardly. "Mr. Elman did not really refuse to play at the concert," he began. "It was simply that he had an engagement, made a year ago, to play at Carnegie Hall in his own recital two days before the Auer concert. He could not very well appear at both. The committee [that planned the Auer event] knew that he had this date, and the concert should not have been made so close. People would reason that by waiting two days, they could hear not only Elman, but others as well. His decision to refrain from playing at the concert was not due to any personal ill-feeling towards Mr. Heifetz or any other artist. It was due purely to not wishing to jeopardize his own concert."

Endicoff's explanation must have struck close observers of the concert scene as weak and ill-conceived. After all, in such a stellar line-up of artists, Elman would have had to play only one or two works, and undoubtedly not the same ones he was planning to play at his own recital. Also, throughout the last decade, Elman had habitually made multiple New York appearances in close succession—a Bagby or Biltmore musicale one day, a Metropolitan Opera performance later in the week, a Carnegie Hall a few weeks after that, and a Brooklyn concert in between. He could fill the Hippodrome once a month.

Besides, the Auer concert was bound to be one of the season's major events, and an appearance at it could only have been beneficial for Elman, for he would be before the public in a concert that would attract considerable notice; and of course, his presence in that exalted company would further confirm his status as one of the great performers of the time. By contrast, his refusing to play made him seem unfriendly towards his colleagues, at best, and ungenerous towards his old teacher, at worst.

At any rate, Elman did not perform at the Auer concert, although he did attend it, and after it he paid his respects to Auer and his colleagues. In the end, the controversy did not have an adverse effect on his own recital, two days earlier. According to the reviews, the hall was "comfortably filled," Elman was in top form, and the enthusiastic audience demanded plenty of encores. The program proper began with the Nardini Sonata in D, and ended with the Vieuxtemps Fifth Concerto, with groups of short works in between.

❖ ❖ ❖ ❖ ❖

As much as Elman and Endicoff denied that temperament or professional jealousy motivated the violinist's non-appearance at the Auer concert, the growing fraternity of managers who had handled his career no doubt suspected that the reports were accurate.

The inordinate distrust of managers Saul and Mischa developed on their first tour of Germany had blossomed into true paranoia, and the violinist's inability to conquer this ultimately caused him innumerable problems.

"I think this is an area where Saul Elman influenced his son's attitudes," recalled Jacob Markowitz, the family's accountant from 1920 on. "Mr. Elman and I were very close in those years. We shared an office together, in the Aeolian building, at 33 West 42nd Street. I did their accounting, and Saul Elman and I used to go out to lunch together and discuss his son's career. Saul Elman was a fairly shrewd businessman, but he was not accustomed to American ways. And one thing he always told me was that he would never allow his son to be managed by a manager who also handled another violinist."

That would explain Elman's first managerial switch—from Wolfsohn, who had handled his career from the time of his debut, to the Metropolitan Musical Bureau, in 1916. The move left some musical journalists puzzled, since the Metropolitan agency primarily handled singers, particularly those who sang at the Met. It was guessed, however, that Elman had come to know the firm's managers during his frequent guest appearances at the Metropolitan Opera's popular concerts, and that the bureau, was interested in expanding into the non-vocal realm. That relationship didn't last long. Soon Elman left Metropolitan for the office of another Russian immigrant who had gotten his start as a manager in 1911 by launching the career of Efrem Zimbalist. This was Sol Hurok, then at the start of a phenomenal career as an impresario.

Elman maintained an on-again/off-again relationship with Hurok through the 1940s. By 1922, though, the Elmans and Hurok had their first falling out, and as a result, Elman left Hurok's roster and hired Max Endicoff—a Hurok employee who had left to start his own office. Endicoff had plenty of connections, thanks to his years with Hurok; and Mischa Elman was certainly a saleable client. But as his business grew, Endicoff naturally wanted to expand his roster, and he was unable to persuade the Elmans that having another violinist on his rolls would not effect his efforts on Elman's behalf. Thus, in 1925, it was back to Hurok.

That was a disastrous year for Hurok, though. In the best tradition of the old-time impresario, he had decided to go for the best and the biggest that year, and in a make-or-break effort, he brought over the Russian Grand Opera, with Feodor Chaliapin as its star. It broke him. Hurok lost a staggering $150,000 on the deal, and ended up sleeping on New York park benches, having been evicted from his hotel. He did manage to maintain his office and secretary, though, and with his remaining resources, he got back on his feet.

Chief among those resources were his recital artists, some of whom were pressed into service on Hurok's behalf. Elman was one. When he returned from his honeymoon trip to Europe in September 1925, Hurok was at the dock to meet him. "Mischa," he said, "you've got a concert tomorrow evening. It's a benefit."

"A benefit," Elman asked, "for whom?"

"For me," Hurok told him, and then conveyed the saga of the Russian opera.

Elman played the recital. At times, though, the antics of managers and promoters tried his patience, and he found pointed ways to retaliate. During one American tour in the late 1920s, a Denver-based manager, Arthur Oberfelder engaged Elman for a series of concerts around the midwest, and although he did not tour with the violinist, he kept in constant communication with him via telegram. Elman found this irritating, for the telegrams were invariably lengthy and full of superfluous instructions, and Oberfelder always sent them collect. Elman waited until the end of the tour, and the morning after his last concert, he sat down to breakfast with Bonime, took out a pencil and pad, and composed a telegram to the manager. He began by thanking

Oberfelder for his daily instructions, and said that he followed each of them to the letter. Then he noted that he was having breakfast with his accompanist, and went into fine detail: they had just finished their orange juice, and had ordered eggs, coffee and toast with marmalade. He said that the food was fabulous, and that the weather was too, and that he was sorry he could not stop in Denver on his way home. He then provided the details of the various train connections he would make in order to get back to New York. "And now," he concluded, "how do you like collect telegrams?"[3]

CHAPTER ELEVEN:

From Chamber Music to the Silver Screen

Early in 1926, Elman launched the Mischa Elman String Quartet. The roots of this idea can be traced back to the Friday evening musicales at the Elman family's Claremont Avenue apartment, more than a decade earlier. Elman loved chamber playing, quartet playing in particular, but he regarded it as a private pleasure, to be enjoyed in the intimate surroundings of a dinner party or an evening with musical friends. In 1916, he made an experimental foray into public chamber playing, assembling the first incarnation of the quartet with three members of the Boston Symphony—the violinist Adolf Bak, the violist Karl Rissland, and the cellist Rudolf Nagel. Given Elman's solo commitments, and the rest of the quartet's Boston obligations, touring was never considered. But the quartet did make some recordings.

Early in 1917, after rehearsals and a string of private performances at Elman's dinner parties, the foursome traveled to Victor's studios in Camden, and recorded movements from quartets by Haydn, Mozart and Dittersdorf. A year later they returned to record more Mozart, and works of Schubert and Tchaikovsky. These discs, released in 1917 and 1918, were well received critically, and they sold respectably, although only the *Andante cantabile* from Tchaikovsky's Quartet, Op. 11—already an Elman favorite in a violin and piano arrangement—could be called a best-seller. Chamber music was a minority interest at the time, even with a star violinist's name attached.

Before leaving for his honeymoon, in the summer of 1925, Elman thought about reconvening the quartet, this time for public performances. The original members were not available, so Elman brought together a second ensemble, with Edwin Bachmann on second violin

143

and Horace Britt as the cellist. The violist's chair was occupied by several players during the group's life—Louis Bailly at first, Nicola Maldovan and William Schubert later on.

Stepping before the public as the member of a quartet, theoretically the most equal of musical democracies, was an unusual experience for Elman, but he clearly relished it, for he toured with the quartet for the better part of two seasons, rarely playing alone during that time. Quartet playing offered a great deal to Elman. It was a welcome change of pace, after 22 years of solo touring, and musically, he found the quartet tours positively uplifting, for much as he loved playing those groups of short crowd-pleasers between the sonatas and concertos at his recitals, the quartet's programs were built of solid repertoire, with nothing that could be dismissed as fluff. Moreover, Elman's intuition told him that spending time and effort in a different discipline would not only be refreshing, but would probably pay dividends in his solo playing when he returned to it.

During its two seasons together, the Elman Quartet worked up a compact but solid repertoire, and in most of the cities the group visited on its American and Canadian coast-to-coast tour, it played a two– or three–concert series. The quartet's standard programs were a pairing of the Beethoven Quartet in F, Op.95 with the Franck in D major (certainly a study in contrasts); a Haydn D minor Quartet, followed by Beethoven's Op.74 in E-flat and Tchaikovsky's Op.30, in E-flat minor; or one comprising a Mozart in D major, the Brahms C minor, Op.51, No.1, and the Ravel quartet. At times these combinations were shuffled, with other Mozart works, or one of the Mendelssohn quartets substituted.

The first performances, a three-concert series at the Aeolian Hall, in New York, were tryouts: if they were poorly attended or harshly reviewed, Elman might have reconsidered undertaking a tour. But the reaction was strongly favorable, so the tour went forward. Not surprisingly, the promoters, parts of the audience, and even some of the critics around the country were unsure how to respond to this ensemble and its famous first violinist. One midwestern concert manager decided to hedge his bets by printing posters announcing "Mischa Elman," in huge letter, with "and his quartet" underneath and much smaller. "It never occurred to him," Elman later quipped, "that as advertised, we would have to be five rather than a quartet." In another town, the ensemble was feted by the mayor, who raised his glass and said, "My congratulations to Mischa Elman, and I hope that by the time he returns next year, his little band has grown."

Elman expected two contradictory kinds of criticism to be leveled at him during the tour, and as the reviews poured in, his expectations were confirmed. On one hand, some reviewers insisted that Elman shone out above the other players, as a soloist rather than as an equal quartet member; but other critics expressed disappointment that within the quartet context, Elman subdued his personality too much. No doubt preconceptions had a great deal to do with these perceptions, and few critics managed to override them fully. One who did was Olga Samaroff, the concert pianist who took up the critic's pen for the *New York Evening Post* for a couple of seasons. Samaroff's review is an odd one: in two columns of rumination about the ideals of chamber playing, she neglects to mention any of the works the quartet played. She does, however, provide some insight about its style.

"I will frankly confess that I expected to find Elman's solo violin sticking out like a sore (even if lusciously euphonious) thumb," she wrote, adding that "the actual playing I heard last night effectually banished [this expectation].... In quantity of sound, he was as unobtrusive as any veteran quartet player. He only emerged when the music demanded that he should. What still remains as somewhat of a handicap is the actual color and quality of his tone. For him to blend into a quartet is almost as difficult as for a woman with a head of burnished Titian red-gold hair to be inconspicuous in a crowd.

"Elman's tone is as personal as the shape of his face," Samaroff continued. "As a solo player, the sensuous quality of it, beautiful as it is in itself, often stood in the way of style by introducing into any music he played regardless of its character, the same element of a certain voluptuous coloring. There is always vermilion in it. I felt last night that he had already accomplished wonders in subduing and modifying this natural state. Quartet playing is obviously increasing his sense of style."

The second incarnation of the Mischa Elman String Quartet made a few recordings as well, but released only two—remakes of the Tchaikovsky *Andante cantabile* and the variations from Haydn's "Emperor" Quartet. One work the group recorded but did not release is the Mozart Quartet in B-flat, K.458, or at least, a large patch of it. Several sections of the work can be heard in a set of test pressings, which are currently held, along with the violinist's score library, in the Mischa Elman Room at the Manhattan School of Music. Surviving are discs containing the exposition of the first movement, an abridgement of the *Adagio* third movement, and the complete *Allegro assai* finale. Whether the missing sections were recorded, and why either Elman or Victor might have rejected the performance is uncertain. But these discs are the closest we have to a rendering of a complete work by either of the Elman quartets, and they make fascinating listening.

In this Mozart score, the group plays in very much the way Olga Samaroff described—although none of the contemporary concert reviews prepares one for the group's tight, finely polished ensemble sound. No-one could fairly accuse this group of sounding like an *ad hoc* chamber collaboration, for they move together uncannily. They are also quite faithful to the score in many respects (although not in all). Every dynamic indication is followed, the instrumental balances are perfect, and there is surprisingly little *rubato*, even in the slow movement. Ornamentation is quick and neat, and although the tempo of the *Allegro assai* is somewhat speedier than it would be played today, the set, all told, is elegantly proportioned.

The group's deviations from the printed text are confined to the slow movement, the most radical of these being a sizeable cut, no doubt prompted by the time constraints of 78rpm recording. Otherwise, in sections where the first violin line had either an accompanying figure, or merely the top voice in a chordal section, Elman took the part down an octave, possibly as a way of blending into the texture more fully. And at the end of the movement, the four players agreed to disagree with Mozart: instead of closing the movement *staccato*, as marked, they play they apply a sensuous *legato* to the final notes; but they do observe the score's *pianissimo* indication.

Did Elman blend fully into the quartet's texture? This is a difficult work to judge by, and the rest of the quartet's discography makes that task equally tough, for the movements that were set down were often those in which the first violin part had a natural prominence. This Mozart quartet, however, tells us a great deal about Elman's ability to shift from lead to ensemble playing, something he seems to have been able to do with ease. Here, the first violin has the lion's share of the melodies, plus much of the punctuating filigree. In these sections, Elman's vermilion tone, as Olga Samaroff put it, shines out from the group's texture. He does not overpower his colleagues dynamically; rather, he adopts a form of coloration that sets his line apart from the more homogenous accompaniment figuration provided by his three colleagues. He also tends to burnish his lines in these passages, giving them a feeling of silkiness, created partly through his bowing and partly through an unusual *glissando* technique that he applied not only to leaps, but to quick runs of consecutive notes.

When Mozart builds the first violin line more firmly into the ensemble setting, though, Elman shifted his tone to match that of the others. Most impressive in this regard are the passages, particularly in the last movement, where Elman and second violinist Bachmann play in tandem. They accomplished this by meeting each other half way: Elman softened his personal coloration, while Bachmann added a touch of *glissando* in certain of the passages to match the effect Elman applied. What emerges is a performance that is obviously well-considered, carefully rehearsed and, in the end, quite effective.

Elman returned to solo performing with a long European tour at the end of 1926. But between tours with the quartet, he continued to make recordings with Bonime. Their recordings of the early 1920s were, as in the past, confined primarily to the popular end of the repertoire, the works Elman played either as encores or in the middle short works sets on his recital programs. As in the past, these were mostly arrangements, but an increasing number were arranged by Elman himself, in a rather freewheeling style that put the music at the service of the violin rather than the other way around. Elman, of course, would have argued for the validity of this approach. To him, an arrangement that delighted the ear with the beauty of the violin's tone, and which caught the attention with interesting technical devices inevitably focused the listener's attention on the beauty of the music itself. Thus, he recorded his arrangements of the *Passapied* from *Le Roi s'amuse*, by Delibes, Rubenstein's *Dew is Sparkling*, one movement from Grieg's set of *Lyric Pieces* for piano, Op.54, and even a Rode *Etude*. In his hands, they were miniature gems.

There were also a few works with more varied accompaniment: With the organist Herbert Dawson, he recorded a stately Handel *Largo* (from the opera *Serse*), plus an arrangement of a Tchaikovsky song, *None but the Weary Heart*. And accompanied by an unidentified orchestra, he recorded a handful of pretty, nostalgic pieces—Marie's *La Cinquantaine*, Popper's *Fond Recollections*, the Cui *Oriental*, and a lovely 19th century song arrangement, Ascher's *Alice, Where art Thou?*

To a large extent, Elman still had a free hand in choosing his recording repertoire through the 1920s, but this freedom was beginning to be eroded, partly because of Victor's financial troubles. Despite some $5 million a year spent in advertising, the bloom seemed to be off the record and phonograph business. Midway through the decade, though, a technological breakthrough helped the company back to its feet. The breakthrough was electrical recording—a recording process that used a microphone and electrical impulses, rather than a recording horn and mechanical impulses, to capture and etch the sound into the grooves of a disc.

There were several benefits to this system, not the least of them being that recording sessions would henceforth be more comfortable for the musicians. The days of crowding around the horn were over; now microphones would capture performances of players deployed more naturally. Also, the new process captured a bit more of the sound the players produced than the old acoustical horn. It was still far from perfect, but with extensions in both the treble and bass ranges, the sounds of the new electrical records seemed richer and more natural than their predecessors. The musical ramifications of this varied. Obviously, the improvement would be a more dramatic boon to, say, orchestras and conductors than to violinists, whose instruments recorded fairly well through the acoustic horn. And since the disc speed and the side length remained the same, the new process didn't broaden the repertoire possibilities much. What electrical recording *did* mean for artists like Elman—those whose large catalogues contained many popular items that had been steady sellers for years— was that their "greatest hits" could all be remade electrically, and sold to the public again.[1]

If Elman found this repetition wearying, the recordings don't show it. Rather, he rose to the challenge of improving upon his previous discs (some of which were now more than a decade old), and although there is much to be said for the youthful freshness of the earlier versions, the remakes of this period show the dividends of experience. They also show the extent to which Elman's ideas about the music had changed. Consider, for instance, Elman's first two recordings of the Schubert-Wilhelmj *Ave Maria*—the first with Percy Kahn, from 1913; the second accompanied by Joseph Bonime, from 1929.

In the first version, Elman takes a slow, devotional tempo, and aims for sheer sonic richness—an effect he achieves by manipulating his dynamics on the long notes at phrase ends, and by shifting strings to give repeated notes different shadings. To this he adds a personalized *rubato* that gives each phrase a feeling of spontaneity. The remake is

an entirely different kind of picture. The tempo is brisker, and although in this version Elman tends to lean into the strong beats more
heavily than in the first account, his articulation is more varied and
his coloration less ostentatious. He applies his unique *rubato* here
too—the arrangement, after all, seems to cry out for it; yet here the
work's rhythms and melodies are pushed shorter distances. The
double-stop playing, gorgeous in the first account, nevertheless
sounds more solid and more firmly under control in the later version.

The two performances are so different, and embody so many features unique to each, that one is hard pressed to voice a preference. In
strictly sonic terms, of course, the 1928 version has the edge: unlike its
predecessor, it conveys a realistic balance between the violin and the
piano, and both instruments benefit from the greater definition and
sense of dimension the electrical process yields.

Electrical recording led to another technical innovation, one that has
changed the 20th century entertainment world—the invention of
sound films. Until 1926, moving pictures moved, but they didn't talk,
and although attempts had been made to synchronize cylinders and
other sound-playing devices with film, these were never fully successful. In 1926, a company called Vitaphone, a subsidiary of Warner
Brothers, worked out a way of synchronizing the filming process with
an electrical recording and playback system. For its first public
demonstration of this process, Vitaphone decided to film performances by some of the leading musicians of the day; and in early 1926, a
representative from the firm called on Elman and persuaded him to
play a few brief selections before the cameras and microphones.

Elman readily agreed to perform for Vitaphone. He liked films, he
liked recording, and he thought it would be a fine way to reach a new
and potentially massive audience. The process would also give him
an opportunity no musician had before him: he could actually see and
hear one of his own performances, almost as if he were in the audience.
He called Bonime and persuaded him to come along (although as it
turned out he would not be shown on the screen), and on the way to
the studio, they selected the two works they would play: Dvořák's
Humoresque, and the bouncy little *Gavotte* by Gossec.

The production was simple. The camera is trained on Elman at the
start, and on Elman it stays, yielding an excellent, if brief, glimpse of
what he was like as a performer during this period, still the height of
his career. One thing that's immediately striking is his physical com-
portment. Serious and intense as he waits to begin, he becomes a pic-

ture of only partially controlled energy when he puts the bow to the string. Compared with the accounts published by reviewers a decade earlier, he is fairly still; yet, one can see traces of the swaying to the left and right, and the twisting from the waist that they had complained about then. In fact, Elman may even have tempered his movements for the sake of the camera. Yehudi Menuhin, then a young boy with violinistic aspirations, heard Elman for the first time during this period, and he recalls seeing the older violinist actually execute a full-circle turn while playing a piece. In the film, Elman keeps his feet anchored, and his eyes, much of the time, turned towards the ceiling.

More inherently interesting, though, is the amount of technical detail these films capture, not to mention the magic of the performance itself. Immediately captivating is Elman's approach to bowing here, an approach that is for the most part surprisingly economical. Rather than changing the bow between phrases, he often lifts the bow from the string at the end of one phrase, then begins the next phrase at the very end of the same bow. The bowing change comes, rather, at a point within the phrase that Elman wants to emphasize. This effect is demonstrated particularly clearly in the Gossec, where he takes the main melody, with its minute twists and turns, all in a single up-bow— all, that is, except for the last note in each phrase, which has a down-bow to itself.

The first eight Vitaphone films, including Elman's performances, were unveiled on August 6, 1926, in New York, and the reaction was, not surprisingly, overwhelmingly enthusiastic. The success of the experiment (from both a technical point of view and in terms of public response) encouraged the Warner company to continue refining the system. These refinements led to the making of *The Jazz Singer*, a milestone in the history of sound film.

This was a particularly active period in Elman's professional life, and at the same time, his personal life was more tumultuous than usual. In 1926, he and Helen had their first child, a daughter, Nadia. Around the time of Nadia's birth, Elman decided it was time to revise the family's financial plan. At the start, Saul Elman handled all money matters, with some investment help from the Rothschilds in London. Later, when the violinist came of age (and after Saul's prewar investments were lost), he took on the finances himself, but continued providing for his family, which had no other source of income. This involved not only covering his parents' day to day expenses, but underwriting his sisters' education. Now that he had a family of his own, he felt it would be convenient to separate the accounts, so he opted to make a $250,000 investment, the proceeds from which would be used to sustain his parents and sister.

He selected a traditionally safe avenue, real estate; but either the firm handling the transaction misrepresented the sale to him, or he misunderstood the terms of the agreement. He thought he was buying second mortgages on a group of Manhattan buildings. These, as he understood it, would yield an extraordinary 18.5%—more than three times greater than the 6% first mortgage bonds he had preferred to invest in until then—and at minimal risk. Before leaving for an extended tour of Europe, Elman explained the investment to his father, who in turn discussed it with his accountant, Jacob Markowitz. Markowitz thought the terms sounded odd, and looked into the matter. He found that many of the investments were actually in third, fourth and even fifth mortgages, and were therefore quite risky.

Saul had power of attorney in Mischa's absence, and he decided it would be prudent to withdraw from the deal. He sent his son a wire to this effect, and the violinist cabled back that he was ready to cancel the rest of his European engagements and return to the United States if he were needed. Unfortunately, by the time Saul tried to withdraw the funds, several of the properties had been seized in foreclosures, and the investment looked irretrievable. Elman's attorneys filed a complaint with the Attorney General's office, and by early August 1927, the matter was to be set before a Grand Jury. By then, it had emerged that the Elmans were not alone, and that other investors working with the same firm had sustained similar losses. In the end, the Elmans recovered a small percentage of their investment, and the violinist resolved to hire an investment counselor and to have nothing further to do with the world of finance.

Since there was clearly nothing he could do in this crisis, Elman continued his tour abroad. He had been away since the end of 1926, and he was accompanied on his 18 month journey by Helen and Nadia. The voyage did not begin auspiciously. Elman had hired a new accompanist for the tour, and on shipboard he discovered that the man was precariously balanced. Halfway across the Atlantic, the pianist began speaking of suicide, and Elman spent several full nights awake, trying to talk him into a calmer state. When they reached Europe, he and Elman parted ways.

In May 1928, Elman and his family returned to New York, and the violinist announced his arrival through a press release in which he took issue with a comment his friend Stokowski had made upon giving up the podium of the Philadelphia Orchestra. Stokowski, in his typically provocative way, had complained that American audiences were more interested in a conductor's clothes than in his musicianship. "Leading European musicians I met on my recent tour," Elman countered, "emphasized that American audiences are not only musically intelligent, but are supercritical because they command the greatest talent of the world today." Elman added that in his estimation, the top American orchestras—he cited the New York Philharmonic, the Boston Symphony and the Philadelphia Orchestra—"are far superior to any European symphonies," with the sole exception of Willem Mengelberg's Concertgebouw Orchestra, in Amsterdam.

Because of his European tour and his quartet playing, Elman had not played a New York solo recital since 1925. His October 1928 Carnegie Hall recital was, therefore, greeted as a long-awaited return by the press, and particularly by Olin Downes, whose lengthy review in the *Times* covered the performance in minute detail. The program leaned more heavily on large works than usual—along with a Handel sonata, a Brahms sonata, three movements from one of the Bach solo works, and the Ernst Concerto, there was only one set of short pieces.

As Downes reports it, the opening movements of the Handel showed "the suggestion of exaggerated expression, such as a slight excess of *rubato*, or the tendency to be overemotional." But the critic attributed this to the tension of returning home, and found that by the third movement, Elman had settled down and adopted a style marked by "a glory of tone, a nobility of line and feeling, that matched the music. It was the best of the style of the young Elman," he wrote, "ripened and deepened in its meaning." He was even more rhapsodic about the rest of the program.

Downes was particularly supportive of Elman's new approach to programming, and several other critics praised the violinist for reducing the number of brief showpieces without entirely eliminating them. Elman had, it seems, undertaken something of a repertoire renovation during his European trip, for while his recitals of the early 1920s were showing a tendency towards repetitiveness, he was now holding fast to some of his old favorites while freshening his programs with works that were either new to him, or which he hadn't played in a long while. In his second Carnegie Hall recital, in November, for instance, he offered the Handel D major Sonata, the Vieuxtemps Fifth Concerto, and the Saint-Saëns *Introduction and Rondo Capriccioso*—all old friends, but joined by his first performances of the Beethoven "Spring" Sonata and a few of the shorter works, most notably, a movement from Ernest Bloch's *Baal Shem*, Kreisler's Corelli Variations, and a spirited, modal piece called *Danse Hebraïque* by Josef Bonime.

Bonime was no longer Elman's accompanist—Marcel van Gool held that post from 1928 through 1930—but they remained friendly, and Elman had taken up some of Bonime's music. His rendering of this one, with its ethnic folksiness and the virtuosic *Scheherazade*-like cadenza towards it beginning, captured the Carnegie Hall audience's imagination, and the applause it earned was so warm and prolonged that Elman repeated it. A quarter of a century later, in 1963, he took it up again, offering it as the opening selection in an LP entitled *Hebraic Melodies*.

Elman's third New York concert of the season followed along similar lines. This time he began with Nardini, but the next work, the Franck Sonata (in which his sister Liza was his accompanist), was still a rarity on his programs. The Mendelssohn Concerto added further weight, as did another pair of Bach solo movements. For his group of short works, he again blended warhorses (the Wieniawski *Polonaise*, and a Joachim arrangement of a Brahms *Hungarian Dance*) with less frequently played works (including his own *Tango* and Leopold Godowsky's *Danse Macabre*).

The *Times*, in an unsigned review of this concert, noted that Elman's "superb musicianship has never been more splendidly revealed than in his recitals this year."

CHAPTER TWELVE:

The Touring Years Continue

In 1929, Elman's second child, Josef, was born. Although Helen had toured with the violinist after the birth of Nadia, now that there were two children, it was decided that the violinist should again travel on his own, except during the summers. During their earlier European tours, the Elmans had enjoyed spending their vacations on the southwestern coast of France, and they returned there several times, renting a house complete with a staff of Basque servants. They found, too, that many of their musical and theatrical friends—including Charlie Chaplin and the Russian bass Feodor Chaliapin—had taken houses nearby.

Elman used these summer retreats to recuperate from the previous season, to prepare his programs for the season coming up, and to relax by pursuing a few favorite pastimes—specifically, playing with his children at the beach, reading, playing chess, and socializing with the other members of the artistic community there. Parties were plentiful. During the summer of 1931, when they took a house in St. Jean de Luz, the Elmans threw a party attended by a few dozen playwrights, authors, musicians, actors, and artists, with Chaplin, Chaliapin, Jacques Thibaud and Toscha Seidl among the guests. Dinner courses alternated with various forms of entertainment—not only chamber music by Elman and his colleagues, but an exercise in role reversal between Chaplin and Chaliapin: Chaplin sang a group of Basque folksongs with, according to the Elmans' five servants, a perfect accent; then Chaliapin embarked on Chaplin's specialty, pantomime, acting the role of a woman of the early 19th century trying to tie herself into a corset. It wasn't until four in the morning that the last of the guests left.

The next day, Chaplin met the Prince of Wales, who was visiting nearby Biarritz, and told him about the party. "Tell Mrs. Elman I'd like a party like that too," he said, and Chaplin returned with the message. Helen Elman did not find this particularly exciting news. "Our household at St. Jean de Luz was not very formal," she reminisced. "The servants, who were darling people and fantastic cooks, walked around in tennis shoes, which was fine with me since it was only for the summer; but if the Prince were going to be there, that would have to change. We'd also have to find the cigars he smoked, the brandy he drank—there are dozens of details to see to, and it really would have been quite a chore."

Feodor Chaliapin's wife, however, heard that the British prince wanted the Elman party repeated, and asked if she could throw it at her house. "I was thrilled," Helen Elman says, "although I pretended I wasn't, and said that it would be a terrible sacrifice. But of course, since the Chaliapins lived in Paris and had a very ritzy entourage, it really made sense." The Chaliapins had the party, and invited some of the same artists who had been at the Elmans' house a couple of weeks earlier, although the guest list was considerably shorter this time. When the Prince arrived, he made it clear that he did not want to stand on ceremony—which meant, essentially, that he wished to be addressed merely as Sir, not by his titles.

After dinner, Elman and Thibaud collaborated on the Bach Double Concerto, with accompaniment on the piano by Emmanuel Bay—a Russian-born pianist who had been Zimbalist's accompanist from 1922 to 1929, and who had just started what would be a 20 year stint with Heifetz. Elman and Bay were quite friendly; in fact, they were born on the same day and year, and in 1951, when Bay and Heifetz ended their association, Elman came close to signing the pianist on as his own accompanist. Elman was between pianists, at the time, and he invited Bay over for lunch, a game of chess, and a discussion about their future together. It became apparent to Elman that the association would not be satisfactory when he asked Bay to read through the Mendelssohn Concerto with him. "I'll read it with you once, Mischa," the pianist said, "and that will be it. You know the piece and I know the piece—we've each played it a thousand times." That was not an acceptable response for Elman, who loved to practice no matter how well he knew the scores. "Emmanuel," he said, "I'm glad you told me that now, because we can still be friends, but we can't work together."

After the Bach performance with Thibaud and Bay, Elman spent a few moments in idle conversation with the Prince, who asked him, "do you always play from the music, or do you sometimes play by heart?" Elman assured him that he sometimes played by heart, and asked the Prince to suggest an encore piece that he could offer as proof. The Prince selected Dvořák's *Humoresque*. But, as the evening progressed and the liquor flowed the party got stranger. Eventually, Prince Edward was moved to challenge Chaplin to a headstanding contest. With 1,000 francs per round as the prize, each stood on his head while the other held a stopwatch, with the cash going to whoever was the more tenacious. This went on for hours, with the same 1,000 franc note passing back and forth between the contestants.

"Mischa, who never touched a drop of liquor, and who didn't find this very amusing, came to me and said, 'I can't take this anymore, let's go,'" Helen recalls. "He was an innately refined person, and he hated to see people drunk, particularly friends of his. But I hesitated, because I didn't think one was allowed to leave a party before royalty. But Mischa was very well versed in the rules governing this sort of thing, and he said, 'no, he didn't want to be called Prince, so technically he's here incognito. And if he's incognito, then we can leave first.' The next day, I called Mrs. Chaliapin, and she said, 'do you know that those fools were standing on their heads until seven in the morning?' I was glad we left when we did."

❖ ❖ ❖ ❖ ❖

At the end of the summer, Elman played a series of concerts in Europe, and went as far east as Latvia—a republic from which, he sadly reported upon his return to New York, "the old Russian atmosphere has disappeared entirely."

Elman and his family landed in New York just before Christmas, 1931; and within a month, he found himself once again at the center of a well-publicized dispute, this time with the management of the New York Philharmonic. The disagreement centered around the music Elman would perform at a pair of appearances scheduled for the end of January. Elman's management (the Metropolitan Musical Bureau, that year) had approved the contract with the orchestra while Elman was in Europe, and cabled the violinist that he would probably be playing the Glazunov and Tchaikovsky Concertos. Actually, the contract had specified "a short concerto," offering those two as possibilities.

Upon his return, Elman asked the orchestra if he could switch to the Brahms Concerto, and there the trouble began. "I have not played with any orchestra in New York for 12 years,'" the violinist told a *Times* reporter during an interview that was published on his forty-first birthday, "and I thought that it would be right to ask to be heard on this appearance in a work of major significance." Five or six days passed before the Philharmonic responded—and both their response and their reasoning rankled. They regretted that they could not have Elman play the Brahms, the orchestra said; but they had already scheduled an appearance in that work by young Yehudi Menuhin, later in the season.

Elman countered by offering the Beethoven, but that work had been played only a few months earlier. "Finally," he told the *Times* reporter, "I suggested the Tchaikovsky Concerto, and the answer was that it was 'too long.' Whereupon I told them to look for another soloist." When queried about this, the Philharmonic's manager, Arthur Judson, confirmed that Elman's contract called for performances of either the Glazunov or the Tchaikovsky, but that the conductor, Bruno Walter, had requested that the violinist play the Glazunov in order to keep the program within a prescribed time limit, since the concerts were broadcast live and had to conform to a fairly rigid schedule. When Elman said he preferred not to play the Glazunov, Walter suggested that he select another work of about the same length (roughly 20 minutes).

"Admitting that they demanded a 'short concerto,'" Elman said, "what is a short concerto and what is a long one? The Brahms Concerto requires about 35 minutes to play, and the Beethoven a little more time. Granted that there are shorter concertos, but should not something be left to the soloist? [The Philharmonic's] only concern appeared to be that the concerto should be short. What was in it, its music, didn't seem to matter. After all, it is a difference of five or ten minutes. I do not see why I could not be allowed to play a work of significance, and to me, the most significant violin concertos that have been written are by Brahms, Beethoven and Tchaikovsky."

Elman and the orchestra were not able to work out the difference, and Elman held firm to his withdrawal. The public reaction, or at least some of it, indicated sympathy for Elman's position. "May I add a few words of comment to the Elman-Philharmonic episode?" one correspondent wrote in a letter to the editor of the *Times*. "As a musician and subscriber to the Philharmonic concerts for a number of years I feel a bit resentful at the treatment accorded so sterling an artist as

Mischa Elman. Why is not the artist permitted to choose his own concerto? Why must he submit to a so-called time limit?"

The Philharmonic ended up engaging the cellist Gregor Piatigorsky
to play the Schumann cello concerto instead, and Elman quickly
scheduled a Carnegie Hall recital for January 31, the date of what
would have been his second Philharmonic performance (which was
to take place in Brooklyn). His program was in the same form it had
recently taken—three larger works plus a group of short pieces. This
time, the large works were Handel and Mozart sonatas and, ironically, the Glazunov Concerto that had occasioned the Philharmonic battle. There was a message there, of course: Elman wanted to emphasize
once more that he had nothing against the Glazunov, but that he felt
strongly about playing a grander concerto in his first New York orchestral appearance in so many years. Elman's accompanist at this
point (from 1930 until 1934) was Carroll Hollister.

According to the review published in the *Times*, the audience was
large and enthusiastic. Clearly, Elman had won a great share of the
popular vote this time. It remained only for his managers to patch
things up with the Philharmonic. Eventually they did, and within a
few seasons, the relationship between the violinist and the orchestra
was renewed.

Another unfortunate brush with the darker side of celebrity led
Elman to cancel the tail end of his 1932 season, as well as his plans for
another European vacation. In the early spring of that year, Helen
traveled to San Francisco to be with her mother, who had undergone
a cancer operation. Elman remained East, continuing to play the
engagements on his schedule, and planning to join his wife and her
family in May, when the season ended. The children were no problem:
at the time, the Elmans retained a governess and a cook, who looked
after Nadia and Josef; and of course Elman's parents looked in on them
too. Nadia was going to be in a school play, so Helen sent her a
telegram from San Francisco, wishing her luck.

The day the telegram arrived, Elman returned from Washington,
where he and Hollister had given a recital. Sifting through the pile of
mail awaiting him, he found the telegram and set it aside for Nadia,
who was at school; and he found a letter addressed to his wife and
marked "personal and private." He opened that one, and found an unsigned letter that read, "unless you pay us $15,000 by the end of this

week, Nadia and Josef will be kidnapped and probably disposed of."
The letter went on to say that further messages and instructions would
appear in the personal columns of one of the New York newspapers.

At the time, the Lindbergh kidnapping case was a major item in the
news, and that tragedy seemed to inspire a number of blackmailers,
who realized that threatening the safety of a celebrity's children was
a quick way to round up cash. Elman checked to see that three-year
old Josef was safe in the care of the governess, and immediately left
the house to collect Nadia from school. Upon their return, he and the
governess packed a few bags, and Elman, the children and the governess took a cab to Penn Station and set off for San Francisco. Before
leaving, Elman telephoned Liza and asked her to let the Kattens and
Helen know that they were on their way. He also called Hollister, with
whom he was about to embark on a tour, and told him that he had to
cancel their plans indefinitely. He conveyed the same message to his
manager, promising to call from San Francisco and fill him in. And
finally, he telephoned his attorney, explained the situation, and asked
him to hire a detective.

"I had no idea why they were leaving," Helen says. "Mischa knew
that my mother was dying of cancer, and that I adored her; but he also
knew that I wasn't the hysterical type. It seemed very peculiar to me,
because he was about to go on a big tour, and he knew I wouldn't have
wanted him to cancel it on my account. I thought perhaps he had only
cancelled a concert or two in order to bring the children out to me, but
even that made no sense.

"When I met them in Oakland—you had to take a ferry from Oakland to San Francisco in those days—my husband hardly paid any attention to me, but instead, he took my brother off to the side and spoke
to him privately. That was very strange too, since he was usually the
most attentive person in the world, and everybody used to kid us because we were holding hands all the time. So, I knew something was
wrong. When we arrived at the hotel, Mischa continued to behave
strangely. He took us all up to the desk clerk and said, 'this is my
father-in-law, this is my brother-in-law and sister in law, and this is
my aunt. Besides these people, absolutely *nobody* is to come up to my
apartment without being announced.'

"That was usually the case, of course, but I'd never seen him so em-
phatic about it. It gave me the jitters. When we got upstairs, Mischa
and my brother went into another room together, and I thought, alright, now I'm going to see what's what. So I went in and asked what

all the secrecy was about. 'It's nothing, don't worry about it,' Mischa said; and for some reason, I don't know why, I said, 'I bet you've had kidnapping threats about the children. Is that it?' He hesitated a minute, and then said, 'yes it is.' And from then on, our lives were miserable."

Elman became fanatical about the children's safety, accompanying them to the park and prohibiting them from playing behind trees or in any way moving out of his sight, or the governess's. Every day, Elman's attorney would send him, airmail, the potential kidnapper's newspaper messages—usually something like, "Josef and Nadia, where's the money you owe me?" The coincidental imposition of a bank moratorium bought some time for the Elmans, who could legitimately say that they didn't have access to their funds. Eventually, another letter, delivered to the Elmans' apartment and forwarded by their maid, instructed them to wrap $15,000 cash in a pair of trousers, which they were to mail to a post office box.

Through his attorney, Elman had learned, by then, that three university professors had received messages so similar as to make it clear that all four came from the same person; so he instructed his lawyer to make the professors an offer: Elman would pay the detective and court costs if the culprit were caught and prosecuted. All he wanted in return was anonymity. The professors, after all, were not public figures, as he was, and given the rash of kidnapping threats, it would be unlikely that a court case involving a threat against the children of three professors would receive much publicity. If Elman were involved, on the other hand, the case would get into the newspapers from coast to coast; and once the ordeal was over, someone else might threaten the Elman children again.

The professors agreed, and a decoy package was sent. The post office cooperated by informing its employees to watch out for someone collecting a package from that box number. Eventually, the blackmailer turned up, took the package and was arrested on his way out of the building. Unfortunately, since he had not actually kidnapped any of the children, he could not be prosecuted under the laws of the time.

The Elmans remained in San Francisco for the summer, but they were not able to while away their vacation pleasantly. Mrs. Katten had died, and Mr. Katten had a stroke soon thereafter; and both Nadia and Josef came down with childhood diseases.

❖ ❖ ❖ ❖ ❖

That fall, Elman and Hollister resumed their touring, starting in Europe and returning to New York at the end of 1932. Elman opened his season with a rather stellar collaboration at Town Hall, under the auspices of the Beethoven Association. The Beethoven Association meant its performances to be chamber music among equals in the true sense, and its organizers usually arranged for some glamorous pairings. This time, Elman shared the stage with the pianist Harold Bauer, with whom he played the Franck Sonata and the Brahms Sonata in D minor. The Franck began inauspiciously, according to the *Times* review; but by the third movement "their interpretation struck fire...and from that moment on, through the entire Brahms sonata, the playing had enkindling warmth and impressive nobility.

"A word must be said," the critic was moved to add, "about the surpassing depth and sensitivity of Mr. Elman's playing, without belittling Mr. Bauer's masterful share last night. In the last years, Mr. Elman has grown enormously in artistic stature. There is a deep humanity in his playing, revealed most movingly last night in the third movement of the Franck and in the *Adagio* of the Brahms. There is also a lofty passion and delicate grace. And all these wedded to his sure technique and rich tone. Assuredly he is one of our first violinists."

In February 1933, Elman made his long delayed return to the New York stage as an orchestral soloist. He was not a guest of the New York Philharmonic this time; rather, he was accompanied by the Musicians' Symphony Orchestra, an ensemble of some 300 otherwise unemployed players, led by Sandor Harmati. The concert took place at the Metropolitan Opera House, and for those who would have settled for hearing him play the Glazunov with the Philharmonic, 13 months earlier, Elman provided a dividend for patience: he played the Bach Concerto in E major, plus the Brahms and Tchaikovsky.

The critics remained kind to Elman through early 1930s, and as younger violinists like Heifetz and, more recently, Menuhin and another Auer student, Nathan Milstein, were winning their own audiences, Elman's technique and interpretive warmth continued to serve him well. He remained in demand, and he retained a large following. Financially, he was doing better than ever, for his tours were taking him far and wide, his records were selling well, and he had recently signed a contract with Victor that guaranteed several broadcast recitals a year, each at a princely fee. Thus, even after sustaining considerable losses in his recent real estate transaction, as well as having had to cancel a tour and spend a fortune on detectives in the matter of the kidnapping threat, Elman remained comfortable enough not to worry about his fees—except as a matter of principle. He did, quite often, find himself engaged in heated arguments with managers and promoters about everything from commission percentages to foreign currency exchange rates, for it was his feeling that when he played for a certain fee, he should take home as much of that fee as possible. On the other hand, his activities during this period show that at the same time he could be quite generous with his time and talent. When his tours took him through vast stretches of the country, where several days of train travel fell between two concerts in large cities, he would arrange recitals in small towns or colleges along the route, at greatly reduced fees. "The money wasn't the important thing to Elman" Carroll Hollister recalled in an interview shortly before his death, in 1983. "For Elman, the important thing was to play as much as possible. He loved to play, and he loved to rehearse. As I recall, he was a very good person to work for. He wasn't bossy or unpleasant, and although as an accompanist I accommodated myself to his way of playing, there were times when he deferred to me on musical matters. We would discuss things. It was quite a nice working relationship, really."

Besides giving cut-rate impromptu concerts in small towns that could not otherwise have afforded him, Elman played numerous benefits for causes he considered worthy. In 1930, for instance, he and Ossip Gabrilowitsch teamed up for a Carnegie Hall concert to raise funds for the Society for the Advancement of Music in Palestine. Together, they played sonatas by Beethoven and Franck, and then each played a group of shorter solos (Elman's were accompanied by van Gool). Similarly, Elman's first New York appearance in 1931—one of his standard recital programs—was for the benefit of the Women's Trade Union League.

The cause he began concertizing for at the end of 1933, however, was one that went beyond charity for Elman. Rather, it was a cause that left him startled, and which hit close to home. Earlier that year, Adolf Hitler had become Chancellor of Germany, and in his drive to establish the thousand year empire he had promised his followers— one in which a racially pure, superior, Aryan Germany would rule the world—he instituted anti-Semitism as a policy of state. Jewish businesses were boycotted, and harassment of Jews was encouraged. Germany's Jews reacted with disbelief, at first, but by the end of the year, thousands had fled Germany, leaving all their possessions behind. Those who remained had found themselves with nowhere to turn.

At the end of the summer, the American Joint Distribution Committee proposed a benefit concert to help raise funds for needy Jews who were still in Germany—a lost cause if ever there was one, although they could hardly have known that. Elman, who was spending the summer in San Francisco, was contacted and asked to perform on the program, which was to be held in White Plains on September 28, and which also featured his friend Gabrilowitsch and the soprano Hulda Lashanska. Elman didn't hesitate for a moment, and in announcing his participation in the recital, he delivered a heartfelt statement to the press.

"During the course of my entire career," he said, "I recall no request for my services as an artist with which I complied more readily or wholeheartedly, or with such deep feeling. People who have not felt the sting of actual persecution can hardly realize the physical and mental torture through which the German Jews are now passing."

Much was made of the similarity between the Russian form of anti-Semitism Elman and his family had suffered, and the variety just unleashed in Germany. But as varieties of hatred go, these were really quite dissimilar, with only their targets in common. In Russia, the prejudices were rooted in the Orthodox Church view that the Jews had murdered Christ, and there were ways around it—i.e., a Russian Jew who elected to forsake his faith and embrace Orthodox Christianity could enter society freely. So, for that matter, could an exceptionally talented Jew—witness the success enjoyed by young Elman, Heifetz, Zimbalist, Seidl and countless others.

But none of this was possible in Germany, where the hatred was racial, not religious. There, even born Christians with Jewish family backgrounds were at risk, and artistic talent bore no privileges: Germany's Jewish composers and performers were banished from the concert halls, no matter how great their contributions to the great German musical tradition had been, and no matter how highly they were esteemed around the world. Stranger still, long dead composers of Jewish origin were expunged from the repertoire. The music of Mendelssohn, Bruch, and Mahler, for instance, was not to be countenanced.

Elman recognized the distinction between the Russian and German forms, and in announcing his participation in the White Plains benefit, he added a clarification. "The present atrocities in Germany," he pointed out, "are far more subtle, mean and cruel than any ever per-petrated in Russia during the Tsar's regime. I make this statement with a pang in my heart because, personally, I have every reason to be grateful to Germany. I cannot and will not believe that the majority of the German people are in sympathy with Hitler. However, an irreparable damage has already been done, and it is our duty to come to the aid of the innocent and helpless Jews still remaining in Germany."

About 4,500 people filled Westchester County Center the night of the concert, and more than $50,000 was raised from ticket sales, donations, and the sale of souvenir programs. As in the salon concerts of old, the starring artists played sets of their own, as well as a few collaborations. The centerpiece of Elman's solo set was Lalo's *Symphonie Espagnole*, with Sanford Schlussel as his accompanist; but undoubtedly more interesting were his renderings of Beethoven's "Kreutzer" Sonata, with Gabrilowitsch, and a Handel *Largo* performed by Elman, Gabrilowitsch and Lashanska.

Elman never recorded with Gabrilowitsch, but in 1939, he collaborated with Hulda Lashanska on some vocal chamber music. The sessions yielded but a single disc—a pairing of an arioso from a Handel cantata, and Schubert's *Litanie auf das Fest aller Seelen*. Joining Elman and Lashanska here are the pianist Rudolf Serkin, and the cellist Emanuel Feuermann. To be sure, these are Lashanska's recordings, and the celebrated instrumentalists provide little more than an accompaniment. But it is a glowing, warm sound they produce together, and here again, no-one could accuse Elman of stepping beyond the bounds of the chamber context. His sound is gorgeously blended with Feuermann's, and both string players move as one with Serkin.

Elman's own recordings of the early 1930s, meanwhile, were hardly as self-effacing. The centerpiece of his discography from this period is his first concerto recording—a marvelous rendering of the Tchaikovsky, with John Barbirolli conducting the London Symphony Orchestra. Elman approved of the cuts Auer had made in his edition, and he continued to play the work in that form; but he does not stint on pyrotechnics or passion here, nor on nuance. His opening phrase is graceful and easygoing, and marked by a leisurely *rubato*. As the movement unfolds, Elman plays with the shapes of the phrases, manipulating their internal emphases and using dynamics to give them unexpected contours. None of this hints at the storminess that will emerge by before the movement reaches its halfway point, let alone that of the work's energetic finale; rather, Elman allows these elements to evolve as part of the work's natural dramatic flow. Of course, the high-point of the recording is the slow movement—not surprisingly, given Elman's tonal and interpretive inclinations, and the opportunities this movement offers for indulging in them.

Fascinating in a very different way is Elman's recording of the Prelude from Bach's E major Partita, the only unaccompanied Bach he recorded during the mature part of his career.[2] By today's standards, this is a subjective account, yet it cannot be said to deviate wildly from the letter of the score. He lavishes a good deal of attention on the repeated bass notes, rarely playing those in a series twice exactly the same way, and sometimes adding a minute touch of *portamento* to help alter them. Yet, his use of *rubato* in this piece is subtle. He retains the Prelude's perpetual motion quality, and plays upon its energy, but he does not do so nearly as ostentatiously as Sarasate did in his jet-speed account. Elman is poetic and colorful here, but he keeps within arm's reach of the music's spirit and style.

The rest of Elman's recordings from this time were of short pieces with piano accompaniment, and they were, again, divided between remakes of old favorites, and new additions to the Elman discography. Some of these—his own arrangement of a Beethoven *Country Dance*, and transcriptions by Wilhelmj and Hullweck of Chopin's *Nocturne No.8* and Schumann's *Träumerei*—were updates. With them came Elman's first recordings of Espejo's *Aires Tziganes*, Ysaÿe's *Rêve d'enfant* and Mendelssohn's *O for the Wings of a Dove*.

Few though they are, each of these discs spotlights a different side of Elman's art; and taken with the slightly larger batch of discs Elman made with Hollister, they convey a good deal about the breadth of style Elman commanded at this time. The Beethoven, for instance, is the lightest-spirited of the collaborations with van Gool, and the two cruise through it at an athletic clip. Elman plays the opening sections with a bouncy staccato, and the middle section with a broader sweep, yet still playfully. Espejo's *Aires Tziganes*, composed in 1926, gives Elman a chance to paint in broader strokes, and he meets the opportunity dazzlingly, playing the soulful, minor mode opening with agility, yet in a gently manipulated *pianissimo*. This little piece also calls for more outgoing gypsy-style fiddling, though, for which Elman shifts gears, adds a measure of paprika, and launches into a display of quick, energetic bowing. Before it ends, the work shifts back and forth several times in this manner, and each time, Elman negotiates the shift with astonishing skill. As showpiece recordings go, this is one of Elman's finest.

For Ysaÿe's *Rêve d'enfant*, Elman calls on the darker, richer side of his tone, and he suffuses his interpretation of the gentle work with a nostalgic and decidedly French flavor. For the Mendelssohn and Chopin selections, he puts forth a more soulful sound; and Schumann's *Träumerei*, played quite slowly, emerges as nostalgia of a different sort—a look back at the by now old-fashioned vignettes from the Elman encore collection. Elman had recorded the piece twice before, and he would record it twice more. This version retains many of the hallmarks of the earlier ones, the chief of them being a tendency to overcome the simplicity of the piece by sliding to and from each of the melodic peaks, and generally basking in the warm resonance of the violin's sound.

Elman went into the studio more frequently with Carroll Hollister, who—at least so far as the recordings show—was a more outgoing player than van Gool, with a brighter sound that meshed more fully with Elman's. Together, they recorded 13 selections, seven of them remakes. Of the remakes, in fact, three had already been remade at least once before: His new recording of the Drigo *Serenade* was his fifth (the first having been made during one of his earliest sessions, for Pathe), while he had previously recorded Tchaikovsky's *Melodie* and the Drdla *Serenade* twice each. Among the new additions to his catalogue, meanwhile, were a few standard works that had long been featured on Elman's recital programs, but which he had not yet released on disc. Among these are Ravel's *Piece en forme d'Habanera*, Wieniawski's *Legende*, and perhaps most surprisingly belated of all, given Elman's fondness of it, Sarasate's *Zigeunerweisen*—a work that gets a sizzling performance. In this recording, one hears all of Elman's finest qualities—some of them the very traits that eventually made his style seem antique, but as convincing as ever here. In every bar of the piece, he applies his coloration sensitively, and his manipulation of each phrase's contours and dynamics are both thoughtful and deeply personal.

So are Elman's tempos, which may strike many as radical, both in the context of today's performances and in comparison with others of the 1930s. The slower sections of this fragmented display piece are taken at an extraordinarily slow pace, and provide a context in which Elman's tone sings all the more sweetly. He plays the fast sections, however, at demonic speeds. For Elman, this was a work almost tailor-made for a subjective performance—one that cried out for an artist's personal vision, and the interplay between Elman and Hollister here shows that the performance is hardly a capricious or serendipitous one, but rather, the product of considerable discussion and rehearsal. Even in the sections in which Elman takes the greatest liberties, the two players move in tandem, precisely. Interpretively and technically, this *Zigeunerweisen*, recorded in 1931, conveys a sense of complete assurance—and complete mastery.

CHAPTER THIRTEEN:

Exotic Touring—New Worlds, Return Visits

In 1934, as the thirtieth anniversary of his Berlin debut approached, Elman longed for a change of scenery. So, instead of taking a summer vacation, he decided to accept some long standing offers from concert promoters in South America. He had considered visiting the exotic continent a few years earlier, but ended up visiting Europe again instead.

This time, though, he also had a practical reason for touring a place that was new and a little out of the way: he wanted to break in a new accompanist. In the past, Elman had taken on his accompanists less carefully, but after a run of bad matches in Europe a few years earlier (a problem he ultimately solved by prevailing once again upon Waldemar Liachowsky), he began to give the matter greater consideration. His best accompanists had been men like Gordon, Bonime, van Gool and Hollister, pianists who understood his interpretive approach, shared his enthusiasm for rehearsal, and stayed with him several years and many tours.

Hollister, unfortunately, had been primarily a vocal coach before joining Elman, and the two had an implicit understanding that when the right singer came along, Hollister would return to the repertoire he loved best. In 1933, Hollister agreed to accompany John Charles Thomas, the baritone, and he gave Elman notice. The violinist immediately began auditioning accompanists, and of those he heard, the most promising was a young Russian immigrant named Vladimir Padwa.

Elman had some doubts about Padwa, though. He was not as experienced as Hollister and some of the earlier accompanists had been, and Elman wasn't keen on the idea of having his accompanist learn on the job. The musical chemistry between soloist and accompanist had to be perfect, and the South American tour could be something of an extended practical audition for Padwa—although Elman was, in effect, giving him the benefit of the doubt, for a European tour was scheduled to begin less than a month after Elman's return to the United States, in the fall. During this Latin tour, Padwa could internalize Elman's mannerisms, and mold his responses outside the scrutiny of the European and American musical publics, which were more demanding and had higher standards for comparison.

Elman had little doubt that he'd be well-received in South America, where American and European musical stars were bankable commodities for Latin promoters. They were also comparatively rare, for while many players did pay visits to the major South American cities, the rigors of travel through this gigantic but technologically underdeveloped continent were still daunting, and for many performers, South America remained off the beaten path.

The wealthier South Americans took their culture where they could find it—usually during their annual visits to Europe. The situation was, in fact, not unlike that which prevailed in the United States a century earlier, and in both cases, this cosmopolitan cultural elite invariably returned with elements of European culture that could be copied for home consumption. By the 1930s, recordings had become important tools in this transplanting of culture (and not incidentally, in the making and sustaining of international musical careers). Elman's recordings were selling briskly in the Latin countries, a point the South American promoters used in persuading the violinist to venture south.

Unlike today's performers, who follow an itinerary planned two years in advance as they travel the world, Elman and his colleagues often made their way with fairly vague ideas about when and where they would be performing. As in the early days, when he and his father arrived in a town, announced a concert for a week hence, and then either practiced or performed elsewhere in the interim, Elman left New York at the end of May with a few solid commitments and a great deal of flexibility. His intention was to sail to Argentina, kick off the tour in Buenos Aires—then, as now, the musical capital of the continent—and then slowly work his way north.

But that was not to be: Jascha Heifetz and his accompanist, Emanuel Bay, had left for South America some time before Elman, and when they were performing in Brazil, Heifetz got word of Elman's tour plans. When the prospect of head-on competition arose, Heifetz invariably adopted an aggressive battle plan—something Elman found mystifying and more than a little annoying, for he considered touring and performing matters of enjoyment, not opportunities for battle. This sort of challenge could only take the pleasure out of it. But Heifetz meant to capture the hearts of the Latin public first, and when Elman's ship put in at Rio, on June 14, he learned that Heifetz had abandoned his Brazilian travels and taken an airplane to Buenos Aires. Elman wasn't about to give chase; in those days, he preferred to travel by ship and rail, and he promised Helen that he would not fly.

He therefore made the obvious tactical decision: he contacted his manager, who arranged for a recital in São Paulo, five days later. "The audience," Padwa wrote to Saul Elman, "listened to the very serious program with an almost pious concentration, and their enthusiasm was great and genuine."[1] Two more São Paulo recitals followed, as did three in Rio. Between those concerts came seemingly endless social obligations. Evenings, they would be wined and dined at the homes of prominent businessmen and politicians, and afternoons, they would invariably be taken on sightseeing tours by their hosts, each of whom, it turned out, showed them the same Brazilian panoramas.

More interesting to Elman and Padwa were the nights they spent with Brazilian musicians and artists. One, a poet, played them dozens of Brazilian folk songs—music Padwa and Elman found entrancing. After two weeks in Brazil, Elman and Padwa made their way to their original destination, Buenos Aires, realizing that by allowing Heifetz to play there first, they might have put themselves at a disadvantage. The reports they heard confirmed their fears. Heifetz, not surprisingly, had dazzled the Argentineans. It was said that they had never heard a violinist as brilliant, nor had they seen one who could surmount the difficulties of the virtuoso repertoire with such extraordinary facility. By the time Elman arrived, Heifetz had played five recitals in the Teatro Colón, the largest hall in Buenos Aires. Each concert was sold out, and at each, hundreds were turned away. Elman's arrival set the Argentinean musical world speculating about who would prove the better violinist—although most doubted that Heifetz's performances could be bettered.

"The dramatic moment came on July 7," Padwa reported. "Mischa Elman stood for the first time on the stage of the splendid Teatro

Colón. The theater was packed and an unusual tension was in the air. Mrs. Heifetz and [Emanuel] Bay were among the audience. Mr. Elman must have had the kind of feeling a general would have before a decisive battle. The program was quite unusual for Buenos Aires— among other numbers, a sonata by Handel, a sonata by Mozart, the *Chaconne* by Bach! Poor Schraml [the manager] was sweating blood of fear—and who could blame him?

"The concert began. The audience listened breathlessly and Elman talked to them on his violin; his 'golden tone' carried his masterfully simple phrases straight to the hearts of the people.... When he finished, the tension changed to an unheard of enthusiasm, and we felt at once that this was the success, the victory, the open road to South America."

Padwa's account may be colored by his own involvement in the events, and by his loyalty to his new employer, or even his eagerness to ingratiate himself with the violinist's family; but the exuberant newspaper reviews lend credence to it—in fact, some of the dispatches published back home in the *New York Times* make Padwa's descriptions look modest. Add to these the crate full of poems, letters, songs, art objects and other testimonials Elman shipped home from Argentina, a collection which confirms that Elman's audiences held him in an esteem that Padwa's flowery descriptions did not exaggerate. Meanwhile, Heifetz remained in Argentina to take up the gauntlet, and for as long as the two violinists were there, the rivalry remained the hottest topic in musical circles.

Elman followed his first concert with seven more at the Teatro Colón, all packed to the doors, and each enthusiastically received. Between these, he played in some of the smaller towns outside Buenos Aires, and according to one of the reports published in the *Times*, on July 21, these concerts were hardly the decorous affairs that Elman's Carnegie Hall recitals were. Apparently, Elman had established a rule about encores: he would play as many as the audience demanded, but he would not *repeat* any of the works. At Rosario, Argentina's second largest city, that policy crumbled. As one of his encores, Elman played his *Tango*, and the flattered Argentineans loved it—or, as the *Times* reported, they "went wild and demanded that he repeat it."

"Then ensued a long endurance contest between the audience and the violinist," the report continues. "He responded with a total of 12 encores, but he declined a repetition of *Tango*. The lights finally were extinguished and the violinist retired to his dressing room. Then hundreds of persons swarmed over the footlights and rushed into the dressing room. They dragged Elman on the stage and the lights were relit. He surrendered and replayed *Tango*. When he reached the street he found practically the entire audience awaiting him. The crowd marched to the railroad station behind his automobile, cheering him wildly."

Elman did, however, run into one problem in Buenos Aires. While he clearly had no trouble filling the Teatro Colón, he had discovered that many of those who occupied the seats had not paid for their tickets. There was, at the time, a traditional form of gate-crashing, apparently accepted by the theater managements, particularly when they felt they needed to fill seats—rather like the practice of "papering" halls today. In this South American version, the practice was to bring in an entire family on a single concert ticket.

When Elman found out about this, he was furious, for there were mobs of people unable to buy their way into the hall each time he played. He demanded that the gatecrashing be halted immediately. "When there are so many outside, willing to buy a ticket," he argued, "why should we let five or six people in on a single ticket? This is nonsense—there is no need for us to allow it." He did, on the other hand, spend a considerable amount of money having publicity photographs printed, so that he could comply with requests for autographed pictures.

Heifetz, meanwhile, forced a direct confrontation by announcing a concert at the same date and hour as one of Elman's Teatro Colón recitals. Elman was clearly the victor, according to Padwa, who writes that while the ushers at the sold-out Teatro Colón were busy turning away gate-crashers, Heifetz failed to fill a considerably smaller hall across town. Heifetz and Bay returned to Brazil, taking up their tour where they left off and leaving the south to Elman. Finding victory over Heifetz gratifying, Elman made Buenos Aires his base of operations for six weeks, alternately performing at the Teatro Colón and setting off for short jaunts to other Argentinean towns, and to Uruguay, where he gave three concerts in Montevideo and declined an offer to present a fourth.

Even after his considerable success, Elman was astounded at the pandemonium surrounding his final Teatro Colón concert. Tickets were sold out days in advance, and after the second of the program's three parts, the audience was so demonstrative that Elman and Padwa had to return to the stage to play two encores. Even then, the applause continued through the entire intermission, stopping only when Elman returned to the stage for the final group. Elman would certainly have stayed in Argentina longer, had he not already arranged to play some recitals in Chile. As it was, he played 15 concerts in Argentina during his last four weeks there.

There was only one bitter note. In mid-August, Elman was supposed to appear as the soloist in an orchestral concert led by the German conductor Fritz Busch, who was in Buenos Aires to conduct opera. The concert was abruptly cancelled, though—the official reason being that Busch did not have sufficient time to rehearse. The word spread, however, that Busch had cancelled the concert under official pressure from the German government. According to the rumor, the German Minister to Argentina had told Busch that if he performed with the Jewish violinist, he would not be allowed to return to Germany. Busch denied this, pointing out that his touring schedule would keep him out of Germany the following year anyway.

Indeed, of all the German conductors working at that time, Busch was among the few who could scarcely be accused of being a Nazi sympathizer. His open distaste for the Nazi party had led to his dismissal as director of the Dresden State Opera the previous year, and as it turned out, he would spend the war years primarily in South America. Whatever the reason for the cancellation, though, the rumors of anti-Semitism were enough to make Elman decidedly uncomfortable.

A more indisputable case of official anti-Semitism occurred just after the Latin tour, when Elman and Padwa went to Europe. Several years earlier, Elman's British manager, Harold Holt, had arranged a duo tour of England for the violinist with the German pianist Wilhelm Backhaus. This was a resounding success, and they repeated the collaboration several times. In 1934, a nine city tour had been arranged, but when Elman arrived in London, he found that Backhaus had sent him a telegram that began "due to circumstances beyond my control...." Elman played the dates with Padwa.

In the few days between the last Teatro Colón concert and their departure, Elman and Padwa gave a few private recitals—one at the American Embassy, and another at the home of Argentina's Vice-President. Upon their departure from the country, their local hosts wished them "a *bon voyage* and a good mule." The latter, it turned out, was more than a quaint figure of speech: it was on mules that they crossed the Andes into Chile, while Heifetz—against the advice of his manager, who found the Elman/Heifetz rivalry too costly to perpetuate—flew to Santiago. The voyage by mule put Elman and Padwa—not to mention Elman's precious Stradivarius—in a precarious position, although they later looked back on it as an extraordinarily beautiful ride. Mostly, Elman and his pianist were able to peacefully take in the natural grandeur of the passage through the mountains, marvelling at the endless expanses of deep, pure snow and the thrusting walls of rock. Now and then, however, the mules would lose their footing, leaving the musicians struggling to remain in saddle. "We crossed rivers, where we had to pull up our legs not to get wet," Padwa wrote, "and just hoped the mule wouldn't slip at that moment."

Before Elman left, his manager, Schraml, had done his best to prepare him for the journey, promising that at the end of the day's ride, they would arrive in the town of Puente del Inca, which would have a modest but comfortable hotel. By nightfall, there was no sign of anything but snow and rocks, and Elman began to doubt the wisdom of his promise not to fly. Eventually, the lights of Puente del Inca shone in the distance, and the party rode towards them. The next morning, Elman and Padwa got back on the mules and rode until noon, arriving at last at Las Cuevas, where they could switch to the dining car of a train for the rest of the voyage to Santiago.

Chile welcomed Elman as warmly as Argentina had. Elman's Chilean presenter, buoyed by reports of the violinist's triumphs in Argentina, Uruguay and Brazil, had decided to raise the ticket prices. Nevertheless, Elman quickly sold out a run of five performances. As in Brazil and Argentina, the concerts were punctuated by a certain amount of diplomatic partygoing, including a command performance at the President's palace on September 1. It was the President's name day, and the occasion was attended by the entire diplomatic corps, all of Chile's ministers, and the cream of Santiago society. Elman played a brief program in an atmosphere that was nearly as electric as that of his public concerts; and at the end, he was decorated with the "El Merito" star, an honor normally reserved for foreign statesmen, and never before conferred on a performer.

Several days later—the day before Elman and Padwa left Chile—they were invited to play at yet another public function, this time a celebration of the fiftieth anniversary of the country's National Savings Bank. The celebration was held at the Teatro Municipal, where Elman had played his five concerts; and of the various attractions offered on the program, Elman's performance was clearly the one the audience was waiting for.

Given the gala nature of the event, he chose to set aside Handel and Mozart, and offer dazzlers only—fireworks by Sarasate and Wieniawksi that let him wow the audience with the warmth of his famous tone. When he finished playing, the President of Chile gave him another gold medal, this time on behalf of the Bank and in honor of his visit to the country. The audience, which had calmed down for the presentation, gave him another standing ovation, and shouts for encores floated over the rhythmic clapping and footstamping.

The President nodded to Elman, who held up his right hand for silence. "I cannot speak Spanish," Elman told the crowd. But holding his violin out towards them, he added, "I *can* thank you with this." He raised the instrument to his chin, glanced over his shoulder to see that Padwa was ready, and then sent the sweetly melancholy strains of Schubert's *Ave Maria* out into the packed theater. Before the audience let the National Bank's festivities continue, Elman played two more encores.

It was going on four months since Elman had seen his family; and Padwa, too, confessed to being homesick. So from Santiago, they set out for home, figuring on arriving just after the start of the New York concert season. Along the way, they made an impromptu stop in Lima, Peru, where they gave two concerts in three days. "Leaving [these] South American countries," Padwa wrote one evening on board the New York bound S.S. Santa Elisa, "we felt that the hearts of the people, as well as the doors of their homes, were always wide open for Mischa Elman. For them, his visit was the big event of their lives. For him, it was a great, beautiful experience."

For his part, Vladimir Padwa had passed his audition. During the next six years, he would accompany Elman on several European and American tours, trips to Japan and the Middle East, and a return trip to South America. His work, in fact, had only just begun: Elman and Padwa arrived in New York on October 2, and 17 days later, they presented a recital at Carnegie Hall. They stayed in town long enough to read the reviews, and on October 24, they set sail for London, where they began a three month European tour, with stops in Spain, France and Holland.

The reviews of the Carnegie Hall recital were mixed—surely a let-down so soon after his Latin American triumphs. His program in-cluded the Brahms Sonata in D minor (which Heifetz had played in the same hall earlier in the week), the Bach-Nachez Concerto in G minor, and Lalo's *Symphonie Espagnole*, with a group of short works that included the Wieniawski Polonaise, Wilhelmj's paraphrase from *Siegfried*, and a Rumanian novelty that quickly disappeared from his programs, a *Bagatelle* by Scarlatescu.

The *Times* and the *Sun* each printed a lengthy review, but although they agreed about which works Elman played best and which were less successful, their approaches to the concert were almost diametri-cally opposite—not necessarily a remarkable circumstance in itself, but in this case, a clear indication of the divergent views of interpreta-tion that had developed over the last decade, and which were now joining battle. The *Times* critic was sympathetic to the old school, and noted that Elman's "conceptions are sometimes tinged with sentimen-tality"—not necessarily a flaw, he suggested, but rather, a product of "excessive ardor." Overall, he was charmed by the performance: "Mr. Elman," he wrote, "is a violinist who communicates his own deeply emotional nature to the music he plays. He is, without question, one of the most gifted of the romantics, and the thrice-famed 'Elman tone' is a peculiarly expressive manifestation of that aspect of this musician's art." He praised other qualities of Elman's stage persona, too—"passion, sincerity and unvarnished forthrightness." Overall, he felt the Bach Concerto worked the best, for Elman played it "with restraint, conveying by the breadth of his line and the warmth of his tone" the work's intrinsic beauty. The Brahms he found less fully con-vincing. "Mr. Elman gave the work a persuasive reading, marred oc-casionally by eagerness to stress the sentiment of a passage, where the feeling would have come through more forcefully if the proper proportions had been observed." The Lalo and the rest were taken less seriously. According to the critic, these "were performed in the spirit of the evening," and vigorously applauded.

A few noteworthy points emerge from between the lines here. On one hand, we see a critic sympathetic to Elman's personal style, and to his way of bathing the music in warmth. Yet, he is no longer entire-ly comfortable with at least one specific aspect that remained an Elman hallmark for the rest of the violinist's life—the tendency to linger over a note or a phrase that he especially liked the sound of, even if em-phasizing that phrase distorted the composer's longer line.

The reviewer for the *Sun* agreed that the Bach was the evening's high point, and he singled out the Largo as a "particularly impressive" rendering, and "a truly masterful handling of the violin's resources, in which the possession of endless 'breath' through a beautiful handling of the bow was a token of Mr. Elman's understanding of this style." The two Allegro movements, he reported, were also "consummately well-played." The critic's reservations about Elman's Brahms were more acute than his colleague's, though.

"Doubts set in at the entrance of the second theme in the first movement," he wrote, "and a not merely over-romanticized but undisciplined and highly personalized reading of the work eventuated. The glow of tone for the Adagio could not be disregarded, nor could the leisurely shifts and arbitrary swells be overlooked." Further, he added that "Vladimir Padwa, his accompanist, brought a fine technical prowess and ample musicianship to his undertaking, with the result that he was frequently at odds with Mr. Elman in the subtle details that bulk so large in ensemble playing."

The most telling part of the review, however, was the critic's summary of his feelings about Elman's interpretive style: "In the final analysis, it was Mr. Elman giving a violin recital, a circumstance not exactly a boon to Brahms, Lalo or even the hyphenated Bach-Nachez. This reversion to proclivities of an earlier period of his career was particularly regrettable last night, for Mr. Elman was in superb violinistic form, the master of a splendid technical dexterity, an unfailingly obedient bow-arm, and, of course, his magnificent tone. But the will to employ these to the precise ends of the composer's indications was peculiarly lacking last night, in sharp distinction to certain recitals he has given here in the not very distant past."

❖ ❖ ❖ ❖ ❖

Elman and Padwa remained on the road for virtually the entire 1934–35 season. After their fall tour of Europe, they returned to New York and then set out on a cross-country tour; but by the summer, they were again on their way across the Atlantic, this time for a string of dates in Europe and a tour through Palestine and Egypt. Elman was particularly interested in Palestine. The historical center of Judaism, it was now also a land of refuge for the persecuted Jews of Germany. In the two years since Elman had played his charity recital, the situation had deteriorated quickly. By 1935, Germany had repudiated the Treaty of Versailles that ended World War I, and had embarked on rearmament. The same year, the anti-Semitic Nuremburg Laws went into effect. Elman met many German refugees during the tour, and the stories they told horrified him. He was, however, pleased to find that in British-governed Palestine, they were "happy and prosperous," as he told one reporter after his return to New York, and that they considered Palestine a place "where they can hold their heads up and have peace of mind."

Elman returned to New York on the S.S. Washington, along with Efrem Zimbalist, who had just completed an eight-month tour of China, Japan, Russia and various European countries. They docked in New York on December 12, and Elman immediately began his preparations for a special series he would be giving at Carnegie Hall during the first 11 weeks of the new year. This was an extraordinary undertaking—an overview of the violin concerto literature, with 15 works to be presented in five Saturday afternoon concerts. Elman was accompanied in these by the National Orchestral Association Orchestra, with Leon Barzin conducting, and the proceeds from the series benefitted the Association's scholarship fund.

The concertos Elman selected for the five concerts were Bach's in E major, Mozart's in A major, and the Beethoven (January 4); Spohr's in A minor (No.8, the *Gesangszene*), Paganini's in D major (arranged by Wilhelmj), and the Mendelssohn (February 1); Bruch's in G minor, the Dvořák, and Lalo's *Symphonie Espagnole* (February 22); the Saint-Saëns in B minor, the Glazunov and the Brahms (March 7); and finally, the last Vieuxtemps, Chausson's *Poème*, and the Tchaikovsky. The series was a triumph—Carnegie Hall was packed for each of the concerts, and both the audiences and the critics showed unalloyed enthusiasm.

The programs, of course, gave Elman a great deal of interpretive leeway, while conveying the impression of a broad stylistic scope. Actually, the scope of the series was smaller than a quick glance at the works list might suggest. With the exception of the first program, most of the works Elman played were the grand essays he was famous for, and which generally served as excellent showcases for his trademark tone. Even the Spohr was a favorite from Elman's repertoire, although he hadn't played it for some time, and to many in the audience it was a novelty. Only the Dvořák was new to Elman, and it was a rarity for many listeners, not having been heard in New York since Milstein played it four years earlier (and, for that matter, more rarely offered than others of its caliber since those days).

With the series complete, Elman again teamed up with Padwa for an American tour, and returned to New York to close out his season with a reprise of the Tchaikovsky, with the New York Philharmonic for a crowd of more than 11,000 listeners at Lewisohn Stadium. These were popular concerts in the time-honored style. The orchestra played a warm-up (Berlioz's *Rakoczy March* in this case), and was then joined by the soloist for a concerto to conclude the first half. In the second half, the orchestra would play again (Rimsky-Korsakov's *Capriccio Espagnole* at this concert), and would then cede the stage to the soloist. Jose Iturbi—who was better known as a pianist, although he conducted throughout his life—was on the podium that night. He and Elman would team up again for a series of more energetic orchestral collaborations in the mid-1960s. In the second half of the concert, after Iturbi and the orchestra left the stage, Elman and Padwa offered a Chopin *Nocturne*, Sarasate's *Zigeunerweisen*, Elman's Beethoven *Country Dance* arrangement, and, among the encores, a folksy rendering of *Turkey in the Straw*.

After a summer in San Francisco, and another run of American concerts, Elman and Padwa were joined by the erstwhile chronicler Fred Erion for the violinist's second tour of the Orient. Elman completed the arrangements by cable just before he left, and as it turned out, a run of concerts in China was added at the last minute. Since these would keep him away from home another couple of months longer than he had planned, he telephoned Helen in New York and invited her to come along. "I'd love to come," she said, "but I have to think it over. If I stay here, I'll be lonesome, and if I come with you, I'll be worried about the children." "That settles it," Elman told her. "It's much easier to be lonesome than worried. I'll call you when I get to Japan."

They left San Francisco on the steamer Chichibu Maru on Christmas Eve 1936, and after suffering a particularly rough crossing, they stopped briefly at Hawaii, where Elman played a Honolulu recital. They arrived at Yokohama on January 8, and were greeted royally: on the pier were singers, musicians, reporters, photographers, and women laden with flowers to be delivered to the violinist.

"I never knew that an American could be so popular in Japan as you were," Erion wrote to the violinist, some years later.[2] "It reminded me very much of the stories we read about Paganini. Just as the crowds followed him on the streets and after concerts, so did crowds follow you. It made no difference where you went, whether on a shopping jaunt or just out for a walk, they were right there with Victor Records and autograph books for you to John Hancock."

The hearts of the Japanese did seem to grow fonder during Elman's 15 years absence from the Orient, although the violinist was not always thrilled about the way this affection was manifested. In particular, he objected to the unauthorized use of his name in commercial connections from which he did not benefit. One day, for instance, he was visited by a delegation of executives and salesmen from the Taiyo Radio Manufacturing Company, Ltd., who brought with them a line of combination radio-phonographs bearing the name ELMAN proudly across the front. Elman was neither flattered or amused. He asked them who had granted them permission to use his name, and demanded that they desist. On another occasion, one of the contractors who had presented a string of Elman's recitals had attempted to abscond with the box office receipts, but Elman, ever-vigilant in such matters, managed to prevent him from doing so.

Elman's principal impresario for this Oriental tour was a transplanted European named Strok, who lived in Tokyo and had arranged a grueling schedule. Elman's first appearances were in Tokyo, where five concerts—each with a different program—were scheduled for the 2,700 seat Hibaya Public Hall between January 21 and 27. The programs were similar to those he played in America, but in some cases even a bit more demanding. At the first, he began with sonatas by Handel and Mozart, plus the Lalo *Symphonie Espagnole*. At home, this last would have come after intermission, and would have been followed by the concluding group of shorter works. This time, all three were played in the first half, and after intermission, Elman offered the Bach *Chaconne* and a set of short works—his Chopin-Wilhelmj *Nocturne*, Joachim's arrangement of the Brahms Hungarian Dance No.7, and some Vieuxtemps.[3]

The tour took Elman around Japan, where he, Padwa, and Erion were feted by local mayors, Victor Records representatives, and American ambassadors. From there, the violinist and company left for Korea, where Elman was chagrined to learn that Strok had contracted him into a large new concert hall, but had done so for the fee normally paid in the older, smaller venue. He vented his annoyance in a sarcastic cable that reached Strok on the impresario's birthday. Strok cabled back, "Thank you very much for your birthday greetings."

From Korea, Elman continued on to China for concerts in Peking, Shanghai and a number of other cities; and after a few weeks on the

Asian mainland, he returned to Japan for a final string of concerts before returning home. Some of these were orchestral dates—or, more precisely, combination concerto and solo programs, similar to those he gave at Lewisohn Stadium (but without the intervening orchestral offerings). These were billed as farewell concerts, and were gala affairs. In Osaka and Nagoya, he offered the Beethoven and Mendelssohn Concertos on one program, and the Mozart A major, the Tchaikovsky and the Saint Saëns *Introduction and Rondo capriccioso* on another.

CHAPTER FOURTEEN:

Closer to Home

Elman and Padwa spent virtually the entire concert season in the Orient, returning to New York in May, and they had another voyage immediately ahead of them, a tour of South Africa. By now, the two children, Nadia and Josef, were eleven and eight years old. The Elmans agreed the children were old enough to travel, and since the tour was to take place during the summer months, there would be no conflict with their schooling. Helen and the children also accompanied Elman on his second visit to South America, the summer of 1939.

This second South American tour was more extensive and better planned than the first, and took in a few new countries—among them, Panama and Venezuela. However, when they were about to return home (the start of both the school year and the concert season were imminent) Germany invaded Poland, and the shock from the outbreak of the war in Europe was felt even in the comparative remoteness of Latin America. Because of the uncertainty the war engendered, civilian shipping schedules were disrupted; and when the S.S. Argentina arrived to take them back to New York, the Elmans were shocked to see that it was painted with camouflage.

Elman considered this trip as great a success as the last, and when he returned to New York, he was still aglow with enthusiasm about the Latin audience. "I don't know of any part of the world except the United States that supports music as well as South America," he told a *New York Times* interviewer. "[The continent] already has a splendid musical life, but the future will be tremendous. The European war will cause more and more artists to play there."

Elman had plenty to keep him close to home, and he devoted himself to the war effort by playing concerts for American soldiers encamped in forts around the country. In January 1939, he began an extended period of charity touring and spent nearly four months concertizing in the United States and Canada in aid of refugees from Germany, Poland, Rumania, and neighboring areas.

The tour, which commenced with a gala concert at Carnegie Hall on January 21, and ran until the beginning of May, was a non-sectarian gesture: Elman wanted its beneficiaries to include not only Jews, but Catholic and Protestant refugees as well, so the entire project was overseen by the National Coordinating Committee for Aid to Refugees, a New York based organization chaired by the state's former governor, Alfred E. Smith, and embodying three component organizations—the American Committee for Catholic Refugees from Germany, the American Committee for Christian German Refugees, and the American Jewish Joint Distribution Committee.

Elman estimated that his itinerary, which included concerts in 25 cities, would take him over 15,300 miles, and would involve nearly 400 hours of train travel. What Elman derived from this, of course (beyond the sense that he was participating in a worthy humanitarian endeavor) was a tremendous amount of good will. Typical of the response to his announcement of the tour was the telegram he received from Thomas Mann, who cabled, "The way this great artist is taking an active part in the support of his suffering fellow men by his eminent art seems to me one of the most moving examples of human solidarity and his success will not only be a material one but one of highest moral and symbolic importance." On a less exalted but equally heartfelt level, one German refugee already living in New York knitted a pair of gloves for Elman ("to keep warm those precious hands of his when he starts out on his trip," the accompanying letter explained) and sent them via the office of Mayor Fiorello La Guardia.

Early in January, Elman gave a series interviews in his home—some to newspapers and magazines, which carried stories about the tour, and some to representatives of the National Committee, who used his statements in publicity kits. He held these chats in his upstairs practice studio, in his duplex at 101 Central Park West—the private sanctuary in which he spent his mornings practicing when he was in New York, and a perfect setting for these sober talks. The studio was a spacious room, with a piano and a mahogany desk as its centerpieces. On the wall over the desk were signed photographs from many of Elman's musical friends—among them, Auer, Joachim, Ysaÿe, Godowsky, Rachmaninoff and John McCormack. Also on the wall were an etched portrait of Brahms, and a sketch for a stage set used in a production of Rimsky-Korsakov's *Snow Maiden*. Across the room, his windows overlooked Central Park; and to their sides were book-shelves containing scores on one side and music reference books on the other. Off to the side was a table containing a chess board, set and ready for play.

With so much attention focused on him, Elman decided the make his statement as expansive as possible. Thus, in one of these inter-views, just before the Carnegie Hall gala, he announced that the Men-delssohn Concerto would be the centerpiece of his tour program, and that he would be playing it not only because it was a favorite of his, but because the Nazis had banned its performance in Germany.

"On this tour," he explained, "I shall play the Mendelssohn with a new pride and a special enjoyment, because I play it for a great country where artists are free and privileged to play anything they wish, giving no thought to prejudices of politics or creed. In many countries in the world, I would not be allowed to play this great work, because Men-delssohn, its composer, who lived almost 200 years ago,[1] was a Jew."

The rest of the program was chosen along similar lines. "Since the objective of this tour is a cause so dear to my heart," he said, "I want to play only great pieces of music which I love myself. And when I think of the noblest piece of music I can offer my audiences, I know immediately that I will play for them Beethoven's great 'Kreutzer' Sonata. There is such eternal verity, nobility and so much emotional understanding in this great work. One somehow cannot believe in worldly pettiness and in cruelty when one listens to music like this. It is a sonata which has inspired great novelists like Tolstoy, and great painters and sculptors to create works reflecting its exalted mood. And I hope that in hearing it my audiences may be inspired to uphold anew the human and spiritual values, a spirit of tolerance and under-standing among all people, regardless of race or creed."

The rest of the program was less philosophical, and contained the Franck Sonata, a sonata by Valentini, and an interesting group of short works, including music by Tchaikovsky, Sarasate, and Ernest Bloch (also a Jewish composer), as well as Dinicu's *Hora Staccato*, already a popular encore from Heifetz's repertoire.

Music was hardly the only topic Elman addressed in these inter-views. Rather, his discussions with reporters were infused with patriotism. "Do you know the lines on the Statue of Liberty—'Send these, the homeless, the tempest-tossed to me, lift my lamp beside the golden door'?" he would ask rhetorically in interview after interview, whereupon he would continue by pointing out that "today, these lines have an especially vital meaning, when sad, confused and persecuted victims of Nazi hate look to our land of liberty for succor. We artists especially have learned to appreciate the freedom and generosity which America offers us. Many great writers, great musicians and great scientists have suffered at the hands of the Nazis, and it is America's proud record that we helped refugees from persecution throughout our history. This land was founded by refugees from religious oppression, and since then, we have established a feeling of respect for, and idealism about, their noble purpose. Today, conditions are critical indeed for more than five and a half million oppressed people, and I believe that we in America have a responsibility and an opportunity to offer a gesture of help. We, who live in a free country, must realize how vital are the rights of citizenship, the right to earn a living, and the right to think, and speak, and to make music. We have these privileges; we must therefore help those who are less fortunate."

A great deal of publicity accrued to Elman during the months he toured for the refugees, and even his detractors gave him credit for spending the bulk of the concert season so selflessly engaged. What was not publicized, though, was the fact that Elman's involvement with the refugee cause went beyond the public gesture of donating his concert fees to the cause. While he was undertaking this tour, he and Helen personally sponsored and helped establish in New York about 30 European refugees, and when friends, business associates and acquaintances from Europe landed in New York, traumatized and disoriented, the Elmans were quick to lend a hand.

One of these immigrants was Edgard Feder, a Rumanian attorney who was also a cellist, conductor and music critic, and who came to New York at the start of the war with his wife Jeri, an American who had been raised in Paris. Feder's father had been the Central European impresario for Elman, Heifetz and dozens of other artists; and while his father saw to the business side of these soloists' visits, Edgard was often given then task of seeing to their social needs—taking them to restaurants, nightclubs and shows, or even simply on drives through Bucharest or into the countryside, and arranging whatever other forms of amusement they required.

It was Edgard Feder, in fact, who brought Jascha Heifetz to see the Rumanian violinist Grigoras Dinicu (over Heifetz's protests, at first: he was not interested in hearing another violinist at the moment); and he helped Heifetz transcribe Dinicu's famous *Hora Staccato*. The elder

Feder did not want his son to enter the music business, despite his love for music and musicians, so he sent him to Paris to study law. There he met and married Jeri, and it was from Paris that the Feders left for America.

"When we came to the United States," Jeri Feder recalls, "we were war refugees. But we knew all the artists. When they were in Paris, we played host and hostess. That's how Helen Elman and I became friends. When the war broke out, we found ourselves in America, but my husband could not practice law here. He contacted Jascha Heifetz, who had been like a brother to him in Bucharest—they were together every moment when Heifetz was there. And he contacted Mischa, and whoever else he knew who was in New York. But of all these people, we found that the only real friends we had—the only ones who responded—were Mischa and Helen." "Mischa did many things that showed his warmth and loyalty, and the authenticity of his friendship," Edgard Feder adds. "When I went to Immigration, he came with me as my witness. I was embarrassed about that, because I knew it might take a long time, and I knew he was busy preparing for his concerts. But he came and he sat with me patiently."

Elman did the same for Carl Flesch, who immigrated in 1940. At that time, he provided an affidavit which said of Flesch that "his presence in the United States would be a great asset to our musical culture."

During the charity tour, critics who disliked aspects of his playing either avoided the concerts, or drew a veil of kindness over their descriptions. Many appearances were outright critical triumphs—for instance, a Brahms Concerto he played with Barbirolli and the New York Philharmonic in February was described by the *New York Times* critic as a "searching and soulful interpretation" that was "marked by sensitive restraint," and was in every way a "finely conceived and expertly delivered performance."

This was, however, merely a hiatus in the storm of critical dissent that had gathered by the mid-1930s, and which re-emerged in the early 1940s. By now many reviewers stood firmly opposed to Elman on interpretive and stylistic grounds. In technical matters, the complaints were fewer; indeed, many who wrote searing reviews conceded that Elman was in fine shape technically, and the recordings from the mid-1930s confirm that he continued in good form.

His previous visit with the New York Philharmonic yielded reviews that bear some witness to the change in taste. With Barbirolli on the podium, Elman played on two programs in December 1937 and January 1938, the first featuring him in the Beethoven Concerto, the second in the Tchaikovsky. The reviews did not focus much on the Tchaikovsky: the reviewer for the *Herald Tribune* noted simply that the first movement seemed slow and rhythmically rigid, but that the rest was beyond reproach. The Beethoven performance, though, drew barbs. One was the attack on Elman's cadenzas by Olin Downes, in the *Times*, quoted earlier. Downes's colleague at the *Herald Tribune*, Lawrence Gilman, seemed hardly to notice the cadenzas, but found the account unimaginative and short on insight. "Mr. Elman," he wrote, "unfortunately did not scale [the work's heights] last evening.... Not only did he sentimentalize the nobility of the melodic line, but he distorted the time-values of the notes, so that the purity and elevation of the musical thought were marred and Tchaikovskyized."

A few weeks later, Elman's Carnegie Hall recital inspired another *Herald Tribune* critic, Jerome D. Bohm, to add his voice to those who found certain of Elman's readings objectionable, although his angle of attack was somewhat different. Elman, he opined, "is no longer the fiery virtuoso, whose emotional excesses formerly were wont to cause the more discriminating of his admirers to shake their heads in pained disapproval. On the contrary, his interpretations of [Brahms, Handel, and Bach sonatas] were subdued and almost always without the touches of the sentimentality which formerly marred much of his work.... Yet, despite his discreet treatment of all this music, it was only fitfully that the composer's intentions were veraciously realized."

What the reviewer missed this time was the loftiness and exuberance in the Handel, and he felt that both Elman and Padwa had failed to comprehend the impulses of the Brahms. Elman was also, he complained, unsuited to the stylistic requirements of unaccompanied Bach playing. In 1940, the same reviewer covered another Carnegie Hall recital, and lamented that Elman's playing lacked some of the excitement it had in those halcyon days "when his interpretations, despite their emotional excesses and sentimentality, carried the listener away because of the fiery temperament and astounding virtuosity which pervaded them." What he heard, seemingly, was a performance that retained certain stylistic sins—particularly an excessive rhythmic freedom in the Bach-Nachez G minor Concerto—but which had somehow lost both the zest and poetry he had once found in Elman's readings.

"I would not really say that Elman's approach to music was old-fashioned by that time," Edgard Feder recalls, "but yes, he did have some problems with the critics, who did not understand what was behind his playing. How did he feel about this? Well, I remember once someone asked him what he thought of reviewers, and his reply was, 'why don't you ask a lamp-post what it thinks about dogs.'"

There were, in fact, a few instances where Elman had recourse in the matter of a negative review, and where revenge was available, he took it. The Steinway piano company, for instance, published and distributed the *Steinway Review of Permanent Music*, containing record reviews. In 1941, its reviewer, R. D. Darrell, found Elman's recording of the Fauré Sonata objectionable. Elman, in a letter to Theodore E. Steinway, objected to Darrell's review. Feeling that the goodwill of a major artist (even though he was not a pianist) was more valuable than a relationship with a reviewer or the editorial integrity of the publication, Steinway took a cowardly route, and wrote to Elman that the company would "discontinue sponsoring Mr. Darrell's review, as we can see that it puts us in an anomalous position towards our valued friends." However, the criticism aimed at Elman's playing was hardly a blanket indictment of his work or his style. It was, actually, rather selective and fairly consistent, and reading through the reviews Elman received throughout the 1940s, a clear pattern emerges. In works by the Romantic and early 20th century composers, his readings generally won critical praise, while his performances of Baroque and Classic works were almost invariably censured.

There were exceptions on both sides of that stylistic dividing line, naturally; and there were some critics who could not abide Elman's performances at all, while others continued to write enthusiastically of everything he played. Olin Downes, for instance, returned to the Elman fold immediately after his negative Beethoven review. Noel Straus, another *Times* writer, was also generally happy with the Elman concerts he heard, although he, too, sometimes expressed reservations about the violinist's Bach.

Also in the Elman court, though, were quite a few musicians—not all of them Elman's old colleagues from the turn of the century. One performer of a younger generation who remembers Elman's performances of the early 1940s fondly is Earl Wild, today one of the last champions of the grand Romantic style among concert pianists. Between 1937 and 1942, Wild (who was born in 1915) was working as a staff pianist for NBC, where his duties included orchestral performances with Toscanini and the NBC Symphony, and accompanying solo artists in radio recitals when their own accompanists were unavailable. Wild accompanied Elman in several of these radio concerts, and recalling his encounters with Elman some four decades later, he described their working relationship as quite pleasant.

"He was very easy to work with, very thoughtful and gentle," the pianist says, "although I remember that when he did get angry about something it was amusing, because his voice was high-pitched, and it got higher when he got upset. Between us, though, there were really no difficult times. If, at a rehearsal, I did not comply with his wishes, he would stop and point out what he wanted, and we would try it again. Naturally, I had to give in—there was no question about that. Yes, he would linger on a note if it especially pleased him. He was of the old school, and a pianist working with him had to listen closely and, where possible, anticipate what he would do.

"But I like that kind of flexibility in music," Wild adds. "It's almost gone today. So is the kind of tone Elman produced. Everyone talks about his tone—it's often the one thing people mention in connection with him. But it's true, it was a glorious sound, and I haven't heard anything like it since Elman. I haven't heard interpretations as beautiful as his in certain works he was associated with, either. The Tchaikovsky Concerto was one. He really believed in it, and his performances were so much better, so much more moving than anything you hear today.

"I associated him with Kreisler, in a way. Both of them had such a marvelous, personal way of playing. When they played, it was as if they were playing for you, personally. Milstein falls into that category too, he was the last of that school. I heard all the others, but I was not impressed. Huberman, for instance—I expected a great deal from him, and he performed wonderful technical feats. But he didn't have the style, or the desire to project beauty that the three I mentioned had. Heifetz, of course, was always set aside. His was a different kind of playing. It was wonderful. But it was different."

It was indeed, and if Elman's and Heifetz's styles were diverging in 1917, when Heifetz arrived on the American scene, the chasm between them widened with the decades. Elman believed he was modernizing his own performing style, but he was wary of taking modernization too far. For him, a performance had to be undeniably expressive if it were to be considered truly musical; and it could not be expressive unless the artist branded it with his own stamp. Heifetz undoubtedly believed this too, but the signature stamp he put on the works he played was a more subtle one. And if Elman's seemingly more sentimental approach proved more successful with the South American audiences during the Elman-Heifetz face off in the summer of 1934, it was less popular in the United States. At home, Heifetz was winning the battle for the public, and decisively.

"Elman did resent Heifetz," recalls Edgard Feder. "The rivalry between them was obvious. But no-one could say a word against Heifetz in Elman's presence. He would say, 'No—I can say something, but you cannot.' He knew that Heifetz was a great violinist, there was no question about it. And he was also fully aware that as a virtuoso, Heifetz had it over him. He was younger than Elman, and it showed.

"Of course, there were other reasons Heifetz captured the public's attention in a way that Elman could not," adds Feder. "Heifetz's life was very colorful. He rode horses, he made movies, and in any number of ways, he stayed in the public eye. He was more of a glamor boy, not only as a violinist, but as a person. At the same time, there was an aloofness about him—something that made him seem more mysterious, and therefore more desireable. Elman, on the other hand, lived a very quiet life. This is not to put either of them down; but there are a number of aspects one can look at when considering the difference in their appeal."

❖ ❖ ❖ ❖ ❖

The quiet life Elman led was fairly regimented by this time, and as he spent more time in New York, his daily routine solidified. By 8:30 in the morning, he was reading the *Times* over a cup of coffee, and by nine he would have climbed the circular staircase that led up to the studio, and taken up his violin. Alone, he worked on basic technical exercises, even at that advanced stage of his career, and he continued to do so until the day he died.

"My father was a perfectionist, who never took himself for granted," says Josef Elman, whose bedroom was next to Elman's studio, and who grew up hearing the daily routine. "He would begin with scales and exercises, and he would play these for 45 minutes or an hour before even looking at any of his recital material. And he would play the things over and over again. If, in a scale, there was a slight error that nobody but he would notice, he would play it again. His discipline, and the kind of equilibrium that kind of work must have taken over a period of 60 years, was one of the most remarkable things about him."

Elman's accompanist would arrive at 10 o'clock, and they would either play through their current program or through a concerto. Most days, they would also read through works that weren't scheduled for performance—selections that had appeared on programs in past years, and new works that had either been sent to Elman, or which he had collected on a recent music shopping trip. After three hours, Elman and his pianist would stop work for the day. Elman would head into midtown (sometimes with his pianist, sometimes alone) for lunch at the Russian Tea Room before making his way to an instrument shop, where he would either have some repairs done, have a bridge made, or simply discuss recent concerts and listen to younger players trying out instruments.

Besides practicing, this was Elman's favorite part of the day. Even on tour, he never tired of finding violin shops and having bridges made, and by the time he died, he had collected literally thousands of bridges from around the world, made of German, English, Japanese, Danish, Brazilian and Norwegian wood, among dozens more varieties. These bridges were, for Elman, souvenirs of his travels, and he could reach into the box, pull one out and identify its origin, even if it were 20 years old. He would also discourse on each bridge's usefulness or lack thereof.

"A bridge does affect the sound of the fiddle, depending on the thickness, the height and the wood," confirms Jacques Francais, the New York luthier whose grandfather had sold Elman his 1717 Strad. "And at the end of his career, when he started to use metal strings, he began to place the bridge lower. Metal strings are easier to play, and he resisted using them until the last three years of his life. The gut strings, after all, are more flexible, but they have a tendency to buzz on the fingerboard, so you have to keep the bridge [and therefore, the string tension] high. Metal strings do not buzz, so you can lower the bridge and get away with it. Many violinists switch to metal strings in their later years.

"But Elman was just as fussy, whether using metal or gut strings. He always knew what he wanted to get out of the instrument. In the years before he changed to metal strings, he came in often to have all kinds of repairs done. He was very sensitive to the most minute changes in sound, and would come in to change the bridge, or move the soundpost—he might spend an hour fiddling with the soundpost until it suited him. And by the time he was finished, he had accomplished what he wanted. Sometimes the changes were very small, but he knew what he was looking for. Eventually, we were able to get a feeling for his requirements; but even then, the adjustments were often so minute that it was difficult to satisfy him. After it was done, we could say, 'oh yes, he was right—he wasn't dreaming.'

"One of the interesting things about his playing, though," Francais continues, "was that as fussy as he was about the details of the soundpost and the bridge, he could actually produce that famous tone of his on *anything*. You could give him a wooden box, a $200 dollar fiddle, and he could make it sound like a million dollars. Of all the violinists I've ever met, his sound was the most characteristic, and the most beautiful."

Variations on Elman's daily regimen were few. Weekends, he would work in the morning and spend the rest of the day playing through Wagner or Puccini operas at the piano, playing with the children (who, by now, were beginning to show some interest in music—Nadia at the piano, and Josef on the violin), or reading. Sunday afternoons, he listened (or often dozed) to the New York Philharmonic broadcasts; and late in the afternoon, his accompanist would come by, play a game or two of chess, then read through some music.

Among the few exceptions to this schedule were the Jewish high holidays. While not extremely religious, Elman tried to be observant; but he was not always successful at putting observance before music. One Yom Kippur, when work of any sort is forbidden, he decided to practice in his studio with a mute on the violin. After a while, Helen came in and told him that by practicing on the holiday, he was setting a bad example for the children. He then took his violin and mute into a bathroom, and continued practicing there, even more quietly. "I suppose you think God won't hear you in there," Helen kidded him. But the compulsion to practice was hard to suppress.

Sometimes, friends were invited to his practice sessions, particularly in the weeks before a New York recital. "One thing that always struck me," says Edgard Feder, recalling those private concerts, "was that the music he used never had a mark on it—not a bowing, a fingering, or a phrasing indication. It was entirely clean. I asked about that, and he said, simply, 'I don't need it. Once I have the music, it's engraved, frozen in my head. I know what I want to do, and I use the music only as a guide.' In other words, his playing was not a matter of reflex muscular reactions. He knew what he was doing at all times, and it didn't matter if he used the same bowing and fingerings from one time to the next. It was like watching a cat always landing on its feet: As he went through the musical discourse, the music itself would seem to dictate everything about the performance—what position to use, how he should accent a particular phrase, or whether he should use *portamento*.

"He did all this with a bow arm control that was absolutely incredible, and which I have never seen with another artist. I remember, for instance, watching him play the Mendelssohn Concerto. Just before the second theme, there is a long, sustained G. He would take this G on a single bow, without changing. It seemed like the bow would never end, yet there was no reduction of intensity or in the quality of the sound. Even the so-called steely-fingered virtuoso violinists of today cannot do that. That was part of his greatness."

❖ ❖ ❖ ❖ ❖

A sad disruption in Elman's routine came with the death of Saul Elman, on May 26, 1940. Saul had stepped away from his son's business affairs entirely after the real estate debacle of the late 1920s, and he began his retirement by setting about the task of reconstructing the story of Mischa's rise to fame. In 1933, he published a private edition of these recollections, *The Memoirs of Mischa Elman's Father*, and distributed copies to friends. His retirement was not entirely pleasant, though. Because of complications due to diabetes (which Mischa later inherited), he had lost one of his legs. But to the end, he followed his son's career with the enthusiasm of a fan, and he continued to delight in the letters his son sent him from around the globe. Having shared so many trials together during the violinist's early years, the two remained extremely close until Saul's death, at age 76.

Another shakeup in Elman's life came two months later, when he resolved to dismiss Padwa—or, to give Padwa the option of leaving their partnership or changing the tenor of his family's politics. Padwa's wife was a member of the Communist Party, and vocal about it; but Padwa himself complicated matters by steadfastly retaining his Estonian citizenship despite having lived so long in the United States. Now Estonia was about to come under Soviet jurisdiction, and Padwa would therefore be a Russian subject. It was some time before the McCarthy era and its Communist witch hunts, but even then, the United States government was looking closely at those with radical affiliations. In 1939, Elman and Padwa played at the White House to the applause of the President; but in 1940, the government was sending investigators to question Elman about his pianist's loyalty.

At the end of July, Elman wrote Padwa a pained letter, pointing out that the pianist was about to become a Russian subject, and noting that he had advised Padwa on several occasions to seek American citizenship. "At this particular time," he wrote, "I feel very strongly that though you are ready and eager to accept all the advantages this country has to offer, you are not ready to do your share should this country be in need—and believe me, this country is in need right now of everyone's unquestioned support." He added that "socially, musically and artistically, I could not have wished for a happier association," but in the end, the choice was simple: If Padwa could not see his way clear to becoming an American citizen, Elman would no longer work with him. Padwa declined to seek citizenship at that time, and although he and Elman remained friendly, and even continued to play chess and meet socially, their musical association ended. In his place, Elman hired Leopold Mittman, who accompanied him for the next six years.

CHAPTER FIFTEEN:

The Search for Renewal

Hectic though the touring of the 1930s was for Elman, he tried to keep an ear open for new literature. Within the standard repertoire, he already played the major works, and other scores by the great composers either failed to catch his imagination, or didn't seem to sit well with the other works on his programs. There were, of course, a few exceptions. The Debussy and Fauré sonatas, for instance, were new additions to his repertoire in 1941, when they turned up on the first recitals he played with Mittman. And three seasons later, he added the sonata by Richard Strauss to his list.

What he really needed, though, was some contemporary music, preferably, a concerto or an extended concert work by a composer of stature. Quite regularly, he received works from composers who admired his playing and hoped he would take up one of their pieces, and while he occasionally added one or two of the shorter, more melodic pieces to his tour programs, more often than not he filed away the music after writing the composers notes of thanks, often with a helpful suggestion or two about directions they might pursue in their future violin works.

As the 1940s began, the need for new works began to weigh heavily on Elman's mind. In the abstract, the process involved selecting a composer, requesting a work, coming to terms (both financial and aesthetic), waiting for the piece to be completed, then learning and performing it. But of course, it's often more complicated than that, particularly when the performer's tastes are as strongly defined as Elman's. An avid concertgoer, and a regular listener to both the New York Philharmonic's and the Boston Symphony's radio broadcasts, Elman was well aware of the course contemporary composition was taking. And he didn't like it.

To Elman, the new breed of composers was eschewing the musical values he held most crucial—beauty of sound, transparency of structure, and a sense of communication that allowed the performer to serve as a connection between the composer's heart and the listener's. An indication of his feelings on the matter is embodied in a news release that his manager, Charles L. Wagner, sent to the *New York Times* in February 1933, presumably with the violinist's approval. It begins with an aggressive pronouncement: "Modern music impresses Mischa Elman as nothing but noise and unpleasant discord." There followed a few kind words about the music of John Alden Carpenter and Ernest Bloch, but in bulk the release was an astonishing diatribe against modernism. "Mr. Elman regrets that the violin repertoire is limited, but he will not agree to play modern works which are uninspired, colorless and formless, nor will he extend encouragement to the composer without talent."

Elman's attitudes may have softened by the early 1940s. Still, he detested music that was overtly experimental, and he continued to say so to the end of his days. "Beethoven didn't experiment," he told an interviewer in 1959, "he expanded. He grew out of Haydn and Mozart. He went further, but he still is very close to them. His early works are still like Mozart and Haydn. Now, Gluck started using the leitmotif, and again, Wagner took advantage of it and expanded on it."[1]

Asked, during the same interview, whether music should be primarily intellectual or emotional, Elman replied, "You might just as well ask this: should music be performed to an audience? If music needs and audience, then that audience must feel something. Do you think that an audience will sit there trying to figure out how [a composer] wrote that fugue? How many voices he brought in there? Is the form perfect?.... An audience wants to feel something, and not unless they feel something will they come to hear you. You only drive them away from music.

"I am criticized," he added, "[by those who say that] I don't encourage young composers—that I am not making a contribution. But I say, my contribution is a much greater one, because when they play that terrible stuff, the audience stays away. To bring people back again and to enlarge the audience seems to me a much greater contribution."

In another interview, from 1966, Elman's expression of distaste for modernism went even farther. "Today we are living in a materialistic world, and that materialism is amply represented in the quality of modern music," he said, adding that "there has been a lack of interest, in general in string instruments, because most modern composers don't like melody. A string instrument is the nearest thing to the voice, and must have melody. A violin can't stand cacophony and dissonance. Beethoven and Brahms were original without resorting to ugly harmonies which to us make no sense whatsoever. People in music today, in order to be original, must be phony."[2]

Elman did, on occasion, discuss what he liked and expected in musical works, although his predilections are easily gleaned from his repertoire list. In an article he wrote for the "Sunday Forum" column of the *New York Herald Tribune*, in 1961, he succinctly described the qualities he looked for:

"What 'good music' is defies analysis. For me its essential quality is the ability to touch the heart, and in so doing add to the humanity of the hearer. For others, the essential quality may be its ability to amuse, beguile, capture the imagination or stimulate the mind. Different aspects of our marvelously varied heritage of music will speak to us at different times in our lives, if we will but open our minds and hearts to listen. Some we will treasure forever; some may not awaken a response in us till later; and some we may in time put aside, as children growing up put aside once cherished toys. The important thing, I believe, is to realize that for any individual, good music is that which, because it gives him pleasure, enriches him emotionally, spiritually or intellectually, adds to the sum total of his pleasure in living."

Back in the 1930s, Elman felt that the currents of the Second Viennese School, for instance, were not likely to enrich anyone's pleasure in living. Yet, he was able to admire the sincerity with which the Serialists were capturing the world around them—a world Elman knew was changing for the worse, and which must have been terrifying for artists whose work incurred the Nazis' displeasure, as of course the music of the "decadent" Serialists did. He was curious enough about the music of Alban Berg, for instance, to attend an intimate gathering, in March 1936, at the New York apartment of his old friend Leopold Godowsky. Godowsky had invited Elman to hear the violinist Louis Krasner and his accompanist give a preview reading of the Berg violin concerto, which Krasner was about to unveil at the ISCM Festival in Barcelona.

Krasner met Berg during his student days in Vienna, and had become friendly with the composer; but he recalls that Berg was at first against the idea of writing a violin concerto, suggesting that what a young violinist needed was a Romantic showpiece. Krasner prevailed, eventually convincing Berg with the argument that a violin concerto might be just the thing to persuade an skeptical public that the 12-tone movement could produce works of immediately palpable emotional depth.

Krasner's rationalization appealed to him, and coincided with a tragic, moving event—the death of Manon Gropius, the 18-year old daughter of Alma Mahler and Walter Gropius. What he produced was an almost programmatic piece, and one of the most touching works in the 12-tone style. The first part, a tender *Andante* and a lively *Allegretto*, is meant as a portrait of young Manon. In the second part, the *Allegro* represents her tragic death, and in the closing *Adagio*, the trenchant violin line ruminates on a Bach choral, "Es ist genug," from Cantata 61—a quotation which, juxtaposed amid Berg's 12-tone writing, is an emotionally powerful touch.

The music is also suffused with a brand of melancholy that may reflect Berg's distress at what was happening in Europe; and one current analytical theory suggests that a hidden program within this final work of Berg's indicates that he considered it a Requiem not only for Manon Gropius, but for himself.[3] Upon hearing Krasner play the work, Elman professed admiration for it. "But," as Krasner recalls, he "wondered whether this music, which obviously represented and portrayed the ugly and terrorizing climate now gripping Europe, might not sound more authentic and more convincing if we played it more caustically in sound, i.e. 'less beautifully.' It should be realized that this reaction was not without its logic at the time!"[4]

Of course, even if he liked Berg's concerto in Krasner's hands, it wasn't a work he was keen on getting under his fingers; and at any rate, Krasner had the right of exclusivity for several years.

For awhile, in the early part of 1942, Elman maintained a friendly correspondence with the American composer Roy Harris, who was at work on a violin sonata for him. The work was completed at the end of June, and Elman wrote to Harris that he received the final two movements on July 8. Strangely, there is little in Elman's side of this correspondence to indicate his feelings about the sonata, and although he never performed the work publicly, he read through it at one of his practice sessions with Joseph Seiger some 20 years later. Seiger's impression was that he liked it, but could never quite find a suitable way to program it.

It wasn't until January 1943—and only by chance—that Elman found a composer whose music he could comfortably champion. Arriving in New York at the end of a tour, he took a cab from Pennsylvania Station to his home on Central Park West, but asked the cab driver to take him past Carnegie Hall so he could see what the evening's program offered. He had been hoping, actually, to hear the Boston Symphony play the Shostakovich Seventh, having grown fond of Shostakovich in recent years; but instead, the billboard announced that the orchestra would play the First Symphony of Bohuslav Martinů, a Czech composer who was a year older than Elman, and who had come to New York in 1941. Elman didn't know a thing about Martinů, but he was curious. Stopping at his apartment only long enough to leave his bags with the doorman, he returned directly to Carnegie Hall to hear the performance.

He was impressed with the Martinů symphony, a work that struck him as rooted in its own time, yet which pays homage to the long tradition of symphonic form. Elman was also impressed by the fact that the audience's response was enthusiastic, and the next day he contacted the conductor Serge Koussevitzky, who had conducted the performance (Martinů's First Symphony is dedicated to the memory of Nathalie Koussevitzky), and who agreed that Martinů would undoubtedly provide the sort of work Elman was seeking. Elman contacted Martinů immediately, and broached the subject of a commission.

Martinů was not eager at first. Eleven years earlier he had undertaken the task of composing a violin concerto for the American violinist Samuel Dushkin, with whom he had become friendly in Paris. He had wrestled with the piece for two years, and eventually abandoned it. In its place, he offered Dushkin the *Suite Concertante* for Violin and Orchestra, completed in 1937. Upon his arrival in the United States, he tried again to accommodate Dushkin, but his second attempt at a full-blown violin concerto also ended in a compromise, the *Concerto da camera*, scored for solo violin, piano, percussion and string orchestra. This, Martinů's first American work, was completed in 1941, and had its premiere in Basel, Switzerland, the following January. Meanwhile, the composer and Dushkin reworked the *Suite Concertante*. That was as far as his first attempt at a violin concerto went.

Nevertheless, when Elman called, Martinů agreed to consider the matter, but he naturally wanted to hear Elman play and discuss the projected work with him. They met several times, usually at Elman's home. Their first meeting, however, took place at Martinů's apartment on 58th Street, near the Plaza Hotel, and is described in detail by Miloš Šafránek, in his authorized biography of the composer:

> The two artists had some difficulty in coming to an understanding. Elman was somewhat stumped by Martinů's taciturnity and, in an attempt to bring the conversation to what he had come for, he asked Martinů if he had heard any of the world-famous violinists: Kreisler, Huberman, Heifetz and others. Martinů's reply, though as a member of the Czech Philharmonic in Prague he must have heard most contemporary virtuosi, was in the negative. Hesitatingly, Elman put the question directly: "And have you heard me?" "No," was the answer. And so Elman had no other choice than to invite the composer to his studio and play for him. Martinů listened very attentively and...a general idea of what the concerto should be like took shape in his mind. The impression that he gained was that Elman was "a violinist, heart and soul, and that his tone, which never exceeded the limits of beauty of violin tone, had a special magic." On laying down the violin, Elman naturally expected some comment. But the silence remained unbroken and, as Elman told me afterwards, Martinů looked as noncommittal as a sphinx. Thereupon Elman rose and the two artists took awkward leave of each other.[5]

The ensuing correspondence between Elman and Martinů indicates that at first their relationship was formal indeed—at least, until after the commission was agreed upon and underway. On January 15, 1943, Elman sent the composer a note confirming the commission, setting the price of the work at $1,000, plus $100 for each performance of the Concerto with orchestra. Martinů acknowledged the note with one that says, essentially, "why don't you call me Bo, and I'll call you Mischa?" Thereafter, their relations grew warmer, and in their discussions about the work, Elman wisely left all matters of form and content entirely in Martinů's hands, his only request being that the first movement include a cadenza, towards the end.

Martinů completed the score in four months, and provided Elman with cadenzas for all three movements. Šafránek spent some time with Martinů during that period, and at one point he asked the composer to describe the Concerto's character. "Violin," was all Martinů had to say about it; but as Šafránek comments, that terse response "summed up its whole form and quality."

When he received the finished score, Elman was thrilled. During their meetings, Martinů had obviously assimilated the hallmarks of Elman's interpretive style, and on playing through the work with Leopold Mittman, Elman found it perfectly suited to his temperament and taste. The work's opening bars immediately establish the score's mid-20th century provenance, the first sound heard being a brashly dissonant and widely voiced chord, played loudly by the orchestra. The depth of the introduction's darkness is immediately dispelled, though, by a solo violin line that, from its very first bars, demands both virtuosity and lyricism. The passage work is quick, and its range is wide, but its feeling of line and its sense of urgency mark it as a heady statement, not merely a vehicle for superficial display.

If the brashness of the opening evaporates, the somewhat cloudy mood of the work is retained through the first movement's *tutti* sections, and the violin's long-lined interjections seem to provide an argument of sorts—equally serious and sometimes as troubled, yet more overtly beautiful, as if to assert that hope and humanity were not beyond reach. It seems, in fact, that Elman's playing had the same effect on Martinů than it had on Carl Sandburg some 25 years earlier, for the message here is virtually the same as the one Sandburg encapsulated so succinctly and directly in "*Bath.*"

The second movement, *Andante moderato*, is gentler, yet still dark-toned and thick-textured. Here too, the violin intercedes with singing and often elegant lines, and in the finale the tense mood is punctuated by sections cast in vibrant Bohemian dance rhythms, poured forth by both the solo violin and the orchestra, ending on a vehement, if not entirely optimistic, note.

Martinů's own program note not only describes the work in formal terms, but discusses, at considerable length, the problems facing a contemporary concerto composer:

> The idea for this concerto presented itself to me in the following order—*Andante*, a broad lyric song of great intensity which leads to an *Allegro* exploiting the technique and the virtuosity of the instrument, and has the aspect of a single-movement composition. The definitive form complies with concerto structure. I have preserved its serious character, lyric in the first part; and even in the middle *Allegro* the *Andante* theme returns to end the movement. The second part is a sort of point of rest, a bridge progressing towards the *Allegro* finale. It is an *Intermezzo moderato*, almost bucolic, accompanied by only a part of the orchestra and progress-

ing *attacca* into the finale, which is *Allegro*. This favors the technique of the violin, which is interrupted by broad and massive *tutti* passages. The concerto ends with a sort of *stretto, Allegro vivo*.

I should like to add a few points which came to me as I composed it and which might throw a little light on that most difficult problem—writing a violin concerto. As with all compositions for solo instrument, the solo violin requires a quite special "state of mind." A piano solo allows us to preserve the image of the musical thought in its full scope, that is to say, almost complete with harmony, polyphony, color and the dynamics of orchestral structure. For the violin solo, all that we wish to express must be contained in a single line, which must also imply the rest. To put it differently, the single part of the violin solo must in itself already contain the whole musical scheme, the whole concerto. We have in musical literature certain types of violin concertos which I could define as concertos which exploit beauty of tone against an orchestral background (as in Mozart), or a concerto which exploits the sonority of the solo instrument together with the orchestra; there are also those where the violin is exploited from a professional point of view without much originality of composition. Finally, there are those concertos in which one exploits the orchestra and adds a violin solo, without paying too much attention to its inherent tonal beauties. It is at this point that the problem becomes confused. In working with the orchestra we have lost the capacity of "thinking solo." We become accustomed to having at our disposal the variegated possibilities of the orchestra, which more often than not become an inducement to "express something"; that is to say, the emotional elements, inevitably tending towards intensity of accent and dynamics, result in a confusion, as these elements serve to intensify not the real musical content but the dynamics of tone, sound and power. This we can do with an orchestra, but we cannot do it so easily with a solo instrument, least of all with a violin solo. A melody whose structure fulfills the function of a string orchestra is not necessarily a melody which will be adequate for the violin solo. The dynamics, nuances and the difference between *p-mf-f* of the violin solo are limited and in no way comparable to the dynamic power of the string orchestra. In short, we confound a single violin with a group of violins, with a resulting conflict between desire and ability. It is just here that a composition requires a different state of mind for its whole structure and for the content of the musical idea.

Here the motivation of the actual music—dynamic, romantic—cannot help us much. We find ourselves faced with the old problem of music as music, "absolute music," as against expres-

sive music (in the literal sense of expressing "something"). But this
is a problem where misunderstanding as so often arises from the
confusion of "words." My only wish has been to touch upon one
of the questions which is bound to occupy a composer when he
undertakes a violin concerto, and it is not to be assumed from what
I have said that I have solved this problem in my composition. I
am far from making any such pretension. My wish was to draw
attention to this question which has filled my thoughts, and the
thoughts of many others, during composition.[6]

   With Martinů's violin concerto in hand, Elman had to find a conductor willing to give the work its premiere—something that turned
out to be more of a problem than he had expected. He approached
several conductors without much luck, although there were certainly
a few nibbles. Hans Kindler, for instance, found the score interesting
and hoped to give it its premiere with the National Symphony, in
Washington; but as he wrote to Elman, at the end of June, 1943, the orchestra simply couldn't afford the $1,000 fee Elman was asking. Elman
wrote back that the quoted fee was significantly less than he was paid
by any other orchestra—at least, for Beethoven, Brahms and
Tchaikovsky concertos—but Kindler merely expressed his regrets.
Elman also gave a reading for Stokowski, with the *New York Times*
critic Olin Downes present, and Stokowski expressed admiration for
the score. Unfortunately, he had problems of his own. Having left the
Philadelphia Orchestra in 1938, he was between posts and by no
means at the peak of his ever rising and falling popularity.[7]
   Of course, the natural choice of conductor and orchestra was Serge
Koussevitzky, who brought Elman and Martinů together in the first
place. Around the same time Kindler declined, Koussevitzky accepted, and the performances were scheduled for New Year's Eve, in
Boston, and as part of the Boston Symphony's January 6, 1944 program
at Carnegie Hall. There was one potential scheduling conflict: Artur
Rodzinski had scheduled the New York Philharmonic premiere of
Martinů's previous effort for violin and orchestra, the *Concerto da
camera*, for January 7 and 8. This was, as Martinů could see, a problem,
and in a letter to Elman dated August 8, he offered to speak with Koussevitzky.
   In the event, the *Concerto da camera* performance was cancelled, but
not without a tradeoff: Rodzinski scheduled the Second Symphony for
the last days of December, conflicting with the premiere of the violin

concerto in Boston. The Second Symphony had already been given its world premiere, by the Cleveland Orchestra under Leinsdorf, the previous October; but a New York premiere was important, and the Violin Concerto would be in town a week later—so Martinů stayed in New York for the symphony performances. Backstage at Carnegie Hall, on December 31, he listened to a broadcast performance of the concerto, from Boston; but the New York performance of the symphony ended midway through the Boston performance of the violin concerto, and Martinů was obliged to leave his radio to go on stage to take a bow.

Elman did have Martinů's full attention during his preparations for the premiere, although he was a little surprised to find that Martinů's ideas about how he wanted the performance to sound were somewhat vague. Not that this bothered Elman; rather, it added fuel to one of his own favorite arguments about the creative role of the interpretive artist; and in interviews thereafter, he invoked Martinů's reticence as a parable through which interpretive liberties could be almost universally justified. In the early 1960s, for instance, he complained to an interviewer about critics who attend concerts with scores, citing his experience with Martinů as proof that listeners bearing scores are not always on the inside track:

"As an interpreter, and as one who has played many compositions now in the standard repertory with the composer himself," he asserted, "I can tell you that the composer is sometimes at a complete loss to know what markings he should put down. I introduced a new concerto by Martinů which I commissioned him to write.... I played from the manuscript during rehearsals. On one or two occasions—it is a complicated score, nothing but dissonances—Koussy was not sure whether one of the instruments was playing the right note. Koussy turned to Martinů and asked, 'what do you want there?' Martinů said, 'I don't know.' This is a true story. Later, I was looking over the concerto again and I noticed something which I did not pay much attention to before, that Martinů did not mark the tempo of the second movement, so I called him up and said, 'Bohuslav, tell me what tempo do you want there?' and he said, 'I don't know whether I should make it *Andante* or *Allegretto*.

"Bach never specified tempo. He depended upon the interpreter to feel the music. If you communicate, it must be the right tempo. The moment you don't communicate, then it is not the right tempo. Bach knew he was dealing with good musicians, people who had good taste and musical culture, and so he left it to each one to interpret the way he felt that music. That is the only way to make music. After all, a real musician is not like a wholesale dress store that sells copies. We don't sell copies. We want to be original. But in our originality, we have to show good taste."[8]

The critics—with or without scores—were out in force when Elman, Koussevitzky and the Boston Symphony brought the Violin Concerto to Carnegie Hall on January 6, and the reviews, while generally kind to Elman, were mixed. Paul Bowles, writing in the *Herald Tribune*, offered the most scathing assessment of the work. Saying that it is "not the best that the distinguished Czech composer has done for us," he added that it "gives, on first hearing, the impression of being a hastily conceived and dispatched opus; moreover, the solo writing is rather less brilliant than the orchestral work, and this is true to such an extent that at times one thinks of the violin as an annoying insect whose sound the orchestra sometimes manages to chase away." Arthur V. Berger, in the *Sun* was less caustic: "It works admirably for the interpreter, it fits the instrument, it moves with a natural and unforced suavity, it has a warm and earnest outer coating," he wrote; yet in the final analysis, he found that the score "lacks depth, genuine harmonic direction, and most of all, long melodic lines." In fact, only Olin Downes, of the *Times*, was thoroughly enthusiastic. Calling the work "brilliantly composed," Downes said that it is written "as if the composer...had used the violinists' unique qualities in the expounding of a special kind of music for which their presence is indispensable. The result is a concerto which is a perfect fit, and which Mr. Elman plays with a delight as obvious as his mastery."

Elman dismissed all but Downes's review, and reported in letters to friends that the work was a triumph. Yet, he found it virtually impossible to secure further performances.

Disillusioning as the lack of followup response was, Elman truly enjoyed the experience of commissioning a new work and bringing it to life, and he wanted to keep at it. While working on the Martinů, he embarked on a correspondence with Mario Castelnuovo-Tedesco, a prolific Italian-Jewish composer who came to America in 1939, after the Fascist government of Italy issued its racial purity laws. Castelnuovo-Tedesco's music is appealingly melodic, not particularly challenging harmonically, and generally quite likeable, if hardly timeless; indeed, the only works in his catalogue that are regularly played today are his many guitar works, including a bittersweet concerto composed the year of his exile. But he had also written a violin concerto, in 1933, and perhaps Elman heard Heifetz play its premiere performance in New York.

Since Elman's original request for a work had been casual, and by no means a commission, Castelnuovo-Tedesco responded with a trifle called *Exotica*. As soon as the Martinů premiere was behind him, Elman looked this work over, and quickly realizing that it offered no depths to plumb, and he set it aside. "I don't think the piece is up to your high standard," he wrote to the composer on January 28. "The music is pleasant, but it lacks power.... Since I don't think it is worthy of you, I will not play it." Elman went on to ask, however, for "something more substantial."

Castelnuovo-Tedesco took Elman's criticism in good cheer, responding on February 12 that he "didn't mind at all [Elman's] frank criticism," but pointing out that if the piece "wasn't meant to be anything else" but unassumingly pleasant. He then asked a series of detailed questions about what Elman might want, and he put forth a few suggestions—a three movement *Pastorale*, and a "Christmas Concerto"—an odd suggestion for a Jewish composer to propose to a Jewish violinist. Finally, he wondered whether Elman's request was in the nature of a commission; and if so, what terms the violinist was considering. If the correspondence continued, the further installments have been lost. In any case, Elman did include some of the composer's shorter works on his concert programs—most notably a piece based on Hebrew themes, and a Suite. In later years, he read through the concerto at practice sessions; but he never performed it publicly.

What Elman *really* wanted was a concerto from Dmitri Shostakovich, and in mid-1944, he wrote to the composer, asking him to consider composing one for him. That plan, too, came to nothing: Shostakovich didn't write a violin concerto until 1955, and he gave it to David Oistrakh. But the composer did not reject Elman's request out of hand. In a letter to Elman (which the composer said was his first letter in English) he said he might get around to a violin concerto after completing a group of works he was then composing.

Elman took this to mean that a Shostakovich work would soon be forthcoming, and he wrote to Koussevitzky to convey the news, sending a copy of Shostakovich's letter. Koussevitzky was delighted too, and naturally he agreed to conduct the work's premiere. But he wondered whether Elman was counting his chickens prematurely, and in August, 1944, he gently suggested that Elman refrain from announcing his prospective acquisition until he actually had the work in hand. That was wise advice, for although Elman wrote to Shostakovich again in 1947, the composer was unable to oblige him.

CHAPTER SIXTEEN:

Battles and Resolutions

Beyond the comparatively novel business of seeking new works lay business-as-usual for Elman— the business of securing dates and playing concerts, and therefore, the business of dealing with managers. By the middle of the 1930s, he left Charles Wagner and went to Columbia Concerts; and from there he returned to Hurok briefly. When he departed from the Hurok roster for the last time, in 1943, he wrote Hurok a letter, explaining that he felt a great deal of friendship for Hurok personally, but that he found his staff uncooperative. Apparently, Elman and Hurok maintained at least a cordial relationship for the rest of their lives, for on several important occasions in Elman's later career, Hurok took the time to send him telegrams that were not simply matters of formal congratulation, but warm, personal messages.

While moving from one manager to the next, Elman had grown fascinated with the machinations of the music world's business side, which was now enormously more complicated than it had been during his first years in America, and more than ever, Elman regarded the managerial world as a conspiratorial web. In a sense, his perception was correct: there was a web, and it was spun partly as the result of a jump in the number of artists interested in touring the United States after World War I, and partly as a mechanism through which the demands of the increasingly culture-hungry audiences around the country could be met. As both supply and demand grew, management firms had to find a way of coping with both the increased workload and the increased competition. Thus, a new system of concert management evolved. This new phenomenon had its start in the Midwest in the 1920s, and was known as the "organized audience plan," a brilliant arrangement wherein small towns were offered a series of five or six concerts in a season, with the tickets available by series subscription only. More often than not, the subscriptions were sold-out even before the artists were chosen, such was the trust the communities placed in the organizing managers. Of course, this plan would not have worked for more than a season if the artists offered proved unworthy; so a formula was adopted whereby each series would included one stellar performer, along with several less established ones who offered solid programs of standard works.

This approach proved so successful that it was eventually taken up by firms much more powerful than the small organizations that had pioneered it. By 1930, an organization called Community Concert Service, established in New York, had aligned itself with the CBS broadcasting company and its management firm, Columbia Concerts. Meanwhile, the competing NBC network also controlled an artist management company, and in 1935, it bought an interest in the Civic Concert Service, which competed with Community.

There were several problems with all this, in Elman's view. One had to do with fees. Generally, a manager took a percentage of the performance fee as his commission, but where organized audiences were concerned, different rules applied. In these cases, an extra percentage came off the top for the operation of the concert circuit itself, so the artists ended up with fees that were as much as 30% lower than normal.

Elman complained about this, and he was not alone. Among the other artists who found the practice odd, if not outrageous, was the British soprano Kathleen Ferrier who, in interviews, wondered aloud about the mathematics of the practice. Estimating that her average audience, on a Community Concerts tour, numbered about 3,000, and assuming that this translated to a box office of at least $3,000, she asked why her fee was a mere $800—out of which she was expected to pay her accompanist, her manager's commission, and expenses for travel and hotels.[1]

Fees aside, Elman had concluded that the organized audience plan was ultimately anti-artistic, if only because it inhibited his (and his colleagues') freedom to play in certain towns at will. He had no objection to the idea of a small town having its own subscription series; rather, he found the idea commendable. But as always, he preferred working with a small, independent manager over a large management firm; and now that the large firms controlled the organized audience programs, he found that these local series were closed to him. Eventually, he began wondering whether the name of the game was music or monopoly.

Here again, he was not alone in his views. By 1942, fearing an investigation by the Federal Trade Commission, both NBC and CBS divested themselves of their management arms. Still, the relationships between Columbia Artists and Community Concerts, on one hand, and the National Concert and Artists Corporation and Civic Concerts, on the other, remained firm until 1954, by which time they controlled about 1,900 series around the country. Elman set down his thoughts on the matter rather concisely in a letter to Charles L. Wagner, in July 1935, towards the end of their working relationship.

"The musical business has reached the point in this country," observed Elman, "where it has nothing to do with art, nor with the popularity of the individual artist. These two big trusts give the public not always what the public wants, but what it is convenient for them to give the public, and the public is ignorant to accept their way of doing business."

The situation, naturally, occasioned a certain amount of friction in Elman's relationship with the unaffiliated Wagner, and it only added to problems that had been developing from the start of their affiliation two years earlier. Their first clash involved the terms under which Wagner would represent Elman, the violinist wanting to pay no more than a 10% commission, and Wagner preferring the 15% cut that was, by then, common. Wagner conceded the point, but as he complained in his memoirs, "for the next three years [Elman] bothered the office daily. If we obtained a $1,000 date, the price should have been $1,200; our $1,500 bookings should have been $1,800 in his estimation."[2]

Unfortunately, Elman's correspondence shows that he pursued a similar course with many others among his long list of managers. This remained one of the paradoxes of Elman's personality. He continued firing off lengthy letters about minor fee discrepancies, yet he also continued donating tens of thousands of dollars to charitable causes. In the 1940s—not long after his charity tour for European refugees—he set out on a tour of United States military bases, and he continued to tour on behalf of the military for the duration of the war. He even wrote an article for the *Musical Courier*, setting forth the reasons he found these performances a special joy.

"What has moved and impressed me most is the overwhelming gratitude of the men for the good music given them," he wrote. "Cut off from their former security and embarked upon a new life in many ways strange and hard to adjust to, these audiences of sailors, soldiers and flyers, as many as 7,000 at a time, become so moved by the power of great music as to express gratitude and joy. At such times, it seems that the beauty of art has a special application for our youth today. Under the spell of the Mendelssohn or the Beethoven Violin Concertos, or such perennial favorites as the Schubert *Ave Maria* and the Bach *Air on the G String*, the men in the services are carried above and beyond themselves. They take hold of the greatness of art and hold onto an imperishable bulwark which only ageless values, even if intangible, can provide.

"Every time I have witnessed such a sight," he continued, "I have been moved with the realization that such an experience is as important for the artist as for his listeners. Strained and molded by a routine of constant tours and travel schedules, artists are sometimes apt to lose intimate touch with their audiences. Performances for servicemen can stimulate and inspire an artist to such an extent that he is brought closer to his listeners, and thus to his art, without ever suspecting it. When an artist stands before an audience of men about to embark to fight in a just cause, and perhaps to lay down their lives, he can hardly fail to give of his best. It is not likely that at such moments he will play with indifference."[3]

For many in the music business, though, the generosity of Elman's public gesture was overshadowed by the demanding side of his personality, and ultimately, Elman himself suffered for this in both long and short term ways. In the long term, his reputation for querulousness spread quickly through managerial circles, and eventually, he found it difficult to find representation. Meanwhile, the kind of short term loss he sustained can be seen in the disastrous exchange of letters with the management of the San Francisco Symphony, with which he hoped to perform in 1945. The correspondence begins with a wire from the orchestra, offering Elman a date, followed by another two weeks later, in which it was suggested that Monteux and the orchestra might want to record either a Saint-Saëns or a Mozart concerto with Elman while he was in town. There would also be a broadcast.

Elman believed that Standard Oil would be subsidizing the concerts, and he instructed his manager, Bernard La Berge, to quote a high price for his services. The orchestra's management was shocked at the asking price, and wired back for a confirmation of the fee. Fearing that something might be amiss, Elman's manager replied to the orchestra's query by repeating the figure and noting that it was "$1,500 less than Mr. Elman's usual fee." For the orchestra, though, the asking price was out of the question, and its office wired back that what Elman was asking for a soloist's fee that was more than double what the orchestra and Monteux together would be paid for the concert. Given that, it was decided that Monteux would conduct a strictly orchestral program.

This put La Berge in a difficult spot, for on one hand Elman was expecting him to net a high fee, while on the other the orchestra was upset enough to cancel its invitation. Trying to salvage the date, La Berge wrote the orchestra a long, detailed letter, explaining that Elman thought Standard Oil was footing the bill, and that a large fee would therefore not be beyond the orchestra's means—a point that seemed to clash with the earlier contention that the requested fee was lower than usual. La Berge offered an extremely reasonable deal: Elman would play three concerts with the orchestra, one of which could be broadcast, for $2,500. But the orchestra's management had by then written off the possibility, and wired back simply that La Berge should forget the engagement entirely.

Under normal circumstances, Elman would have found this breakdown in communications upsetting enough, but in this case he was all the more disappointed, because the concert would have conveniently let him finish his season in San Francisco, where he planned to vacation with Helen and the children. Yet, wherever Elman felt the blame for this unfortunate incident lay, one person he did not hold it against was the conductor, Pierre Monteux, nor apparently did Monteux hold the incident against Elman. When the conductor left San Francisco, in 1952, Elman was among those who helped arrange his return to the Boston Symphony, the orchestra he had directed in the early 1920s. And in the 1950s, Elman and Monteux performed together several times at Lewisohn Stadium, in New York.

Elman's relationships with his fellow artists were not always so harmonious though, and in the 1940s, he made a few powerful and influential enemies among his colleagues, several of whom thereafter painted him as a temperamental egomaniac, and circulated stories that gave credence to the tales Elman's managers had already been telling. One relationship that ruptured irreparably around this time was Elman's friendship with Eugene Ormandy. The two had worked together often in the 1930s, and their collaborations were generally well-received. By 1944, though, Elman had not been invited to Philadelphia for several seasons, and he wondered why. So, on a visit to the city, not long after the premiere of the Martinů concerto, he attended one of Ormandy's concerts and took the opportunity to pay a friendly call on the conductor during intermission.

The meeting was tense, but cordial, and after praising the first half of the concert and the sound of the orchestra, Elman said to Ormandy, "why don't we make music together?" Ormandy took exception to this. Whether or not he were inclined to invite Elman to come to Philadelphia as a soloist, he could hardly make a commitment then and there. He could, of course, have said, simply, "oh yes, Mischa, we should," and then either follow up or let it slide; but at the moment he considered Elman's visit, with its offer of his services, an imposition. He also seemed angry that Elman had played the Martinů premiere with Koussevitzky, so his response to Elman's question was, "well, you've gone to Boston now, haven't you?"

Elman was puzzled by the exchange, and upon his arrival home, he wrote Ormandy a friendly note, asking him to explain the Boston comment, and suggesting that they have lunch together when Ormandy next visited New York. He was not prepared for the vehemence of Ormandy's response. They could have lunch, if Elman liked, the conductor wrote, but he refused to comment further on their discussion in Philadelphia. Ormandy added that he was shocked that Elman would use an intermission to ask for an engagement.

Elman wrote back immediately: "Your astonishing letter received. My coming in to see you during the intermission was the result of my enthusiasm for your performance, and my saying to you 'why don't we make music together' was meant as a compliment from one artist to another.... I never knew there was a reason why we have not played together for a long time. If I had any idea my remark would be embarrassing to you, I assure you I would not have exposed myself to a reproach such as you express."

That was virtually, although not entirely, the end of their association. Ormandy invited the violinist to play the Tchaikovsky concerto at a Hollywood Bowl concert in 1948; but he never invited him back to Philadelphia, and Elman was hurt by this. In later years, he looked into the possibility of patching up the rift through friends who were on good terms with Ormandy, and even through Ormandy's brother Martin, a cellist in New York. But the word came back, time and again, that Elman would never play with the Philadelphia Orchestra while

Ormandy was on the podium. Elman did play with the ensemble again, and he even made a recording with the orchestra not long after this exchange. But his appearances were confined to the orchestra's summer Robin Hood Dell series, under a guest conductor's baton; and the disc, a recording of the Wieniawski Second Concerto, is conducted by Alexander Hilsberg, with the orchestra listed as the Robin Hood Dell Orchestra of Philadelphia.

Elman's popularity with his audiences held firm, though. He was one of the artists selected to participate in a broadcast radio tribute in memory of Franklin Delano Roosevelt after the President's death, in 1945; and that August, when he played the Mendelssohn Concerto with Alexander Smallens and the New York Philharmonic at Lewisohn Stadium, 11,500 listeners turned up to hear him. Noel Straus, in his *New York Times* review, noted that Elman's audience was one of the largest crowds the series had attracted that summer. Young violinists were still buying his arrangements, too. In 1945, Schirmer renewed its copyrights on a group of these, as well as on a couple of Elman originals, *The Departure* and *Thro' the Lonely Garden*.

In 1946, Leopold Mittman left Elman to accompany Nathan Milstein, and Elman signed on a new pianist, Wolfgang Rosé. Rosé, a nephew of Gustav Mahler, was thoroughly devoted to his employer, and rather starstruck. On July 31, 1947, he wrote to Elman, who was vacationing in San Francisco, noting that they had met exactly a year earlier, and confessing that it was his ambition "to become the best accompanist you ever had." Elman felt warmly towards Rosé, and it's clear from both their recordings and the reviews of the time that Rosé was a solid, enthusiastic accompanist.

Eventually, though, Elman came to find Rosé's veneration exasperating. While on tour in Mexico, in 1948, he wrote home to Helen that as much as he liked Rosé, he was "tired of being constantly followed and imitated" by him. "His sense of obedience and desire to please me," he complained, "makes me feel uncomfortable. I don't know how I will be able to tell him that he doesn't have to walk when I walk, stand when I stand and turn when I turn." Before the lengthy section about Rosé ends, Elman complains that he hates his pianist's aftershave, and says that he went to the movies just to get away from him. Their relationship came to an amicable end a little more than a year later, to Elman's relief.

As a recording artist, Elman saw his world change radically through the 1940s and into the 1950s—for the better at first, but eventually for the worse. With Padwa, he had recorded only a few short selections. He did, however, record a few orchestral discs during Padwa's tenure. Having scored a success with his Tchaikovsky Concerto recording, in 1930, Elman wanted immediately to make another recording with orchestra, his first choice being the Mendelssohn. Concerto recording was still a complicated business, though, his label told him. Besides being more expensive in terms of session personnel, concertos posed a marketing problem, for these were still the days of short-playing 78s, and extended works had to be offered in multiple disc sets, which were naturally more expensive.

In the Victor Company's view, Elman's appeal had been, traditionally, to the single disc buyer, so by way of compromise, Elman and the company settled on a few shorter works for violin and orchestra—the two Beethoven *Romances* and the Bach E major and Vivaldi G minor Concertos, which he recorded with Lawrence Collingwood and the London Symphony in 1934, and Tchaikovsky's *Sérenade mélancolique*, for which he was accompanied by an unidentified orchestra, conducted by Nathaniel Shilkret.

Of these, the Tchaikovsky is of particular interest, for Elman's emotional approach is perfectly suited to its elegiac character. From the first phrase, he applies a subtly shifting coloration that gives the performance a heartfelt, singing quality. Brief though it is, it is one of Elman's most beautiful recorded performances, one that fully captures the spirit of his art.

It was not lost on Elman, however, that other artists were recording concertos by the handful: Kreisler had recorded the Mendelssohn in 1927, and the Brahms in 1929, both for HMV, RCA Victor's British affiliate; and the pianist Artur Schnabel had recorded all five Beethoven piano concertos between 1932 and 1935. And there was Heifetz. He had done the Glazunov in 1934, the Wieniawski Second in 1935, the Prokofiev Second in 1937, the Brahms in 1939, and the Beethoven in 1940. And while Elman couldn't win any enthusiasm for the Martinů at RCA, Heifetz had been able to convince the label, in 1941, to record the new concerto composed for him by William Walton.

It was quite natural for Elman to find Heifetz's activity upsetting in the face of RCA's refusal to let him pursue a similar course, and in his repertoire meetings with the label's executives, he made his feelings clear. In 1947, the company finally agreed to record him in the Mendelssohn, with Desire Defauw and the Chicago Symphony, and a few years later, his Wieniawski Second with Hilsberg and the Robin Hood Dell Orchestra followed. These are fine, sweet-toned and rather vigorous performances in the classic Elman style.

As a solo recording artist, meanwhile, Elman recorded more frequently with Mittman than he had with Padwa, but the full extent of their recorded collaboration turned out to be rather sparse, largely because the American Federation of Musicians had imposed a recording ban from 1942 to 1944, the two middle years of their six year association. The reasoning behind this ban is easy to understand, if you see it from the union's point of view. To the union and its leader, James Caesar Petrillo, recorded music, mechanically reproduced on jukeboxes and disseminated over the radio waves, posed a great danger to the welfare of musicians who made their living performing live. Petrillo saw the dance bands of the 1920s and 1930s fade away. If jukeboxes and recorded radio programs were to displace the dance band, what would become of the musicians who had earned their livelihoods as nightly performers?

Clearly, the union's concern here was with musicians who worked day-to-day for fairly low wages, and whose metier was popular music. The same problems did not apply to classical players. In the classical world, records furthered reputations and led to more concert engagements. For both the rank-and-file orchestral player and the star soloist, they were unquestionably beneficial. What Petrillo wanted, though, was a royalty fund for musicians, to be established through a blanket levy on record sales, and to be administered by the union. This was to apply to both classical and popular recordings—and so did the recording ban the union imposed when the record labels refused to entertain Petrillo's idea.

Elman had mixed feelings about the union. Early on, he had been inclined to join, but he had been paid a visit by Heifetz and the baritone Lawrence Tibbett, who persuaded him that joining the union was not in the interest of the important soloists. Elman stood aside, but soon found that his non-membership caused difficulties, particularly when he sought engagements with unionized orchestras. Heifetz and many other soloists undoubtedly experienced the same thing, and many of them therefore abandoned the anti-union stance and joined. But Elman remained steadfast, unaware that he was one of a dwindling group who held to that position. Eventually, he asked an orchestra manager why he had not been invited to play lately, and it was then that he learned that Heifetz had not only joined the union, but that he had become active in it. Elman joined too; but when the recording ban was imposed, he wondered whether union membership was beneficial after all, and he soon resigned.

Years later, Elman had occasion to tell the union what he thought of it in the direct, point-blank fashion he employed when he felt strongly about something. It was November 1948—four years after the end of the recording ban, a year after the Taft-Hartley Act rendered the union's royalty fund illegal, and not long after the union attempted a second, less successful recording ban. He received a letter inviting him to perform at a concert sponsored by the American Guild of Musical Artists (AGMA), and in declining the invitation, he pointedly added that he had resigned from the union. Having joined enthusiastically, he wrote, "as time went on, I became more and more disappointed as to its actual accomplishments. Instead of making the artist more independent of the monopolies and their way of business," he charged, "you have allowed the monopolies to expand to the extent that talent, ability and reputation are of no value unless you 'play ball' with them."

The recording ban had affected Elman in a number of ways, for his label, Victor—by then a subsidiary of the Radio Corporation of America (RCA)—had held out to the bitter end, as had virtually every major company but Decca, which capitulated in 1943. RCA had to meet a consumer demand that was hardly dampened by the ban, and it was able to do so by emptying its vaults of performances that had not yet been issued. This was fine with Elman, for there were several recordings of his in the icebox, and now it looked like they would be released. Or did it? It seems there was also a counterforce at work, a function of the war effort. Materials for making such frivolous consumer items as gramophone records were scarce, and the labels therefore had to be conservative in their release plans. Important catalogue items from the past were discontinued, and new discs were released only after the record-buying public's pulse had been taken.

It was at this time that a marketing philosophy still common among the major labels today was first articulated: "We must give very careful consideration to our releases from now on, and must confine them primarily to material of a rather popular or mass appeal nature," an RCA executive wrote to Elman in 1942, when the violinist wondered why the company had been holding back his Debussy Sonata, one of his first full-length sonata recordings. "I am sure you will agree with us," the executive continued, "that you cannot consider a Debussy sonata a truly popular type of piece."

Elman could not agree that there was much point to the label's argument. He had recorded the Debussy because he found it a beautiful piece of music that deserved to be more of a "popular type of piece" than it was. One of the attractions of recordings, he argued, was that they helped make this kind of popularity possible; besides, he added, he had been playing the Debussy in concert a good deal lately, and his audiences genuinely enjoyed it. Moreover, he felt he had done his part in making records that were quintessentially popular, and he continued to do so, even though these discs reflected only a small part of his repertoire. He longed to present his public with recordings that documented the more serious side of his art, a side his audience heard in concert, but with the exception of his Tchaikovsky, Bach and Vivaldi concertos, could not relive at home. Surely, he reasoned, after decades of supplying Victor with a stream of vignettes that had by then sold millions of copies, the company owed it to him (and to his audience) to issue something more substantial.

Eventually, RCA came around, and the Debussy recording was issued. But this was neither the first nor the last of Elman's run-ins with the firm's Artists and Repertoire department. Two years earlier, before the threat of the recording ban, Elman had suggested recording another new additions to his repertoire, the Fauré Sonata. The reply he received utterly astonished him. "I have checked the Fauré sonata and regret that we do not feel this should be duplicated in our catalogue since it was done only a couple of years ago by Heifetz with Emanuel Bay at the piano. This is an excellent recording judged by present-day standards, and we find that the sale has not been great enough to warrant a duplication at the present time."

That Elman suggested the Debussy next was logical enough. He wanted to document something of the French repertoire, to which he had lately come, and of which he was quite fond; and he knew that Heifetz had not yet recorded the Debussy. But he found it objectionable that he should have to consider Heifetz's repertoire in making his own plans, and in the coming years, his objections on this count grew more intense. But for the moment, the fact that there was no Heifetz recording of the work helped him win the point, and RCA gave him the green light to record the Debussy.

Nor did it hurt Elman's case that he remained loyal to RCA through the period of the recording ban, while Heifetz quickly signed a short-term contract with Decca. It may have been partly because of this that when Elman continued to press his desire to record the Fauré, RCA relented. By the middle of the decade, both sets were on the market.

These were the only works of this scope Elman recorded with Mittman. The rest of their joint discography was devoted to short selections, and indeed, it was a small sampling, a mere nine pieces. Three of these were remakes—Dvořák's *Humoresque* and Schumann's *Träumerei* for the fourth time each, and Massenet's *Méditation* for the third time.

The other six items were not only new additions to Elman's catalogue of recordings, but with the sole exception of Achron's *Hebrew Melody*, which he later remade twice with Joseph Seiger, these performances remain unique in his discography. Besides those already mentioned, Elman and Mittman recorded a traditional Irish dance, an arrangement of a song by Balakirev, Fauré's *Après un rêve*, a Grieg *Album Leaf*, and most interesting of all, an outgoing showpiece by Jeno Hubay, *Hejr Kati*. Technically and interpretively, these performances are akin to those Elman recorded with Hollister in the early 1930s—outgoing, emotional, fully secure in intonation, and endowed with Elman's trademark warmth of tone.

During this period Elman renewed his recording ties with stars of the vocal world, his efforts here consisting of a handful of short selections in which he played *obbligato* for Jan Peerce, Rosa Ponselle and Risa Stevens. On the Peerce recordings in particular—Braga's *Angel's Serenade* and del Riego's *O Dry Those Tears*—his violin is placed further forward than it had been on his earlier vocal discs. The interpretive impulses are unmistakable: Elman varies his vibrato expressively, and using a combination of dynamic swells and a touch of *portamento*, he sets a gilded web around Peerce's voice. Yet, his tone is different here. Gone is the broad, throaty tone of old, and in its place is a thinner, reedier-sounding thread.

This change of timbre continues through the recordings he made with Rosé, who accompanied him into the LP era[4]. To a degree, changes in recording technology or microphone placement may account for some of this, for in his recordings of the 1950s and 1960s, one finds certain collections infused with something akin to the grand tone of his earlier recordings, while others veer towards this leaner sound. Interestingly, the sound that pours forth from live recordings of Elman, preserved in television and radio broadcast tapes, suggests that in person his tone was far richer and more commanding than his post-war discs convey.

One disturbing tendency emerges in the series of recordings Elman made with Rosé—an increase in his use of *portamento*, along with a change in the *way* he used it. In some works, he used the effect simply as an expressive device, as he always had. The fact that musicologists were advocating less of this sliding in the works by Mozart and Handel he was recording didn't bother him in the least, and in some cases, Elman's counterargument, preserved on disc, can be quite persuasive. In the *Larghetto* of Handel's Sonata in D major, Op. 1, No. 13 (one of three Handel Sonatas he recorded with Rosé), his slides and dynamic play make for a reading that speaks from the heart and turns the movement into a glorious introspective essay. Within his own aesthetic, historical exactitude is rendered superfluous.

But his newer, stranger use of *portamento* turns up in the very next movement, and even more pervasively in the Brahms Sonata in D minor, recorded during this same period. Here Elman incorporates the effect into his basic mechanism for getting around the fingerboard. He does not use it as a crutch—his passage work, when he plays it without sliding, is still fastidious and crisp. Rather, he has turned his *glissandi* into a lubricant of sorts, combining it with his normal fingering shifts in order to produce a seamless, smooth backdrop over which individual notes are placed.

It's an interesting notion, but it doesn't always work. In the finale of the Handel sonata, he takes this approach to some of his trills, making them sound oddly rubbery; and in the Brahms, similarly, some of the more traditionally applied slides are quite effective, while the newer application inevitably distracts the ear. Hearing this reading, the listener's attention is focused on the sound of the instrument and the style of the reading, rather than on the flow of the music itself—a complaint critics had made earlier in Elman's career, and one that would haunt Elman for the rest of his life.

CHAPTER SEVENTEEN

A Look at Elman's Style—
Taking Stock and Shifting Focus

Elman spent the war years and the half decade that followed close to home, but with the start of the new decade, he was eager to resume his global travels. First on his agenda, though, was finding a replacement for Wolfgang Rosé. One of those he auditioned was a young Israeli-born pianist named Joseph Seiger. Then in his late twenties, Seiger had been working as a freelance accompanist for artists on the Columbia Artists roster.

Seiger was born in 1924 in Rishon-le-Zion, a small town south of Tel Aviv. In 1942, Seiger joined the American army (his father was born in San Francisco, and had retained his American citizenship), and since he was fluent in Arabic, Hebrew and English, he did a good deal of work for G2, the army's intelligence unit, while serving in the Mideast and North Africa. He was also active in the Palmach, an elite strike force of the Jewish militia, the Haganah. As he explained to a newspaper interviewer in the late 1940s, "any member of the Palmach can change his identity to that of a Palestinian Arab at a moment's notice. Part of our training was to live three weeks in Arab villages, learning their customs."

After he was discharged from the American army, in 1945, Seiger moved to New York, resumed his musical studies at the Manhattan School, and pursued a modest career as a concert pianist. He also continued working for the Haganah, which was then engaged in liberating his homeland from British rule. Among his tasks was the procurement of munitions, something that could not be handled openly. And in 1948, when a shipment labeled as machinery turned out to be 20,000 pounds of explosives, Seiger and his partners in the Oved

Trading Company were arrested. With some intercession from the United States government, the charges were dropped, and Seiger continued his studies and his performing career.

When he auditioned for Elman, in 1951, he was 27 and the violinist was 60. But Elman felt he was the most promising of the pianists he had heard, and offered him the post on a trial basis. It was tempting: Elman's immediate itinerary included not only a visit to Europe, but a tour of the three-year old state of Israel. Seiger also had a strong memory of having seen Elman perform when he played in Palestine, in 1935. He was 11 at the time, and had been so taken with the *Rondo* that closes Mozart's A major Concerto that he went home and practiced it endlessly on the piano. He also remembered Elman's own *Eili, Eili*, which, not surprisingly, brought down the house in Rishon-le-Zion.

But the salary Elman offered him was less than he was making as a freelancer, so he respectfully declined. "You will be sorry young man," Elman told him as he left his studio. "You're missing a great opportunity." Elman's next choice was Erwin Herbst, who accepted the job at the salary Elman offered, and joined him on his voyage to Europe and Israel, and in a New York recital on his sixty-first birthday that was something of a departure from his normal programming. Here, for the first time, he left the encores off the program proper, offering instead a Bach partita (with an accompaniment by Nachez), Beethoven's "Kreutzer" Sonata, the Vieuxtemps Fifth Concerto, a new sonata by Werner Josten, and a bit of razzle-dazzle for the finale, the Saint-Saëns *Introduction and Rondo capriccioso.*

Musically, Elman was perfectly satisfied with Herbst, but their personalities did not gel. For other performers, this might not have been a problem. Heifetz, for instance, maintained a strictly business relationship with his accompanists. He did not travel with them—he flew first class, they went by train—nor did he encourage familiarity. Elman liked to maintain a measure of formality, but since he did travel with his pianists, and often shared meals, played chess, and rehearsed with them for at least three hours every day, he wanted to like them. He had, in his career, been lucky on that count, but Herbst proved unsatisfactory.

Elman was able to put that problem on the back burner for the moment, though, for on February 9, less than three weeks after his 1952 birthday recital, he embarked on another survey of the concerto literature with the National Orchestral Association and Leon Barzin, a slightly more compact one than his 1936 cycle with that same organization. This time he played nine works in three concerts, the earliest being the Bach E major, with Brahms and Tchaikovsky at the end of the cycle, in mid-April.[1]

When the series came to an end, Elman renewed his search for an accompanist, with little luck. One day in May, he tuned into a recital of Mozart violin sonatas broadcast live on WNYC. Elman was impressed with the pianist, who turned out to be Joseph Seiger. He pulled Seiger's resume from his files, and looking it over, he found that a friend of his, Dora Zaslavsky, was listed (along with Harold Bauer) as one of Seiger's principal teachers. The day after the radio recital, Seiger visited Zaslavsky, and was having cocktails in her garden when the phone rang.

"Guess who that was," Zaslavsky said on her return.

"Mischa Elman," Seiger replied, half-joking, but his teacher confirmed that it had indeed been Elman, and that the violinist had asked her to put Seiger in touch with him. "Be a *mensch*," she advised. "Call him tomorrow." Seiger obeyed.

"Oh, Mr. Seiger, how nice to hear from you," Elman said when Seiger called at 11 the next morning. "What are you doing now? Would you like to come and play?"

As Seiger recalls, they played sonata after sonata, then Elman took him to lunch at Fine and Shapiro, on West 72nd Street. They talked about music, and about Seiger's background; and when they finished, Elman asked the pianist if he felt like playing some more. Several sonatas later, they decided to call it a day, but as Seiger left Elman's apartment, the violinist told him to expect his call at noon the next day.

Elman called promptly at noon, and asked Seiger to come to his studio once more, this time, as he put it "to talk some business." When he arrived, Elman came directly to the point, and asked Seiger what he would like as a salary. "The same salary I asked for last year would be fine," the pianist replied, and this time, Elman put his hand forward and said, "It's a deal. Come back this time tomorrow. I'll have my lawyer here, and we'll sign an exclusive contract."

Thus began the most fruitful association in Elman's career. In the 15 seasons they played together, from the summer of 1952 until Elman's death in 1967, Seiger took on responsibilities considerably broader than those normally expected of an accompanist, and over the years, their relationship became almost familial; in fact, Seiger was only a few years older than Elman's own children. Yet, his unusual range of experience, and the musicality that Elman admired in him, served to diminish what might have been a generation gap. And if Elman took a fatherly interest in Seiger, the pianist reciprocated with a kind of filial protectiveness. Virtually from the start of their association, Seiger began looking for areas in which the forward motion of Elman's career had flagged, and when he found them, he worked behind the scenes to correct them—sometimes successfully, sometimes less so.

For example, not long after they began working together Seiger realized that his employer's recording career had come to a standstill. Elman had made no recordings with Herbst, and the single LP of Tchaikovsky and Wieniawski works he and Seiger recorded at the end of 1952 stood as an island amid years away from the studio. Elman wanted, as always, to record concertos and the major sonata repertoire, but RCA consistently declined. So far as Elman was concerned, Jascha Heifetz was at the root of this problem. He had heard a rumor to the effect that Heifetz's contract with RCA included a clause giving him first refusal rights on major works, as well as a period of exclusivity in the works he recorded. During a luncheon with David Sarnoff, the chairman of RCA's board of directors, Elman asked whether this was so. Sarnoff deflected the question diplomatically, explaining that although the record label was a subsidiary of the larger RCA corporation, it had its own management, and that repertoire was the label management's province.

Elman took this to be a confirmation through non-denial, and he told Seiger that the report had indeed been confirmed. In fact, whether it was true or not, the effect was the same: RCA was restricting the breadth of repertoire he could offer his public on disc. Elman left the matter there, a source of frustration and an artistic dead end. So Seiger took up the gauntlet. "Mr. Elman," he said one morning during a break in rehearsal, "you must make more recordings. My generation doesn't know you. It isn't right." Elman agreed—but what was he to do about it? "Leave RCA," Seiger suggested, pointing out that Nathan Milstein had been in the same situation at the label, and had finally left it for Capitol. "But Joseph," Elman responded, "I've been with RCA for nearly 50 years."

That, Seiger pointed out, apparently didn't mean much to RCA, and while Elman retained his unrequited sentiment for the firm, he was getting older and his interpretations were not being recorded. Seiger began making inquiries, and found that the British Decca label (marketed as London in the United States) was interested. It took him some time persuade Elman to consider the proposition, but once he agreed, the path was smooth. Elman told his British manager, Holt, that he was interested in recording in Europe; and the next day, a representative from Decca called, offering him a free hand to record whatever repertoire he chose.

Seiger worked as an advance man for Elman in other ways too. Since they rehearsed concertos together, it was often Seiger rather than Elman who first met with conductors to convey the violinist's wishes regarding tempo, and to alert them to Elman's particular approaches to phrasing. Seiger also did his best to intercede when Elman's observations ruffled the feathers of managers and promoters. And towards the end of Elman's life, Seiger tried hard to persuade him to teach.

Seiger's initial contract with Elman ran for a year, starting in May 1952, with an option for renewal. As in the past, Elman made it clear that this first year was to be a trial period, and as often was the case when he took on a new accompanist, the first hurdle was a tour of distant parts—this time, South Africa. Elman and Seiger rehearsed for a few weeks and then went their separate ways until the middle of the summer, when Elman (who was vacationing with his family in a rented cottage near Los Angeles) summoned Seiger westward to prepare the tour programs.

From the start, their relationship was easy, if formal. "I worked with a man who belonged to another generation," Seiger recalls, "and he acted that way. He was proper, polite, and honest. When we were on tour, we travelled together, and we stayed in the same hotel. Yet, there were times he needed his freedom, and times I needed mine, and we each respected that."

Seiger was familiar with Elman's interpretive aesthetic, having grown up listening to performances by Ignaz Friedman, Alfred Cortot, and others whose performances embodied pianistic applications of the style Elman's violin playing represented. But learning to play that way himself was another matter.

"It was three or four years before I really felt comfortable," Seiger says of the musical side of their collaboration, "and at the beginning, it was a little strange, because I didn't always understand why he did certain things the way he did them. I was learning the repertoire, or more precisely, I was learning the Elman way to play the repertoire, and in many cases I was performing major works for the first time, all over the world. It was not an easy experience—it was a matter of hard work and constant rehearsal, which I liked. I was willing to learn, and I learned a great deal."

Seiger found Elman's rehearsal technique particularly enlightening. "Every rehearsal was a performance," he says. "You must understand that Elman was an artist of the stage—that was where he really blossomed. So in rehearsal, we played as if we were in the concert hall, and his method of rehearsing was to bring up the level of the performance from day to day. We rarely stopped to repeat a passage, or even a movement, although that happened on occasion. I remember one funny experience with him, rehearsing Lalo's *Symphonie Espagnole*. I started the *Rondo* at a brisk tempo, and when he came in everything was fine. But something happened when we got to the sixteenth note section, and suddenly we were a beat a part. He turned around to me and said, 'Joseph, what's the matter with you? You're not playing in time. Let's try it again.' We started again, and I played steadily, without giving an inch.

"When he stopped again, I said, 'Mr. Elman, you always tell me I have a wonderful sense of rhythm. I'm playing exactly at the tempo we started.' But he turned and said, 'My dear boy, you may be playing in time, but you're not playing in *my* time.' He was entirely serious, and I knew just what he meant. He was practicing, and he wanted me to give him the time to play those sixteenth notes so that each would come out with a specific sound. When it came to the performance, everything was in strict time. But in rehearsal, I would know that if on a Monday he lingered on an E, then he would linger on that E each time for the next four days.

"In general, our rehearsals were chamber music sessions, and my job was to be prepared. If I would have had a technical difficulty, he would have thrown me out. It had to be perfect, it had to fit with him, and I had to have the control to make the necessary changes. If he had a different idea about tempo, or if he wanted to slow down in a particular place, I had to be ready to anticipate that. After all, as I tell my students today, ensemble playing is 90% listening, combined with knowing both your own part and the other one. If you're involved only in your own part, that's already bad.

"So," Seiger adds, "if a piece did not work out to his satisfaction, we'd try it again the next day. What we would *not* do, however, was make written notations. He never marked anything in his music, nor would he let me mark mine. Why? Again, that was his style. He felt that if I marked what he wanted in my scores, I would simply be following the indications. He preferred to keep playing the work over and over, day after day, until I became *convinced*. He wanted his interpretation to become part of me, not something I was producing by rote."

Elman's objection to writing the fine points of his interpretation into the printed music was often mirrored in a disinclination to launch into long discussions of these matters. Musical interpretation, he insisted, was something that had to be felt rather than intellectually understood. Once, when they were flying between cities, Seiger fortified his courage with a couple of martinis, and asked Elman why he made a *ritard* at a certain point in the second movement of the Brahms G major Sonata. "While he lingered over that passage," Seiger explains, "he changed his coloration. It was really gorgeous and effective. But there was nothing in the music to indicate that."

Seiger said as much to Elman. "I wonder," he added, "whether we're not overdoing it. It makes the music come to a complete stop."

Elman looked at him and said, curtly, "Don't tell me what's in the music, Joseph. I know what's in the music."

"Yes, I know that, Mr. Elman," Seiger replied, "but it does not say *ritard* at that point."

"My dear boy," Elman said, "you look again. You'll find it. It's there." He then offered a parable. When he was about Seiger's age, he heard Ysaÿe play the Mendelssohn Concerto. In an exposed passage, Ysaÿe added an attractive ornament that was not in the score, and which caught Elman's ear. He wondered about it through the rest of the performance, and later asked Ysaÿe, "why do you do that? Mendelssohn didn't write it." Ysaÿe smiled at him and said, "but if Mendelssohn had heard me do it, he would have written it."

Seiger took the point, and continued pondering Elman's Brahms. "And the more we played it," he says, "the more I became convinced that this was the only way to do it. Even if it wasn't written in."

Another interpretation Seiger was moved to question was Elman's reading of the Franck Sonata, the first movement of which they took at an exceedingly slow tempo. This time, Elman cited the authority (albeit indirectly) of Franck himself. Elman had played the Franck on one of his British duo tours with Backhaus, and during the intermission of a Queen's Hall concert, in London, he and Backhaus were visited by an elderly Belgian musician who said to them, "Gentlemen, I was with Ysaÿe and Franck when they played that sonata from manuscript, and they took it at exactly the same tempo you did." "So you see," Elman added, "I'm not so far from the composer."

In fact, Seiger especially admired Elman's way with music of the French school. "He could make it sound more French than many French musicians I've heard," Seiger offers. "I thought he had a special feeling for the Debussy Sonata. His interpretation of that was unique, but when I asked him about it, he said, 'Joseph, I am not doing anything the composer didn't write.' He took pains to translate every word of Debussy's instructions. And when we discussed the music, he'd say, 'look, he wants this section to sound *dirty*, or, 'here he wants it to sound *clumsy*,' or even, at one point, 'he wants this slide to make you think of a prostitute.' He not only verbalized, but he characterized the mood of each phrase and each effect. The music suggested pictures to him, and most of the time, it worked.

"A lot of people accused him of being an intuitive player—of being very talented, but without rules or boundaries," says Seiger. "But I found, after working with him, that everything was thought out very carefully, in *addition* to being intuitive and musical. He used a lot of common sense. I never questioned his taste, purely out of musical respect. There were things I didn't necessarily agree with—things I thought were overdone. But everything he did was done with great sincerity. And what came out could not be duplicated."

Elman's and Seiger's first tour together was a substantial one, with a stop in London for a Festival Hall concert, and then two or three recitals, plus concerto appearances, in each of the large South African cities. The performances went easily, but the tour itself was not without its share of drama. In Durban, both Elman and Seiger received telephone calls from blacks who had seen Elman perform in London, but who, because of the apartheid laws, would not be allowed into the South African concert halls. "We're great fans of yours," they told the violinist, "and we would love to hear you play." Elman said he was flattered, and that he would see what he could do.

He took it up with his manager, whose reaction was to stare in disbelief. "Mischa," he warned, "stay out of trouble. You want to finish your tour, and you want to get your money out of South Africa, don't you? In that case, you never received those telephone calls, and you've never heard about the problem." Elman thought he'd better take his manager's advice, and returned to the hotel with instructions for

Seiger. "Joseph, don't answer the telephone until after we've played this concert. And don't call my room. If you want something, knock on my door."

The day after the recital, Elman and Seiger were having breakfast at their hotel when they were approached by a well-dressed black man who told them that he had telephoned a few days earlier, and that he was very sorry not to have been able to hear the concert. Elman looked around the dining room, where he saw a few other blacks awaiting their spokesman. "How many are you?" Elman asked, adding, "I will be rehearsing in my suite in an hour. You are welcome to come and listen." An hour later, Elman and Seiger gave a private concert for a dozen blacks who could not buy tickets to the public concerts.

In Johannesburg, Seiger caught his first glimpse of the clash between Elman's ego and the commercial realities of the record world. After their morning rehearsal, they went out for a walk, and Elman suggested visiting the largest local record shop. Seiger didn't think that was such a good idea: he had been there alone the previous day, and noticed that the store's window display contained recordings by other violinists, with none of Elman's. In fact, there weren't any Elman recordings in stock. But Elman was not to be deterred, and when they reached the store, Elman asked Seiger to go in and ask for his recording of the *Rondo capriccioso*. Seiger went through with it, and then reported to Elman that they didn't have the disc.

Elman didn't believe him. He went into the shop, asked to see the manager, and asked him for Elman's recording of the *Rondo capriccioso*. "I'm sorry sir," the manager said. "We can give you Menuhin, Heifetz, or Milstein, but we don't have Elman." He tried a few other titles, but the response was the same. The two left the shop, and walked down the street in silence. "You see that, Joseph?" Elman finally observed. "They've sold out all my records."

The next day, Seiger returned to the shop and persuaded the manager that since Elman was playing in Johannesburg, it made sense to have his records on hand. Within 24 hours, the shop was well-stocked with Elman discs, and the window display was changed to one featuring the recordings as well as posters advertising the concerts.

Meanwhile, there was drama at home. Helen Elman had accompanied her husband on his pre-war tour of South Africa, but this time she stayed behind, and it wasn't until the tour was well underway that Elman found out why. In the weeks before the tour began, her doctor had diagnosed a cancerous tumor, and told her she would have to have a mastectomy. She knew Elman would have cancelled his tour if he'd known about the impending operation, so she kept it a secret, and entered the hospital as soon as he left. By the time he found out she'd had an operation, the family was able to assure the violinist that his wife was through the worst and was recovering.

In the brief time between the end of their South African tour, and the start of a brief trip through Scandinavia, Elman returned home and Seiger made a visit to Israel. By November, they were back in New York for a Carnegie Hall recital that featured the Sammartini-Nachez *Passacaglia*, a Brahms sonata, Mozart's Fourth Concerto, a suite from Korngold's *Much Ado About Nothing* incidental music and a set of miniatures.

This time, some of the reviewers thought they noticed a healthy updating of Elman's style. "The amplitude of the violinist's tone never ceases to be a source of wonderment," wrote the *Tribune* critic, "and in recent years, since he has cut down on some of the throbbing quality and since he indulges less in his tone for its own sake, he has had more success than ever before in placing it at the service of music." As had been case since his first concerts, Elman's playing on the G string made the greatest impression, from a purely sonic point of view. "Last night," the critic continued, "the tones of his lowest string filled the large reaches of the hall impressively with the dark hue and resonance of the tones of a cello."

Interestingly, the reviewer cited the Mozart concerto as the high point of the program, even though concerto performances with piano accompaniment were by then regarded as antiquated and unnecessary. Elman, actually, agreed with the new view to the extent that he naturally preferred to play concertos with orchestra. Still, he felt that works like Lalo's *Symphonie Espagnole*, the Saint-Saëns *Introduction and Rondo capriccioso* and the Chausson *Poème* worked well with piano, and he continued to play them that way until the end of his life. He also revived the Spohr Concerto No.8 for recital use on several occasions in his last decade; and in 1960, he closed a New York recital with the Khachaturian concerto, although this was an anomaly. For the most part, though, his New York concerto-with-piano repertoire was limited to small-scale works.

"When we played the Mozart Fourth and Fifth Concertos," Seiger explains, "we approached them as if they were sonatas. He was very sensitive about balances, and about bringing out orchestral sounds in the right registers, but many of the published arrangements of these concertos were too heavy. It seemed almost as if the editors wanted to give the pianist something to do, but we didn't feel that worked to Mozart's advantage, so we redid them, restoring the flute lines to the top, the clarinet lines to the middle, and so on. Beyond that, there were things he added and deleted in order to make them feel more like sonatas. And in the concertos we played out of town, we would make certain cuts in the orchestral *tuttis*. For instance, he never let me play the orchestral introduction to the Wieniawski First.

"But playing the concertos didn't bother me at all, except at the beginning, when I wondered why we were doing it. Once I got used to the idea, I actually enjoyed it, because it gave me an opportunity to play with orchestral timbres. Mostly I was on my own in that regard, although there were times he would sit down at the keyboard and show me what he wanted. He had a lovely sound on the piano. He knew the quality of sound he wanted, and he knew how to produce it."

In late September, Elman and Seiger made their first and last joint recording released by RCA, an LP containing seven Tchaikovsky movements and five Wieniawski selections (a Brahms Second Sonata, recorded two months later was unissued). It was a colorful disc, certainly. As a collection, it runs the gamut of late 19th century virtuosic style, and Elman, who had played most of these works since his childhood, was in fine technical and interpretive shape. Passages in multiple stops sing out with a lush vibrato, and the upper harmonics have a pure, bell-like ring. In the more ostentatious display pieces— the Wieniawski *Polonaise Brilliante* that closes the disc, for instance, or Tchaikovsky's zesty *Russian Dance*—his phrasing is as tempestuous as ever, and it's clear that Seiger had, by then, mastered Elman's way of letting these pieces breathe according to their impulses (or his view of them) rather than according to the divisions of the bar line.

Even in the more subdued pieces (the Tchaikovsky *Andante cantabile*, for one) he adopts an outgoing stance, and no matter what the music's character, the variety of timbre he draws upon is impressive. The recording itself has its flaws, the chief of which is that it fails to do Elman's tone full justice. On the top string in particular, the sound is thin and one-dimensional, a far cry from that of the lower strings.

The sound is good enough to convey one especially heartening sign, though. The set shows that Elman had returned to his older and more purely expressive use of *portamento*. Gone are the connective slides he experimented with on his recordings with Rosé. Instead, each note is rendered distinctly.

From Elman's point of view, the collection was fun to make, but it was recovering old ground. All around him he saw younger violinists recording sonatas and concertos, and being regarded as more "serious" than Elman; yet, RCA steadfastly refused to let him take on larger works. His relationship with the label was deteriorating rapidly. In 1950, Elman picked up a set of discs by another RCA violinist, and was shocked to see a condescending reference to himself in the liner notes. He immediately complained to Alan Kayes, the commercial manager of RCA Red Seal, who assured him that the set was no longer in production, and that if it were revived, new jacket notes would be written.

Then, scarcely a week after he had received a profuse apology from Kayes, he noticed that RCA's Home Instrument Department had embarked on an advertising campaign to push RCA's 45rpm player. Adorning the advertisement were pictures of many of the best known and most highly regarded RCA Red Seal artists. The ads ran in the *New York Times*, *Life* and dozens of other newspapers and magazines, and none included Elman.

"I think you will pardon me if suggest that I am still among the living and that I belong to the category of famous artists," he wrote to Kayes, "at least, that is what all the encyclopedias say and what a lot of newspapers the world over have said for 40 years. The books also say that my art represents an historical contribution to the art of violin playing." He then leveled a rather serious charge. "I cannot help but consider this particular omission of my picture as a deliberate affront. By this omission, the Victor Company casts an aspersion on my standing as an artist."

What was just a record player advertisement to RCA was a point of honor to Elman. He noted his long-standing place on Victor's roster, and his loyalty to the label these many decades, and he added that "the Victor Company, in making a recording contract with an artist of my attainments, assumes a moral obligation, if not to help further his career, at least to do nothing to injure it. Injure me is precisely what the company has done." Yet, while the wording of his complaint sounds almost litigious, in the end all he asked for was "the assurance that it will not happen again."

He quickly received those assurances from Samuel Chotzinoff, RCA's General Music Director, as well as a lengthy and assuring letter from Chotzinoff's assistant, George R. Marek, who pointed out that RCA did indeed take pride in having Elman on its roster, and that a biographical portrait of Elman, written by Billy Rose, had been included in a new booklet, *Words and Music*, that RCA was distributing. To further demonstrate the label's sincerity, Marek invited Elman to RCA's offices to spend an hour looking over the promotion plans the company was mounting in his behalf.

But RCA's assurances of their regard for Elman were not borne out in their repertoire discussions. Indeed, the fact that Elman had not been allowed to record some of the major concertos—the Beethoven in particular—proved an extra thorn in his side when he joined battle with WQXR, the radio station of the *New York Times*, in July 1953. Scheduled to play the Beethoven in a Lewisohn Stadium concert with Pierre Monteux, he learned belatedly that WQXR planned to broadcast the performance live, one of several the station was picking up that summer. Elman insisted on a separate fee for broadcast rights, and when the station declined, he refused to give it permission to carry his performance.

So the broadcast that evening was an odd one. The first half, featuring Monteux, was piped in live from the stadium. But after intermission, the station announced that Elman had not granted permission for a broadcast of his performance; thus, in order not to disappoint listeners intent on hearing the Stadium Symphony's all-Beethoven concert, the second half of the program would be offered on disc. Given the disagreement, the station might have opted not to play an Elman recording of the work even if there were one; but that wasn't an option, so while Elman fiddled at the Stadium, the listeners at home heard Heifetz and Toscanini.

The next morning, right under the review—which was positive, overall, and which called Elman's cadenza "one of the evening's highlights"—the *Times* ran a story about the dispute and WQXR's change of programming. As far as Elman was concerned, this added insult to injury, and it focused his attention once more on what he considered RCA's prohibitive recording program.

Seiger had already started trying to persuade Elman to consider other labels. And soon after the Stadium concert, one of RCA's more harebrained marketing plans helped drive an even larger wedge between Elman and the company. Early in July, he learned of RCA's plan to issue a "condensed version" of his Mendelssohn Concerto recording. "This," he wrote to Alan Kayes, "is the type of performance that would normally be used for a children's concert." Kayes assured him that RCA hoped the record would have a broader appeal than that, and even sent Elman a test pressing of the edited version.

"Frankly," Elman replied in a letter from San Francisco, dated August 10, "I don't understand the object of releasing such merchandise. This needs a lot of explanation, since I don't off hand see anything educational about it.... Do you intend to release more works in abbreviated form? I would like to know what artists have given you the permission or approval for this sort of thing."

The condensed Mendelssohn disc was never released. But by the time he wrote this to Kayes, he had already resolved to leave RCA, and had communicated his decision to the label chief, Emanuel Sacks. At the same time—in a letter dated August 7—he expressed his displeasure in a heartfelt letter to David Sarnoff.

"I cannot tell you how much I regret this, not only from a financial point of view, but from a purely sentimental point of view," he wrote. "The reason I am leaving the company is very simple. I have not worked hard and built up a big reputation to be held back on repertoire so as to enable another distinguished violinist (his name is no more and no less than Mr. Heifetz) to record whatever his heart desires, in spite of the big expense involved in recording with orchestra. It seems perfectly ridiculous, when people come into a record shop and ask whether they have the Beethoven concerto, the Brahms or the Tchaikovsky by Elman, and the answer is always, 'No, but we have it by Heifetz.' And this applies to many other concertos. As a real music lover, nobody knows better than you that there is more than one interpretation of a great work, and it seems that it is much more to the credit of the artist when the public chooses their favorite interpretation. What the company is doing is to eliminate the competition in order to sell the record or records of the one the company favors."

He went on to note that his repertoire discussions with Sacks and Kayes invariably ended with his being told "sorry, but we have made commitments," and he wondered about the basis on which those commitments were being made. "If the argument is that Heifetz brings in more money," he suggested, "then I say, give me the same privileges and promotion, and the sale of my records will at least double and treble. I cannot tell you how much was said to keep me in the dark as to why they could not comply with my request to record certain works that go with the prestige of my name. I do not mind telling you, and this, believe me, is not boasting, that the consensus of opinion is, excuse my immodesty, that I am at the height of my artistic power. What a pity that sooner or later another company will benefit from it!"

Sarnoff wrote back promptly, saying that he, too, would be sorry to see the association between Elman and the label end, and suggested that Elman meet once more to meet with Sacks, Markek and Kayes—who, he pointed out, had to exercise their authority as the management of the record label according to their best business judgement.

In early October, Elman met with the company as Sarnoff requested, but the results were predictable. Elman insisted that the renewal of his RCA contract was contingent upon a commitment from the company to record him in orchestral literature; and the company responded that they could not justify the expense, and that they would be happy to record Elman in the literature for violin and piano. Elman was not to be appeased—how could he be, knowing that between 1950 and 1953, RCA had let Heifetz record a pair of Bach concertos, the Beethoven *Romances*, Sarasate and Saint-Saëns dazzlers with orchestra, the Bruch First and the Conus and Korngold concertos, as well as his second versions of the Beethoven, Tchaikovsky and Walton? It was, as he told Sarnoff, time to take his talents elsewhere. And the British Decca firm was waiting with open arms.

CHAPTER EIGHTEEN:

A Career Revitalized

The end of 1953 was a troubling time for Elman. In July, his mother died, and by October, his longest-standing business relationship, his affiliation with RCA, had come to an end. Other than through his sisters, his links to his child prodigy years were now severed. He didn't dwell on this. "My husband never thought about the past," Helen Elman says. "He saw himself as a man who lived in the present and looked to the future."

On that count, he had plenty to look forward to. Seiger was working out perfectly, and his touring schedule was as solidly packed as he wanted it to be. Besides his regular performances in England, France and Scandinavia, he planned return trips to South Africa, Latin America, Japan, Australia and New Zealand. His American tours continued to take him coast to coast, with visits to the larger Canadian cities along the way. And when he submitted his first list of proposed sonata and concerto recordings to Decca/London, the company agreed to the lot and arranged session dates to coincide with his visit to London that year.

So as the 1953–54 season began, Elman threw himself into his daily practice routine, and in no time he was back in good spirits. The start of each season was a special time for him, a time to browse through the literature once more before settling in on the year's recital programs and concertos. Seiger, too, found this the most interesting part of the year.

"Those were wonderful times," Seiger reminisces. "We would try different combinations of works, and every day he would go to his library and take out pieces he hadn't played for years. One day he came in and said, 'Joseph, do you know the Goldmark concerto? Wait, I'll get you the music.' We'd play through it, and it would be very refreshing. Another time, he decided that we should read through all the Mozart sonatas. We did, but when it came time to select one for his program, he would always choose one of the two big B-flat sonatas [K. 378 and K. 454]."

That season, Elman settled on two programs. The main one was built of four extended works (a Nardini sonata, the Beethoven "Spring," the Bach *Chaconne* and the Glazunov concerto) with only a pair of short pieces (Kreisler's infrequently played *Malagueña*, and the Vieuxtemps *Rondino*). The program as a whole took on greater proportions than those Elman had offered a decade earlier, and even the vignettes were a bit broader-scaled and less overexposed. His alternative program, offered in smaller towns, was closer to the old-fashioned variety, and included the Sammartini *Passacaglia*, the Mendelssohn Concerto, Korngold's *Much Ado About Nothing* suite, and a different selection of little works, familiar (*Zigeunerweisen*) and novel (Marsik's *Poème de Mai*, and Charles Miller's *Cubanaise*). And he ended the season with a performance of the Mendelssohn Concerto at Lewisohn Stadium, with Sir Adrian Boult on the podium. Only a few months earlier, in London, Elman and Boult had collaborated on Elman's remake of the Tchaikovsky Concerto, and on a pairing of the Bruch First and Wieniawski Second.

The critics, by and large, were at peace with him now, although New York critics continued to note that his style was at odds with current conceptions of the music of certain eras. Elsewhere, Elman's reviews in the mid-1950s were quite enthusiastic. "Elman may be almost 63," wrote a reviewer from the *Toronto Daily Star* at the start of the 1954–55 season, "but he showed he still has youthful fire, vigor and romance and has lost nothing of the golden tone for which he is famous around the world." And in Winnipeg, on the same tour, the critic's only complaint (and not an unreasonable one) was that the major works on Elman's program—a Handel sonata, the Beethoven "Spring," and Lalo's *Symphonie Espagnole*—were the same he'd played on his last visit to the city, in 1946. As for the performance, the reviewer noted a special vitality. "The final group," he reported, was "played with all the zest and impulse of a youthful genius."

Elman's luck with the critics persisted through the next few seasons, even when the concert circumstances were less than ideal. In June 1955, he was reunited with Monteux and the New York Philharmonic for an all-Beethoven concert at Lewisohn Stadium. According to Olin Downes's *Times* review, the performance was a triumph of "the native warmth and humanity of (Elman's) playing." But the concert could just as easily have been a disaster, for Monteux had come to New York directly from a conducting engagement in Amsterdam; and because of delays occasioned by his insistence on traveling with his poodle, he did not arrive until just before curtain time. The concert took place unrehearsed.

"When it came to playing concertos," Seiger explains, "Mischa Elman was a no-nonsense musician. He was prepared, he knew what he wanted to do, and if the conductor was with him, it was a pleasure. Monteux was one who understood him, and I think of all the conductors he worked with, Mischa liked performing with Monteux the best. When they played together—even at that concert they did with no rehearsal—it was like chamber music."

His collaborations with conductors were not always so easygoing, though. In some cases, basic disagreements over the intrinsic value of the music led to performances he considered less than ideal. "He told me once about playing the Glazunov with Rachmaninoff conducting," Seiger recalls. "All through the performance, Rachmaninoff was shaking his head, saying, 'dreadful music, dreadful music.'" His collaboration with Beecham, in the Tchaikovsky, was equally unsuitable, "the coolest collaboration you ever heard," Seiger says.

Beyond that, differences in approach sometimes led to a face-off between soloist and conductor. "There were some conductors who came to the rehearsal and continually stopped the orchestra to lecture about what they wanted. That didn't appeal to him very much. He just wanted to play, and the analysis made him impatient. Besides, no matter what their explanations were, when Elman came in with the solo line, he played it *his* way, even if that meant taking an entirely different tempo.

"These were, however, established conductors, and some were flexible enough to know immediately that they had to adjust. But I never saw him have an open disagreement with a conductor in front of the orchestra. If it wasn't going well, in rehearsal, he would stop and say, 'Let's start again,' and sometimes things settled in. If not, he would give in to the conductor, but at the break he would speak with him privately and say, 'look, I'd like a little more time here,' or, 'I like to take this section a little faster.' And nine times out of ten, the orchestra would catch on and follow him, regardless of the conductor."

If he failed to reach an agreement, or when the performance was especially important to him, Elman found other means of imposing his will. In June 1958, for instance, he was invited to play the *Méditation* from *Thaïs* at Covent Garden's centennial gala—a concert that featured dozens of luminaries from the world of opera and dance, including Maria Callas, Jon Vickers, Jussi Bjorling, Joan Sutherland and Dame Margot Fonteyn. The *Méditation* was one of Elman's early signature pieces, a work he'd played at many galas of this kind in his youth; and so far as Elman was concerned, the fine points of interpretation were simply not open to discussion. When he first met with the conductor, Georges Prêtre, in his suite at the Savoy, there seemed no disagreement. "Tres romantique," Prêtre commented when Elman and Seiger played the work together, "tres magnifique."

At the dress rehearsal, though, Prêtre took a quicker tempo. Elman stood fast, entering at the pace he preferred; but Prêtre did not modify his accompaniment. Soon it was obvious that Prêtre was not going to defer to the violinist. When the rehearsal ended Elman telephoned his manager and said, "you tell this young man that if he does that this evening, I'm walking off the stage." At the performance, Prêtre conducted it at the speed Elman preferred.

Conductors who understood Elman's style and who were willing to give him the room he required, on the other hand, found working with him an uplifting experience. One who cherishes fond memories of his collaborations with Elman is Efrem Kurtz, a Russian-born American, nine years younger than Elman. Kurtz had studied with Glazunov, and held a number of posts in the United States and Europe over the course of a long career.

"I played with him many times," Kurtz recalled, "but I think the best of the performances he gave with me was in Palermo, in the early 1960s. He played the Beethoven, and he played it like a god. Palermo has a very beautiful old theater, and a very bad orchestra; but that didn't bother him. He went out and showed them what he wanted, and we spent a lot of time rehearsing. What did we discuss? Well, he didn't discuss tempo. But he did talk about his phrasing. He would take the violin and say, 'I will begin this way,' and play it. One phrase flowed into the next in the most ingenious way. The breathing was always there, and of course there was that fantastic sonority of his. His playing was like a painting by Rubens or Rembrandt, and never dull for a moment. It may not have been stylistically 'acceptable'—but who is to determine what is acceptable and what is not? I never had a moment's doubt. He was full of power and energy. He sent out a message that was *his* interpretation of this bible."

❖ ❖ ❖ ❖ ❖

Seiger was fully at ease with Elman and his way of playing by now, but in 1954, he was faced with a tempting offer that tested his allegiance. Emanuel Bay had left Heifetz's service, and Seiger was among those Heifetz invited to audition. "I'm honored, but you know I have a contract with Mr. Elman," Seiger told his representative at Columbia Concerts. "Yes," she said, "Mr. Heifetz is aware of that. However, he would like to hear you play." It was not certain he would be hired, of course, and if Elman found out that he'd auditioned (as he inevitably would have), their relationship would likely have suffered. On the other hand, an offer from Heifetz was a career prospect that could not be immediately dismissed. He sought the advice of Dora Zaslavsky and several friends, who confirmed his own instinct—that he should write Heifetz a letter, politely declining. Heifetz hired Brooks Smith, with whom he worked until his retirement.

"Yes, I do think one reason Heifetz invited me was that he knew it would upset Mischa," Seiger guesses. "On one hand, quite a few of the things Mischa perceived as predatory moves by Heifetz were really just coincidental. But when he looked at what was happening and added everything together, he saw Heifetz as a monster."

One such coincidence occurred on their 1955 summer tour of South America. Since the Heifetz-Elman battle of 1934 had caused such a stir in Brazilian, Argentinean and Chilean musical circles, the biggest impresario in South America, Ernesto de Quesada, decided to recreate it. He invited both Elman and Heifetz to tour extensively in South America that summer, scheduling them in close proximity in virtually every major city on the continent. From an impresario's point of view—and from a culture-hungry audience's—it was perfect. Elman left from New York, and traveled down the eastern part of the continent, while Heifetz left from Los Angeles and started in the west. Their paths crossed, finally, in Chile.

It was a strenuous tour, with concerts in Brazil, Uruguay, Paraguay, Argentina, Chile, Peru, Ecuador, Venezuela, and Columbia, plus a few of the major Central American cities on the way back. Elman and Seiger prepared five programs, a necessity, since their itinerary included that many concerts at the Teatro Colón, and multiple recitals in several other large cities. Seiger was not prepared for the magnitude of Elman's popularity in this part of the world. "His name was magic there. When we played at the Teatro Colón, in Buenos Aires, all five concerts were oversold, and there were people sitting in the orchestra pit and on the stage. Outside the hall, it was wild—we had to be ushered in with police protection."

When they traveled to Japan, in September, they found audiences that were far more decorous than those of Argentina; but there too, it was clear that Elman's stature had not diminished during his long absence. Even the publicity for the concerts surprised him. Along with the standard posters and newspaper advertisements, his promoters had printed up matchboxes that bore a picture of the violinist, fiddle at his chin, with a message in Japanese on one side, and the legend "Supreme Master of Violin Virtuosity!" plus information about the local concert dates and venues, on the reverse.

His records were popular there too—more popular, in fact, than they should have been, for it turned out that many of them were illicit pressings of his old RCA discs. Seiger happened upon some of these one afternoon while patronizing a coffee bar that played classical records. On each table, there was a menu listing the music that was being played, and as he sipped his coffee, he heard several of Elman's earliest discs. Curious, he stopped at some record shops on his way back to the hotel, and found that there were many more Elman records available in Japan (and many of them in seemingly recent pressings) than at home.

"You know, Mr. Elman," he said that evening at dinner, "it seems to me that there are recordings here that you are not collecting royalties on." They engaged a Japanese attorney, who found that RCA in America had no idea that these pressings existed, and no accounting of them. After some negotiation, and an audit of Japanese Victor's books, extending back through the war years, Elman's attorney was able to win a royalty settlement that Seiger describes as "a fortune."

"He was very shrewd in his business dealings," Seiger elaborates. "He always protected himself very well. He had to—he had learned the hard way, by being hurt financially during some of his early tours. He did not like feeling that promoters were taking advantage of him, and by the time I began to work with him, he was very wary of this. Our trip to Japan was the first time he actually showed me one of his contracts, discussed the negotiations with me, and explained how the arrangements worked. I was very impressed. He had been invited over by one of the Japanese newspapers to play 18 or 20 concerts. But since the sponsors were people he didn't know, and since he had no guarantee that they'd come through, he made them sign a fabulous agreement under which the fees for half the concerts were deposited in his bank in San Francisco before we left the country."

Elman and Seiger returned to the United States in mid-October. On their South American and Japanese tours, they had used the programs they had toured the United States and Europe with over the previous three seasons, with a few additions and recombinations. These programs had worked well for them, and they would take them up again the following summer, when they toured Australia. In the meantime, though, they needed fresh programs for American and European consumption, so as soon as they arrived in New York, they began their annual process of reading, sifting and selecting works. As it turned out, they kept the Beethoven "Spring" Sonata in active repertoire, along with the Handel D major Sonata and the Franck; and they added the Vitali *Chaconne*, the Mozart Sonata in B-flat, K. 378, and a new group of short works that included a few novelties—a *Romance* by Tcherepnin, and a *Zapateado* by Gianneo.

In November, Elman's performing season began in earnest with a New York Philharmonic appearance. He played the Bruch First Concerto, with Monteux on the podium. "The slow movement was Mr. Elman at his best," Howard Taubman mused in his *Times* review, "not in the sumptuous manner of his middle years, but in a different and more rewarding way. The tone was mellow, but always pure. It was as if the old opulence had been burnished and was throwing off new and fascinatingly subdued and subtle tints." Taubman admitted that he was no fan of the Bruch First; but he found that the collaboration between Elman and Monteux transcended the work's weaknesses. "In a program of classics," he wrote, "the concerto, which looked to be the weak spot, turned out to be the surprise of the evening."

The week in late November that Elman joined Monteux at the Philharmonic was a banner one for violin aficionados in New York. One of the Philharmonic repeats took place on Sunday November 20, at 2:30 pm, in Carnegie Hall. Three hours later, the Russian virtuoso David Oistrakh made his American debut, in the same hall, and that evening, Nathan Milstein played there.

The enthusiasm for hearing others among the world's great violinists that Elman showed as a child remained with him, and even at this stage of his career, he retained a curiosity about both important rivals and newcomers whose reputations had preceded them, as

Oistrakh's had. Ever since he took first prize at the Ysaÿe competition, in Brussels, in 1937, Oistrakh was widely considered one of the supreme Soviet violinists, perhaps the best the country had to offer. His work had been known here through recordings, and Elman had liked much of what he'd heard. So, fresh from his own afternoon performance, Elman returned to Carnegie Hall to hear his colleague, and was heartily impressed. Here was a violinist who played with the individuality and communicative passion he prized so highly—one for whom depth was more important than speed, but who could call upon a magnificently polished technique when the music demanded it.

Elman enjoyed discussing performances by important violinists almost as much as he enjoyed hearing them. When he liked them, he could be effusive, as he was about young Michael Rabin. Rabin had played for Elman when he was a child, and although at the time he expressed some fears about Rabin's penchant for seemingly undisciplined flashiness, Elman found him extremely promising. Later, his reservations were fewer, and whenever he heard Rabin's recording of the Wieniawski First Concerto on the radio, he would call Seiger and ask, "did you hear the boy? *That's* violin playing. It's the only way to play."

Whether or not he enjoyed a performance, he tended to be diplomatic in his discussions with strangers; but with friends, his morning-after analyses could be comprehensive and entertaining. And they were especially colorful when his idea of what happened at a performance was at odds with the critics' view—as was the case when Henryk Szeryng made his first orchestral appearance in New York, playing the Brahms Concerto with George Szell and the Cleveland Orchestra, in 1957.[1] The reviews were disastrous, and it was said that Hurok was considering dropping Szeryng from his roster. Elman, who thought Szeryng had played fabulously, was outraged, and telephoned several of his friends in the violin world to gauge their reactions, and to offer a few words in support of Szeryng.

"I saw you at the concert last night," he said to the luthier Jacques Francais, "how did you think he played."

"I thought he played wonderfully," Francais responded.

"Did you see the reviews?"

"Yes," Francais said, "it's a shame." Elman, at that point, launched into what Francais describes as a "harangue against critics" who could write so negatively about so fine a performance by an artist of Szeryng's caliber.

"Of course," Elman added, "Henryk Szeryng doesn't play the Brahms Concerto the way Mischa Elman does. For example—wait a minute." He put down the phone and walked across his studio to get his violin. Picking up the receiver again, he told Francais, "this is how Szeryng plays the solo violin entrance," and played the passage just as Szeryng had done the night before. "And this is how I play it." The conversation continued for another hour, to Francais's amusement.

"That morning I heard the entire Brahms violin concerto twice over the telephone—once *a la* Szeryng, once *a la* Elman," Francais recalled, "Can you imagine? That was typical of him. I only wish I'd had a tape recorder."

It was during Oistrakh's first visit to New York—and, in fact, as a result of it—that Elman began considering a trip to the Soviet Union. He was not especially nostalgic about Russia, and he had some misgivings, chief among them being the assumption that the Russia he would find upon his return would be nothing like the country he remembered. Yet, he felt a certain bond with the people there. After the war, when the Soviet government set about repairing the wartime damage to the Tchaikovsky Museum at Klin, Elman donated a set of his Tchaikovsky recordings to the museum's library, at the invitation of the Soviet government. But that had been the extent of his contact with Soviet officialdom.

Until Oistrakh's visit, actually, the idea of going to Russia had played on Seiger's mind more than on Elman's. From the pianist's point of view, the Soviet Union represented fresh and mysterious ground, and he was anxious to see it. And the fact that Elman was the first of the Russian violin school to establish himself in America had a romantic appeal to Seiger, who felt it was time Elman re-established himself there.

That dream came within reach at the end of December 1955, when Oistrakh returned to New York to make his New York Philharmonic debut. For the occasion, a special concert conducted by Dimitri Mitropoulos, he played the Beethoven, Brahms and Tchaikovsky concertos. Eight days later, after a visit to Philadelphia for some performances and a recording session, Oistrakh again joined the Philharmonic, this time for the American premiere of the Shostakovich Violin Concerto No.1, the work Elman had tried so hard to commission during the 1940s.[2]

Elman's concert schedule took him out of town the week Oistrakh played the Shostakovich; and when he finally caught up with the work, several years later, he did not find it entirely to his taste. He did, however, attend the Beethoven, Brahms and Tchaikovsky concert; in fact, he was so eager to hear Oistrakh play these pieces that he arranged to sit in on the dress rehearsal. His impressions were mixed: he found the Tchaikovsky was surprisingly pedantic, and in the Brahms, he found Oistrakh's slow pacing of the middle movement unconvincing. On the other hand, he loved the way Oistrakh played the opening movement, and he liked the finale. He thought Oistrakh's Beethoven was exquisite.

Elman wanted to meet Oistrakh, but he was hesitant to approach him and decided not to go backstage after the rehearsal. Still, he felt they had a good deal in common, and a lot to discuss. Oistrakh had been born in Odessa, where Elman had spent his formative years, although Elman was on his way to America at the time of Oistrakh's birth. And like Elman, Oistrakh had recently presented a series tracing the history of the violin concerto—a difference between them being that Oistrakh's Moscow series spotlighted the modern end of the spectrum, while Elman's explored the classics. And both violinists were avid and accomplished chess players.

The morning after Oistrakh's dress rehearsal, Elman rehearsed with Seiger as usual, and when they were finished, he stood in the middle of his studio, lost in thought. "Joseph," he asked, "do you think I should call Oistrakh?"

"I think it would be nice," Seiger replied, adding "he's staying at the Essex House."

"Alright then, get on the phone and call the Essex House." As Elman packed away his violin, Seiger began making his way through the maze of agencies that separated Oistrakh from the world—security agents from the CIA first, then those from the KGB. Once he got to the Russian end of the chain and said he was calling on behalf of Mischa Elman, the wall of security dropped, and Oistrakh came to the phone.

Elman, speaking in Russian, came directly to the point. "When can you have dinner with me? I'd like to give you a dinner party." Arranging to have the Soviet violinist attend a dinner party meant dealing with considerable bureaucratic and administrative red tape, but both Elman and Oistrakh were anxious that the party take place without hitches. It turned out to be the sort of cross-discipline, starry evening that the Elmans' dinner parties typically were: among the guests were Edward G. Robinson, Helen Hayes and celebrities from virtually all corners of the arts world. Oistrakh arrived promptly, accompanied by a KGB man who checked behind the living room curtains for hidden microphones.

Oistrakh was only fleetingly familiar with the work of the other luminaries among Elman's guests, having been insulated from the American film and theater world. What he really wanted was to hear Elman play; and as these gatherings invariably ended with either chamber music playing or performances of the works Elman was preparing for his next run of recitals, he was quite prepared to accommodate his guest. In fact, that morning, he and Seiger had put in an extra couple of hours polishing the works they would play for their distinguished colleague.

They began their after-dinner recital with the Vitali *Chaconne*, one of Elman's favorite Baroque concert openers. A slowly unfolding set of increasingly complex variations over a simple, descending bass line, it struck him as a perfect way to wade into an evening's program, just as it was in the concert hall. Next came the Mozart Sonata in B-flat, K. 378. The Debussy sonata was a change of pace, its misty Impressionistic textures lending themselves to Elman's coloristic shaping. And the Vieuxtemps Fifth Concerto let the violinist pour forth all the lugubrious emotion his instrument was capable of producing.

A few shorter works—Kreisler vignettes, and some old Elman encore favorites requested by the violinist's friends—rounded out the performance, which came to an end about one in the morning. But Oistrakh was not ready too call it a night. He wanted Elman to try out a violin he had brought with him—a Stradivarius that he was thinking about buying from a dealer in New York.

Oistrakh's request reminded Elman of a warning he had received only a few weeks earlier from a violin dealer. One afternoon, when he was visiting the shop, a young player who was considering an instrument asked Elman to play something on it. He did, and the young violinist, convinced of the instrument's quality, took the violin home. The next time Elman went to the shop, though, the dealer seemed upset with him. "Look," he said, "don't ever play our instruments for the customers."

"But why?" Elman asked. "What do you mean?"

"Do remember that kid you played for—the one who seemed so pleased with the violin after you played it?"

"I remember."

"He came back the next day and told me, 'I just can't seem to get that same kind of tone out of this violin. I think I'll keep shopping.' You ruined the sale!"

Of course, the violin wasn't a Strad, and the student wasn't Oistrakh, but all the same, Elman declined to try Oistrakh's prospective purchase. "Why don't you play it yourself?" he asked. "Here's an audience that would love to hear you."

"Alright," Oistrakh agreed, "but only if you play with me. How about the Bach Double Concerto?" Seiger retrieved the music from Elman's studio, and the two violinists brought the evening to an end with a rousing performance of the work.

The next day, Elman and Oistrakh met again. They spent half the day looking at violins, and the rest playing chess. Their discussion naturally turned to Odessa and Leningrad; and Oistrakh told Elman as much as he could about the country's current musical life. He also asked, casually, whether Elman would be interested in playing in Russia again. "Of course," Elman said. "But you know, I've never been invited."

Oistrakh promptly got in touch with the Russian cultural attaché in Washington, who forwarded an official invitation for Elman to the Soviet Union. The call from the cultural attaché came a few days later, while Elman and Seiger were in the middle of their daily rehearsal. Elman confirmed that he was indeed interested in visiting the Soviet Union, and honored to be asked; and he supplied the dates he would be available to undertake a tour.

Back in the U.S.S.R, the State Concert Agency (Gosconcert) took over, and negotiations regarding the dates, cities and repertoire went fairly easily. Even the discussions about Elman's fee were quickly resolved: Gosconcert would pay Elman the same fee Oistrakh was then receiving in Russia. But there was a catch. Elman, like all artists who visited the Soviet Union, was to be paid in rubles; and rubles could not be taken out of the Soviet Union.

Elman contacted colleagues who had played in Russia, and asked them how they dealt with the currency restrictions. It turned out that there were two ways around the ruble rules. One, as the conductor Charles Munch told him, was to spend the fees there: "They sent me to the store, and I bought a few fur coats. There's nothing more you can do," Munch told him.

The other was to negotiate with Sol Hurok. Hurok had cornered the market for Russian artists, ballet companies, and opera troupes, despite the financial woes these had caused him in the 1920s. He regularly brought them to the United States, and in return, his own artists toured Russia. His influence in this cross-cultural exchange was impressive. When he and his artistic charges travelled between countries, he prevailed upon government connections and managed, both in the United States and in Russia, to get through Customs and Passport Control without the usual formalities, declarations and baggage searches. He was also able to arrange for currency exchanges, so that the rubles an American artist earned in Russia could, through a paper transaction, be exchanged for the dollars a Russian troupe earned in the United States.

Elman had left Hurok's management a dozen years earlier, but he was excited about the prospect of a Russian tour, and he hoped his old manager would make an accommodation for him. "Not a chance," was Hurok's response. "Mr. Elman is not one of my artists. There is no reason I should go out of my way to secure dollars for him." It was nothing personal, Hurok went on to explain; but while arrangements of this sort were in his power, they were not easily achieved, nor was there a guarantee that every one of his requests would be honored. He was not about to waste this particular courtesy on an artist who was not on his roster. As it happened, the star violinist on Hurok's roster, Isaac Stern, had also become friendly with Oistrakh, and he too was contemplating a Russian tour, which he undertook the following May.

Elman wasn't pleased about Hurok's refusal to help, but he understood it from a purely commercial point of view. The real problem, he felt, was the Soviet government, which surely had the power to arrange that he be paid in dollars. The more he pondered this, more annoyed he became. "You know Joseph," he said one morning between sonatas, "this is ridiculous. Why should I put up with this?" He picked up the phone, and called the Russian cultural attaché. "I was born in Russia, and I was proud to have studied there and to have started my career there," Elman told him. "But I have been in the United States since 1908. I am now an American citizen, and I make my living here. And if your great government cannot find a way to pay me in dollars, then cancel the whole thing."

The next day he wrote to the embassy confirming that these were his final thoughts on the matter; and he never again expressed an interest in returning to Russia. But if the exchange put an end to Seiger's hope of paying a visit to Russia, there was one more touring idea close to the pianist's heart—a visit to Israel with Elman. Elman had played there in 1935 and in 1950, and throughout the early 1950s, he played benefit concerts to raise funds for the new state; but there had been no talk of a tour there during Seiger's first few seasons with the violinist. Around the time the Russian negotiations collapsed, Seiger asked about touring Israel.

"Let them invite me," was all Elman said at first, but upon further discussion, it emerged that he'd had a falling out with the management of the Israel Philharmonic just before Seiger signed on. During his 1950 tour, Elman had played the Tchaikovsky Concerto with the orchestra, which was preparing for its first visit to the United States. Elman provisionally agreed to be soloist on that tour, but when negotiations were being finalized, he learned that Koussevitzky was to conduct. Elman liked Koussevitzky, personally and professionally. But Koussevitzky had converted from Judaism, and as Elman understood the orchestra's by-laws, Jews who had converted to other faiths would not be invited to appear as soloists or conductors.

"I don't understand this," he told the orchestra's manager, Zvi Haftel. "You've invited Koussevitzky, who is denying that he is Jewish, and you want me to appear with an Israeli orchestra under a converted Jew?" Haftel did not take kindly to Elman's questioning. "Do you mean to tell me," Haftel asked angrily, "that *we* accept Koussevitzky, and *you* don't? You're going to tell us who we should have?" The exchange grew more heated, and in the end, Elman declined to play with the orchestra, and Haftel resolved never to invite him again.

Seiger found this tale depressing, for a tour of Israel would not be very practical if it were to be all recitals and no concerto appearances; and if Elman was not going to be invited to play with the country's major orchestra, the chances of their touring there were slim. Early in 1957, when Haftel was in New York, Seiger met him at the Russian Tea Room and broached the subject. "Listen," he said in Hebrew, "you've had Heifetz, Francescatti, and everyone else, why don't you invite Mischa Elman?"

"We don't need that kind of playing in Israel," replied Haftel, who had studied the violin with Huberman, and whose playing Seiger had not found especially impressive when he had heard it in Israel. "When two Israelis talk," Seiger explains, "they talk straight." So he did.

"*You* say *that*?" Seiger asked. "I remember hearing you play the *Symphonie Espagnole*, and my ears still hurt. What do you mean, 'we don't need that kind of playing in Israel?'"

"You know what?" Haftel responded with equal directness, "As long as I'm manager, Mischa Elman won't play with this orchestra." Over the next decade, Elman and Seiger made several attempts to get around Haftel, but each failed. One involved the mayor of Tel Aviv—a native of Odessa—who came to a party at the Elmans' apartment and volunteered to take a hand in the matter. "I'll sponsor you," he said. "You'll come as my guest."

"I'll tell you what," Elman countered. "I'll play for free. My performance will be a benefit for Tel Aviv University." The university engaged the Jerusalem Symphony to back Elman, and the concert was scheduled to take place in the new Fredric R. Mann auditorium, the Israel Philharmonic's home. At the last minute, the Israel Philharmonic notified the University that the hall was not available, nor could a new date be found. The visit was cancelled. Abba Eben and Moshe Dayan had, likewise, volunteered to unravel the situation; but they too were unsuccessful.

"This hurt him terribly," Seiger says, "because although he was not particularly religious, in terms of ritual observance or synagogue attendance, he had a deep feeling for the Jewish tradition. It would have pleased him very much to have played in Israel during his last years, and of course it would have pleased me too."

But as he had done in the past, Elman quickly put these disappointments behind him and set his sights on the hurdles that lay ahead—visits to Europe, for both concerts and new recordings; and in the summer of 1956, an extended trip to Australia.

CHAPTER NINETEEN:

Jubilee

Elman's triumphant returns to South America and Japan whetted his appetite for foreign travel, and after a string of American recitals in January 1956, he flew to Europe for recitals and concerto appearances in Spain, Italy and France, returning to America in time to close out the concert season and refurbish the four programs he planned to take to Australia in August. These were, with some alterations, the ones he and Seiger had played elsewhere over the last few seasons. But taken together, they represented a strenuous active repertoire:

The first program brought together the Handel Sonata in D major, Beethoven's "Spring" Sonata and the Mendelssohn Concerto, with the Chausson *Poème*, Achron's *Hebrew Melody*, Benjamin's *From Santo Domingo* and the Wieniawski *Polonaise Brillante* after intermission. Program No.2 began with the Vitali-Charlier *Chaconne*, and the Beethoven "Kreutzer" Sonata first, followed by Lalo's *Symphonie Espagnole* plus the Chopin-Wilhelmj *Nocturne*, Miller's *Cubanaise*, and Sarasate's *Zigeunerweisen*. The third opened with the Nachez arrangement of Bach's Partita No.1, BWV 1001, then the Franck Sonata, with the second half comprising the Bruch G minor Concerto, Elman's own *Tango*, and the Saint-Saëns *Introduction and Rondo capriccioso*. Finally, the most demanding of the programs began with the Sammartini-Nachez *Passacaglia*, the Brahms A major Sonata, and the Vieuxtemps Fifth Concerto, and concluded with Korngold's *Much Ado* Suite, the Chopin-Wilhelmj *Nocturne* and the Wieniawski *Polonaise Brillante*.

The tour was presented by R. J. Kerridge, a company that ran a cinema chain. Kerridge devoted greater attention than many another of Elman's impresarios to fine details, and printed an attractive program book, distributed throughout the tour, heralding Elman as the "Supreme Master of the Violin." Two advertisements within the

257

booklet listed Elman's three most recent Decca recordings. Even Shell Oil took out a violin-oriented advertisement; and Kerridge had alerted record stores to the possibility of tie-ins with the tour far more efficiently than his managers in other countries had done, so that nothing like the embarrassment of the South African record store visit would occur again.

On the other hand, since Kerridge was an independent company in competition with the larger Australian Broadcasting Corporation, some problems emerged around the larger details. The ABC, it seems, was resolutely uncooperative, and not only managed to prevent Kerridge from obtaining any orchestral dates, but declined to allow Elman and Seiger the use of the Steinway pianos it controlled along the route, leaving Seiger to make do with a string of imperfectly maintained Baldwins and Yamahas.

The welcome accorded Elman by the audience was warm, but the critical verdict was mixed, and even some of the more enthusiastic notices left Elman dissatisfied, for they began from the premise that his stylistic mannerisms were reminders of the distant past. Some wrote in praise of this; others tempered their admiration of Elman's legendary tone with condescending reminders that violinists no longer played this way.

Complicating matters was the fact that a violinist 41 years Elman's junior, Christian Ferras, was touring at the same time, and also included the Beethoven "Kreutzer" on his program. When their paths crossed (in Sydney, for instance), some reviewers found the temptation to write "old versus new" reviews irresistible. This irritated Elman and when one reviewer who had written this sort of comparative study sought an interview, Elman refused to see him. Interestingly, the comparison this reviewer had made was by no means at Elman's expense. In the first part of the review, Elman was praised for his suppleness, warmth and vitality; and although the critic marvelled at Ferras's dexterity, and defended the 23-year old's interpretations as sufficiently mature, he took him to task for some overheated dramatic mannerisms which, he added, "didn't succeed in getting any more emotion out of his violin than did the older man." What Elman objected to was not the substance of the review, but the idea of making a comparison at all.

Overall, Elman did not enjoy this trip much, nor did Helen, who found Australia appallingly out of touch with the modern world, and was sorry she came along. When Elman had visited there in his younger years, the country's frontier profile hadn't bothered him. But now he was 64 and diabetic, and its roughness was inconvenient. In one town, for instance, he checked into a hotel and asked Helen to order him a bottle of seltzer, only to learn that the hotel not only didn't serve liquor, but refused to serve any beverage that would normally be mixed *with* liquor. They suggested Coke, but since it contained sugar, Elman couldn't drink it.

As these inconveniences mounted, combined with the great distances that had to be traversed between major cities, the tour began to take a toll on Elman, and apparently this weariness could be heard in at least a few of his performances. For the first time in his career, he read reviews that described his playing as dull—not wayward, overly Romantic, or shaped in a way that defied the limits of current taste, but simply *dull*: "[The works on the program] were listlessly played," observed one critic, "as if Elman were too tired to have strong convictions about them."

By the time Elman left Australia, though, one more circumspect reviewer put his performances in perspective rather artfully:

> It is said that the Universe is only as old as each of us, and the most dangerous experiment is to attempt to regenerate it. Elman preserves the idiom of an epoch almost departed. He is wise, although character and style are difficult to share with a younger generation, to teach us from the inexhaustible mind of the past, but as we are self-styled more intelligent than sensitive, our critical voices are out of tune. Today, we look for faults in others with a pompous unwillingness to see them in ourselves. We are ungracious and lack the courtesy and respectful flexibility due to finer things. It may be this lack which prompted a Sydney newspaper to print a double concert review concerning two individual artists (Elman and Ferras) in one notice! Surely each is sufficiently worthy of separate mention? This was sheer journalistic bad manners and discourtesy! The playing of the Beethoven "Kreutzer," the Brahms A major, or the Cesar Franck; either would be sufficient to show Elman's musical and architectural authority. Those who missed hearing Elman missed an Australian session of the Twilight of the Gods, and if they missed out because they thought he was too old, or that a critic or two were not enthusiastic, their musical education should be watched over with solicitude.[1]

Elman did not return to Australia; in fact, this tour and the previous year's visit to Japan mark the end of Elman's distant travels. Thereafter, he divided his time between Europe and the Americas.

❖ ❖ ❖ ❖ ❖

His recording career, meanwhile, had experienced the rebirth he had hoped for, but by the time his contract with Decca/London came up for renewal, in 1958, there was enough mutual dissatisfaction with the fruits of the relationship that Elman and the label agreed to part ways. At the start, the company's open offer thrilled Elman, and during his first couple of trips to Decca's studios, he recorded the Tchaikovsky and Beethoven concertos, as well as the Mozart Fourth and Fifth. For the Tchaikovsky—and later for the Bruch First and Wieniawski Second—Decca matched him with Sir Adrian Boult and the London Philharmonic. For the Mozart, he was joined by Josef Krips and the New Symphony, and for the Beethoven, he was again joined by the London Philharmonic, this time led by the rising star on the Decca roster, Georg Solti.

Decca also suggested that Elman record some Beethoven sonatas with Solti as the pianist, but Elman preferred to record them with Seiger. "We've rehearsed them, we've played them together, and we understand each other," he explained, and the label let him have it his way. Together, Elman and Seiger recorded a healthy selection of their repertoire during those three and a half years, including Beethoven's "Spring" and "Kreutzer" Sonatas, the Grieg First and Third, the last two Brahms sonatas, and the Franck and Fauré—plus three discs containing works from his recital programs. The first brings together Korngold's *Much Ado About Nothing* Suite, Achron's *Hebrew Melody*, the Josten *Sonatina*, and Bloch's *Ningun*; the second, called *Elman Recital* offers the Sammartini-Nachez *Passacaglia*, the Vitali-Charlier *Chaconne*, the Handel D major Sonata, and Bach's *Air on a G String*, and the third, entitled *Elman Encores*, contains short selections by Dvořák, Mendelssohn, Kreisler, Espejo, Sammartini, Wieniawski, Benjamin and Smetana, along with Elman's own *Tango*.

These recordings run the gamut of compositional styles, from the Baroque through the more conservative side of the 20th century, and from works of sublime seriousness to those lighter in spirit. Some are brilliantly rendered. On the *Encores* disc, for instance, one hears some truly dazzling, high-wire playing that attests to Elman's still considerable dexterity—and to his special ways with the literature's display pieces. The disc of Korngold, Achron, Josten and Bloch gives us a valuable look at pieces that were staples of Elman's repertoire in the mid-1950s, but which have rarely been heard since his time. They are not works of enormous consequence; but they represent the most modern pieces he played, and they allow him to show sides of his art that the standard repertory does not. In the Korngold particularly, contemplative moments, played with gorgeous expressivity, alternate with more colorfully outgoing and even lightly humorous turns. And elsewhere in the recital, the music invites him to engage in unabashed soulfulness, a challenge he was always ready to accept.

The Baroque pieces on the *Recital* LP are more troublesome. They are wonders of timbral beauty, yet they are presented with such gravity, and in so stentorian a fashion, that they grow unduly ponderous. In the concerto discs, his slow, broad tempos also make for weighty and not entirely successful readings; and in the sonatas, particularly the Beethoven and Brahms, not only does he freely apply his characteristic *portamento*, but he alters the rhythmic shapes of the main themes upon their reappearances in the recapitulation sections.

For the critics of the time, it was difficult to reconcile this headstrong interpretive individuality with current notions about the degree to which a performer may recast a phrase without perverting the composer's message. Thus, while these discs had their champions, the preponderance of critical opinion ran against Elman's approach.

One of the first notices was published in the *New York Times*, in March 1955. Written by John Briggs, who had written with understanding and sympathy about several of Elman's recent recitals, this is basically a positive review, but with some reservations. "In this new disc," he wrote of the Tchaikovsky, "Mr. Elman's famous tone is, as usual, an exciting sound. The performance is conceived along Elmanesque lines, on a big scale, with sweep and a disinclination to worry over trifles (some of the flaws of intonation in the opening movement, for example, might have been corrected by a more meticulous performer). Mr. Elman's many admirers will not worry about such minor matters, however, for the essential Elman fervor and lyricism are abundantly present."

In those few sentences, Briggs captures both the pleasures and the problems of virtually the entire series. Indeed, a truer and more expansive barometer of critical feeling about the series emerges from the pages of *High Fidelity*.[2] Three reviewers addressed Elman's recordings in the magazine's pages—Paul Affelder, C. G. Burke, and Harold C.

Schonberg—each with a somewhat different point of view. Affelder was the most accepting. "Elman and Seiger approach both sonatas with the utmost care and discretion," he wrote of the Grieg disc. "They allow the music to speak for itself, setting it forth in simple, sensitively phrased fashion."

But Affelder was not consistently in Elman's camp. Upon the release of the Bruch and Wieniawski concerto coupling, the following year, he observed that "with a certain degree of nostalgia, we speak of artists of the 'old school.' Mischa Elman may or may not care to be placed in this category, but it is here that he belongs." He went on to note that since the works on the disc are also of the "old school," the combination should be ideal—but that in this case, it's not. He found the Bruch somewhat disjointed, and marred by what he calls "debatable liberties," and the Wieniawski on the slow side, but better than the Bruch: "The *Romanze* is particularly congenial to the violinist's talent; here he has a chance to sing with freedom of style and beauty of tone, and he takes full advantage of the opportunity."

A year later, Affelder reviewed the Fauré and Franck sonatas, and the *Recital* and *Encores* discs. The latter two he found thoroughly pleasing—"the performances throughout are of a caliber to lift nearly everything onto a high artistic plane," he wrote of *Encores*, and *Recital*, he reported, was "one of the best of [Elman's] recent efforts before the recording microphones." The French sonata disc fared less well. "As an interpreter," wrote Affelder, "Elman can be a sensitive stylist or a rank eccentric. Both facets of his musical personality are revealed here." In effect, he felt that the Fauré reading was played with "fine polish and rare musicianship," but that the Franck was ruined by "all sorts of liberties in tempo and phrasing."

But if Affelder blew hot and cold according to the work at hand, the other *High Fidelity* critics wasted no ink on diplomacy. Writing about the Brahms sonatas, Harold C. Schonberg observed that Elman's "big, thick style sounds clumsy here, and his constant interest in bringing out melodic lines and his own magnificent tone at the expense of other elements of the music does not make for the purest style imaginable."

Even more scathing were the comments of C.G. Burke: "It would be sadism to deride this astonishing pair of performances," he wrote of the Beethoven sonata disc. "The violinist strings together some thousands of lovely noises in a quite personal and unfamiliar way, although there are reminiscences of Beethoven in many measures and in the *Adagio* of the 'Spring' Sonata we hear Beethoven absolute."

Burke also tackled the Mozart concertos. "The stylization suggests a sure grounding in Coleridge-Taylor. It is the work of a free man, a little dazed," he observed. "The pace is languid, inclined to swoon, the phrase unshaped, as if stuck in molasses on the bow." The Fifth Concerto, he added, was "a hymn to melting butter, an apotheosis of goo."

One can argue that some of these views, particularly Burke's, are extreme and perhaps gratuitously harsh, and perhaps three decades distance provides a sense of perspective that makes it easier to admire the distinctiveness and individuality some of these performances show. Yet, complaints were not entirely unfounded—something Elman, Seiger and the Decca/London production teams realized at the time, although they disagreed about the roots of the problem.

For all concerned, the great frustration of these recordings was that while they capture the contours of Elman's interpretations, and a hint of the tone he produced in the concert hall, the gulf between these discs and his concert playing was huge—a point that is made startlingly clear when concert tapes of these same works, recorded in the mid-1950s, are compared with the versions on the discs. In the Baroque works particularly, the concert versions embody a lightness and transparency that the disc versions simply do not approach.

The reasons for this are many. In the concert hall, Elman's warm, lush tone took on a special character as it resounded through the room, and the distance between Elman and his listeners (or between Elman and the live recording microphone) played a part in the way the sound was perceived. On many of the Decca/London discs, Elman is recorded closely, and the breadth of his tone seems overwhelming and unnatural; and after a while, the recordings take on a glutinous, cloying quality that poorly represents Elman's sound. At that, the closely placed and unforgiving microphones also magnified some occasional flaws in the fabled tone—a harsh attack here, a wavering of intonation there. These were unacceptable blemishes to many listeners, and certainly to many critics, to whom these discs sounded rough-hewn when set aside the crystalline recordings of Heifetz, Oistrakh, Milstein and Stern released in the same period.

"Yes, there were some problems," admits Seiger. "Partly, I think it was too much of a change. You have to remember that he had not made many recordings for RCA in the years just before we went to Decca, so he was not familiar with the new methods of recording. He was not comfortable with them. Another difficulty was that the Decca crew was constantly changing. We might record a couple of sonatas one day, and then when we returned to the studio a few days later, the producer and the entire engineering team would be different. So he was never able to build a rapport with the technical staff—he had to keep adjusting himself.

"The real problem, though, was that he felt constrained in the studio. In his concert performances, and even in our rehearsals, he liked to really let it out. He was completely free, and that made all the difference. But he didn't feel that freedom in the studio."

It bothered Elman, Seiger adds, that in the studio he had to try his best to stand still as he played, and after decades of twisting at the waist and wandering along the stage, this restriction was a heavy one for him. There was no rebelling against this, for when he moved, the sound on tape was inconsistent. Eventually, the engineers drew a square on the studio floor, and instructed him, "stand here, please, and don't move." As Seiger recalls, "When they told him not to move, he didn't move. But it affected his playing."[3]

Hearing the recordings and reading the reviews, Decca's Artists and Repertoire department had second thoughts about the series; indeed, decades later, in a memoir of his years as one of Decca's premier producers, John Culshaw referred to the Elman discs only in passing, noting that "an attempt to record violin concertos with Mischa Elman late in his career proved little short of disastrous."[4] Moreover, there were feuding factions within the Decca/London organization at the time. One side stood by Elman, while the other preferred another of the label's violinists, Ruggiero Ricci. It did not sit well with Elman that his recording of the Brahms Second and Third Sonatas was issued at the same time as Ricci's, a circumstance that invited comparison reviews.

Ultimately, the company cast its lot with Ricci, a decision Elman saw reflected in both artistic and purely commercial ways. Commercially, he began to notice that in the United States, his recordings were not being distributed as widely as he expected them to be. Even in New York, he found it much easier to find Ricci's recordings than his own. Artistically, the problems multiplied. At repertoire meetings, he encountered resistance that brought to mind his dark final days at RCA. His original *carte blanche* had been rescinded, and when he suggested works he wanted to record, he was told that Ricci was about to undertake them, and that they wanted to avoid duplication.

Equally frustrating was the fact that when Decca finally agreed to another concerto project, a proposed coupling of the Mendelssohn and

Bruch Second, the label did not pair him with one of its top flight conductors, as in the past, but sent him Anatole Fistoulari. Elman didn't
know Fistoulari's work, and he didn't care for it when he heard it at
their sessions. With the London Symphony, they made their way
through the two concertos, but Elman was thoroughly dissatisfied
with both performances, and argued against releasing them. In the
end, he managed to suppress the Mendelssohn and reluctantly approved the Bruch. Surprisingly, whatever Elman's problems with Fistoulari might have been, the Bruch recording is one of the few
Decca/London discs that captures the full bloom of his sound, if not
quite the expansiveness of his interpretation. Elman realized, by the
middle of 1958, that his days with Decca/London were numbered. But
it didn't matter, for by the time his contract lapsed, he had received a
better offer. Seymour Solomon, the president of the New York-based
Vanguard label, had been in Vienna to oversee some orchestral recording projects during Elman's European tour, and he caught one of
Elman's performances. "I've never heard you play better," he told
Elman after the recital. They arranged to meet again, and to discuss
the possibility of making some recordings together.

Solomon's proposal was even more attractive than the original
Decca/London terms. Along with the promise of a free hand in selecting repertoire, Vanguard provided a healthy advance on royalties, and
Solomon immediately set his mind at ease on two points that had become bothersome at Decca. First, he assured the violinist that he would
personally oversee his sessions. "That worked out wonderfully,"
Seiger recalls. "Seymour knew how to relax him, how to work with
him, and how to get the best out of him. He took charge, but he did
not constrict him, and you can hear that in the recordings." Second,
Solomon assured Elman that the discs would be well-distributed, and
that the label would do its best to win them attention in the press. He
was as good as his word on all those points, and he elicited from Elman
a series of performances far better than those embodied on the
Decca/London discs.

Elman began recording for Vanguard in 1959. In the meantime, he
embarked on a celebratory season that marked the fiftieth anniversary
of his Carnegie Hall debut—his golden jubilee. Elman marked the occasion itself with a Carnegie Hall recital on December 8, a couple of
days short of the actual anniversary. Elman's managers (now the National Concert and Artists Corporation—he had left Columbia in 1956)
made the most of this, heralding the anniversary with an extensive

publicity campaign and a full schedule of special events. An honorary Doctorate in music was conferred on the violinist by Combs College, in Philadelphia. Mischa Elman Day was duly proclaimed in both New York and San Francisco. And in a ceremony at City Hall, on November 24, Elman was presented with a testimonial commemorating his "fifty years of service to music" by the mayor of New York, Robert F. Wagner.

There were also feature interviews in all the New York newspapers. This was the most attention the press had lavished on Elman since the 1920s, and he loved it. He took the opportunity to bring his public up to date on the personal side of his life. "I am fortunate to have married the right woman," he offered. "Helen sympathizes with my moods, and helps me to think clearly in moments of disappointment and distress. She assumed many responsibilities, and enabled me to devote myself undividedly to my art."

By now, Nadia and Joseph were grown, and both had moved to California. Nadia had married a San Francisco businessman, Mel Mack, and had gone there to live. They had two daughters, ages four and seven at the time of the jubilee concert. Josef had moved to Hollywood, where he was pursuing an acting career, with modest success. Elman had, by then, long since given up his secret hope that Josef would become a musician. It wasn't something he had pushed, Josef Elman said, but it would undoubtedly have pleased Elman to know that the line of violinists that started with his great-grandfather would continue.

"I guess he wanted me to follow in his footsteps to some degree," Josef Elman said. "In fact, the Amati was supposed to be for me. When I was a kid, he put it in a safe and told me that when I'd practiced enough, I could have it. But I wasn't about to become a violinist. It was too much of a challenge. Maybe if I'd been somebody else's son, it might have been different. But I had some good teachers, and I guess some talent; and every now and then he would listen to me play. That was nerve-racking, because he was a perfectionist, and he expected everyone to be like him. That's why I didn't think he'd make a very good teacher. I don't think he had the patience.

"At any rate, I also didn't like to practice much, and he didn't understand that, either, since practicing was one of his favorite occupations. You see, when my father was growing up, he didn't have many distractions. There was the violin, and that was his life. When I grew up, I loved sports. I'd go to school with my violin case in one hand and a basketball in the other. My father didn't understand that, but my mother was my savior in that regard. She'd say, 'Mischa, you have to understand that if he's being brought up in this country, he can't play the violin all the time. He has to play basketball.'"

Of course, much as Elman enjoyed telling his visitors from the press that he was happily married and proud of his children, he really got going when given an opportunity to air his views about music and the music world.

"In my day," he mused in a *New York Post* interview, "personality made the publicity. Today, publicity makes personality. Today, when a personality comes along, the public lacks confidence in its own opinions. It lacks discrimination. It needs publicity to tell it: here, look—a personality. Take Van Cliburn," he added, referring to the pianist who had been catapulted to celebrity status after a victory in the Tchaikovsky Competition, in Moscow, earlier that year. "Isn't it a reflection on us that we didn't know he was supposed to be good while he was in our midst—but that he had to be lionized in Russia before Americans got the signal to say that he was 'great?'"[5]

It was during this series of interviews, in fact, that Elman coined an expression that he would repeat often in the future. "We're living in an age," he told an interviewer who asked him for an assessment of the performing world, "in which the standard of mediocrity has been raised."

He also used the occasion to say his piece about the management world, and what he felt was its outrageous abuse of power; and about music critics and musicologists, who he felt had little right to take issue with his readings. Generally, though, even his complaints were delivered in a light-spirited way, and the reporters spiced their stories with descriptions of his infectious laugh. Several concluded their accounts with Elman's encomiums to life in the United States. "In 50 years of playing here, I had my knocks as everyone else has," he told one interviewer. "All in all, though, I'm grateful to this country for what it has given me. I feel I have received more than I gave."[6]

In the weeks before the jubilee recital, Elman made a string of television appearances, something quite rare for him. On an earlier occasion, he had appeared on a variety show and played a few works, only to learn that the station had gone to a commercial in the middle of one of them. Outraged, he vowed never to perform on television again. "He felt that by going on television, artists were cheapening themselves," Josef Elman recalls, "He thought it was a vulgar way of making a big reputation quickly." Yet, the invitations were there, and in the spirit of the jubilee celebration, he consented to go on a few programs, including the Ed Sullivan Show, on which he and Seiger played a couple of encore pieces, and the Patti Page Show, on which he played a thoroughly Romanticized version of the Bach's *Air on the G String*, set over an unusual choral accompaniment.

The golden jubilee concert itself was a much more formal affair, naturally, the program comprising a Handel Sonata in A major (arranged by Gevaert), the Brahms D minor Sonata, and the Spohr Concerto No. 8, plus the Chausson *Poème*, a Sarasate *Nocturne*, a movement from Falla's *La Vida Breve*, arranged by Kreisler, Tchaikovsky's *Melodie*, and the Wieniawski *Souvenir de Moscow*—this last being the only remnant from the original debut program. At intermission, Paul Cunningham, the president of the American Society of Composers, Authors and Publishers, presented Elman with a gold medallion, in recognition of "his contributions to the musical culture of America."

Elman's following turned up in force for the concert, and when he came on stage to begin, his listeners greeted him with a prolonged ovation. The performance went well until the finale of the Brahms, when in the excitement of the moment, Elman had a memory lapse and was forced to stop, look at Seiger's music for a few seconds, and then take up where he had left off. With the Spohr, the proceedings were back on track, and Elman surpassed himself in the short pieces that closed the evening.

The reviews were composed in the spirit of the occasion, and were generally congratulatory, although the basically supportive tone did not prevent Howard Taubman from mentioning the memory lapse in his *Times* review, or Francis D. Perkins, in the *Herald Tribune* from describing the Spohr work as dated, "more contrived than convincing." Perkins added, however, that the work is "an excellent vehicle for Elman's tone and also for his technical deftness," and that the violinist "played it with persuasive devotion, fully realizing the atmosphere of the music and the style and period it represents."

CHAPTER TWENTY:

Venerable but Vulnerable

For the remaining nine years of his life, Elman kept a grip on the attention that was focused on him during his jubilee year, for if one intangible but important asset accrued to him from these festivities, it was the press's realization that whatever one might say about Elman's style, he was venerable—an elder statesman. Better still, he was outspoken, and journalists quickly realized the eminently quotable violinist could be a useful source of off-the-cuff observations about the state of the music world, or for comments about the ways in which modern times differ from times past.

He was also invited with increasing frequency to expound upon his views and experiences publicly and at length, both as a guest speaker at dinners and ceremonies, and as the author of his own articles. The latter were occasionally constructed from a reporter's interview notes, and published under Elman's by-line; but more often than not, Elman did his own writing. He even around toyed with the idea of writing his memoirs, a project he alluded to in a few of his speeches. Ultimately, the memoirs plan was permanently shelved.

Many of these articles and speeches, particularly the earliest of them, were fairly innocuous. In a piece called "Fifty Years of Concertizing,"[1] he expressed gratitude for the public's support, adding, "I strive continually to evince my appreciation by giving my best whenever I perform." He reminisced about his early years under his father's wing, and about Liachowsky, who was then 84 and living in New York. He mused briefly about his love for chamber music, and mentioned that while he enjoys playing the piano, he avoids the viola. "Unlike some of my colleagues, Ysaÿe, Kreisler, Heifetz and others who love to play the viola in quartet, I shun the instrument. Due to its size, I am sensitive to the differing measurements between the viola and

269

violin and always felt that my intonation suffered a bit after playing viola."[2]

He offered some advice, as well, beginning with a few words on his approach to life: "I am grateful to God for good health. I neither smoke nor drink, nor do I waste energy on the unnecessary things of life. Whatever I do is with a purpose. When so motivated, accomplishment is bound to ensue. This accomplishment promotes a healthy outlook. I believe that if you are mentally healthy you will be physically healthy."

And at greater length, he conveyed his views on a few technical matters:

> As for practice, the trouble with the young generation today is that they are sophisticated before they are mature. In my opinion maturity is the key to overcoming handicaps and inhibitions. I believe that eight to ten hours a day of practice brings lesser results than practicing three or four hours a day. Results come not from the number of hours practiced, but from the way you feel and think. If mentally tired, all the hours put in will not bring good results. People who exercise their muscles without thinking remain icebergs. When practicing, you have to involve your emotions, and three to four hours' practice, putting your mind and heart into it, will bring greater results than practicing ten without the emotionalism necessary to improve your playing.
>
> Tone production, which many think is a purely technical thing, comes from emotions. You produce that which you feel more than others. The degree of emotional feeling is something individual. That is why we have good artists, great artists and—others. I never practice much in terms of hours but rather in terms of concentration.

On other occasions, his discussions were prescriptive in a more general and speculative way. In April 1963, he was invited to speak at a luncheon given by the National Women's Club, in Washington, D.C., where he was joined by the architect Philip Johnson, the choreographer George Balanchine, the writer Paul Horgan, and the actress Cornelia Otis Skinner. David Brinkley served as host. Each speaker was invited to expound for roughly five minutes upon the question, "what would I do for the arts if I were president for a day".

Elman took an unusual approach, delivering a speech that was not a call for more arts funding, as such, but rather, a proposal for a tax allowance that would take the special problems facing performing artists into account. It was an interesting idea. After pointing out that talent was a highly personal and potentially finite asset, and that the income-generating life of a performer was limited both by the short duration of the concert season and by the increasing frailty of the physical mechanism, he drew a parallel between artists and oil wells. The tax codes, he reasoned, gave the owners of oil wells special depletion allowances; so, he reasoned, why not structure the tax law to allow for the depletion of artistic resources as well?

Later in the talk, he offered a few briefer suggestions, including sponsorship of regional opera companies and music schools, and funding for new works; and he suggested that a group of fact-finding committees be set up "to report on the state of each of the arts in our country today, possibly with a view to establishing a Department of the Arts within the Cabinet." In concluding, he returned to his tax proposal. "The arts flourish best where the artist is cherished—at least sufficiently to give him the economic peace of mind necessary to concentrate on his art."

But not all of Elman's articles and lectures took this constructive or advisory tone. In some, he preferred to explore sides of the music world that bothered him, and when he decided to address these matters, he did so in his characteristically unvarnished manner, lambasting those who, in his view, behaved improperly. One of the strongest and most revealing of these is an essay Elman entitled "25 Years of Fiddling: As Seen Over the Frog, or, A View from the Bridge."[3] "What has happened to the music world these past 25 years?" he asks rhetorically at the start of the article, and then warns his readers, "I am going to speak harshly concerning this." After a brief (and, in the context of the piece, rather pointless) anecdote about Auer and the Tchaikovsky Concerto, he launches into an assessment of the music business that was every bit as harsh—and relentless—as he promised it would be:

> Musicians have become commercial. Musicians are no longer artists in the deep sense of the word. They're *artisans*—like a carpenter who makes a chair—their music is made, almost *manufactured*.
>
> When I started, no one would have thought of taking up music, whether to be a performer, teacher or composer, unless he had an extraordinary talent for it. In the past 25 years music has become a mechanical product of the technical age. Many "musicians" have

taken up music just to make money, not because they're interested in giving it *sincere expression*. The younger generation knows all the mechanics but that's *not enough*.

They make tremendous strides in technique but the feeling, the *emotion*, is lacking. They practice many hours a day to accomplish something, but they all work according to a certain pattern. There is no longer any individualism in performance.

A good deal of the blame for this, he continued, fell to critics, who he charged with having "too much power and too little knowledge," a description he would use frequently, thereafter. He then turned his attention to other matters of concern to him at the moment—among them, Russia, arts funding, contemporary music, managerial monopolies, and record company practices:

> Regarding the cultural explosion in the past 25 years, I'm afraid it's not the culture that has exploded, it's the people who give money to the projects; *they* are exploding. Most of these people who handle the distribution of funds don't know what they're doing; they have no feeling for, or understanding of, the art. What sense does it make when a well-known foundation gives grants to performers and composers who have reached middle age? Those musicians have had opportunities to achieve success. If they haven't achieved it by middle age, I believe there is no chance for them to reach the top. Foundations seem to think these musicians can reach the top by giving them grants but, in so doing, the foundation is more often promoting mediocrity.[4]
>
> It's almost unbelievable; the American people are very naive and kindhearted; they're taken in by people who are good salesmen.
>
> Composers never "had it so good" as they have it today. Most of them are making a good living teaching in fine schools. Lully had to come in through the kitchen door. Haydn had to wear a uniform like the stable man. How times have changed! (But so has the music.)
>
> Don't let them tell you about this cultural explosion business. The composers in this country have a clique. Together they have strength in influencing orchestras to perform their works. In all my career I never had to confront a situation like this; but the condition has grown worse in the past 25 years, and I feel genuinely sorry for the young artist—the *real* artist—who must hurdle these almost insurmountable obstacles.

And more about composers. Many present day composers admit that their own works may lack beauty but they say they are "entitled to 20th-century expression!" They have driven many truly musical people away from concert halls, despite the cultural explosion so widely discussed. In my opinion, the whole thing is artificial. You can't buy genuine culture. (And the general public, for social reasons, will attend almost any highly publicized cultural event, especially those held in the glamorous new halls.)

To me, culture is something *national*. Every nation, every section of the world, has its own behaviors and aesthetics. It takes centuries for a nation to develop its own way of life and manners. For instance, the Japanese: the greatest compliment they can pay a host and hostess is to slurp their soup when they eat; they even go so far as to burp. This seems strange to us but look at it from the other point of view.

We're so naive in this country! Good people are willing to give money because it's deductible, but they give it indiscriminately. I believe sincerely in helping young people develop, and I'm strong for giving them opportunities, but there must be a better way of doing it.

Back to composers. Among Russian composers, for example, not every one of them is a Tchaikovsky or a Rimsky-Korsakov, but even compositions written by lesser composers than Tchaikovsky and Rimsky-Korsakov have a *feeling in them*. They have *emotion*, which is much more than just putting dissonances together to prove they "belong to the 20th century." The great Russian composers didn't have to prove they were living in a certain age—they wrote from the heart. Today many Russian composers still write from the heart. I am amused when I hear talk about the cultural exchanges between our country and Soviet Russia. Our artists who go there get paid in rubles which they cannot take out of Russia but the Russians can take out our dollars. That's no cultural exchange; the Russians benefit monetarily, the Americans don't! The Russians take out the good American dollars—and they're also paid higher fees than artists from other countries!

The entire Russian system is different from ours. According to Russian standards of living, their artists are extremely well paid. Russian artists live there much better than people in other professions, by comparison, so they have plenty of money for their own standard of living. When an American artist goes to Russia to perform, his expenses continue here in America where there is an entirely different standard, and he is living up his earning capacity.

Russia is a country which does not believe in private enterprise, yet it turns over practically ninety per cent of its attractions to one

manager[5] here in this country. While I certainly have no objection
to giving the American public the opportunity to attend some of
the Russian attractions which they send over here, I do object to
the *prices charged for tickets* and the *fees* some managers are obliged
to pay because the attractions are being sold as a package. Besides,
high ticket costs are prohibitive for the average customer who is
unable to derive any benefit from either the so-called cultural exchange or the so-called cultural explosion.

I'm sorry to say that the public is taken in 1) by clever publicity
and 2) because of politics between the two countries. I repeat: I
have no objection to artists coming here from other parts of the
world to show us what they have accomplished, providing admis-
sion fees are charged according to their merit, not because we have
to show our friendship to the country from which they come. Even
before they play a note, the audience often rises and cheers! This
misleads the laymen as to the real value of the artist. Incidentally,
I wonder why the foremost artists from other countries besides
Russia are not more often brought to the U.S.A.

The musical situation in this country is not a healthy one. It's
not healthy because it's controlled, monopolized. It's monopolized by managers who wield great influence in this country from
a business, not a cultural, point of view. Many managers are out
only for business. If they try to tell the world they are helping
young artists, I can point out how many young artists they ruin.
Often completely impersonal in managing an artist, they're frequently interested only in the turnover. That's why so many young
artists have nice tours and many concerts *in the beginning* of their
careers, and, three years later, they're played out. (No pun intended.)

If a young artist is successful, if the public accepts him, that
doesn't necessarily mean that the manager will accept him. Why?
Because managers (with very few exceptions) don't sell an artist;
they sell a *package*. When they sell a package they choose an artist
who fits into the package. They don't consider the public at all.
The public is thereby forced to hear performers they never asked
for or never heard of. In selling packages, the manager decides that
so-and-so should appear and the public has no way of voicing an
opinion. They may do so but it doesn't help. Quality is lost and I
believe the public is entitled to hear whom they wish. The public
is being taken for a ride.

This way of doing business now dominates even orchestras and
their conductors; the orchestra boards have little to say. Some conductors behave the way they do concerning this problem because
they too are slaves to the managers. The manager influences the

conductor to engage artists who are often under the same management as the conductor. Back-scratching is what it is, and it's all arranged before it gets to the board of directors. Thus, since the orchestras are obliged to buy packages, they're in a greater predicament than the local managers who run concert series. Why? Because the orchestras engage soloists the conductor wants. And why does the conductor "want" certain artists? Because he is under pressure from managers to engage soloists who are under the same management as he.

The concert manager, conductor of the orchestra, and manager of the orchestra concoct the package and when it's presented to the board of directors it is usually a *fait accompli*. Most boards function that way; they're mostly businessmen and society women who don't question such tactics because they don't realize that there are such behind-the-scene maneuverings.

When the music committee of the board of directors happens to ask for a special artist as soloist, they are often told (after an ostensible investigation!) that the artist they request is not available, that he's in Europe at the time, or some other excuse. Often, the artist's fees are *deliberately misquoted* to the board as being exorbitant so the board will consider the fees too high for its budget.

Also, orchestras are obliged to engage soloists who *record for the same recording company for which the orchestra records* because the recording company *saves money* that way. How? The soloist and the orchestra must rehearse thoroughly for the symphony concert. Soon afterward they get together again and make the record. This way the recording company doesn't have to pay for extra rehearsals which would be necessary if both soloist and orchestra were not with the same company. Recording companies exert a tremendous influence on orchestras because of this.

So the public, who makes it possible for the orchestra to exist, is deprived of hearing many of their favorite artists. This is a great injustice.

Orchestras are not particularly interested in promoting the careers of rising young artists. Why? Because when a young artist is engaged to play with an orchestra, he is seldom asked to play a standard work which might already be in his repertoire. They expect him to play a modern work which the public doesn't understand and doesn't feel; and who suffers by it? The artist. The young artist is under a terrible disadvantage when playing a modern work because the audience doesn't listen to the way the work is performed; it listens to try to get something out of the composition the artist is performing. When the audience doesn't like the composition it doesn't like the performer because it can't judge the performance.[6]

From there, Elman devoted a few paragraphs to the competition phenomenon, which he considered unhealthy and unmusical. He then concluded on a slightly more consonant note.

> Some people may think I don't look at the situation from the other side of the frog, that I don't point out some of the good things. The good things don't have to be explained. I'm trying to point out what's going on because there is so much camouflage.
>
> On the credit side, it is heartwarming to observe how, in the past 25 years, colleges and universities have taken such a tremendous interest in developing their music departments. When I came to this country very few large schools had such departments. It is wonderful now. I praise the music departments because they engage outstanding teachers, quartets in residence and composers. Even though I may not like the composers' music, I admit most of them are very knowledgeable. It is good that the schools have broadened their music departments to teach all phases of music properly.
>
> I urge every college and university student, regardless of his major, to avail himself of the opportunities to learn about music through courses offered by the remarkably fine music departments. Every student should take as much music as he can, for that is something nobody can ever take away from him; it is something he will have to enjoy all his life.

Elman based many of these observations about the machinations of the music business on personal experience. Several times, he and Seiger found themselves at post-concert receptions, at which a member of a presenting organization or an orchestral board would remark that they had tried to engage Elman in previous seasons, but that his manager had said he was not available. When that happened, Elman asked what part of the previous season they had tried to get him; and when he was told, he diplomatically agreed that he had been performing elsewhere. But he was livid. "Did you hear that Joseph?" he would ask Seiger when they left the reception. "We weren't in Europe at that time last year. We were home, between engagements!"

Still, in other parts of the discussion, Elman does exaggerate the evils of the practices he describes—a case in point being his description of the workings of record companies, and the linkage between concert engagements and recording sessions. This has never been a clandestine matter, and in fact, from both the commercial and artistic points of view, the relationship Elman outlines makes perfect sense. As Elman knew, recording with orchestra in the United States had become an enormously expensive undertaking, even under the best of circumstances. And the best of circumstances were those in which the soloist, conductor and orchestra knew exactly what to expect of each other by the time the recording light went on. From a strictly artistic point of view, it also made better sense to record an interpretation that had recently been rehearsed and performed before the public, than to convene the forces independently and let the interpretation evolve before the microphones.

To Elman, though, this linking of performance and recording schedules meant that a certain number of slots in an orchestra's season were automatically taken, and that artists not affiliated with the orchestra's record label were therefore frozen out. A glance at the schedules of the major orchestras, however, shows this conclusion to be vastly overdrawn, for even in the 1950s and the early 1960s, when orchestral recording in this country was still a lively business, orchestras were careful to alternate their soloists from season to season, if only to avoid repetitiveness. There were, to be sure, soloists who were invited back more regularly than others, and certainly recording relationships sometimes played a part in this scheduling. But soloists who were popular with audiences, or who were favorites of the conductors, were frequently re-engaged as well, regardless of their recording affiliations. Elman himself benefitted from this kind of preferential treatment in his early years, and to the end of his days he appeared annually at the Lewisohn Stadium summer concerts.

The root of Elman's complaint, actually, was that as the 1950s waned and the new decade began, he found that he was not being invited to play with the major American orchestras as often as in years gone by, a situation he ascribed to a series of conspiracies between managers, conductors, record companies and orchestra managements. In objecting to these cabals publicly, he cast his complaints in altruistic terms—"these orchestras are depriving the public of the artists it wants to hear." But even the least astute of his listeners could see the subtext, which read, "these orchestras are depriving the public of Mischa Elman."

This polemical approach did not win Elman many friends. To the dispassionate observer, the overstated scenarios he painted seemed silly, and ultimately overshadowed some of the more substantial points he made. And to those in the businesses of promoting concerts and managing orchestras, Elman's complaints were ill-founded and ill-advised, and only alienated him further. "The real problem," Elman's accountant, Jacob Markowitz, confided, "was that Mischa had gotten into battles with so many managers and promoters that there 'were certain cities he just couldn't play in, because the important managers there simply wouldn't touch him. I remember that Emma Feldman, in Philadelphia, would not deal with him for any money. And until they more or less made up their differences, Harry Zeltzer, in Chicago, felt the same way. When you make enemies in the major cities, you run into problems."

Thus, as the 1960s began, Elman found himself still fighting the same two-front war that had occupied him, on and off, since the 1920s. On one hand, the endless skirmishing with managers had now erupted into full battle; and at the same time, the promoters who disliked him could easily boycott him, for the larger part of the public preferred a more modern interpretive style.

Even Heifetz was not immune to shifts in the public's taste, however. In the mid-1940s, Heifetz's detractors called him a "cold" interpreter whose playing was "all head and no heart."[7] In 1951, the composer and critic Virgil Thomson cited Heifetz's "disembodied violin playing," in a *Herald Tribune* review, going on to describe the performance as "completely disengaged from any semblance of personal responsibility to the music it was draped over."[8.] These brickbats were mirror images of those hurled at Elman. But by the late 1960s, Heifetz was being charged with some of the same interpretive sins that had long been ascribed to Elman.

"Heifetz does not play music. He uses it," Alan Rich complained in a 1966 *World Journal Tribune* review. "Last night he used one genuine masterpiece, and a few works of far lesser quality, to show off his way with the swooning phrase."[9] But Rich went on to observe, as Thomson had, that Heifetz seemed detached from the music—that he cared about it only as a vehicle for his playing, and that he was "a master of non-involvement." Whatever criticism Elman endured for his outsized Romantic gestures, non-involvement in the music was not typically among the reviewers' complaints.

In fact, Elman had chalked up an impressive number of critical triumphs in his first recital tours of the 1960s. For the 1959–60 season, he put together a hefty program—a Nardini concerto, the Fauré Sonata, the Bach *Chaconne* and, as the complete second half, the Khachaturian Concerto. There were no vignettes this time, other than as encores. John Briggs, lately Elman's champion at the *Times*, found the *Chaconne* a particularly compelling "demonstration of how great freedom within the phrase can be combined with an overall rhythmic pulsation that keeps the music going."

"His playing," Briggs summarized, "is fascinating for its economy of movement. As usual, there was extraneous bobbing and weaving, but the actual bow stroke was just enough, no more and no less. Mr. Elman's performance, mannerisms and all, is individual. It is the playing of an artist so assured that he dares to be wholeheartedly himself, carp who will. And to judge by the applause, carpers were in the minority."

Elman played the program coast to coast with equal success, and in some cities, he was engaged for orchestral performances, in which he offered both the Mendelssohn and the Khachaturian concertos. At the season's end, just before heading west for a family vacation, he made two appearances at Lewisohn Stadium, the first with the Tchaikovsky Concerto, the second with the Beethoven. In the latter, he held firm to his cadenzas, which reviewers by now took in stride. "They are not very Beethovenian," wrote Ross Parmenter in the *Times*, "but they enabled the violinist, who two years ago celebrated the fiftieth anniversary of his debut, to show that he can still accomplish formidable technical feats."

A year later, he returned to Lewisohn Stadium to play the Mendelssohn and Tchaikovsky concertos in a single performance. In the interim, he played a Vivaldi Concerto with the National Symphony as part of John F. Kennedy's inaugural celebrations; and he played a recital for Kennedy at a dinner given by the Washington press corps. He was doing well in Europe, too; and in London, where reviewers had lately been sharply critical, a Festival Hall concert in October 1961 signaled a decisive change. "On this occasion," Hugh Merrick wrote in an appreciation in *The Strad*, "the London papers for once acclaimed him as the master violinist he still is."[10] Merrick had first heard Elman in 1906, a year after his London debut, and in the intervening 55 years, he had kept an eye on Elman's progress—and, naturally, on the progress of the violin world in general. He was an enthusiast, and in his article on Elman, he also writes of the excitement of hearing Ysaÿe (albeit in his decline), Kreisler, Heifetz, Menuhin, Oistrakh and Szeryng. From his point of view, Elman's playing, that October evening at Festival Hall, was no different from his norm, and he guessed that Elman's age may have made the critics more open-minded.

"Whatever the reason," he concluded, "it was good to note from the morning press of October 17, 1961, that Elman has, overnight, been widely recognized by the pundits of London as a master violinist of long standing world renown, whose rendering of major classical works was not only worthy of serious evaluation, but of almost unanimous approbation."

In the course of his encomium, Merrick endeavors to put Elman's style and the press's reaction to it in perspective. "It is true," he conceded of the most common criticism leveled at the violinist, "that from a purist's point of view, he would at times do unorthodox and even irritating things, on which the London critics seemed to fasten avidly. He would—very often achieving thereby an effect which only his incredible tone and technique could encompass—select an unusual tempo, pull a phrase out of shape, carry *portamento* to the jarring-place, introduce embellishments such as a high octave or harmonic repeats. But even when he had offended with some such momentary aberration, the lapse was almost immediately erased from the mind by a magical beauty of playing, of tone quality and of dazzling technical perfection."

The crux of the matter, from Merrick's point of view, is that what Elman did with the instrument defied analysis. "In the ultimate event," he wrote, "Elman is perhaps a violinist's violinist *par excellence*; maybe no-one who has not wrestled with the difficulties of producing an acceptable sound, let alone the technicalities of a perfect intonation and clean notation in a work of major difficulty, from that intractable instrument, could ever appreciate him to the full."

❖ ❖ ❖ ❖ ❖

But critical praise was not what Elman craved most at this time. He wanted to pursue a full schedule of concerto appearances to match his recital itinerary—just as it had been in the early years. With the exception of the Lewisohn Stadium concerts and occasional invitations from smaller orchestras, though, concerto dates were getting to be few and far between. So, a few months after his seventieth birthday, he devised a way of by-passing the orchestral managers who were his bane.

His plan was audacious. He would engage independent local promoters, who would assemble freelance orchestras, to be paid by Elman. Elman would also supply his own conductor—his old friend

José Iturbi. Elman liked the pianist's conducting, and he knew that as friends of long standing, and interpreters raised in the same Romantic tradition, they would see eye to eye. Besides there was a mutual understanding about the nature of the performing relationship: Elman was to be the master, Iturbi the accompanist.

Their program for the Elman/Iturbi concerts consisted of three violin concertos—the Bach E major, the Mendelssohn and the Brahms. Playing three concertos in an evening was nothing new for Elman. He had offered such programs often in his youth, and as recently as October 1959, he played the Bach E major, the Beethoven and the Tchaikovsky on a single Royal Philharmonic program, conducted by Norman del Mar. Still, the gesture was a grand one, for he was now over 70, and instead of slowing his pace to accommodate his age, he was intent on going into higher gear.

More startling than the ambitiousness of the plan itself was the fact that it worked. Elman and Iturbi began in the northwest in the fall of 1961, and made their way east. When there were long stretches between concerts, Elman gave recitals, including his annual Carnegie Hall concert in February 1962—a performance at which he paid homage to Fritz Kreisler, who had died the previous week, by adding an especially tender performance of Kreisler's *Preghiera* to his program. In the spring, Elman and Iturbi took up the tour again, playing their concerto program in the larger cities on both coasts.

Financially, Elman would have been better off simply playing recitals; but the expense of engaging full orchestras and hiring halls was nothing compared to the joy he got from showing the public that he was still up to such marathon feats of stamina and concentration. And from the start, the tour won the hearts of both the critics and the public. Some of the performances turned into gala events. In Portland, Oregon, for instance, the conductor of the Portland Symphony, Jacques Singer, took the podium after intermission and had the ensemble (drawn largely from his own orchestra) play "He's a Jolly Good Fellow" for Elman. A brief ceremony followed, highlighted by the reminiscences of a local architect who had attended Elman's first Portland recital, some 51 years earlier, and who had been chosen, for that reason, to present the violinist with a plaque commemorating his visit.

The music editor of the city's newspaper, the *Oregonian*, found the performance "a source of amazement to witness this artist, who has been playing in public more years than most of us have been alive, and whose ability to lead his violin through an interpretive discourse of the most searching and revelatory kind, and in the process to exhibit vitality of a disarmingly youthful sort."

Elman was thrilled with the response to these performances, and he was particularly gratified to find that the critics in the larger cities were equally generous. When he and Iturbi unveiled their program in Los Angeles, in March, Walter Arlen, in the *Los Angeles Times*, waxed poetic. "Mr. Elman's playing was like old wine: rich, smooth, heady and mellow. It also had its clearness and purity. He oversees each work from the mountain peak of accumulated knowledge, feels every nook and cranny of its topography and charts its course with unerring directness."

A few days later, Elman and Iturbi played again in San Francisco, this time with the San Francisco Symphony at the Opera House, under the sponsorship of the California Music Foundation. In the *San Francisco Chronicle*, the veteran critic Alfred Frankenstein recalled that the first concert he had ever attended was an Elman recital. "Elman's way with a violin has not changed over the years. He is still king of the Romantic violinists, with a gorgeous, big tone, fiery technique, and a highly individual style of interpretation, unfettered by the tyranny of the bar line."

The tour gathered its own momentum as it continued, for the local promoters were as enchanted with the performances as the critics and audiences were, and on occasion they called colleagues in distant cities to suggest that they import the event. One promoter who decided to bring Elman to his town was Eugene Jelesnick, of Salt Lake City. Jelesnick was an all-around impresario: he presented an extensive recital series, conducted the Salt Lake City Philharmonic and a pops orchestra, and was the host of a program on the local CBS television affiliate.

Jelesnick was put on to the Elman/Iturbi program by a colleague in Seattle, and he was not skeptical in the least, for he had been an Elman fan since the late 1920s, when he came to New York from Budapest, where he had studied the violin with Hubay. "I used to save my pennies to hear him at Carnegie Hall," Jelesnick remembers. "I even got to meet him once, when I went backstage after a recital to ask for his autograph. There were many greats, of course, but there was something Elman had that no other violinist could equal—a special quality of warmth, that magnificent tone that came directly from the heart. Even Kreisler didn't have that kind of warmth, at least, not when I heard him. And Heifetz always struck me as, well, ingenious, but mechanical. For me, Elman was the king."

Jelesnick contacted Elman; and after the initial arrangements were made, Iturbi's requirements for the makeup of the orchestra were conveyed to him. "I started with my own Philharmonic, but I had to augment it, because Iturbi would not have any fewer then eight basses. Essentially, I had to put two orchestras together to form the orchestra for that concert." Naturally, Jelesnick attended the rehearsals.

"Elman and Iturbi had a rapport unlike any I've ever seen," he recalls. "The interaction and communication between them was truly inspiring. I also found Iturbi quite commanding as a conductor. He and Elman had clearly worked out the kind of interpretation they wanted, and they knew what to expect from each other. Elman played like an angel.

"But he was also quite excitable. After all, the orchestra was an excellent one, but it wasn't a top notch ensemble like Philadelphia or Boston, and during the rehearsals, when he asked for certain things and didn't hear them, be blew up a bit. And rightfully so. A man of that magnitude deserves to hear what he asks for.

"I recall, too, that one of the music writers came backstage to talk to him, and said, 'Mr. Elman, aren't you playing the second movement of the Brahms a little slower than it should be?' Elman just looked at him for a moment, and then said, 'how do you know how fast it should go? Were you there when Brahms wrote it? I think our conversation is over.' He was very upset."

By curtain time, the orchestral problems were ironed out, the curtailed interview was forgotten, and the concert went without a hitch. "It was everything I'd hoped it would be," Jelesnick says, "a monumental event. People here were elated, and the newspaper ran a story about the concert on its front page."

Elman, meanwhile, had been taken with the way Jelesnick had handled the event, and during his stay in Salt Lake City, he and the promoter began a friendship that lasted the rest of Elman's life. A couple of seasons after the concerto concert, Jelesnick invited Elman back to Salt Lake City to play a recital on his series—a concert that got an extra promotional boost through an interview on Jelesnick's television show; and Elman invited Jelesnick to visit him in New York. "I'll never forget that," Jelesnick says. "In the morning, when he was ready to practice, he said, 'come on up and tell me if I make any mistakes.' I stood there watching him practice for an hour and a half, with my mouth wide open.

"When he was finished, he said, 'now you play for me.' I didn't dare play any of the standard literature, but when he insisted, I played one of the Hungarian gypsy pieces that had been my specialty since my younger days. And he said, 'that's very nice, but why do you keep your thumb so high on the fingerboard?' He was right, of course, and I should have known better: one of the first rules a violinist learns is not to keep his left thumb too high. But I was so nervous, I'd forgotten even that elementary point of technique."

CHAPTER TWENTY-ONE:

A Return to Germany and a Change of Pace

Elman's new relationship with Vanguard got off to a fine start with the release of three LPs in close succession, in 1960. The first two were concerto discs, with Vladimir Golschmann and the Vienna State Opera Orchestra, one of these a coupling of the Khachaturian concerto and the Saint-Saëns *Introduction and Rondo capriccioso*, the other a remake of the Mendelssohn, paired with Lalo's *Symphonie Espagnole*. The third was a sampler of Elman encores, a baker's dozen of them in a package entitled *Elman Jubilee Record: Celebrating Fifty Years of Violinistic Triumph*.

All three must have come as a surprise to listeners who thought they knew Elman's playing on the basis of his RCA and Decca/London recordings. The Khachaturian, composed in 1937, was among the most contemporary works in Elman's repertoire, and in the first movement he made much of its is aggression and angularity, adopting a throaty tone, and supporting the line with all the power at his command. There are moments of tenuous intonation in this opening *Allegro con fermezza*, but unlike the intonation problems that afflicted some of the London discs, this seems controlled and almost purposely done, as if a concession to the harshness of the movement's atmosphere.

Indeed, the purity of tone he brings to the other two movements make it seem all the more likely that he was trying to give the first movement a purposely harsh edge. In the lyrical *Andante sostenuto*, he is more at home: here he casts the solo line in the loveliest and richest of timbres, and he manipulates its shape as freely as if he were playing the Tchaikovsky. And in the playful closing *Allegro*, his deft bowing makes the lively solo line dance rapturously.

The Saint-Saëns, Mendelssohn and Lalo works come across as old friends with which Elman was fully at ease technically, interpretively and temperamentally, and in the case of the Mendelssohn, the improvement over his earlier RCA disc is vast. Here, his tone is fuller and better rounded, his pitch is flawlessly centered, and his interpretation flows more smoothly and freely than on any recording he'd made since the late 1930s. It would seem, too, that the chemistry of the sessions made a great difference in the success of these orchestral recordings. In Golschmann, Elman found a sensitive collaborator who carefully molded the orchestral textures to respond to the impulses Elman conveyed in his solo playing; and Seymour Solomon, the producer, found a way of setting the performance in the most realistic, three-dimensional perspective Elman's sound had ever enjoyed on disc.

Solomon also found a way of compensating for the problems Elman's tone had posed for recording engineers ever since the advent of magnetic tape, undoubtedly by experimenting more vigorously than his predecessors with microphone placement. On these discs, the details of Elman's carefully nuanced, personalized interpretations emerge, but the noise of the bow being drawn over the strings that afflicts several of the Decca discs is banished.

These improvements, notable in the concerto recordings, are even more telling on the *Jubilee Record*, the biggest hit of the initial series. This was a collection of chestnuts Elman had recorded over and over since his early years; but in the past, the constraint of the short 78rpm playing side lingered over him, making it necessary for him to abridge some of the pieces, and to play through others slightly more briskly than he did on stage. This time, Elman had thorough freedom to play the full texts, and to stretch the contours of his interpretations. Some of these performances are slower than the previous accounts; others are at roughly equivalent tempos. But the impression one gets listening to the old and new versions side by side is not so much of a change in tempo as of an increase in spaciousness.

In these souvenirs of an earlier age and performing style, Elman lets his Romantic taste and temperament rule, spicing the works with deftly executed roulades and ornaments, and manipulating the shapes of his phrases in even more extreme ways than he did in the early decades of the century.

What makes this first series of Vanguard recordings so magical is the number of interpretive paradoxes they embody. They are clearly rooted in long experience; yet they do not sound like the performan-ces of an old man. One hears fleet, precise playing, secure intonation, and complete control of the bow here; and the performances show Elman as a supreme colorist. In piece after piece, he shifts from a creamy, smooth tone to a brightly illuminated one, or from a coarse, thick sound to one with a razor-sharp edge, in a way that seems en-tirely original, yet inevitable within the context he establishes. Every slide, nuance, and tempo shift, every touch of *rubato* and dynamic shading, seems carefully considered; but one also gets the impression that this is music Elman could abandon himself to, and a special sense of freedom shines through these performances.

The season after the Iturbi tour, Elman returned to his normal reci-tal schedule, again with a program of full-size works, the short selec-tions reserved for the encores. This year's mixture included the Handel D major Sonata, the Beethoven "Kreutzer," the Debussy Sonata, and the Wieniawski Second Concerto. And at the season's end, he made his annual appearance at Lewisohn Stadium. Elman had become one of the most popular attractions at these outdoor stadium concerts, his performances regularly drawing between 7,000 and 8,000 people and sometimes as many as 11,500, even in seasons where critics noted that attendance had generally been down.

Elman was also, by a long lead, the most frequent visitor to the stadium's stage, and on the occasion of his 1963 performances, it was noted that he had performed at Lewisohn Stadium about 25 times since the series was inaugurated, in 1918. It had also, by then, become traditional for Elman to offer the Tchaikovsky Concerto there. He had departed from that tradition in 1962 (when he played a Vivaldi G minor Concerto plus the Mendelssohn, with Vladimir Golschmann on the podium), but he revived it in 1963.

The year ended badly, though. On a December afternoon, two days before Christmas, he went into a garage at Amsterdam Avenue and 76th Street to use a public phone, and tripped in a stairwell, bruising his right shoulder and fracturing his right ankle. He ended up spend-ing three weeks at Roosevelt Hospital, where he was put in an ankle to hip cast. Naturally, his concert engagements for the next several months had to be cancelled.[1]

While he was incapacitated, however, Elman turned his thoughts to Europe—specifically, to Germany. In 1964, he would celebrate the sixtieth anniversary of his professional debut in Berlin. But Elman had not played in Germany since the early 1930s, and his feelings about returning were mixed. He had always loved the German public, and during the first three decades of his career, the Germans had returned the sentiment. But much as he longed to return, he had not been able to reconcile himself with the idea of performing in the country that had been the center of the most murderous campaign of anti-Semitism in history.

Now he was reconsidering. Many other Jewish artists had returned by the early 1960s, and even President Kennedy had gone there, a gesture that impressed Elman, and ultimately helped him resolve his own conflict. "I stayed away for 32 years," he told an Armed Forces Radio interviewer, in Munich. "But when our good President Kennedy decided to visit Germany—I was a great admirer of Kennedy's, and since he thought that it's about time that we should try to forget our prejudices, *et cetera*—I felt it was my duty and my mission as an artist to come back here and see whether I cannot create a better understanding and a better feeling between our nations with my art. The world must live in peace. And we have to use nicer weapons, for that, than nuclear weapons. With art, you can do something."[2]

But he could not thoroughly banish his uneasiness, so when he entered into negotiations for his first post-war German tour (arranged to follow his British and French engagements in the fall of 1964), he established a set of ground rules, the most important being that he would not play with orchestra. He did not want, even inadvertently, to share the stage with musicians who had worn Nazi uniforms.

Elman felt so strongly about musicians' participation in the regime that he refused even to attend performances by prominent musicians who were known to have been party members during their younger years. On a few occasions, friends who felt that this prejudice only deprived Elman of some magnificent musical experiences found ways of getting him to attend. On one occasion, Seymour Solomon and Joseph Seiger managed to get him to a performance of *Die Walküre*, in Vienna, without telling him that Herbert von Karajan was on the podium. Elman had particularly strong feelings about Karajan, who joined the Nazi party in Austria in 1933, long before the Nazis were a prevalent force there, and who left his homeland for Germany when the Austrian Nazi party was banned. Whether Karajan was a committed Nazi or merely a young opportunist didn't matter to Elman, who wanted nothing to do with the conductor.

He was entranced by Karajan's performance, though. An avid Wagnerian since his youth, he found the precision of the orchestral playing and the contours of the performance beyond his dreams. "This is what Wagner should sound like," he told Seiger and Solomon. But when he found out that Karajan was in the pit, he shook his head and quietly left the hall. The same thing happened on a visit to Italy, when Seiger persuaded him too attend a performance of Mozart's *Le Nozze di Figaro* at La Scala. Seiger arranged for a box, and hoped it would be too dark for Elman to read the program. "Who is this girl?" he kept asking Seiger. "What a beautiful voice, what phrasing." Seiger professed ignorance of the cast, but Elman became more and more fascinated. At intermission, Seiger managed to distract him, but during the next act, Elman recalled seeing a newspaper article about Elisabeth Schwarzkopf, and made the connection. "You stay here Joseph," he whispered to his accompanist midway through the second act, "I'm going back to the hotel." His only comment, the next morning, was "why did she have to be a Nazi?"

When he arrived in Germany, Elman was nervous about his reception after so long an absence. In Hamburg, where the tour began, he spent the day of the concert telephoning his manager to check on ticket sales. The assurances of the manager, Seiger and Helen were enough to calm him down only temporarily, and he grew particularly restive on the way to the concert, when his limousine got caught in a traffic jam near the hall. "They're all going to the Elman recital," Seiger joked, but Elman, still tense, snapped, "that's not funny, Joseph." Seiger may have been right. When they walked onto the stage that evening, they found a packed hall, with a section of seats added on the stage; and it was only when he saw that the full house had risen to its feet to greet him that Elman's humor returned. "You see, Joseph," he said, turning to the pianist, "just like Tel Aviv."

Elman's Munich-based impresario arranged plenty of publicity, and thanks to his early years under Liachowsky's tutelage, Elman spoke perfect German and was therefore able to reminisce and discuss his return on a number of German radio and television programs. He also did some English interviews, for the use of the Armed Forces Radio network. He was in fine spirits for these, and in brief spots lasting between 10 and 15 minutes, he discussed his attitudes about the music world far more congenially than he had been doing in his speeches and articles. "I don't like to speak about my past," he responded to an interviewer who asked him to cite some of the highlights of his career. "Not that I'm ashamed of it, but I always live in the present, and the present takes care of the future. I don't know how many people know my age. Some people don't like to speak about their ages, but I don't mind, for the simple reason that I have reached my seventy-third birthday, and I really don't know what it is to be 73. I know that as a young man, when I met someone my age [now], I considered him finished—I was even surprised that he was still around. But now that I am 73 myself, I can tell you that nobody feels younger than I feel right now."[3]

To the question "what do you feel you owe the audience that pays to hear you play," he responded calmly, "I owe them my integrity. My honesty. I owe them my gratefulness that they're willing to listen to me. But they are entitled to disagree with me." About contemporary music, a topic on which he had made scathing remarks in the not too distant past, he was now diplomatic: "I must say I am reluctant, very reluctant, to play some so-called modern music. Maybe it's my limitation. Maybe the young people have a right to say 'our time is a different time, we have our own expression.' I am by no means against studying new things. But I have to like it. If I don't like it, I'm not going to play it."

He even handled the interviewer's questions about publicity and the commercialization of the music business with delicacy and forbearance. "There has never been a time when publicity didn't help some of the young people to make their way. But let me tell you this: It doesn't last very long if it's built [only] on publicity. In the final analysis, it's the talent that wins out. And it's only through your talent that you can last and endure." Radio and television, he added, can be "of great value, providing the people who engage you for these kinds of appearances ask you to give that which you give best. And again, the sponsors have their own taste—and sometimes their taste is not a very good taste! We do get into conflicts with sponsors [when] they want us to do something which will have a 'popular appeal.' Now, what they call popular appeal and what we call popular appeal is not the same thing."

The interviewer pursued that one, wondering whether a classical artist performing a popular selection on television might not win himself a larger following—a theory that was eventually adopted in its extreme form by record companies in the 1970s, under the banner of "crossover music." Elman didn't see the point of this. "In my personal experience," he replied, "it isn't worth the bother of belittling yourself, in your own estimation, by playing that kind of music."

At every stop on that tour, Elman was in the news, heralded as a legendary figure long absent from the German concert stage. As a result, the houses were invariably full, the crowds were enthusiastic, and the reviews were, by and large, written with a combination of respect and appreciation. Now and then, a critic would frown upon Elman's style. But only one review really bothered him. It was written by a critic in a small city, who pointed out that other violinists were touring with full Bach unaccompanied sonatas, works by Hindemith and other contemporary composers—and in general, more sophisticated programs than the one Elman gave. He took particular exception to Elman's performance of the Mendelssohn Concerto with piano accompaniment, and noting Elman's long absence, he accused him of treating the audience as if it were provincial and unimportant.

Elman thought he detected a current of anti-Semitism in the review. "You know, Joseph," he said to Seiger, "I think I smell a fire here. I'd like to look into this." Seiger telephoned the newspaper and said he was visiting from out of town, that he'd enjoyed the review and wanted to speak with the critic. The newspaper gave Seiger the critic's home telephone number. Elman called, and to the reviewer's shock, he invited him to their hotel for tea. He turned out to be a young man, with blonde hair and classic Aryan features.

"I'm very sorry you did not enjoy my recital," he told his guest, speaking in German and stopping to emphasize points he wanted to be sure were clear. "But you know, I've come to Germany reluctantly, and on the condition that I play only recitals with my pianist. I am, however known here for my concerto performances, and I felt that at least one of these should be included on each of my programs. I also selected the works I am playing here very carefully, for some of them—for instance, the Mendelssohn and Bruch concertos—are works that were not played in Germany for some time." Elman and the critic spoke for several hours, and parted friends.

By the end of the tour, Elman decided to relax his restriction on orchestral performances, or to at least consider the offers on a case by case basis. After his first Berlin recital, he was approached by the manager of the Berlin Philharmonic and the orchestra's concertmaster, Michel Schwalbe. Elman was offered his choice of repertoire and dates, and he eventually agreed to appear with the orchestra two years hence, so long as Karajan, the orchestra's director, was not on the podium. The orchestra conceded this point, and Elman returned to play the Khachaturian Concerto under Karel Ancerl's baton.

❖ ❖ ❖ ❖ ❖

Elman was elated by the response he found in Germany, and he was impressed with the efficiency of his impresario there, a sharp contrast to the situation at home. The firm that had managed him from the mid-1950s into the 1960s, NCAC, had disbanded, and since he was wary of the larger firms, he opted to employ a string of independent managers. He also occasionally tried his hand at arranging for performances that his managers seemingly hadn't thought of, by writing personally to some of the local promoters he had worked with during the Iturbi tour. Often these letters yielded recital engagements, for the promoters found it flattering to think that an artist of Elman's stature had taken the time to contact them himself.

But this was not a satisfactorily efficient mode of operation. He was playing well and he felt up to extensive touring; but the spotlight was focused on violinists of the younger generation—or two, or three—and he felt that to recapture it, he needed an aggressive manager who was thoroughly and unquestioningly devoted to his interests. He talked to several, including Eugene Jelesnick, the promoter, conductor and television host from Salt Lake City. Almost immediately upon his return from Germany, Elman invited Jelesnick to New York, and the two of them, along with Helen spent an evening discussing the problems Elman was facing.

"He was quite distressed with the way he was being handled," Jelesnick explains, "and it seemed to me that he was at a low point then, as far as management was concerned. It still bewildered him that Heifetz had been able to do whatever he wanted and that he could not, back when they were both at RCA. He also felt that if a manager booked another violinist instead of him, the manager was being dishonest. I don't think he understood that sometimes the local impresarios requested other violinists, and that they might do so for a variety of reasons—either because they were younger and the audiences were curious about them, or because they had been particularly visible in the press, and were therefore in greater demand. I felt for him, though. I idolized the man, and when he was in Salt Lake City I did all I could to make him comfortable.

"But after we spoke for a while, he asked me whether I'd be willing to drop everything and manage him. Money was no object. He said,

'I'll pay you whatever you want.' I was in a state of shock, and there were tears all around; but what could I say? I would love to have managed him—I *wanted* to—and I was flattered that he had that much confidence in me. But I had my own life, and I had contractual obligations in Utah. What he desperately needed was immediate attention, and I just wasn't in a position to do what he required."

In the summer of 1965, however, Elman's health rendered his management dilemma a moot point. After an exhausting tour of Europe that culminated in two weeks of orchestral recording sessions in Vienna, he flew back to New York, two days before his scheduled appearance at Lewisohn Stadium. He was pushing himself hard. For a man of 74, with diabetes and high blood pressure, two days was scarcely enough time to recover from jet lag and prepare for a performance of the Beethoven Concerto in the heat of a New York summer evening. He played the performance, and he and Seiger played a few encores. But as soon as he reached the artists' room after the final encore, he collapsed. His friend Edgard Feder was there, and brought his car around so that Elman could be transported home without having to walk any distance.

At home, Elman felt better, but before leaving for his summer visit to California, he paid a visit to his doctor, who diagnosed a mild heart condition and informed the violinist that he would have to treat himself more gently. Elman cancelled the concerts that had been arranged for later in the summer, but otherwise kept his heart problem a secret. "One day, when he was in California," Seiger remembers, "I got a call from him, and he said, Joseph, you're the only one who knows about this, because you're involved. But I have to take it easier from now on. Doctor's orders." The doctor also ordered a strict diet, which he adhered to; and when he returned to begin the following season, he was trimmer.

The main effect of the doctor's warning, though, was a reduction in Elman's schedule. In fact, he had been playing only 40 or 50 concerts a season during the last three or four years; now, 40 concerts a year was to be his limit.

Otherwise, Elman's life continued on the course it had always taken. He continued to rehearse with Seiger every morning at 10, and in the afternoons he still made his way from the Russian Tea Room to the violin shops and music stores on 57th Street. But now he began devoting more time to his less strenuous sideline interests, one of which was the musical theater. Since the 1950s, he had been investing in Broadway shows, as something of a business-related hobby. Among those he backed were *The Pyjama Game, Damn Yankees* and *West Side Story.* In most cases, his ear for prospective successes had proven accurate and, therefore, lucrative—although he did turn down an opportunity to invest in *Fiddler on the Roof,* suspecting that it would never catch on beyond the Jewish public.

The works Elman recorded in Vienna that summer were the three Baroque concertos he had been playing on his recital programs the last several years: the Bach E major, a Nardini in E minor, and Vivaldi's Op.12, No.1, in G minor. As performances of Baroque works, these renderings might be faulted on a number of points where Elman's sensibility clashes with current notions about the era's performing techniques—for instance, his use of a lush, buttery vibrato in the slow movements, his interposition of *portamento* for effect, even in quick passages, and his tendency to expand and compress phrase shapes in a way that renders the impulse of the line secondary to the performer's will.

As documents of Elman's style, though, these—his final concerto recordings—are as fine as the initial releases in the Vanguard series, and on their own stylistic terms, they are electrifying. At that, the Bach and Vivaldi sound streamlined and modernized compared with the recordings of them Elman made three decades earlier. In both cases, the new performances are strikingly tighter, more firmly controlled, and a great deal more subtly nuanced than those of the 1930s. The tempos are brisker too, and although the orchestral accompaniment in the Nardini is rather grandiose, Golschmann keeps the orchestra reasonably trim in the Bach and Vivaldi.

Naturally, Elman continues to phrase according to his own lights. He retains some of his swooping slides in the outer movements of the Bach, and in the slow movements of all three concertos, he unleashes the full compass of his vibrato-laden, almost cello-like tone, giving the performance a lovely Romanticized glow. Yet, if a few carryovers from his original rendering remain, several of the stylistic affectations of the 1930s have been jettisoned—most notably, Elman's habit of accenting beats that are not naturally stressed in the music, and which make for a jumpy reading rather than a flowing one. Expositions on musicological findings may have been far from Elman's agenda, but as these performances make clear, his approach was by no means calcified.

This concerto disc was preceded by two thematically programmed recital albums. The first, *Caprice Viennois*,[4] is a tribute to Fritz Kreisler, and contains a dozen favorites by the violinist-composer—original works, arrangements, and pieces that Kreisler had formerly identified as Baroque discoveries (here identified as such with the notation "in the style of..." appended to their titles). This lovingly played performance is not as fully successful as the *Jubilee Album*, but its flaws are few—a couple of harsh attacks, a moment or two of intonational imprecision, and occasionally a strident chordal passage, all nearly (but not entirely) disguised by a layer of studio echo applied to the stereo mix.

The rough moments, though, are the exceptions. For the most part, these are vibrant, outgoing, rather celebratory readings, and when Elman is at his best, he turns these lightweight but thoroughly violinistic little pieces into glimmering gems. *Liebesfreud, Schön Rosmarin, La Gitana* and the arrangements of Dvořák's first two *Slavonic Dances* jump off the disc with an opulence of spirit; and in the *Variations on a Theme of Corelli* and the jaunty *Rigaudon in the style of Francoeur*, Elman plays with speed and grace, using a variety of bow-strokes to alter the coloration along the way. By contrast, in the gently muted *Preghiera*, he makes the violin whisper dolefully.

The second recital, *Hebraic Melodies*, collected some of the works on Jewish themes he had recorded before (his *Eili, Eili*, Achron's *Hebrew Melody*, and Bloch's *Ningun*) along with a couple of previously unrecorded pieces that had long been part of his encore repertoire (Bonime's *Danse Hebraïque* and Lavry's *Yemenite Wedding Dance*), plus a few selections new to his repertoire (the violin version of Bruch's *Kol Nidre*, George Perlman's *Dance of the Rebbitzen*, Julius Chajes's *The Chassid*, and Abraham Goldfaden's *Raisins and Almonds*).

Like the Kreisler selections, these are character pieces, far removed from the Olympian heights of the "Kreutzer" Sonata or the Brahms Concerto, or from the rarefied air of the Franck and Fauré sonatas. But it's clear from Elman's lavish, detailed coloration that he considered them important musical portraits of a different sort. For him, these (and, for that matter, the Kreisler, Ysaÿe and Wieniawski chestnuts he played) were essays in national spirit, concisely drawn but deeply felt; and it was his role to evoke both the ethnicity at their core and the universality of their emotional underpinnings. In this music, he was thoroughly at home, and entirely uninhibited. Let the critics say what they would about his *portamento* or his free *rubato* in the classics; there could be no argument about their propriety here.

One can catalogue the devices he draws on easily enough. The careful regulation of dynamics and timbre, and the sliding from note to note in the slower, more introspective modal melodies—sometimes traced by a doubling in harmonics—creates the music's accent. Add to that the practice of hovering tenuously around important melody notes before settling on their centers, and you have the suggestion of a music that is vocal rather than instrumental, and which is improvised within a solid framework. In the dance pieces, the techniques are different. Lively *staccato* bowing alternates with more rapid, differently enunciated slides, and the moods shift quickly, from the joyous to the wistful and back.

But no description the music and the way Elman plays it can do full justice to this recording, for there's more here than meets the strictly analytical ear. Through the simple, soulful melodies that fill the disc, Elman was glancing back at his roots. As a man in his seventies, with six decades of touring the world behind him, he stood in a modern, New York recording studio, and recreated the sounds of the cantor and the *badchen* that he'd heard as a boy.

CHAPTER TWENTY-TWO:

The Last Years—Trials and Triumphs

After his heart condition was diagnosed, Elman could have retired from the stage and devoted his energies to teaching, or to writing the memoirs he planned in the late 1950s. At 74, he had lived a full life, and although there were frustrations that certainly weren't likely to be dealt with decisively at this late date, he had enjoyed a satisfying career. But the idea of putting down his violin and never facing the public again was out of the question for Elman. Performing was the focus of his life, and he fully intended to keep touring until he could no longer lift the violin to his chin.

He was not unique in this; indeed, many musicians consider performing to be of an elixir of youth, and most have said as much in interviews. Artur Rubinstein, for instance, performed into his nineties. Andrés Segovia gave concerts until only a few months before his death at age 94, and when asked why he continued, the guitarist replied, in his charmingly philosophical way, "because when the waters remain still, they become stagnant."

Elman would certainly have agreed. When he walked into the spotlight, he could forget about the rigors of age—his failing eyesight, his diabetes, his heart problems—and bask in the music. But now, in addition to his problems with managers and the critical battles over his performing style, Elman's age was creating an image problem. The question, lingering in the minds of those who saw pictures of the bald, rotund violinist on concert posters, was, can a violinist in his mid-seventies still be worth hearing?"

In 1985, Donal Henahan, the senior critic of the *New York Times*, discussed that very question in a Sunday "Music View" column. Noting that in his youth he had avoided Elman's annual recitals because, he said, "critics had been writing for years that his intonation could no longer be counted upon, and that his old-fashioned style was not to be taken seriously." But in 1958, he decided to overcome these prejudices and attend one of Elman's golden jubilee recitals, in Chicago.

"I cannot pretend that Elman on that afternoon put on a recital to shame Paganini," Henahan recalled some 27 years later. But he added:

> With his shining bald head and 5-foot-3-inch stature he was not a glamorous figure to begin with. When he came on stage puffing out his little chest, he looked like Erich von Stroheim without the monacle. I noted with disdain that his program included a concerto (Khachaturian's) played with piano accompaniment, something as out of date as celluloid collars.
>
> But then Elman put his bow to the strings and, without seeming to draw it more than an inch, suddenly filled the house with as big and sensuous a tone as I have ever heard from a violin. It was startling to hear so much sound produced with so little discernible effort. Yes, he played off pitch at times and his rhythms could be eccentric or indulgently flabby, but I could hear the residue of a noble, serene style of playing that had passed from favor but retained its own assurance and integrity. I could not care too much that I might be overvaluing or undervaluing his performance. I was listening with other, more innocent ears than people at the recital who had grown up with Mischa Elman and his generation of fiddlers.[1]

Elman's visit to Minneapolis, in March 1966, typifies both the backstage machinations involved in arranging an appearance—and the way the performance was received, once the non-musical hurdles were cleared. Towards the end of 1965, the Women's Auxiliary of the Minneapolis Symphony Orchestra was casting about for a fundraising idea, and one of the board members, a young violinist named Shirley Thomson, suggested that instead of holding a bazaar or a bake sale, as they normally did, they ought to sponsor a concert.

The board agreed, and set Thomson the task of finding a suitable artist and as a result of a chain of coincidences, she ended up engaging Mischa Elman. Around that time, a colleague had loaned her a handful of Elman records. She didn't know anything about Elman: she had heard his name, and had some vague ideas about his early reputation. The records sat in her living room unplayed for nearly three months, until one day not long after the WAMSO board meeting, when she decided to give one a spin and return them. The album that looked most promising, in an old-time violinistic sort of way, was *Caprice Viennois*. She took the disc out of its bright orange cover and listened to side one as she gathered her violin and music for the evening's rehearsal. She couldn't believe what she heard.

"His style is so *personal*, I've never heard anything like that," she told the violinist who had loaned her the discs. Meanwhile, she was doing a bit of historical reading, trying to catch up with a few other violinistic legends, namely Leopold Auer and Carl Flesch. In books about both those players, Thomson kept running into Elman's name. Even then, she never considered suggesting Elman to the WAMSO board. She had assumed he was dead. But she soon learned otherwise. Her search for an artist took her to the offices of James Lombard, an local concert presenter. Lombard was cordial—he asked Thomson what sort of program and performer she thought would bring in enough money to make the benefit successful. Then he got down to business: "Have you given any thought to what this benefit will cost to put on?" he asked. She said they had a budget of $1,500.

Lombard saw this benefit as the solution to another of his current headaches. He had arranged for a performance by Mischa Elman, to be presented under the auspices of another Minneapolis organization that was also holding a benefit. That group, however, had not signed its contract, and was still haggling about the violinist's fee.

This put Lombard in a difficult spot. He was not anxious to negotiate with Elman for a lower fee. "I'll tell you what," he told his Thomson. "I have Mischa Elman under contract for an appearance elsewhere in Minneapolis. But the people who were having him come are getting to be a problem about the fee, and I just don't want to bother Mr. Elman with that. I have to honor my contract with Mr. Elman anyway; so for $1,500, I'll let the Minneapolis Symphony present him. What do you say?"

Delighted at the prospect of hearing a performer whose work she had just discovered, she said that having Elman play for the Minneapolis Symphony benefit would be perfect—provided, of course, that the rest of the board agreed. She gathered as much publicity material as she could find, rounded up a few recordings, and called a meeting. Most of the women in the group knew as little or less about Elman than Thomson did a few weeks earlier, but the recordings, the background material and Thomson's enthusiasm carried the day, and the group voted in favor of inviting Elman.

Thomson returned to Lombard's office with the news, and a March recital date at the Guthrie Theater was set. There was one problem, and not an inconsiderable one: the contract for the benefit had to be approved by Richard Cizek, the manager of the Minneapolis Symphony, and Cizek began asking around about Elman.

Elman did have some fans in the orchestra, and one of them was Norman Carol, its concertmaster (and later concertmaster of the Philadelphia Orchestra). "I had seen Elman play on many occasions," Carol recalled, years later, "and I really looked forward to him coming to Minneapolis, as did many of the violinists. I think we knew this would be one of his last concerts." In fact, several years earlier, when Carol was in the army and stationed in San Francisco, he spent an evening playing chamber music with Elman ("it was the Schubert A major Quartet," Carol recalled).

Yet, somehow Cizek came away from his investigations convinced that Elman was so far past his prime that a recital would be a disaster. Calling in the representative from the Women's Auxiliary, he said, "from what I hear, Mischa Elman couldn't play in our orchestra's second violin section. What kind of benefit concert would that be?"

In shock, Thomson undertook a survey of her own, hoping to hear that Elman was still in good shape (but prepared to hear confirmation of Cizek's information). At the time, she was also on the concert committee of the Schubert Club, another organization that brought in guest artists. One day, the committee met with Sheldon Gold, then a young executive working for Sol Hurok (and later the head of ICM, one of the principal heirs of Hurok's empire). When the meeting broke for coffee, Thomson asked Gold about Elman.

Gold was a little perplexed by the question: Elman was not a Hurok artist, and Gold was certainly aware of Elman's stormy relations with the Hurok office. But he said, simply, "He has never played better." Thomson returned to Cizek with Gold's opinion, but he remained against the idea of an Elman recital. Meanwhile, Lombard was calling to remind her that he needed a signed contract.

Ultimately, the WAMSO board broke the impasse itself, for it controlled its own funds and was willing to pay Elman's fee, Cizek's objections notwithstanding. Lombard, for his part, had a contract with Elman, and he decided to let the concert go on, without the signed contract.

Meanwhile, Elman sent ahead his program—the Handel D major Sonata, the Brahms G major Sonata, Lalo's *Symphonie Espagnole*, Chausson's *Poème*, and short pieces by Kreisler, Chopin (via Wilhelmj) and Wieniawski. Thomson shuddered when she saw it. This was, after all, a benefit concert, and although she had no doubt that this program would delight violinists, she wondered whether a general audience could sit through it. She expressed her doubts to Lombard, who deleted a movement of the Lalo and one of the short works before sending the program to the printer.

Thomson and her committee then set about the rest of the business of putting on the concert—seeing to ticket sales, arranging for local television and newspaper interviews, getting an advance interview from New York, and arranging for the various forms of hospitality that ought to be extended to Elman while he was in town. Whatever Cizek's doubts, tickets sold quickly, and the Minneapolis Symphony turned a healthy profit.

Elman left New York blissfully unaware of the infighting his engagement had occasioned in Minneapolis. For him, this was going to be a return to a town whose orchestra had invited him often in his younger years, but which, like so many others, had neglected him of late. It was, in a sense, a mission of reconquest.

The evening of Elman's arrival, a delegation from the Women's Auxiliary drove out to the airport to meet the him. Watching from the tarmac, they saw Joseph Seiger leave the airplane first, carrying Elman's violin and occasionally glancing back at Elman and Helen, who had been persuaded to come along, although she usually joined him only on foreign tours, and generally preferred to stay in New York when he was touring the United States. The Minneapolis women did think Elman looked old. He walked down the ramp gingerly, giving an impression of frailty that disappeared once he reached the ground.

Thomson stepped forward to meet the entourage, and was astounded by the quickness with which Elman began to size up her town. "Who is the orchestra's concertmaster?" he asked first; then, "who are the best violinists here?" And so on for teachers and violin makers. In the few moments' walk from the airplane to the car, Elman had solicited and absorbed an annotated inventory of the Minneapolis violin world.

Thomson had some questions of her own, and the next day, between interviews, she went to lunch with the Elmans and Seiger, intent on asking him about his colleagues, past and present. She was a stranger, though, and Elman wasn't in the mood to comment on living players. About Heifetz, for instance, he held his tongue: "Heifetz plays beautifully," he said, and left it at that. But when the conversation turned to the violinists who walked the stage in the early years of the century, Elman reminisced freely. "You know," he chuckled, setting his cup of tea on its saucer, "I recall going to a concert of Kreisler's, where Kreisler played a passage in a piece incorrectly. So a few days later, I played the same piece, and because Kreisler was in the audience, I played the same phrase incorrectly, in the same way he did. It was an innocent joke; we had a lot of those." Thomson asked him about Kreisler's recordings, noting that Elman's interpretations of Kreisler's works thrilled her in a way that Kreisler's own did not. "But those recordings of Kreisler you've heard," Elman responded, "were not Kreisler at his best. You had to hear him play his own pieces for an audience of a thousand people eagerly awaiting them. Those same pieces that you don't like so much on record really came to life in the concert hall."

Oddly, when questioned about Ysaÿe, Elman didn't say much. "Ysaÿe really didn't have such a big sound," Thomson says he told her, "but he was such a big man that everybody thought he had a big sound." He did, however, offer several anecdotes about Carl Flesch. "His approach was very rigid," Elman said, "very cerebral. And his tone always struck me as rather thin. I remember once—oh, long ago, in Paris—we were playing for each other, and Carl said to me, 'Mischa, I wish I could figure out how you get that wonderful tone.' And I told him, 'Well, Carl, if you spent less time *thinking* about it, and more time *feeling* the music, it might come to you!'"

He noted, however, that Flesch was more a pedagogue than a performer, which brought the conversation around to teachers and teaching. Thomson asked him what Auer had been like as a teacher, and Elman replied vaguely, saying only that one of Auer's greatest assets was his ability to let his students develop freely.

"Do you teach?" Thomson asked him.

"Not really, I've listened to some young players on occasion, but I don't think they really want to hear what I have to tell them. Besides," he added, "having skipped the normal course of technical exercises when I was a child, I would find it difficult to set a student on the right track. In my case, a great deal was intuitive. But that's a personal thing, and it would be impossible for me to make intuitive decisions on behalf of another violinist."

As Elman protested his feelings of unsuitability as a teacher, Thomson noticed that both Seiger and Helen were encouraging her to pursue that line of inquiry. Both had been trying to convince Elman to cut back on his touring and consider teaching, but he resisted. Thomson pressed on. "I think a violinist of your experience, and with your personal approach, could offer a good deal to a receptive student," she insisted. "You have a gift. You're the living representative of a whole era of violin playing, and you really *have* to pass that on to other players."

"That may be," Elman tentatively agreed. "But you know, the young players in New York call me, and when they come up to play for me; and I tell them, 'oh yes, that's very good.' I listen to them. But they don't ask me to play for them. They don't ask me for interpretive or technical advice. They don't ask me for anything, except—like Flesch—what the secret of my sound is. If I wrote a book, 'How to Produce the Mischa Elman Sound in Six Easy Lessons,' I could make millions. But I just don't think it works that way. It's something that comes from inside, something every violinist has to find for himself."

In mid-afternoon, Elman returned to his hotel for a pre-concert nap. At around 5, he awoke and got ready for the performance, warming up casually, and having the tea and toast that was his typical pre-concert meal. Thomson arrived at his hotel an hour later, and drove him to the Guthrie Theater.

Elman, on the way to the concert hall, was not at all the ebullient, anecdotal character he had been at lunch and during the day's interviews. He sat in the back seat of the car, his attention turned inward as those around him chatted. Helen, who had been watching her husband's pre-concert withdrawal for nearly 40 years, knew how to balance his need for privacy with his need to be slightly diverted; and she could also see their hosts wondering if he was alright.

"Mischa," she said, in a gently teasing way, "don't tell me you're nervous."

"I'm only nervous when I'm not nervous," he replied—a retort she'd heard often before, but which had the right blend of irony and truth to lighten the moment.

Out in the hall, older violinists debated the merits of Elman, Kreisler and Heifetz, and exchanged some of the Elman anecdotes they'd collected over the years. Younger players who had turned up on their teachers' recommendations wondered what all the fuss was about. And of course, there were many doubters. Some came solely to support the orchestra, despite the negative reports they'd heard about Elman's playing. Some came out of respect for Elman's reputation, but not expecting much. And some expected the worst.

At 8:15, the stage door opened, and from the wings the audience heard the brusque, loud bowing of the four strings as Elman checked his tuning. A few seconds later, Elman strode to center stage, with Seiger behind him. He bowed quickly, looking around at the audience surrounding the Guthrie Theater's thrust proscenium, and without a wasting a moment, he launched into the Handel. Those in the audience who had met Elman at the airport couldn't believe their eyes: the bald, frail bespectacled old man who set them worrying as he slowly stepped off the airplane was standing in the spotlight, playing as if he were 20 years younger and a foot taller; and the burnished tone he was famous for poured forth from his Stradivarius.

Elman's approach to the Handel was very much as it always had been—which is to say virtually unornamented but for the occasional slide, and slower than one heard at younger players' recitals. But it conveyed fire, passion, and personality, and as the program unfolded, Elman quickly won over the Minneapolis audience, including those who had doubted his powers before the concert began.

He was, even at 75, a consummate showman, and the intensity he conveyed in the way he carried himself on stage compensated for some of his eased tempos. As he had done these past 60-plus years, he accompanied his performance with a personalized ballet. He would shift his position on the stage, occasionally taking a step towards the audience, or back towards the piano. He would turn at the waist as he bowed the start of a phrase. And he would lean towards the front rows as he played certain passages, as if some of the notes he tossed off in bravura showpieces like Wieniawski's *Polonaise Brillante* were aimed at specific listeners.

By the time he made his way through the Kreisler piece that closed the program, no-one in the Guthrie Theater doubted his ability to dazzle an audience—let alone to make his way fluently around the fingerboard; and the audience kept him playing encores until nearly 11:30. "I know Elman was always known for having a lush, fantastic sound," recalled Norman Carol. "And he did. But what stood out in my mind about that concert was the extraordinary elegance of his playing."

When the house lights went up, the discussion in the aisles was animated. And Richard Cizek, the orchestra's manager—who still hadn't signed the contract—conceded that he had been wrong. "Well," he told Thomson, "it was wonderful." A few weeks later, he invited Elman to return to Minneapolis as a soloist with the orchestra.

After the concert, Elman attended a reception thrown by the orchestra in his honor. "What I don't understand," he told Thomson, "is why Lombard made those cuts in the program." "That's entirely my fault," she admitted. "But I had no idea *any* violinist could keep an audience so enthralled through a program that long. I've never seen anything like this before." Elman did not stay at the reception long. He was hungry after his lengthy concert, and the food at the reception was non-dietetic. So, with the Thomsons leading, the Elmans and Seiger went to a diner, where Elman settled for a plate of eggs and a cup of tea, and answered a great many more of Thomson's questions about the violin world, past and present.

Eventually, the party ended up at the Elmans' hotel, where they said their goodbyes. "Mrs. Thomson," Elman said as the Minneapolis couple headed towards their car, "do you ever come to New York? If you do come, please contact me. I'd like to hear you play."

Two months later, Thomson took him up on the offer, and arrived in New York with a Handel Sonata and a few French works. "I deliberately chose very simple things," she recalls, "because I knew that most people probably went to him with Paganini *Caprices*. But I didn't want to impress him; I wanted to learn music from him."

Thomson's lesson was set for the morning after her arrival, and Seiger was given the day off. "What do you want to do?" he asked her as she unpacked her violin. "What I'd really like to do is hear you play," she responded, but he explained that they would be having a dinner party that evening, and that she could hear him play then. So she played her Handel sonata.

Thomson's recollections of that first session are vivid: "He listened with a great deal of intensity. He had me play each piece all the way through, and then he asked me questions about my intentions for particular phrases. He also commented about specific technical things. At one point, he leaped up, imitated my bowing arm position, and asked me why I was playing that way. I was keeping a straight wrist. I had been taught otherwise; but somehow you get to a point where for forget why you do things. He spotted that immediately and corrected it."

Thomson asked Elman if he would play so she could have a close look at both his bow arm and his left hand fingering. "His bowing style was gracious and flowing," she says, "although actually, what I watched most was his left hand. I had never seen a left hand like that.

He used his fingernails, which were very long. In fact, I noticed the length of his nails the first time I saw him, at the airport in Minneapolis, and it made me nervous, particularly since I still didn't have a signed contract. When I watched him play that afternoon in New York, I noticed that he used the nail to stop the notes and to produce his vibrato up in the highest positions, where the notes are very close together. Using his nail, he was able to stop the note at the exact, precise place.

"Down in the lower positions," she added, "the thing I noticed was that he played very flat on his fingers, instead of on the tips—a technique that produces a really voluptuous sound. Using the flat part of the finger, I've found, also makes for much greater dexterity. Instead of picking the fingers straight up, he would pull them off the string more gently and to the side. These things were part of the secret of his sound."

Thomson's contention that Elman used his fingernails in the higher positions is controversial. On one hand, she bases her comments on having watched him play at close range that morning in May 1966; and as the current owner of his Amati violin, she adds that the higher reaches of the fingerboard bore indentations that she cites as further evidence.

But virtually everyone else who knew Elman and his playing techniques intimately doubt that he used his nails in this manner. Both Mrs. Elman and Joseph Seiger deny having noticed any such thing, although Seiger noticed that Elman's nails were generally a bit longer than his own. "I used to ask him how it was possible that he didn't hit the string with the nail," the pianist recalls, "and he explained that it was because he played on the flat part of the finger, so that the nail wasn't really in the way."

Jacques Francais also doubts that Elman played with his nails, and he adds that the hard ebony of the fingerboard cannot be scored by something so comparatively soft as a fingernail. Some slight depressions, he suggests, might have been caused by the strings, which are pressed hard against the fingerboard. Those who dispute the fingernail theory also point out that Elman rarely used the Amati after he acquired the "Madame Recamier" Strad, in 1925.

Of course, the secret of Elman's tone has long been a matter of speculation, and Thomson's observation about his use of the fleshy part of the finger to stop notes lower on fingerboard is confirmed by several of his friends and colleagues, including Francais and Seiger.

Others who observed Elman closely offer further conjecture, and perhaps when taken in sum, all these clues point to the technical foundation of Elman's sound—although, as many of his colleagues also point out, the *technique* of his tone production was by no means the essence of his playing; rather, it was merely the means through which he communicated the depth of his feelings to his listeners. "As he explained it to me," Seiger relates, "his tone was based mostly on his ability to hear the quality of sound he wanted to produce in his inner ear before he put his finger on the string."

Indeed, the combination of technical observations and philosophical overlay Elman's friends offer in explanation of his tone is fascinating. Henryk Szeryng, for instance, theorized that the secret of Elman's sound had a good deal to do with "the depth with which he produced a simple violin sound. He could have been practicing just a long, sustained note, but he was incapable of playing that long note as if it were simply part of an exercise. He would play the note with a beautiful vibrato, and as he approached the tip of the bow, instead of a *decrescendo*, as most of us would do, he always made a *crescendo*. That is one thing that always struck me—that as he came to the end of the bow, when the sound should have been tapering off, he managed to give it greater intensity."

Perhaps the most probing, all-encompassing description and explanation of Elman's tone is that provided by one of the violinist's closest friends in New York, Edgard Feder:

"I would say it had to do with the length of his bowstroke, his total control, and with his *knowing* what he wanted to do—how much vibrato, how much pressure to put on the strings. I think his tone was probably the product of an uncanny balance between the left and right hand. Tone is something very personal. You produce a tone that is related to the way you sing. And Elman could sing: he had an extremely pure tenor voice. He also knew a good deal of music that was outside the violin literature, and he could sing almost any opera aria, on pitch. He was in awe of Caruso, and I believe he took a lot of this into his playing. His playing was very vocal, very songlike, and you could feel that singing quality. There was also, of course, the expressiveness of his vibrato.

"Now, what creates a tone, I don't know," Feder continues. "The fact that he had a great violin was not enough. I have heard him when the strings were not good; and I have heard him give concerts when, after one of his own strings broke, he took the violin of the orchestra's concertmaster and produced a sound no different from that which he produced on his Stradivarius.

"A couple of things that struck me as unusual, though, had to do with his bow. First, it was not very heavily rosined. Second, the bow hair was not very tight. Kreisler's, by contrast, was extremely taut, but Elman's wasn't. Elman also preferred a light bow, so he could produce a juicy tone, but you would never hear the scratch of the bow. Speaking about physical qualities, he was a short man, and not fat, but heavyset; and his fingers were like sausages. Yet, his intonation was superb, and his facility with those short fingers was remarkable. Also, his fingers never had callouses, which is unusual because he never missed a day of practicing. This too, I believe, was because of his extraordinary sense of balance."

Shirley Thomson stayed in New York for four days, and each day she had either a long lesson, or two separated by a few hours of practice. After the first lesson, she returned to her hotel to get ready for that evening's dinner party; and when Seiger arrived, he asked Elman how the lesson had gone. "If only she played as well as she looks," Elman told him. "But you know, I think there's hope." The next day, Elman and Thomson worked through the morning, and when Seiger arrived, Elman had her play for him. "You see?" he asked. "Now she's a totally different player."

During her lessons, Elman also gave Thomson a short course in the fine points of presentation. "When you play a recital," Elman told her, "you should never leave the stage, except at intermission. I never do. When you leave the stage, you have to get your audience's attention back. While you're offstage, they begin to think about where they're going for dinner, or what they're going to do tomorrow. If you go out and make it a complete, unified performance, you're giving your audience a much more vibrant and personal experience."

Upon her return to Minneapolis, Thomson arranged an invitation for Elman to give a series of master classes under the auspices of the local university the following summer. The plans proceeded smoothly at first: Elman and the school agreed on a fee and a program, which was to include three weeks of recitals and classes that summer. At the last moment, though, the funding for the series fell through, and the course was cancelled. Elman spent his summer in California, as usual, and in the fall he toured Europe. But upon his return to New York, he invited Shirley Thomson to return for another run of lessons, in January 1967.

CHAPTER TWENTY-THREE:

The Final Seasons

Through most of 1966, the prospect of teaching was hardly the most pressing of Elman's concerns. At 75, he was beginning to think about mortality, and as the year drew to a close, he had some premonitions that his death was imminent. He confided this to his sisters, Liza and Esther, during a visit to their home in Philadelphia, in November 1966. One evening, after dinner, he stood in their living room and looked at the painting of the thatched roof house he was born in, and then at a grouping of family photographs.

"How old was father when he died," the violinist asked Esther. "He was 76," she told him. He stood silently for a few moments, then walked into another room. Esther recalls the scene as an eerie one. When Elman returned to New York, he asked his attorney to prepare a revision of his Will, and in January, on his seventy-sixth birthday, he signed it.

Elman's visit to Philadelphia came towards the end of a year of activity that, despite his cutback in engagements, was hectic and no doubt stressful. After a series of American performances, he spent a week in the recording studio, followed immediately by a European tour. He was to return to Europe in a few weeks, but had scheduled a few more American concerts between trips. Just before the first of these European jaunts—and about six weeks before his visit to Esther and Liza—he had experienced another coronary scare.

Elman's last full season had begun with a handful of concerts around North America that led to his Carnegie Hall recital, on February 2, 1966. For these, he played the same program he would perform a month later in Minneapolis—Handel, Brahms, Lalo, Chausson and short works. The reviews were kind; in fact, after several years of leaving Elman's concerts to other critics on the *Times* staff, Harold C.

Schonberg, then the paper's senior critic, decided to assess the violinist's strengths for himself. In his review, Schonberg observed that the concert had "its labored moments and its dubious ones." He noted, too, that Elman's Brahms was never particularly to his liking; and that his Handel was rooted in another age. Most of the review, though, was a paean to the Romantic, personalized style that Schonberg had always admired in pianists, and which Elman personified among string players.

"His place in the history of violin playing is secure," Schonberg wrote, "and it is a high one. To this day Mr. Elman represents a tradition that just about has disappeared—the concept of the Virtuoso-as-Hero. He stands for golden tone, for dazzling fingerwork and the long, soulful phrase, and in him is echoed the great nineteenth-century virtuosos who thrilled audiences with a kind of literature that today is altogether out of fashion.

"It was a school," Schonberg added, "in which the instrument was more important than the music, the player more important than the composer." He continued by setting forth examples of the style, both of playing and programming, which set it apart from the mid-20th century norm, and from there on, until the brief discussion of the Brahms and Handel towards the end, his stance was more observational than judgmental. At that, the slow movement of the Lalo was singled out as particularly delicious: Elman's violin, wrote Schonberg, "still sounded like a cello when he bore down on the G string."

"He is Elman," Schonberg concluded, "and he still can dazzle, still can bewitch, still can produce a tone that melts the violin, and still can reproduce the technique—with all of its slides, its fast vibrato, its rhythmic oddities and personal quirks—that brought him everlasting fame in his great days."

The New York recital was followed by a brief rest, but soon enough Elman was again making jaunts around the country. During one of these, he ran into an interviewer who brought Carl Sandburg's poem *Bath* to his attention. Elman was astonished not to have come across the poem in the half century since Sandburg wrote it. Upon his return to New York, in late March, he wrote the poet a contrite note: "I shall live in shame for the rest of my life," he confessed, "but it is absolutely true that through peculiar circumstances I only recently found out that you honored me with a most beautiful poem called *Bath*. In spite of the English language being so rich, I cannot find words to thank you and tell you how proud I am that my performance left such a deep impression on you."

In his interviews during these trips, he retained his posture as an outspoken observer of the music world's commercial decline. In a *Montreal Gazette* interview, for instance, he discussed the media age uncompromisingly. Radio and television, he said, are "influenced by advertising and the consequent necessity to exaggerate, praise too many of the performances they present as 'great' and create a distorted standard of what is exceptional and what isn't. The result is that the average person watching TV today no longer really knows what is 'great.'"[1]

Later in the season, on a visit to Tampa, Florida, where he was about to play the Mendelssohn Concerto, he found himself at a rather crowded interview—one attended not only by the journalist, but by the young conductor, George Cleve, and by the president of the Tampa Philharmonic Association, Mrs. Charles Ford. He decided to make the most of his built-in audience. First, he deplored the loss of artistic individuality. "Shaking a finger at George Cleve," the journalist from the *Tampa Times* reported, "he said, 'Watch out, do not lose your individualism. Do not belong to the herd. The small fellow with little strength is being devoured by the powers of the big fellow.'"

Then turning to Mrs. Ford, he launched into an exposition on managerial monopolies. "You are giving your time, your efforts, your knowledge and your money to bring culture to your city," he told her. "I could kiss you for that, but unfortunately, you are being taken for a ride by these booking agencies. You are really being pressured into hiring only the artists they are 'pushing' at the time. This maneuver is being carried on so subtly you are not aware of it, but we in the field can see it so plainly."[2]

Elman did not confine these observations to small town newspapers. Even in the country's most visible forum, the *New York Times*, Elman went out on a limb. Speaking to Murray Schumach for a Sunday piece that appeared just before his Lewisohn Stadium concert at the end of June, the violinist covered most of his pet topics. He wondered, for instance, what all the fuss about the State Department's cultural exchange program was. "We have here at least as good as what they bring us," he offered, "but people here are very naive. They fall before things." Asked about music education, he theorized that teachers were no longer sufficiently devoted to their craft—that they don't give their students enough time, and that they are more interested in money than in furthering musical art.

Other observations were equally harsh. "Just because we live in an ugly age is no reason I should not give beauty," he said, following it with a rhetorical question that reduced the shift in the century's performance style to a question of quality: "If Romanticism is better than ugliness," he asked, "why should I abandon Romanticism?" About the new Lincoln Center complex, he was equally unyielding. "I don't like shopping centers for the arts," he insisted, noting that, to his taste, opera houses, concert halls and theaters should have their own distinct characters, whereas at Lincoln Center, the halls struck him as too similar. The audience bothered him too: "When I go to Lincoln Center," he said, "I don't feel I am among musical people. I don't feel that way at Carnegie Hall"—an observation that must have puzzled both Lincoln Center's and Carnegie Hall's administrations, who hoped to appeal to the same segment of New York's musical public.

He also restated his old charge that record companies exerted a monopolistic hold over orchestral scheduling, making the arrangement sound even more conspiratorial this time. "Certain artists," he pointed out, "play every year with certain orchestras. This is because the artist and the orchestra happen to record for the same company and that company wants to save on rehearsals. Famous artists do not perform with orchestras that record with different companies."

In his younger years, Elman's outspoken views about the music world often made him seem a daring crusader; by now, though, many even-keeled readers took his complaints as those of a disappointed, frustrated performer with a personal ax to grind. In fact, after listening to Elman's complaints for nearly two hours, the *Times* interviewer felt moved to ask the violinist if he were bitter about the music world.

"Elman was astonished," Schumach wrote. "Me, bitter?" Elman replied, "Hah! I get a great kick out of life. I know how to enjoy. Thank God I'm not a frustrated artist." He then noted the joys of his marriage and his family, and concluded, "I have more pleasure today from performing than ever. Oh, no, I am not bitter. But I have integrity."[3]

Elman closed his season with a Lewisohn Stadium concert on June 29, a performance that bore the trappings of a great, celebratory event. This was to be the final season of these summer concerts, and Elman had not only been its most frequent guest, but it was calculated that his appearance there would mark his five thousandth concert performance.[4] Telegrams arrived at the stadium from politicians and luminaries of all sorts—including Senators Robert F. Kennedy and Jacob Javits, New York's mayor, John Lindsay, and the state's governor, Nelson Rockefeller. President Johnson sent a cable, which was read aloud to the crowd. There was even a wire from Sol Hurok, whose message of "heartiest congratulations" carried a touching, personal note:

"[This concert] serves as a reminder of our pleasant days together," Hurok wrote. "It was an honor having the pleasure and satisfaction of promoting your concerts. No one has done more to further the cause of fine music in America than you have. Let someone else try to do what we accomplished at the Hippodrome."

The concert was billed as a "Russian Night," and featured the Metropolitan Opera Orchestra, conducted by Joseph Rosenstock, in works by Tchaikovsky and Mussorgsky. Elman played in the second half—the Tchaikovsky concerto, of course—his performance preceded by a brief tribute, delivered by Martin Bookspan, then the program director of WQXR. "As is his habit," Theodore Strongin wrote in the *Times* "[Elman] gave it a throbbing, sentimental performance, full of freedom in phrasing. His tone was as juicy as ever." There were, Strongin reported, some intonation problems in the first movement; but he allowed that these were beside the point, given the emotion Elman projected.

To the end, Elman's Tchaikovsky remained an embodiment of the Romantic style; yet, his last performances of the work were very different from those he had given in decades past. In the *Canzonetta*, he now played with an extraordinary serenity and reflectiveness that was the pronouncement of a seasoned veteran, rather than the passionate outpouring of a young firebrand. The finale, too, was a picture of precision and clarity, rather than an essay in daring and speedy dexterity.

Rosenstock and the orchestra followed him closely, and if there were some in the crowd who felt that the work's normally zestier closing movement lacked momentum, they were clearly in the minority, for the moment Elman, Rosenstock and the orchestra brought the concerto to its close, the audience rose to its feet in a thunderous ovation. Elman was pleased, and he turned to applaud the orchestra during one of his curtain calls. For his encores, he played Dvořák's *Songs My Mother Taught Me* and Kreisler's *Schön Rosmarin*. He dedicated the Dvořák to the memory of Minnie Guggenheimer, the founder of the Lewisohn Stadium Concerts.

❖ ❖ ❖ ❖ ❖

Immediately after the Lewisohn Stadium performance, Mischa and Helen Elman left for California. It was not an entirely idyllic time, for their relationship with Nadia and Mel had grown increasingly tense in recent years. They enjoyed the time they spent with their grandchildren though, and they liked the time away from New York. Meanwhile, Elman's ritual of daily practice continued, although it was practice of a different and more leisurely kind.

Back in New York, in September, Elman and Seiger resumed their daily morning routine, this time concentrating on two sets of works—one for the concert performances that were scheduled from late October through the end of January, and another for a disc of short selections they were about to record for Vanguard. The Vanguard sessions were held between October 4 and 10, and yielded Elman's final LP, *The Art of Mischa Elman*, released posthumously the following spring. It's a pity, given Solomon's ability to capture the beauty of Elman's sound, that this final recorded testament was not devoted to the Brahms D minor Sonata, the "Kreutzer," or another of the larger works, which Elman undoubtedly intended to remake for Vanguard eventually. But as it stands, it is a companion disc to the *Jubilee Album*, and it contains all the coloristic variety of that recording, the Kreisler LP, and even the *Hebraic Melodies* collection.

As encore discs go, in fact, this is a collection that relies more on passion than on surface dazzle. In a few cases—for instance, Tchaikovsky's *Russian Dance*, in which Elman seems to be almost defiantly grouping his sliding figures in bunches—manages to run a course between nostalgic intensity and sheer violinistic display. And in a couple of works (Kroll's *Juanita* and Espejo's *Aires Tziganes*), unabashed display carries the day.

But the loveliest moments on the disc are those that demand subtle shading rather than overt finger power. In an arrangement (by Roques) of Debussy's *La plus que lente*, and even more so in Faure's *Berceuse*, he recalls the gentle, *sotto voce* sound that made his recording of Kreisler's *Preghiera* so magical. Even the Gluck *Largo* (arranged by Franz Ries) is a study in intensity, conveyed through a melting tone that breathes with the line; and the second of Smetana's *From My Home* essays is played with an infectious nostalgia—misty at the start, dizzyingly lively at the end, and glowing with warmth throughout.

One morning as Elman and Seiger walked to the studio, the violinist began to feel faint. They stopped, and Seiger held him steady for a moment as he reached into his pocket for his nitroglycerin pills.

"He could hardly stand," Seiger recalls, "I'll never forget it. But when we arrived at the studio, and he put his violin under his chin, it was as if nothing had happened."

The first major tour of the season was a visit to Europe, with concerts in Italy, Austria and Germany. For his solo recitals, he chose a program that began with Handel's Sonata in A major, followed by the Brahms Sonata in D minor, and Spohr's Concerto No.8 in A minor. After the intermission, he offered Tchaikovsky's *Sérenade mélancolique*, and then played Joaquin Nin's *Rapsodia Iberica*, Ysaÿe's *Rêve d'enfant*, and finally, the Saint-Saëns *Introduction and Rondo Capriccioso*.

Throughout the tour, reviewers found that Elman's old fashioned programming had a certain charm, and noted his tone was as beautiful as ever. What particularly pleased him, though, were those reviews that acknowledged the sheer poetry at the heart of his interpretations, or admired the musicality of his playing—qualities singled out by the critics from two of the Vienna newspapers, *Die Presse* and the *Kurier*, in their reviews of his recital in the Musikverein.

He also made a few concerto appearances. One was with the London Philharmonic, which was touring Germany with John Pritchard on the podium. And on November 20, he made another exception to his ban on German orchestra performances, and played both the Mendelssohn and Tchaikovsky concertos with the Munich Opera Orchestra at an Akademiekonzert at the Deutschen Museum.

That was his last stop in Germany until early December, when he was to play the Khachaturian with Karel Ancerl and the Berlin Philharmonic. Rather than spending his couple of free weeks in Europe, he decided to return to the United States, and to visit his sisters in Philadelphia, staying over to celebrate both Thanksgiving and Esther's birthday. He also had an engagement in Tampa on December 1. A few days later, he flew back to Berlin. It was only after this that he allowed himself a few days rest. At the start of the New Year, he and Seiger gave some concerts on the West Coast, returning in time for their Carnegie Hall concert on January 17, four days before Elman's seventy-sixth birthday.

Shirley Thomson returned to New York the day of the concert, and was given a seat in the Elmans' box at Carnegie Hall, joining Helen and the violinist's two sisters. This was Elman's last New York recital.

In the audience that evening was the violist William Primrose, who included a few interesting paragraphs about Elman's late performances in his memoirs:

> I had great admiration for Mischa Elman. He was out of a special mold; his tone was glorious, as recalled by all who heard him.... Elman's annual New York recital, the last one before he died...was to me an instance of what was taking place in the realm of the recital then. He played a handsome program...the kind of program he had played all his life, the kind Kreisler and all the fiddlers of that era played. I was shocked when I took my seat in Carnegie Hall. In the first place, the hall wasn't full, and secondly those in attendance represented the old faithful cohorts who had gathered around Elman for many, many years. Very few young people were in attendance, and I felt it was a great pity that the youth hadn't turned out to hear this man, who at 75 was still playing superbly.
>
> The experience confirmed what I had been aware of for some time—the recital as we knew it during my time, the recital that I loved because I had been brought up on it, was on the way out. The younger generation is not interested. Elman was a bewitching fiddler, no doubt about it, and his death was a tremendous loss to the world of string playing.

Primrose was also among those who tried to persuade Elman to teach around this time, and he closes the passage quoted above with the observation that Elman "had a great deal to impart," adding:

> I lament the fact that Elman didn't teach. One thinks of such a violinist, having achieved his enormous artistry at such an early age and in such a genial and intuitive manner, perhaps being spared the consciousness and often the travail of systematic learning.[5]

After the concert, Elman took his family, along with Thomson, Seiger and a group of friends, next door to the Russian Tea Room where he held court for his entourage and for various visitors to his table, including the handful of newspaper columnists who happened by. Among the other musicians present was the cellist Albert Catell, who joined Elman in a group of vocal duets on the inner voices of their favorite string quartets.

The next day, Thomson went to Elman's apartment for another lesson, which this time covered more daring repertoire—the

Tchaikovsky Concerto and some Wieniawski. At noon, after working for two hours, Elman took her, Seiger and Helen to lunch, picking up the newspapers on the way and looking up his reviews.

Unfortunately, these did not mirror Primrose's enthusiasm for the performance, and the *Times* review, while it was not wholly negative, caused him particular pain. The critic, Howard Klein, began by calling Elman a phenomenon, and it seemed that in some general ways he admired the playing, which he described as "warmhearted, if technically cautious." He also observed that "the control over bow-arm and fingers was never to be doubted," and he praised the eloquence of Elman's Spohr and the persuasiveness of his Tchaikovsky, Nin, Ysaÿe and Saint-Saëns closing group.

Yet, on balance it seemed that this praise was merely the polite veneer the critic felt compelled to apply when writing about a disappointing concert by an aging master; and Klein made his objections clear. He was struck, first of all, by the slowness of Elman's tempos, which he felt "indicated not so much a desire to draw out musical complexities as to be sure all the notes were there." More crucially, he found Elman's interpretations antiquated. "Stylistically, the recital was a complete throwback to violin-playing of several generations ago. There was no change in orientation from Handel's Baroque in A [to] Brahms's wildly Romantic Sonata No. 3 in D minor. Mr. Elman connected melody notes with bold slides up or down the strings. Rhythms were very flexible and the pulse of any given tempo could vary drastically."

From there, praise was mingled with damnation. "By modern standards," Klein wrote, "the Handel was scandalous. But," he added, "a kind of love went into Mr. Elman's playing that let one glimpse a bygone day when performers were like heavenly envoys, blessed with special communications and hence special license." The Brahms, Klein reported, contained liberties that today's players would deem "unthinkable." In the end, Klein found so much to object to, blended with so many likeable qualities, that he was unable to come to an unwaveringly firm conclusion:

"Mr. Elman's sense of involvement with all the music, despite the anachronisms here and there, was not to be questioned. There was no dazzle to the playing, but his audience seemed to be with him in everything. And the way the small, bald figure bent over the violin to coax a long melody out of it, then, after the completion of a satisfying passage, shot a look at the audience to see it the point had been made, persuaded even a modern-eared critic to go along."

Elman was particularly incensed at seeing his Handel called "scandalous." "Why do they write things like that?" he asked. "Don't they understand?"

Evidently, several in Elman's audience that evening felt that Klein had indeed not understood, and a few wrote him lengthy letters to the critic, care of the *Times*, disputing his observations. One writer pointed out that "every artist should have the audience approval that Mr. Elman had at this past concert. The applause after each selection was very heavy, and became thunderous after the Spohr Concerto and the Brahms Sonata. But after the *Rondo capriccioso*, which officially ended the programmed recital, the applause and the shoutings of 'Bravo' from the audience was deafening. Four times the exhausted but gracious Mr. Elman came out for encores, and the audience continued to stand in the aisles and applaud, even after the stage was darkened, and the house lights turned up, and the people knew for sure that Mr. Elman would not come out again."

A more detailed letter came from Rose Heylbut, a music writer who had been the New York correspondent to *The Etude* in decades past, and who took the opportunity to argue against what she saw a trend of modern criticism—specifically, instances wherein, as she writes, "a mature and experienced artist is rebuked for performing 18th and 19th century works according to what your critic calls 'the standards of an earlier generation.'" Pointing out that "the question is not today's standards, but those of the composer," she argues that "when a master interpreter tells us, in effect, that this phrasing or that rhythmic spaciousness is what he believes the composer meant, he is entitled to be judged in terms of his own integrity. The critic need not 'like' the result (or the artist), but he should also be guided by integrity and not a mere fashion of the day. It is no service to music to denigrate what, actually, is a valuable link in tradition."

Heylbut went on to make one further point—"the matter of an artist's power utterly to move his hearers, the intangible magic of his communication, expressed through music yet not explained by rhythm or tone," was something she felt could not be ignored. "This sheer magic," she continued, "for whatever reason, was far more prevalent among the giants of an earlier generation than among the practitioners of today's standards. One seldom finds it now. It was glowingly in evidence when Mr. Elman played, a strange, inexplicable thrust into the deepest human essence, affecting the Beatle-mops in the audience as well as the graybeards. If this reflects a difference in standards, vive la difference!"

Responding to Heylbut's letter, Klein held his ground. "I disagree on several points with you," he wrote, "especially the one you raise about 'intangible magic' of a performer that is not explained 'by rhythm or tone.' This in itself is a romantic notion.... As you say, standards of performance change. What was done in Handel's own day, alas, is a matter of conjecture. But we know what was done in 1900 and we have been through a great period of rediscovery regarding the styles of earlier eras. The current taste in Baroque music is antithetical to what Mr. Elman did, however sincere his emotions in doing so were. I concur with the prevalent tastes in Baroque performance and merely pointed out how far from today's (who really knows what the composer's standards were?) ideas Mr. Elman's were."

Klein's criticism made Thomson curious about Elman's notions of stylistic differentiation, and she pursued the point, asking him how he viewed the differences between the various national schools.

"In general," she recalls of this discussion, "he spoke about his violin style being a singing style—which struck me as a basically Italian approach. 'I never come off the string,' he said, 'and the result is the opposite of the approach where the notes are separate and there's a bite and crunch.' But when he played French music, he preferred a filmier sound, which he produced by moving the bow a little faster, and using a slightly different arm weight. It was almost a question of being French in intent. It was gracious and elegant, but also a little tongue in cheek. And in Russian music, his style was once again a singing one, but with an accent very different from that which he applied to Italian music.

"He also emphasized the importance of keeping in mind the essence of the piece—that is, if it were a dance, it had to have that rhythmic drive. He used to complain that young violinists 'have no sense of style,' by which he didn't mean that they didn't play with flair, but that they didn't understand that you don't play Mozart with the same kind of tone you use to play Tchaikovsky. He certainly didn't: his vibrato, for one thing, was far more restrained in Mozart and Baroque music than in, say, the Tchaikovsky Concerto."

Elman seemed to be enjoying these informal lessons, and they were leading him reconsider his resistance to teaching. In recent months, he had been pondering an invitation to hold a master class at the University of North Carolina, at Chapel Hill. Early in January, he and the school came to terms. He and Seiger would spend a week there, giving a recital and presiding over a small, carefully selected class; and at the end of his stay, addressing the full student body, all for the rather handsome fee of $10,000 (plus expenses).

He looked forward to this residency, and when he told Thomson about it, she was ecstatic. "I felt that my mission was accomplished," she says. "He had come to see that teaching was something he could enjoy, and he had decided to continue."

CHAPTER TWENTY-FOUR:

Valedictory

The University of North Carolina selected five of its violin students to participate in Mischa Elman's class, and each prepared a major piece from the sonata repertoire. Elman and Seiger arrived in Chapel Hill in early March, a few days before the recital that would inaugurate the series, and they found that the school had arranged for lots of publicity, including newspaper, television and radio interviews. Otherwise, the atmosphere was restful. Between rehearsals, Elman and Seiger took long walks in the surrounding countryside, during which Elman rehearsed the speech he planned to deliver at the end of his stay. Elman took this lecture quite seriously, for although he had given dozens of talks for women's auxiliaries, symphony boards, and various arts organizations, he saw this speech to the student body as an extension of his master class. He was there as a master of his art— as someone the students would look to for advice on establishing their own careers. He wanted to be truthful with them; in fact, he decided to be bluntly so, and to avoid painting too rosy a picture of the professional music world.

In New York, he had typed a 29 page draft; and in the weeks before he and Seiger left for North Carolina, he spent nearly as much time rehearsing the talk as he did rehearsing the recital program. One morning, he asked Seiger to listen to the entire address as he delivered it from his sheaf of notes. The next day, when Seiger turned up for rehearsal, he found Elman standing before the mirror, reading the speech to himself.

After a few relaxing days on campus, Elman played a fluent, outgoing concert; and two days later, he sat before the class of music students, with Seiger at the keyboard, and the five violinists seated around him. As it turned out, three of the five players were at too

321

elementary a level for him to do much with. He talked to them about bowing, fingering and intonation, and he treated them gently, but in the end he could only suggest that they improve upon their technical weaknesses before taking up the difficult works they had brought to the class.

The other two students, both young women, impressed Elman more. One played Franck, the other Schumann. Each played a movement at a time, with Elman offering comments, discussing specific points of interpretation, and suggesting alternative solutions without insisting that they change their approach—only that they consider all the possibilities. Much of his commentary centered on bowing. "You must breathe between phrases," he told one. "It's not a good idea to jump so quickly from the last beat of one phrase to the first of the next. Take the time to breathe. Just keep in mind, when you finish a phrase, that the bow has to breathe too."

The class lasted from 10 o'clock in the morning until just after 1 p.m. A couple more days of rest followed; then, on March 12, his last evening in Chapel Hill, he gave his talk. He spoke slowly, calmly and clearly, departing frequently from his written text, yet covering all the material he had outlined. The speech was an extraordinary one, embodying anecdotes, practical advice, and naturally, a survey of his attitudes about the performing world. He addressed his comments not only to string players, but to other instrumentalists, and in some cases, specifically to singers.

This speech, which lasted slightly more than an hour, was Elman's valedictory in a way—a final, sweeping public statement about his art, and a survey of his attitudes about a world that had changed radically during his decades as a performer.[1:]

> Members of the faculty, students, ladies and gentlemen: Dr. Mason has suggested that this talk include various subjects such as my childhood, my years as a prodigy, my father's care; my opinions as a parent, of music for children, outside influences on my career, et cetera. All the foregoing could well comprise a talk which might interest you. But would it help you?
>
> There are many frustrating problems which plague the music world. There are questions which need answering; musical ills which need healing. I believe I can be more useful by assuming the combined role of teacher, counselor and psychologist.
>
> First, I want to talk about mediocrity. Why is there so much mediocrity today—especially in music? Because many young per-

formers are not able to evaluate their own talent. They overestimate themselves.

Second, many young performers are encouraged by well-meaning friends and teachers who see greatness in them before they have had a chance to develop. No teacher, no critic, no group of admiring relatives or friends can predict the future of a student, regardless of his talent. Why? Because musical eminence depends on something far more elusive than talent or ability to perform.

Third, many students work at their music with the idea of achieving greatness. This is unfortunate. Many highly gifted students already consider themselves future Rachmaninoffs, Kreislers, and Carusos. Neither my father nor I had the slightest idea of what my career would become when I was a young student. My father's earliest hopes were that I might have a routine post in a good orchestra. The development of my career paralleled the development of myself. I was watched by my father to prepare my lessons properly. My parents never talked in terms of fame or wealth. And I strongly advise this procedure for parents of other young students.

Young men in medical school work to become fine physicians, not thinking to become world famous doctors. Law students don't feel they have to prove themselves by striving to be internationally renowned lawyers. Potential doctors and lawyers must have special talents too, the same as we musicians must have. But they don't knock themselves out to become famous as soon as they begin to show a little promise. If world fame comes, bravo.

Singleness of purpose is fine. But don't let it ruin your life. One can derive immense joy and satisfaction from music without ever approaching greatness. No possible disappointment can result from an eager, ardent pursuit of music. But much disappointment and bitterness can result from deliberately planning for a goal which the circumstances of life may deny.

There seems to be a false sense of values today. We raise the lower level, but we also pull down the top. And the result is mediocrity. For some time, I have been deploring the lack of artistry in young concert performers, by saying, facetiously, "the standard of mediocrity has been raised." All young people have their idols. Hero worship is good. But do they always choose the right heroes? Not having reached maturity, youth often fails to evaluate properly. A particular idol may enjoy great success, make much money, and draw vast crowds. Observing this, the ambitious young musician concludes that this is a notable artist, and tries to imitate his approach, never realizing that what he does is only glitter. And all that glitters is not gold.

The good performer knows his instrument. And this includes voice. He is technically equipped to express himself fluently. He draws from his technique tones, passage work, shadings, dynamics and effects over which we assume he has perfect control. Most singers are inadequately prepared because they study badly. After a short time, they think they are ready. They force. They try to do more than they can. Once there was a stricter difference between types of voices—*spinto, lyric*, etc. But now, singers want to sing all kinds of music, whether it suits their voices or not. And they want to sing beyond their natural range. Furthermore, they fail to communicate the meaning of their words. They think more of vocalization and production than of the text.

Now I want to talk about criticism. There are several kinds. Some people tell the student that everything he does is marvelous. They encourage him to consider himself a genius, when in all probability he is cable of only giving a good performance. The wise student realizes that he's probably not a genius, and even if he is, there is plenty of time to admit that after he has convinced the music world of its truth. A young performer should place more confidence on those who tell him how he can *improve* his performance— provided those people know something about it and can substantiate their criticism. Some people pick flaws without understanding what they criticize.

Competent criticism is not an ability to pick out flaws. It is a constructive means of correcting them. To say, "he phrases badly" means nothing. But to analyze a composition, phrase by phrase; to give thoughtful reasons why certain phrases should be emphasized—those are helpful things.

All performers are subject to criticism. Sometimes a performer is told that his playing was not in the spirit of the composer. Now, what does that mean? Who, today, can set himself up as being absolutely sure of what was in the mind of this or that great composer at the moment when he conceived a musical idea? It would be miraculously helpful if somebody could do so. But until the spirit of Bach or Brahms remanifests itself, with authoritative certainty, it is fair to assume that the artist who devotes his entire life to the study of great works knows at least as much about the intentions of the composer as the critics.

Once, at a recital of a violinist colleague of mine, while I was still applauding his playing of the Bach *Chaconne*, a lady tapped me on the shoulder. Leaning forward, she murmured, "That was enjoyable, but it wasn't Bach, was it Mr. Elman?" To which I replied, "I'm sorry Madame, but I never heard Bach play it." So, don't say, this is not Schumann, or this is not Mendelssohn. There is no such thing as right or wrong interpretation when you deal with the higher echelon of artists. A conventional interpretation doesn't make it right; and an unconventional interpretation doesn't make it wrong. On one occasion in London, when Rachmaninoff played one of his own concertos, a critic wrote that he had not played it in the style of the composer.

Critics are partly to blame for the lack of inspired performances by many young artists. They think they must perform according to the critics' conception of a good performance, otherwise they don't get a good review. And if they don't get a good review, that's the end. This is deplorable. Young performers are afraid to be original, to be individualistic, even if they happen to have something of their own. They're afraid because they know they would be immediately attacked and criticized. Critics have too much power today. Too much power, and too little knowledge. That's one reason I say that we are living in an age in which the standards of mediocrity have been raised.

Early in my career, the artists were not afraid of criticism. The manager did not shirk from his belief in the artist; and the public did not shirk from attendance because they read a bad criticism. The wisest attitude towards criticism is to investigate its constructive worth. Develop self-criticism. Set yourself an ideal, a standard. Pursue it wholeheartedly, developing yourself and your perceptions at the same time. You should like or dislike music on the basis of your own reaction to it, no matter what the critic says. Their judgments are merely statements of their own listening experience. Yours are just as valid for you. Why? Because among these knowledgeable gentlemen there are often wide disagreements.

Here, I am addressing an audience of aspiring young musicians. All of you are at different degrees of advancement. You have different temperaments, different problems, differently constructed fingers and arms and vocal cords. It's impossible to outline any single set of commandments to unsnarl everybody's musical problems and keep everybody's progress at the highest pitch. But I'm going to try. President Franklin Delano Roosevelt said, "The difficult, we do at once. The impossible will take a little longer." Ready?

Discipline: Nothing worthy is accomplished without discipline. Some do only what they like to do, when they like to do it. Their excuse is that it makes for freedom. These people develop into the least free. They vacillate. They flit from one unfinished task to another. They must depend upon the help of others for all the important things in life. Much of life is made up of doing things we don't especially like to do. The practical person disciplines himself. I take keen pleasure in disciplining myself in my own work. I'm an early riser. I practice in the morning. I remember a pupil of my professor, Leopold Auer, who began to play the Mendelssohn Violin Concerto. After playing a few bars, Auer stopped him and asked, "what time did you get up this morning." "8 o'clock," answered thee pupil. Auer took out his watch and said, "it is now 2 o'clock, and you are not up yet!" This was Auer's way of telling the student he did not understand the piece.

But back to discipline. Almost every day, I play alone about an hour. Then, Mr. Seiger, my pianist, comes and we practice and prepare the next recital programs. Incidentally, string players should practice with piano as much as possible to get the harmonic background. That helps to get color and warmth.

Value of self-criticism: Don't be too much impressed with yourself and your talent. Stay humble. Remember, you have much to learn, and you can learn from every serious artist, regardless of his age or generation. Listen to the performances of great artists with an open mind. No two will be alike, yet all are valuable. The purpose of the artist is not to play louder and faster than anybody else, but to create beauty—to give his listeners that special thrill. I cannot overemphasize the importance of self-criticism. One must learn to divide one's person into two halves, so to speak, one half concentrating on performance, while the other half listens to the results in impartial, objective criticism. The half of you who listens knows exactly what the half of you who plays is trying to express.

Intelligent practice consists of three steps. First, the formulation of what you want to say. Second, the effort to express this idea through your performing. Third, a simultaneous and dispassionate appraisal of the points that go well and the points that go badly. There is an amusing story about a great pianist of the recent past, who should be a shining example of honest self criticism. He [Leopold Godowsky] had just given a concert at which he played badly. A colleague of his [Josef Hoffmann], an equally great pianist, came backstage and remarked, sympathetically, "you missed a lot of notes." The reply was, "yes, but the ones I played were worse."

From my personal experience, I advise young performers, don't take anything for granted. Don't get careless. By careless, I mean, that when something goes wrong during a performance, it is important to restudy that section. A performance can become dirty from an accumulation of accidents. So take a fresh, careful, thoughtful look at the places that accidents occur. In line with carelessness, I say this to string players and singers: good intonation is the basis of string and vocal technique. Practice with sharp, alert ears. Each tone you produce, challenge it for absolute purity of intonation. If intonation is faulty, it prevents the overtones from ringing out and giving carrying power to the tone.

Incidentally, string players: avoid bad shifts. Be careful in your use of the *glissando*. It must be used with good taste. Be careful where you use it and how you use it, for it can either enhance or cheapen. Mere slidings to a note do not put genuine feeling into that note. Cheapness of effect of any kind never succeeds in touching people's hearts.

Now I want too talk about tone, et cetera. To produce a certain color of sound, you must hear the tone mentally, anticipating it before it is produced. Afterward is too late. Train your hands or your voice to go surely and accurately to any note. To produce any tone in any position—to produce the kind of sound you want— you must anticipate it in your mind's ear before you attack it physically. You cannot attack every note with the same weight, or the same stroke of the bow.

Here is more about tone. People often ask me how to produce a good tone. A good string tone should be relaxed, unforced, firm, and one with the proper vibrato. It must involve a complete coordination between the fingers on the strings, and the bowing arm.

A ten-year old boy played for me. I was strongly impressed with the child's talent and ability, and I was curious as to what a certain prominent teacher [Carl Flesch] would say about him. So I telephoned this man, saying, "I have a boy here who has just played for me, and I think he's good. I want you to hear him. Will you hear him now if I send him over?" The teacher said yes, so I sent the boy over to him. An hour later, the boy was at my door again. "Well, what did [Mr. Flesch] say about your playing?" I asked. "He didn't say anything, he didn't even hear me play," sobbed the youngster. "Why? What happened?" I inquired. The boy explained, "He just kept asking me, 'What is a musical tone? What is a musical tone?' I didn't know what to say, so I came back to you, Mr. Elman." I was incensed at his treating the youngster that way, so I telephoned him again, and I said, "Do you want to know what a musical tone is? I'll tell you what a musical tone is. A musical tone is what you haven't got."

Now I want to talk about the microphone. Much harm has been done to young performers by the microphone. It has distorted their conception of tone. Much of the music one hears today passes through the mic, which filters out much of the beautiful quality. A tone should be the expression of a performer's personality. One player may have a larger tone than the next. One player may have a sweeter tone. Still another may have a generous supply of both qualities. The color, the finer nuances that make a beautiful tone, these are disappearing, because most young players and singers concentrate on acquiring a big tone, such as they hear on radio, television and records. They completely forget that the mic can transform a thin, squeaky tone into one that sounds enormous from the loudspeaker. In trying to imitate this big tone, they produce a harsh, loud tone to which their ears become accustomed. Let us not even discuss their quality of tone in a *pianissimo*.

To younger performers I say don't be superficial in your approach to music. Don't sacrifice sentiment. Beauty of tone will come from your conception of music, from your appreciation of its beauties. If you search honestly to find that beauty, your performance will reflect your sincerity and the beauty of your thought. And your audience will respond to it. A great danger of the age in which we live is the immense stress of mechanics and speed. We conquer distance by Telstar, planes, etc., and we call it progress. But we must use great discrimination when we apply it to a completely non-mechanical medium such as music. The fastest plane may be the best; but the fastest performance of Mozart is *not* the best.

There seems to be an overemphasis on the sheer mechanics of performance. Young musicians should think in terms of more inward values, reaching towards the aspects of performance which spring from the heart, rather than from the muscles. In striving for speed, playing becomes mechanical. Not always clear, ethically or musically. Speed is fine if it's in the right place at the right time. But it seldom is. In the classical repertoire, for example, one must consider at what period the composer lived and composed. You cannot apply modern tempos to the tempos which Bach and Mozart etc., felt in their time. There were no fast contrivances in their day, as compared to those of today.

Comparing young performers of today with great performers such as Ysaÿe, Caruso, Paderewski—here is the difference: they gave pleasure to their audiences. They moved people with their message. To attend one of their recitals was an experience never to be forgotten. Most young musicians perform exceedingly well, technically, but lack imagination and individuality. Such great artists show their true greatness by the way they perform slow movements. Today, even some *Adagios* are played twice as fast as they should be. And even at these speeds, the performers are *bored* by *Adagios*, rushing faster and faster. An artist can create beauty in any tempo he feels. But most performers don't recognize beauty, because they perform just notes.

Now about musicianship: Musicianship begins when one's performance reflects not merely correct notes, but a well-planned
inner concept. You get this inner concept by studying the score in
relation to its time and style. From observing and comparing interpretations—but never copying them. My own method of work
begins with a complete reading of a score to find its structure, its
meaning, its moods. When I know it has possibilities for me, I
begin to study it, and at once new vistas open before me. I plan my
interpretative conception as a whole. I hear inside exactly how I
wish the work to sound, both as a whole, and as the individual
phrases which built that whole. I know, from the first to the last
note, the precise picture I want to present; how each phrase must
fit into its context; every shade and color connected with it. Then,
I dissect the various phrases and passages for further study according to the color and nuance they require in their particular
point of context.

The importance of the point of context cannot be overstressed.
Even the handling of purely mechanical details varies with the
phrase in which they occur. A simple G major scale, or arpeggio,
for instance, may be played as an exercise. It may also occur in different pieces. In each case, it has different meaning and demands
entirely different treatment. It can seem extremely easy in one
piece, and extremely difficult in another. And still, it is always the
same sequence of notes. In the Bruch G minor Concerto, there's a
simple arpeggio, which every violinist practices over and over as
a daily exercise. Yet, in this particular context, it becomes a stum-
bling block which the most experienced performer finds difficulty in surmounting. Why? Because that passage must be expressed
in a certain dramatic way, at a certain speed. And the difficulty
lies not in the notes themselves, but in the need of meeting the full
demands of the context in its specific framework of color and
tempo. It's always the context, and not the notes alone which deter-
mines the ease or difficulty of playing. That's why technique as
such can never be the final answer.

More about tone. Along with the mechanics of tone control,
there must be elements which have nothing to do with mechanics.
There must be nuance. A sure and well-planned knowledge of
which note will bring out the expression of a passage; a certainty
of the exact fingering to bring out what you feel. Correct fingering
is a part of both tone and expression. And it is an individual thing.
You feel within you that a phrase must sound a certain way. You
ask yourself exactly what you must do to bring out this sound. Experiment with all possible fingerings until you have the one that
will give you that sound. I spend much time working out correct

fingerings. And by correct fingerings, I don't mean those of some editor, or some other performer; but the ones which will enable my fingers to sound forth the effects I want. Remember, the expression of a passage depends on the fingerings you use.

Again about musicianship. Musicianship is not necessarily bound up with performing surety and security. The knowledge of music, and the taste of interpreting are vastly different. You may know a great deal about music, and not have good taste in performing. For instance, the essence of string or vocal surety is the ability to produce good, true, fluent tones. Yet, we have all heard performers who could do all that without moving us in the least. They may be good musicians, but they have nothing to say. Musically, they project no message.

The common opinion, in such cases, is that such players lack personality. This mysterious quality, personality, is thought to be the source from which springs meaningful expression—the human power to move human hearts. Musicianship is not a mysterious gift. It can be cultivated. But no matter how much magnetism a performer may have—no matter how skilled he may be in technical fluency—unless he bases his message on honest, careful musicianship, he becomes a charming liar, in a musical sense. And we tire of him, because we lose confidence in him.

One of the most serious lapses of good taste—one that can mar an otherwise well-planned performance—is lack of balance, of proportion, of timing within a phrase or between phrases, in fitting together the various parts of the music. For instance, suppose an *Andante* passage is followed by an *Allegro*. The performer must know how—not merely how to play an *Andante* and an *Allegro*, he must know how to conceive this interpretation as a whole, so the balance between the slow and fast parts makes sense. What jars the listener are the inconsistencies in a performer. To attain and maintain your technique, practice slowly, always keeping in mind the content of the music so you don't tire of going over the passage again and again. When you start to study a piece, consider it as a musical whole. Think about it—what mood and meaning it is to you. Which are the important phrases? In a sonata, which are the melodic lines? Which are the chief themes? Where are the inner voices which give greater warmth to the phrase or theme.

As you practice, try to discover meaning in the work which didn't occur to you when you heard it the first time. You may change your mind about it. But never work without a clear picture of what you are working toward. The real artist finds the unity of concept through mood, feeling, shape and color. Above all, he must listen to himself to be sure that what he does is in good taste.

I am opposed to contests. Today, there are contests almost everywhere, with young people entering and hoping to win, and publicize their winning as a stepping stone to a great career. Contests have their place in sports, where it is possible to see an athlete or a horse reach the finish line so many seconds ahead of his opponents, or where one may count the number of successful goal shots in basketball or in hockey. But music is not a sport. It's an emotional experience, something we hear and feel. In sports, if you win, you are the best. In art, winning is a question of taste. And when it comes to taste, judges are free to like or dislike as they wish, whatever personal reasons they may have. So winning a contest is no criterion whether the performer is a great artist or not. I happened to attend a well known international contest a few years ago and I think I know something about violin playing—the player who got that prize should not even have been allowed to enter the contest. The winner wins by a majority; and I question the quality of the judges when I see the quality of people who win the prizes.

The impression a musical performance makes on one listener will be different from that made on another listener. The fact that a performer wins a musical contest doesn't necessarily make him the champion, even though the jury may agree unanimously on their verdict. The very nature of music makes it impossible to watch performances fairly at contests. So never be discouraged at losing a performance contest. In a competition in Russia, years ago, Tchaikovsky received only a silver medal; an unknown composer, whose name completely escapes me, won the gold medal. And the eminent French composer Camille Saint-Saëns failed in two competitions for the coveted Grand Prix de Rome. The winner in both cases was a composer who has never been heard of since. Incidentally, about Saint-Saëns: as a child, his family and friends considered him somewhat of a prodigy. His mother gave an elegant soiree one evening, and invited all the influential musicians and critics to hear little Camille play the piano. After the performance, the mother approached the most prominent music critic and asked his opinion of her son. "Madame," he announced, "your son will never be a musician." "In that case," retorted the mother, "I'll train him to be a music critic."

Contests such as the one in Moscow recently[2] place an enormous burden on the winner, who faces a constantly increasing strain trying to live up to the standards of excellence expected of him. At the same time, that a winner receives world acclaim and clatter can be a source of discouragement to students who may be equally talented. There seems to be room for only one champion in our American way. This is regrettable. Frustration can cause much harm to human beings. Let's avoid it. Sustained consistency in performance quality is the important factor; and this only time can determine.

Judging: There is a tendency of judges, critics, audiences, and young performers themselves to evaluate artistic performances through phonograph records. As an artist who has been recording for more than 50 years, I'm aware of the difficulties inherent in the recording process. Often a performance on a recording is less than authentic. It is really not representative of the artist concerned. So it can't be properly evaluated. Therefore, to draw a comparison between an artist who is known chiefly through his records, and an artist heard in the concert hall, is not fair. Only the concert hall can give you the proper perspective.

Henry Pleasants, the noted musicologist, author of *The Agony of Modern Music*, comments, regarding singers—and this also applies to instrumentalists: "With records being made from a selection of the best of several 'takes', and with more or less splicing, the singer or performer may find himself hard put to live up to his recordings in his public appearances. He is at a disadvantage as his own competitor. And the strain and nervous tension of recording sessions is an additional tax on vocal and other physical resources, not to overlook the frustrations of having a conductor and a good many other functionaries passing judgement on his performance and telling him what to do and what not to do, and of having to repeat certain passages over and over again because of somebody else's mistakes."[3]

By the foregoing I do not mean to suggest that we should devalue recorded music. On the contrary. We should be thankful that we have recorded performances of such a wealth of music available to us, especially for those for whom live performances are out of reach. My point is that recorded performances cannot replace the direct contact with the artist's personality. Only in the concert hall is this contact possible.

If any of you succeed in becoming artists, you should know what you are up against. You should know the inside stories—the injustice, the heartaches, the hardships, the trouble, the trials, the behind-the-scenes intrigue and politics in which you will be involved if and when you enter the concert field. If you are in the top echelon, naturally there is glamor, joy, satisfaction and even relative wealth. Balancing that, however, even for the great artists, are the cold, cruel facts of life in the professional music world. No doubt you have had a taste of the sugar coating. I am now going to tell you about the bitter pill.

Few Americans realize the peculiar financial dilemma of the musician. He spends his childhood, youth and often the early years of his adult life in costly study, preparing for his career. Whether he becomes a famous star, an ensemble singer, or an orchestral instrumentalist, he labors under certain disadvantages peculiar to his profession. The talent with which he earns his living is a highly personal commodity which only he can purvey. Should illness prevent his performing, his income ceases until he recovers. The businessman deals in less personal goods and services, so sickness poses not quite the same problem. His business and his income continue, despite his illness, through the organization he has developed.

Another peculiar disadvantage of the musician's life is the relative shortness of his career. Physical duration is a critical factor, particularly with singers. For the voice, a physical thing, tends to age along with the performer. This is less true of the instrumentalists. A few, like myself as you can see, are a hardy breed. But it can also be true of them. There's also the element of vogue, which has brought many an artist a brief success, only to leave him high and dry when the vogue has spent itself and another vogue replaced it.

Also, for the great majority of musical artists, the music season, which provides the steadiest, most dependable period of employment, is shorter than the employment year of others. For all these reasons, the musician's earning life is crowded into fewer and shorter years than that of people in other professions. The government so far seems little interested in these special economic problems that assail the musician. It has, however, shown keen interest in some of the special economic problems concerning oil wells. Oil wells become depleted; so the government protects oil well owners against this inevitable eventuality, by establishing a preferential tax philosophy for income derived from oil wells. Talent, and the human beings who manifest it also deteriorate with time.

It is proper and reasonable, for the government to help oil well owners. It would be equally proper and reasonable for it to show similar concern for the artist's eventual deterioration, and the decline of his activity and ability to perform. Those who work in the drama, literature, sculpture, painting and the dance, all face similar problems. They are entitled to the same consideration I suggest for musicians—not only because it would help those in the creative arts; but because they too, like oil, are important natural resources which enhance our life at home and bring prestige for us abroad. Properly used, as an instrument of cultural rela-

tions, they can be a unifying influence among nations by em-
phasizing similar tastes and attitudes to create mutual respect and
understanding.

Perhaps in the future, our government may establish a Department of the Arts within the cabinet, which would have the budget
and authority to deal effectively with all these problems. In the
meantime, though, I believe the administration should evolve a
tax philosophy specially tailored to each of the arts. It should be
designed to promote their health and growth, as well as the health
and growth of the artists who practice them.

Concerning singers: Our American singers find it necessary—
indeed they are forced—to go to Europe for their experience because we have so few opera houses, so few outlets for them here
in America. There are two, possibly three exceptions—the
Metropolitan Opera, the New York City Opera, and the San Francisco Opera. There are some fine opera workshops throughout
America; but most of them operate only in summer. We should
have municipal opera houses in all the large centers of our country,
to provide outlets for our deserving and talented American
singers. If our Federal government is not prepared to advance such
a project now, our local governments should be made aware of
this need. As matters stand now, many serious American singers
find themselves in a frustrating position, through this lack of real
theaters.

But we must give credit where credit is due. There is a great up-
surge of music in this country. Many communities now have open
air summer concerts. And they support local symphony orchestras. Music is being made in large quantities. I believe,
however, that we should stress more quality, since quality is art's
great purpose. The commercial epoch in which we are now living
tends to level down the dignity that belongs to great art. You, the
students—and performers of the future—must resist this trend.
The destiny of music in America lies in your hands.

Thank you.

Elman's speech was met with hearty, appreciative applause, and a
brief question and answer period followed, during which one of the
students asked him to play. Elman declined, pointing out that he had
just played a recital a few evenings earlier, and that he hadn't brought
his violin to the lecture hall. "But," he added, "I hope I'll be back again,
and I hope that when I return, you'll all come to my concert."

CHAPTER TWENTY-FIVE:

A Peaceful End

If Elman was disappointed in the performance level of three fifths of his first master class, he nevertheless enjoyed the encounter and looked forward to more. The venture was a success from the school's point of view too, and within a week, word of the master class had spread to other colleges. By the end of March, Elman's manager was fielding offers from several interested schools, and the violinist decided that henceforth, his cross-country tours would be structured to include a combination of concerts and master classes.

But it was not to be. In the weeks following their return from North Carolina, Elman and Seiger settled back into their practice routine, in preparation for another run of concerts out of town.

On Wednesday, April 5, they rehearsed in Elman's studio, and went their separate ways. It was an unusually hot afternoon for early spring, and Elman didn't feel like making his customary trek into midtown. Instead, he had a light lunch at a deli around the corner and then went for a walk. When he returned, at around 4 o'clock, he climbed the circular staircase that led to his studio, and walked past it to the bedroom, where Helen was in bed, recovering from a broken foot. "I feel so funny," he told her. "Maybe it's something I ate." He went back downstairs, unaware that what he was feeling was the onset of a heart attack.

A few minutes later he called out that he couldn't breath, and in a moment he collapsed. Helen could not get to him quickly: on her crutches, she was unable to navigate the circular staircase, and since the front elevator went only as high as the first floor of their duplex, she hobbled to the service elevator, only to find, when she reached the lower floor, that she didn't have her key and would have to be let in by the superintendent.

Meanwhile, the Elmans' maid was seeing to the violinist, who was now stretched out on the couch in the den, unconscious. She was unable to reach the family doctor, and she had been trying desperately to find someone who could help when Jeri Feder telephoned to say that she was going to stop by and visit Helen. "Oh, Mrs. Feder," the maid told her, "I'm afraid Mr. Elman is dying, and I can't get the doctor on the phone." Feder left an emergency message with the doctor's office, and driving through half a dozen red lights, she rushed to 101 Central Park West.

When she arrived, she found Helen in a wheelchair outside the den, where the doctor had been trying to revive Elman with oxygen. But it was too late. Elman never regained consciousness, and at a little after 4:30, he was pronounced dead.

The next day, the *New York Times* began Elman's obituary on its front page, devoting 58 column inches to it—an impressive amount of space for a musical figure. It covered the highlights of his career, beginning with his earliest studies and moving quickly through his Berlin and New York debuts, noting his relief efforts for German refugees, and his golden jubilee. Included, too, was a handful of anecdotes—about the time he suffered gas poisoning on the eve of his Berlin debut; about his search for the "ideal girl" and his courtship of Helen; about his exchange of letters with Olin Downes (here identified simply as "a critic") about the Beethoven cadenzas, and more. And the article was spiced with quotations drawn from Elman's forthright interviews, conveying both his opinionated and his humorous sides.

Set beside this lengthy portrait, the *Times* ran an appraisal of Elman's contributions to his art, by Harold C. Schonberg. Under the headline, "Master of Sheer Sound," it began:

> Mischa Elman, short, somewhat rotund, bald, energetic, would come bustling out on stage in that indescribably cocky walk of his. He would look over the audience with wise eyes that had seen audiences of all kinds for 30, 40, 50 years. Then he would tuck his Stradivarius under his chin. When he did that, the instrument seemed an extension of himself, welded to his body. This is true of all natural instrumentalists. There is never a feeling of strain or effort, and Elman above all violinists except Kreisler played with ease. When he brought that sturdy bow arm down, the hall was

filled with the Elman sound, and audiences—especially in the early days of his career—would promptly go into hysterics.

The Elman sound. It was full, rich, sweet, throbbing. On the G string his instrument sounded like a cello. In the upper positions of the E string, it was a platinum flute. No violinist of the century, and undoubtedly none in history, had this kind of sheer, sensual sound. Elman was never one of the philosophers of music, one of the deep thinkers, one of the learned musicians. But he had something that many of his more learned colleagues would have given anything for, and that was the ability to play the violin with such expression and sweetness that criticism was disarmed.

Schonberg went on to note that Elman was at his best in works like the Tchaikovsky Concerto. "Of course there was nothing wrong with the way he played the Beethoven or Brahms concertos," he added, "but musicians were in general agreement that in such works as the Tchaikovsky, Elman was in a class by himself." He then mused about Elman's style, and his famous, unique tone. And he devoted a few paragraphs to non-musical side of the Elman story—the tale of a child of the Russian Jewish ghetto, who polished his art and made his way in the world.

The same day, in the United States Senate, Jacob Javits, took the floor to pay tribute to his famous constituent. "Mischa Elman was most distinguished by the fact that he was giving concerts literally up to the moment of his death," Javits said. "I saw Mischa Elman in New York not more than 10 days ago, and he was full of plans for the future instead of, at the age of 76, resting on an enormous world reputation.... Mischa Elman in his lifetime was an example of the very finest of concert music and was one of the greatest instrumentalists. His death is a great loss to our nation. As a great artist he brought honor to our country throughout the world."

Perhaps the most touching of the tributes composed in Elman's honor, though, was the one his Russian colleague and friend David Oistrakh sent to Helen.

"The memory of his unequaled playing, his unmatched artistry and extraordinary sensitivity—gifts that throughout his long life captivated the world and brought happiness and joy to untold multitudes of people who loved and appreciated music—will live forever in my soul. My generation has learned a lot from your husband, who has made the Russian violin school famous. That school will be forever grateful to him and will cherish his memory for years to come. I consider myself most fortunate indeed for having had the opportunity to know Mr. Elman personally, and for having been able to hear his inspired music in private."

❖ ❖ ❖ ❖ ❖

When Mischa Elman died, so did the thoroughly subjective style his playing represented. It was a style he had assimilated from the great violinists of his early years, and which he transformed into the basis of his own personal language. Part of that language was a bag of technical tricks and interpretive gestures that, when applied in the right way, could turn both great works and trivial ones into statements that communicated personal warmth and emotional depth—or as Elman liked to put it, humanity.

Of course, other violinists from his era outlived him: Heifetz, for one, had virtually retired from the stage before Elman's death, but he emerged for a few concerts and television productions in the 1970s. And Nathan Milstein continued to travel the world as the violin's elder statesman. But while their Russian, Auer-nurtured roots were similar, neither Heifetz nor Milstein were of the same stylistic mold as Elman. If, in their younger years, they had played with something approaching Elman's ultra-Romantic sensibility, they were taking different paths by the time they came before the public. And as public taste slowly shifted, Heifetz, Milstein, and later, Menuhin, Oistrakh and Stern, not only floated in the same direction as those strong currents, but through the forces of their own personal styles, they helped influence the course the tide of performance style well into this century.

Elman was not that way. When the tides of stylistic preference rose and fell around him, he stood rocklike, like a jetty in the middle of a harbor, changing gradually over the years, yet essentially holding his ground. It was not his destiny to be the spearhead of a new style, but rather, the culmination of an old one; and it is probably because the very essence of Elman's style was widely regarded as old-fashioned long before his death that his reputation faded so quickly once he ceased to walk the world's concert platforms.

In his time, many of Elman's colleagues found his readings suffused with beauty and warmth, while others who had become familiar with the characteristics of the Romantic style through the recordings of Joachim, Sarasate, Zimbalist, Seidl and the few privately circulated discs Auer made, argued that Elman's work, particularly towards the end of his life, was more an exaggeration of the style than a pure example of it. Was that the case? One might ascribe the slower tempos Elman took in the 1960s to his age, and one could suggest that his increasingly personalized *rubato*, his pulsating *vibrato* and his sweeping slides were his reactions against the what he considered the cold, mechanistic and inexpressive side of the modern "objective" school.

But if interpretive leeway and individualistic expression were among the hallmarks of the Romantic style, how can one authoritatively say that Elman's brand of individuality was inappropriate? Ultimately, the question can only be resolved by establishing the boundaries between interpretive individuality and stylistic transgression; and since that involves as many subjective criteria as the Romantic style itself, it's unlikely that any universally acceptable definition will ever be formulated.

What militates in Elman's behalf is the fact that the history of musical performance is full of shifting currents that bring opposing approaches and styles in and out of favor; and that one of the more fascinating aspects of performance history is that as the distance between the present and an earlier era increases, the long-obscured giants of that era sometimes come back into focus and benefit from posthumous re-examination.

In Elman's case that process has begun—slowly, perhaps, and as part of a rebirth of interest in the last phase of the Romantic era and its great interpreters. We are at last able to view that period from a vantage point that makes the personalized renderings of its great artists seem fascinating and magical once again, and perhaps even more than they did in their time, for they speak to us in a language that is alluringly alien at first, but which we learn to understand only by abandoning the prejudices of our time and accepting those earlier musical dialects on their own terms.

Until recently, the resistance to this style has been steadfast, and it's easy to understand why when you look at the musical thrusts of our day. We live in a time where the emphasis has been on either thorough novelty or purified antiquity. On the novel side, the thrust of music has been into new realms of sound and organization, often divorced from the harmonic, melodic and rhythmic traditions of the past. And of course, even our fascination with the antique has a novel edge. We want our performances of old music to be *authentically* old: we want the music to sound as it did when it was written, according to the most current estimations of what that ancient sound may have been.

Thus, the performances that take into account the very latest musicological discoveries and/or speculation are the ones that have been championed—and rightly so, to the extent that these findings are the hard-won products of serious, painstaking research, and ideally bring us closer to each composer's intentions and the spirit of his time. But at today's pace, these guesses are not championed for long before newly discovered evidence leads to new musicological conclusions. What were musicologically appropriate performances recorded in the early 1970s already seem slightly quaint in the light of current theories, while many of the fresh-new-correct performances of the 1950s and 1960s now sound rather ponderous. We can now hear early music discs and accurately guess the decade they were recorded—just as we can hear recordings by the likes of Elman, Mengelberg, Furtwängler, Toscanini or Heifetz, and identify the stylistic schools to which those musicians belonged.

Where does all this leave Elman and his approach? Ironically, the increasingly rapid shifting of theories, tastes and styles may ultimately lead many listeners to see the validity of his stance, if only in a roundabout way, for one need only stand back and survey three or four decades worth of musicologically sanctioned performances to realize, first, that absolute musical truth is a chimera; and second, that in its own way, every style that has been adopted along the road has a usefulness and a set of meanings all its own. A scholarly, "authentic" rendering of a Bach concerto, recorded in the 1950s, gave us a fresh view of Bach when it was new. But when we hear it today, we no longer conjure up that same illusory vision of unvarnished, historically accurate Baroque practice. Rather, we hear it as Bach, with the thumbprint of 1950s-style "authenticity" superimposed. Performances inevitably tell us about their own times, even when the intention behind them is to tell us about the composer's.

Elman and his contemporaries intuitively understood that this always was and always would be the case in musical performance, so they skipped the musicological pretense and went directly to what they considered the root of the matter: expressivity. To Elman's way of thinking, the great works were immutable, and questions of stylistic right and wrong were irrelevant. Style, he felt, was the province of the performer; and while it had to be applied tastefully, taking into account the composer and the kind of music at hand, its primary function was not to help the player recreate the sounds and sensibilities of a distant age, but rather, to help him communicate the music in a personal way to a contemporary audience.

It becomes clear, in the end, that Elman's style is a part of the larger musical continuum, and that it holds a place of honor there. It was superceded by a style seemed more coolly objective to listeners living in a time when cool objectivity was more attractive than steamy Romanticism. In recent years, that objective style has run its course too, at least in certain areas of the repertoire. And in its wake, an approach has emerged wherein personal warmth and individual interpretive initiative are valued once again. Many of the players who are now in the "middle" generation—Itzhak Perlman, Pinchas Zukerman and others of the Galamian school—were perceived as sounding rather alike when they first came to prominence; but the best of them have found their own stylistic paths as they matured. And among the youngest generation of players the variety is already considerable, ranging from the creative eccentricity of Gidon Kremer and Nigel Kennedy, through the more straightforward but equally thoughtful, personalized style of Dmitry Sitkovetsky, to the lush-toned, Romanticized virtuosity of Shlomo Mintz and Cho Liang Lin. None of these players has adopted a style anywhere near as extreme as Elman's; yet, each has a distinct, identifiable personality.

Within their individual styles, these players have found ways to add daring touches of Romanticism to approaches founded in the school of cool, modern precision, thereby blending the two formerly warring influences of the 20th century. But such is the alchemy of the performance continuum, and as we look back, with the help of recordings, at the great artists who thrived nearly a century ago, we can see this process unfolding clearly and inexorably. Styles thrive and fade, successors rise and fall, and hybrids of old and new styles emerge, eventually charting ground that had not been explored in the past, and furthering the development of the art. It is through this constant shifting that musical performance retains its vigor. And as we come to appreciate not only the continuum as a whole, but each of its component historical styles, our understanding of performance as a creative art is inevitably enriched.

Notes

Chapter One

1. There is some question about exactly what kind of violin this was—a minor point, perhaps, but for violin fanciers, an interesting one, and since several interesting violins came into Elman's possession during his lifetime, this seems a good place to try unravelling their chronology. Elman's first violin by a major maker was a 1654 Amati, purchased for him in 1903—towards the start of his time as a pupil of Leopold Auer, at the St. Petersburg Conservatory—by the Grand Duke of Meklenburg-Sterlitz. It was on this violin that Elman made his important European debuts; and Joseph Seiger, Elman's accompanist from 1952 until the violinist's death, recalls Elman telling him that he played the Amati at his New York debut as well.

   According to the publicity material Elman's managers were distributing by the 1930s, though, Saul Elman had acquired a Stradivarius violin especially for his son to play at his New York debut. Was this a publicist's fabrication? Perhaps. Moreover, by the early 1950s, some of Elman's press kits, as well as published articles derived from them, refer to this debut instrument as a "1772 Stradivarius," Antonio Stradivari's death in 1737 notwithstanding. This dating seems to be the result of a transcription error (which passed uncorrected from one press kit and newspaper article to the next), for Elman did own a 1722 Stradivarius, said to have once belonged to Joseph Joachim. Was this violin actually purchased for the New York debut, or at some later date? There is no extant receipt; but the 1722 instrument was apparently the first of three Stradivarius violins Elman owned during his life.

   Elman's second Stradivarius was a 1735 instrument, called the "Count Chapponey," and purchased from the Parisian firm of Caressa and Francais on June 14, 1923. Two years later, just after his wedding to Helen Katten, Elman returned to Caressa and Francais, and acquired (as a wedding gift from Helen) a 1717 Stradivarius, the "Madame Recamier." From 1925 until his death, that was his preferred instrument. In 1926, he sold the 1735

Strad to a dealer, who sold it to Raymond Pitcairn. When it surfaced again, at a March 1980 auction in New York, its documentary materials included a history of the instrument, compiled in 1903 by W. E. Hill and Sons, of London, as well as a 1926 letter from Elman, attesting that "I have used it at all my concerts for two years. I consider it one of the best Stradivarius instruments for tone quality and it is in an excellent state of preservation." He retained the 1722 Stradivarius until the mid-1950s, when he sold it to a collector in the midwestern United States. At the time, he told his sister, Esther, that he felt odd seeing the violin sitting in a glass case, after having used it in concert for several years. Esther Elman could not verify, however, whether this was the instrument he played at his debut. At the time of his death, he owned the Amati and the 1717 Stradivarius. The former is now in the possession of Shirley Thomson, a violinist in Minneapolis; the latter was sold to Ian Stoutzker, a banker and instrument collector, in London, in 1972.

2. Complementing the confusion over Elman's debut instrument is the claim (put forth by Elman's later publicists) that Elman played the American premiere of the Tchaikovsky Concerto—an assertion that, if it were true, would have had a special irony, for it had originally been dedicated to Leopold Auer, who, however failed to perform it and thereby lost the dedication. The commonly given reasons are that he was displeased with the work, and felt that the solo violin part was too difficult. But Elman, in an article entitled "25 Years of Fiddling: As Seen Over the Frog, or, A View from the Bridge" (see Chapter 20, note 2, below), questioned the veracity of this oft-cited legend: "The story spread that Auer told Tchaikovsky that the concerto was impractical and too difficult for the violin and I asked him about this. 'I said nothing of the kind,' maintained Auer. 'I was busy, with no time to look it over; those were not my words. '" However, when Auer did finally perform the work, in 1893, he used (and published) his own slightly simplified edition.

At any rate, the concerto was unveiled by Adolph Brodsky, in Vienna, on December 4, 1881. The American violinist Maud Powell is sometimes credited with giving the work its American premiere: she first performed it in the United States in 1889. Through the 1890s, it was a fairly common vehicle for soloists in New York. The New York critic James Gibbons Huneker, in his *Mezzotints in Modern Music* (1899), wrote that the concerto "has been heard here several times. It is romantic in feeling and a very interesting work, although by no means a masterpiece." The anonymous writer of Elman's debut review in *Musical America* also refers to the score's popularity with visiting violinists.

Nevertheless, in 1952, a splashy brochure printed by Columbia Artists credited Elman with introducing the concerto to the United States. Thereafter, some of his program and record jacket biographies repeated the assertion, which has crept into a few reference works. As with the conversion of the 1722 Stradivarius to a 1772 instrument, this factual flaw may have more to do with sloppy transcription than with an intent to deceive: In Elman's earlier publicity materials, he is variously called, somewhat more defensibly, the violinist "who first won renown for the Tchaikovsky Concerto," and, "the first violinist to popularize the Tchaikovsky Concerto." No doubt Elman's later publicists, in rewriting his materials, construed that the mean that he was the first violinist to *play* the work.

3. Saul Elman, *Memoirs of Mischa Elman's Father* (New York: privately published in an edition of 500 copies, 1933), p. 183.

4. Going by the calendar used in Russia at the time, the date of Elman's birth was January 7. Converting this date to the standard Western configuration has caused some confusion, and some sources list his birthdate as January 21, although Elman and his family celebrated his birthday on January 20. There is also some question about the *year* of Elman's birth. Most reference sources giving it as 1891, but some claim 1892. The Elman family marked the violinist's years from 1891; but interestingly, the case for 1892 finds its strongest support in Saul Elman's *Memoirs*. In this volume of reminiscences covering the period up to Elman's New York debut, the senior Elman never mentions the date of his son's birth, but he offers several clues. On page 16, he notes that they arrived in Odessa in 1897; and two pages later, he relates an anecdote in which he cites his son's age as five—pointing to an 1892 birthdate. Later, on page 29, he describes the performance examinations of December, 1901, giving Mischa's age as nine, again supporting 1892 (although later on the same page, he says that his son was "not quite nine," suggesting 1893!).

Towards the end of the book, though, all this is contradicted—and then the contradiction is contradicted. Saul Elman states that Mischa was 17 (thus, born 1891) at the time of his New York debut; but he goes on to say that in order to circumvent American resistance to child prodigies, he put it about that Mischa was two years older than he really was. Press reports of the time fairly consistently give Elman's age as 18. The elder Elman's memory of what he told reporters some 25 years earlier may have been faulty; but if he did really overstate his son's age by two years—and if the press reported his age as Saul Elman gave it—Mischa would have been 16 (born 1892). It could be that since Elman's debut took place five and a half weeks before his birthday, the press rounded his age up, reporting that he was 18 when he was only 17; but reporters don't tend to do that sort of rounding, particularly in cases where younger subjects make more sensational copy.

Yet, all this notwithstanding, it is difficult to accept that Elman—in his late teens and already quite well-known—would have adopted a new birthdate and stuck with it all his life; and European publications of around this period were using 1891 as his date of birth. For instance, England's *The World*, in a "Celebrities at Home" column dated March 25, 1908, notes that Elman had turned 17 "a few weeks ago." Elman's birth certificate is not extant, and in its absence it seems best to accept the violinist's own belief that his birthday was January 20, 1891.

5. From the manuscript of an unpublished interview by Ben Gross, January 26 and 27, 1959, apparently part of the preliminary research for a planned but never completed biography of Elman. This is one of the few interviews in which Elman spoke in detail of his childhood; and his detailed memories nicely complement those Saul Elman included in his *Memoirs*. Elman's recollection of his house is corroborated by a photograph of the Elman home, published in the *Musical Courier* in 1918, and by a painting by a Russian painter named Borisoff—although the painting, now in the possession of the violinist's youngest sister, Esther Elman, in Philadelphia, looks as if it were copied from the photograph.

6. Gross-Elman interview. The disparity between Saul Elman's recollection of blood-stained lifeless bodies and his son's doubts that anyone was killed is interesting. No doubt Elman's parents would have shielded him from the sight of corpse-strewn streets, although he most likely would have read Saul Elman's account and discussed it with him.

Chapter Two

1. In the *Memoirs* (p. 17), Saul Elman makes it clear that he is giving the violin teacher a pseudonym by adding "as we shall call him" at the first mention of the teacher's name. Actually, the disguise is a thin one, based on a multi-lingual pun: Instead of Fiedelmann, he calls the teacher "Geiger," or fiddle in German. He transforms the teacher's first name, Alexander, into Albert.

2. Gross-Elman interview

3. Ibid. Aside from bringing up a somewhat uncharacteristic incident of his early life that his father left out of the *Memoirs*, Elman's relating of this tale sheds some light on an aspect of his character that remained with him throughout his life. Replace the "other boy" in the story with "other violinists," and replace the report card marks with, for instance, concert fees or preferential treatment by record labels or concert promoters, and you have the root of Elman's life-long battles with the powers of the music business. The child is indeed father to the man.

4. Leopold Auer, *Violin Playing As I Teach It*, (New York: Dover, 1980, after Stokes original, 1921). p. 16.

5. Joseph Szigeti, *Szigeti on the Violin*, (New York; Dover, 1979, after Praeger original, 1969). p. 171.

6. Auer never recorded for commercial release, but in 1920, to celebrate his seventy-fifth birthday, he recorded several works privately and distributed the discs to students and friends. A pair of these extraordinary documents were made available on LP for a brief period by the American Stereophonic Corporation, on a disc entitled *Great Violinists of the Nineteenth and Twentieth Centuries* (ASCO A-123). Also included on the LP are two recordings by Joachim, four by Ysaÿe, one by Jan Kubelik, and eight by Pablo de Sarasate.

7. Saul Elman, op. cit., p. 32.

8. Boris Schwarz, *Great Masters of the Violin*, (New York; Simon and Schuster, 1983), p. 235.

9. The best LP transfers of Sarasate's recordings are those included in the American Stereophonic Corporation disc, listed above; but that recording is long out of print. Currently, nine of Sarasate's recordings (along with five by Joachim) are available on an LP called *The Complete Recordings* (Opal 804). The title notwithstanding, one of the versions of Sarasate's *Tarantella* included on the ASC disc is not included here.

Chapter Three

1. For an idea of Auer's teaching method, or at least, his advice on how to practice and execute both generic types of passages and specific musical works, two books are crucial. The first is Auer's *Violin Playing As I Teach It*, cited above; the other is his *Violin Master Works and their Interpretation*. (New York: Carl Fischer, 1925). The latter has not lately been reissued, possibly because the interpretive ideas embodied in it are rather dated, as are the editions (his own, naturally) he uses as his primary examples. Still, from a historical point of view, it makes fascinating reading.

2. Leopold Auer, *Violin Playing As I Teach It*, p. 76.

3. Ibid, p. 78.

4. Mischa Elman, "Good Music is Timeless," *Music Journal*, March, 1963, p. 19.

5. Mischa Elman, written notes for a speech he delivered at the University of North Carolina at Chapel Hill, March 12, 1967.

6. Saul Elman, op. cit., p. 52.

7. Ibid, p. 53.

8. Ibid, p. 56.

9. Boris Schwarz, op. cit., p. 382.

10. These observations are based largely on a series of recordings von Vecsey made for the Fonotipia label, some years after this 1904 concert (reissued in the Masters of the Bow series, MB 1002); however, other accounts of von Vecsey's early work (including some quoted in Schwarz) suggest that these early discs do represent his early style, technically.

11. From a press kit prepared by Columbia Concerts Corporation in the late 1930s.

Chapter Four

1. Here again we run into the problem of Mischa's age. If he was born in 1891, he would have been 13, going on 14, at the time of his Berlin debut. Yet, in his *Memoirs*, Saul consistently refers to his son as being 12 at this time, as do all the critical notices from this first European tour.

2. Saul Elman, op. cit., p. 87.

3. Elman's early German reviews are collected, in translation, in the appendix of Saul Elman's *Memoirs*.

4. Saul Elman, op. cit., p. 110.

5. Henry Roth, *Master Violinists in Performance* (Neptune City, NJ: Paganiniana, 1982), p. 137.

6. Donald Brook, "Violinists of Today", (London: Rockliff, 1949) pp. 34–35.

7. "Celebrities at Home No. 1554: Mischa Elman at Clapton" *The World*, March 25, 1908, pp. 506–7.

Chapter Five

1. For some reason, Saul Elman consistently refers to Liachowsky as "Liachowetsky" in his *Memoirs*. Elman and Liachowsky, or "Lia," as Elman called him, remained lifelong friends.

2. Selections from Ysaÿe's small discography can be heard on a handful of historical reissue discs currently in print, but the best overview is to be gained from a now rare LP issued in 1963 by the British Delta label (TQD 3033). Entitled *Eugen Ysaÿe: An Historical Recording*, this contains ten selections: "Prize Song" from *Die Meistersinger* (Wagner-Wilhelmj), *Albumblatt* (Wagner), *Berceuse*, Op. 16 (Faure), *Rondino*, Op. 32 (Vieuxtemps), *Mazurka: Lointain Passe* (Ysaÿe), *Caprice Viennois* (Kreisler), 2 *Mazurkas*, Op.

19 (Wieniawski) *Scherzo Valse* (Chabrier), *Hungarian Dance No. 5* (Brahms-Joachim), and the last movement of the Mendelssohn Concerto. All are accompanied by a pianist (C. Decreuse). The American Stereophonic Corporation disc mentioned above contains a few of these pieces.

Among currently available recordings, the Vieuxtemps, Wieniawski and Mendelssohn selections are included on *Great Virtuosi of the Golden Age, Vol. I—Violin* (Pearl GEMM 101). This disc also includes Elman's 1913 recording of the Schubert-Wilhelmj *Ave Maria*, as well as selections played by Sarasate, Joachim and Powell.

3. Margaret Campbell, *The Great Violinists* (Garden City, NY: Doubleday, 1981) p. 137.

4. Kubelik made many recordings, and selections from his discography are included on many historical anthologies. Two interesting discs devoted entirely to his work are *Jan Kubelik, Vol. 1* (Masters of the Bow MB 1001), and *The Immortal Art of Jan Kubelik* (Supraphon 1011 3193 G). These include 18 and 15 selections, respectively, with several in common. Unfortunately, neither disc provides recording dates. However, an anthology—*Great Virtuosi of the Golden Age, Vol. II—Violin* (Pearl GEM 102)—includes four Kubelik selections, dated between 1905 and 1910. The disc also includes accounts of similar vintage by Thibaud, Marie Hall, Kreisler, Drdla and von Vecsey.

5. Included on *Kreisler* (Pearl GEMM 132), along with a 1915 recording of the Bach Double Concerto (with Efrem Zimbalist, accompanied by string quartet), and Kreisler's 1924 recording of the Mozart Concerto No. 4, K. 218. The Bach (but not the Mozart or the early G&T recordings) is included in a remarkable five-LP set issued by The Strad in 1987, *The Art of Fritz Kreisler: The Acoustic Victor Recordings (1910–1925)* (Strad LB1/5). Included in this comprehensive collection are 100 musical selections (including a previously unissued and quite elegant 1914 performance of Dvořák's *Humoresque* by Kreisler as a pianist, as well as several unreleased violin performances) plus a recording made in 1950, at Kreisler's 75th birthday tribute in which the violinist launches into a fascinating lecture about the vagaries of interpretation and the quest to reach an interpretive ideal.

6. George Lehmann, "The Violin" (column), *The Etude*, January 1904, p. 33.

7. Fred J. Erion, *Fiddling Around* (unpublished manuscript, circa 1951), pp. 9–11.

Chapter Six

1. The four Elman-Caruso recordings have been reissued on LP by RCA, in its "Complete Caruso" series. The recordings from 1913 are included on

Volume 11 (ARM1-4047), and those from 1915 are included on Volume 13 (ARM1-4686).

2. The story, called "Some Striking Elman Ideas," is included in the files of the New York Public Library's Music Research Division, lacks the name and date of the publication in which it appeared. Comments made in the course of the story date it to around 1911.

3. Schwarz, *Great Masters of the Violin*, p. 430.

4. A good selection of Zimbalist's early Victor recordings, plus one side he made for Columbia, is included in the Masters of the Bow series (MB 1008).

5. From Clarence Adler's memoirs, from manuscript, pp. 283–284.

Chapter Seven

1. Unsigned review in *Town & Country*, December 20, 1916.

2. Carl Sandburg, *The Complete Poems of Carl Sandburg* (New York: Harcourt Brace Jovanovich, 1969), p. 26.

3. According to Joseph Seiger, Elman had written out roughly half the cadenza, and played the rest from memory. He told Seiger, however, that the cadenza he played at the time he made the Solti recording was the one he had always performed.

4. Sol Hurok, *Impresario*, (New York: Random House, 1946), p. 30.

Chapter Eight

1. Henry Roth, *Master Violinists in Performance* (Neptune City, New Jersey: Paganiniana, 1982), p. 161. According to Roth, Heifetz's audiences in Odessa, during a three concert series in 1911, numbered 5,000, 14,000 and 28,000. The last is difficult to credit: it is the equivalent of nearly 10 fully sold-out Carnegie Hall audiences, or several thousand people greater than can be packed into Madison Square Garden for a rock concert today.

2. Quoted in Schwarz, p. 434. The original review, by Hugo Rasch, was published in the *Allgemeine Muzikzeitung* on June 7, 1912.

3. A good cross-section of Seidl's work is collected on Masters of the Bow MB 1007. This disc contains a few of the standard showpieces (the Brahms-Joachim Hungarian Dance No. 1, Kreisler's *Caprice viennois*, Schubert's *Standchen*, etc.) plus less familiar works by the likes of Provost, Margis,

Burleigh, Balaleinikoff and d'Ambrosio, and Elman's *Eili, Eili* arrangement.

4. This is the accurate version of the story, although one frequently encounters versions with different casts of characters. All of them, interestingly, include Elman as the one complaining of the heat; but some give his companion as Hoffmann, and some give the debuting violinist as Menuhin (etc.).

The story is also, however, the most famous in the genre of musical joke known as "the Mischa Elman story." These virtually defy cataloguing, and Elman quite frequently told many of them himself, at parties and even in interviews. Many of these tales are recounted today by people who never heard Elman and who scarcely remember his recordings. But to those who did know Elman, the stories are irresistible: virtually everyone I interviewed while researching this book stopped talking at one point, chuckled and said, "of course, I'm sure you've heard the story about the time Elman. . . ." and launched into a tale that, in many cases, no-one else had told.

No book about Elman could be considered complete without reprinting some of these stories, yet most are not rooted to specific events of importance, and would therefore find no proper place in the main text. Therefore, I have chosen several for inclusion here:

a) Elman was backstage greeting his public and signing autographs after a recital, and he noticed that one young boy kept coming up to him with a fresh program book to sign. After the fourth time, Elman said to him, "excuse me, but didn't I just sign your book for you?" "Yes," the child replied, "but I have a friend who will trade me one Kriesler autograph for five Elmans."

b) In the restaurant at the Savoy, in London, Elman and Fritz Kreisler were having dinner together, when a waiter brought an envelope addressed: "To The World's Greatest Violinist." Elman passed it to Kreisler, saying "Fritz, it's for you." Kreisler insisted, "oh no, Mischa, it's for you." Eventually, they were both curious, so one of them opened the envelope and took out the letter. It began, "Dear Jascha. . . ."

Elman told this story to Joseph Seiger, who added that the waiter eventually returned to point out the perpetrator of the prank—Charlie Chaplin, who was dining across the room. Chaplin was a close friend of Elman's. They spent several summers together on the French coast, and in the 1950s and 1960s, they met whenever Elman was performing in London.

c) In a taxi on the way home from a concert, Elman and a cab driver got into a conversation about music, and it emerged that the driver was particularly fond of the violin. They discussed a few of the greats—Elman, Kreisler, Heifetz and others—and upon their arrival at Elman's home, the violinist gave the driver an unusually large tip. "Thanks," the driver told him. "Now I can buy a ticket to hear Jascha Heifetz."

d) Towards the end of his life, Elman listened several times to the young violinist Michael Rabin, who he considered a brilliant technician, but who, he feared, was in peril of being seduced by speed and flashiness. At one of their meetings, said to have taken place when Rabin was about 10 years old, the young violinist played a brilliant showpiece for Elman. Elman felt he played it as well as it could be played, yet without much in the way of personal spirit. "Tell me, Michael," he asked, "what does this music say to you? What do you want to *do* with it?" Rabin had no answer, so Elman asked him a more expansive question. "What do you want to do with yourself and your playing, then? What do you want to be?" Rabin replied, "I want to be just like Jascha Heifetz."

e) In the 1950s, when the Elmans' daughter was engaged to a man whose family lived in California, the Elmans decided to send them some salmon from Barney Greengrass, a New York Jewish delicatessen that is still famous for its fresh fish. Helen Elman called the shop to place the order, and was told that the store's limit for long-distance deliveries had already been reached, and that their air cargo load was full.

"We couldn't take another order if it came from the Prince of Wales," Greengrass told Mrs. Elman.

"What if it was an order from Mischa Elman?" she asked.

"Can you prove it's Mischa Elman?"

Mrs. Elman called the violinist to the phone, explained the situation, and asked him to play something. With Mrs. Elman holding up the phone, Elman put the violin to his chin and played the opening phrases of Schubert's *Ave Maria*. Greengrass was convinced, and put the order through.

f) Finally, according to Mrs. Elman, the famous joke wherein one person asks "how do you get to Carnegie Hall" and the other says, "Practice" was of Elman's creation based on a response he actually gave to a tourist one afternoon when he was walking along 57th Street. Elman repeated his quip to a columnist, who published it, and eventually it became generic. In fact, in the early 1980s, Carnegie Hall used a variation on the joke in its subscription advertisements.

5. Quoted in S. W. Bennett's liner notes for *Mischa Elman Plays Kreisler Favorites*, Vanguard Everyman Classics SRV 367 SD.

6. Reissued on Pearl (GEMM 132) and in the strad set, cited above.

Chapter Nine

1. Wagner, Charles L., *Seeing Stars* (New York: G. Putnam's Sons, 1940), p. 350.

2. "Elman Enjoying a Rest Year Here," *New York Times*, January 23, 1915.

3. The manuscript score and parts are in Mrs. Elman's possession, and she has kindly loaned them to me for examination. It is virtually impossible

to construct a full picture of the play from these however, for Elman seems to have saved only the music and none of the auxiliary materials. The words embodied in the text setting alone do little more than suggest relationships between some of the characters—they offer little help in establishing the work's plot. For that matter, the pages of the score are not numbered, so aside from the title song (which we may presume to have been the opening number), and the sheaf of pages labeled "Finale," there's no way of determining the proper order of the songs and instrumental movements. It may be, too, that Elman at some point discarded or mislaid sections of the score along, perhaps, with the libretto. It's odd, for instance, that a work with two instrumental interludes is missing a formal overture. At any rate, the available materials make it difficult to guess, let alone judge, what the full work might have been like.

4. From Elman's typed notes for a speech to the members of the Lamb's Club, which gave a dinner in his honor and presented him with a cup, in 1961. In a variant of this story, Elman sometimes added that Ziegfield threatened to bring the worst orchestra in New York to court to play the work and show that it wasn't very good, to which Elman replied that he would bring his violin.

5. "'London a Graveyard' Says Mischa Elman," *Musical Courier*, August 21, 1919.

6. Erion, op. cit., p. 44.

7. Ibid, pp. 20–21.

8. Ibid, pp. 21–22.

Chapter Ten

1. "Mischa Elman's Fiddle Not Tuned to Play "Here Comes the Bride," *New York World*, June 29, 1922.

2. Schwarz, op. cit., p. 422. Schwarz was among those detained with Auer at that time—as was Jascha Heifetz.

3. Wagner, op. cit., p. 352.

Chapter Eleven

1. The repetitive patterns and relationships in the history of technology and commerce are interesting. The switch from acoustical to electrical recordings, coming during a slow sales period, revitalized interest in recordings, and led to a grand reduplication of the catalogue as performers remade

their (and their buyers') favorite works from the acoustical days. The move from 78rpm discs to LPs, in the late 1940s, didn't quite accomplish this, since batches of 78rpm discs could be transferred to LP without necessarily having to be re-recorded. But in the late 1970s, when record sales were slow again, digital recording arrived on the scene, and once more performers were encouraged to remake their catalogues wholesale. The introduction of CD in 1983 extended this progress, but as with the switch from 78 to LP, this was at least partly a changeover of convenience. As with the LP changeover, it meant that recordings already sold could be sold again without necessarily having to be remade. And best of all, from a record company's point of view, there were buyers for CD incarnations of recordings from all eras--going all the way back to the days of acoustically recorded 78s.

Chapter Twelve

1. Perhaps Elman was misquoted in the article: he may have said that he hadn't played a concerto with a *major* orchestra in New York, or the reporter may have erred in the amount of time Elman mentioned. But that statement, as it stands, is not quite true. It had only been eight and a half years since the afternoon of concertos with an orchestra conducted by Auer, at Carnegie Hall.

2. In fact, Elman recorded only two movements of solo Bach, the other being the Gavotte from the Partita No. 3 in E major, recorded for Pathé during his youth. It's interesting, given his passion for Bach, and particularly his love of the *Chaconne*, that he did not commit more of this music to disc.

Chapter Thirteen

1. Letter from Vladimir Padwa to Saul Elman, dated September 21, 1934, from the Santa Elisa. It was composed on board the ship, which was taking Elman and Padwa home, and given the density of detail Padwa conveys, it seems to have been the only such letter he wrote during the tour. Perhaps he kept a diary: the letter itself is set out in nine neatly handwritten pages on thin airmail paper, and seems so carefully composed as to suggest that the pianist had kept notes during the journey.

2. Letter from Fred Erion to Mischa Elman, December 9, 1946.

3. The ambitiousness of this particular program may, however, have been accidental. In a letter to Elman dated May 8, 1942, Erion reminisces about

the concert and recalls that Elman had instructed Strok to remove the Bach *Chaconne* from that already hefty program. Strok neglected to do so, and Elman elected to play the full printed program, along with his typically generous selection of encores.

Chapter Fourteen

1. Elman may have gotten carried away with the rhetorical spirit of the moment: Mendelssohn was born in 1809 and died in 1847. The two hundred years Elman gives him would have put him at the end of the Baroque era.

Chapter Fifteen

1. Gross-Elman interview.

2. Mark Starowicz, "Modern Music Reflects Today's Materialism, Says Mischa Elman," *Montreal Gazette*, May 14, 1966.

3. An article by Douglas Jarman in the Fall/Winter 1982 edition of the *Alban Berg Society Newsletter* elaborates on what he calls "an equally authentic, but more private programme" hidden beneath the publicly acknowledged tribute to Manon Gropius.

4. Louis Krasner, "The Origins of Berg's Violin Concerto," *Keynote*, October, 1983, p. 22, in an article condensed from a talk given by Krasner at a 1980 Berg symposium in Vienna, originally published in *Alban Berg Symposium Wien 1980: Tagungsbericht*, (Vienna: Universal Edition, 1981).

5. Miloš Šafránek, *Bohuslav Martinů—His Life and Works*, trans. Roberta Finlayson-Samsourova (London: Allan Wingate, 1962), p. 232.

6. Quoted in Šafránek, op. cit., pp. 233–234, also published in the Boston Symphony's program book at the time of the premiere.

7. According to Mrs. Elman, Stokowski was one of several musicians invited to a dinner party on Long Island soon after the premiere of the Martinů, and since the Elmans had an automobile, they offered Stokowski a ride. When they reached Stokowski's apartment, he was waiting outside—in brisk weather but without an overcoat, Mrs. Elman recalls. The conversation in the car centered around the premiere of the concerto, the circumstances of which were by no means obscure: Koussevitzky led the work with the Boston Symphony, first in Boston, then in New York, and the occasion was accorded a good deal of publicity, ranging from pre-concert fanfare to reviews in all the major newspapers, and a broadcast performance. Stokowski offered that he heard the broadcast, and that he was

delighted with Elman's performance. "But tell me, Mischa," he added, "who was conducting?"

8. This excerpt is drawn from an undated clipping in the Elman collection at the Boston University Library, from *Bravo*, circa 1961. A few of the points he raises beg comment. It is true that Bach's scores do not bear the detailed tempo and expression markings that composers of later eras lavished upon their works, but that has less to do with his trust in his players than with the scoring conventions of his time; in fact, in the context of those conventions, Bach's manuscripts are often surprisingly detailed. As for tempo markings, Bach did label his movements with either general character indications (*Allegro, Andante*, etc.) or as specific dance movements (*Allemande, Courante*, etc.)—all of which defined the tempos fairly specifically for the musicians of Bach's day.

No doubt taste did enter into interpretation in certain kinds of works, and accounting for taste was certainly part of the Baroque tradition. In the preface to his *Toccate e Partite d'Intavolatura di Cimbalo* (Book I, published in Rome, 1615), Girolomo Frescobaldi (a composer whose works Bach studied in his youth) gives several broad clues about tempos, but notes, in a section on Partitas, that "it is left to the good taste and fine judgement of the player to select the right tempo." But of course, taste is not a fixed concept, and one of the musicologist's tasks is to discover the parameters of taste (regarding tempo, dynamics, and expression) common in given eras. In dealing with the music of Bach, for instance, the musicologist endeavors to learn how fast a movement marked *Allegro* might normally have been played, and what the nature (and therefore the tempo) of a *Gavotte* was, so that today's performer—if so inclined—can recreate those works in the spirit (i. e., according to the presumed taste) of their time. Elman was not of the school that strove to resurrect those conventions. Rather, he felt that if his own speeds and inflections made the music come alive for his listeners, then musicological data, whether it contradicted his views or supported them, was beside the point.

Putting it that way would not have won him friends among the purists, but it would have been convincing in a way that his usual argument was not: Elman's contention, voiced frequently in his lectures, interviews, and articles, was that if one did not hear the great composers perform, one could not possibly know how they wanted their music played, and one therefore had no right to criticize Elman's interpretations on stylistic grounds.

Chapter Sixteen

1. Milton Goldin, *The Music Merchants*, (New York: MacMillan, 1969), pp. 164–172.

2. Charles Wagner, op. cit., pp. 349–350.

3. Mischa Elman, "Why Playing for the Armed Services is a Privilege," *Musical Courier*, August, 1944.

4. In RCA's case, this transition was actually made via the 7-inch 45rpm disc, which RCA considered superior to the LP. Several of Elman's discs of this period were issued in a variety of formats—on 78, on 45 (sometimes in boxed sets), on 10-inch 33rpm discs, and finally, on LP.

Chapter Seventeen

1. Program 1, presented on February 9, included the Bach E major, the Mozart A major and the Beethoven; Program 2, presented on March 22, included the Bruch First, Lalo's *Symphonie Espagnole* and the Brahms; and Program 3, presented on April 12, included the Wieniawski Second, the Mendelssohn, and the Tchaikovsky.

Chapter Eighteen

1. Actually, Szeryng had played a concerto in New York in 1943, in a concert for the Polish Relief Fund; but as this was a wartime charity event, Szeryng and his managers considered it his "unofficial" New York debut, and listed the 1957 appearance his "official" debut, as do most violin reference books.

2. Oistrakh recorded the Shostakovich with Dimitri Mitropoulos and the New York Philharmonic just after the series of performances, which ran from December 29 through New Year's Day. This extraordinarily evocative performance was reissued just after Oistrakh's death, in a two-LP set (CBS MG 33328, *A Tribute to David Oistrakh 1908–1974*) containing the Philadelphia recordings he made during the same trip—the Mendelssohn Concerto, the Mozart Fourth, and Bach Second, plus double concertos by Bach and Vivaldi with Isaac Stern.

Chapter Nineteen

1. From *The Canon*, September 1956. The clipping, from Joseph Seiger's collection, is otherwise unidentified.

2. All *High Fidelity* reviews quoted herein come from the 1956 through 1958 editions of *Records in Review* (Great Barrington, MA: Wyeth Press), annual compilations of reviews published in the magazine over the previous year.

3. One can only wonder, though, how Elman managed to make such magnificent records in the days when a soloist had to play into an acoustic horn—a process that allowed for much less freedom of movement than microphone recording.

4. John Culshaw, *Putting the Record Straight*, (New York: Viking Press, 1982), p. 132.

5. Joseph Wershba, "Daily Closeup: Mischa Elman," *New York Post*, December 5, 1958, p. 58.

6. Peter D. Franklin, "Elman Starts 2d 50 Yrs. On U. S. Stage Tomorrow," *New York Herald Tribune*, December 7, 1958.

Chapter Twenty

1. Mischa Elman, as told to Ralph Lewando, "Fifty Years of Concertizing," *Music Journal*, April/May, 1958.

2. Another of Elman's views on the viola: Elman heard that William Primrose had recorded some of the Paganini *Caprices* on the viola, and during one of Primrose's visits to Elman's home, Elman asked whether this were true, and if Primrose would play a *Caprice* for him. Primrose complied. Elman was silent for a moment, and then said, "it must be easier on the viola!" Primrose included this story in a letter to the violinist Sergiu Luca dated December 30, 1978.

3. This seems to have been intended as a speech, although there is no record of where and when Elman delivered it. The section quoted in the text, however, comes from a printed version, found among Elman's papers in the Boston University Library. The article carries no publication name or date, and the typestyle and layout are not similar to those used at the time by *The Strad*, *Music Journal* or *Musical America*, the magazines most likely to have published this sort of piece. In any case, the article seems to have been printed without editorial tampering, for in all matters of style, organization, syntax, and italicized points of emphasis, it bears all the hallmarks of his lecture style, as one finds it in the typescripts he prepared for various speaking engagements.

4. Presumably, Elman is referring to National Endowment grants, Rockefeller Foundation grants and the like, but he seems confused as to their purpose—and his confusion throws an interesting light on his own view of the musical world. The point of these grants is not, of course, to help performers or, particularly, composers, "reach the top," as Elman puts it, but to help defray the expenses involved in, for example, writing and performing new music in a world where, because of the very commercializa-

tion that Elman decries, such endeavors have become prohibitively expensive. Interesting, too, is that while Elman here takes what seems an almost Spartan view—that middle aged composers and performers have had their opportunity for success, and therefore should not receive public subsidy—he frequently gave cash gifts (or made loans he did not intend to collect) to colleagues who had failed to achieve success comparable to his own.

5. The reference is to Sol Hurok. The Russian currency exchange matter was clearly still a sore point for Elman.

6. The reasoning here is even more muddled than in the rest of the diatribe. Surely if there's one thing orchestras can't be accused of, it's subverting young talent by forcing newcomers to play contemporary works. Rather, young players occasionally select new concertos as their introductory vehicles themselves, as a way of attracting attention and standing out as unique in a concert world that has its share of warhorse performances. Of course, Elman's own debut vehicle, the Tchaikovsky, was a recent, if not quite new work then—and it was not one that was generally liked at the time. Interesting, too, is the dichotomy Elman draws between two activities that are ideally united—listening to the music versus listening to the performer.

7. Herbert Axelrod, *Heifetz*, (Neptune City, NJ: Paganiniana, 1976/81), pp. 405–6.

8. Ibid., p. 418.

9. Ibid., p. 448.

10. Hugh Merrick, "Elman at Seventy," *The Strad*, December 1961, p. 273.

Chapter Twenty-One

1. The account given is drawn from the first published story about the accident, from the *Times*, December 26, 1963. According to a followup story, published in the *Times* on August 24, 1964, Elman sued the garage owner, Anthony Buoncore, for $100,000; and by then, the story had changed somewhat. This report, based on the court papers, says that Elman went to the garage to inquire about parking space, and that he was directed by an employee into an area where he "was caused to slip, trip and fall" into a grease pit. The suit was settled nearly three years after the fall, when Elman accepted $25,000 in damages (*New York Times*, October 12, 1966).

2. Interview with Sgt. Pat Patrick on the Armed Forces Radio series, *Munich By Day and By Night*, broadcast on November 16, 1964.

3. Ibid.

4. *Caprice Viennois* is the LP's original title. When it was reissued on Vanguard's Everyman Classics series (SRV 367 SD), in 1977, it was retitled *Mischa Elman Plays Kreisler Favorites*. This was also the first Elman recording to be reissued on Compact Disc.

Chapter Twenty-Two

1. Donal Henahan, "On Playing the Game of Musical Reminiscence," *New York Times*, May 26, 1985, Section 2, p. 13

Chapter Twenty-Three

1. Mark Starowicz, op. cit.

2. Mary Coolidge, "Violinist Mischa Elman Speaks His Mind," *Tampa Times*, December 1, 1966, p. 6-A

3. Murray Schumach, "Elman 'Is Like a Good, Old Wine,' *New York Times*, June 26, 1966.

4. Undoubtedly the number was close to correct, although it must have been an approximation, since Elman did not keep a personal or professional diary of any sort. Starting from his professional Berlin debut, in October 1904, Elman had been performing for nearly 62 years. A believeable average of around 80 concerts a season (there were more in his prime, fewer in his later years) brings the figure close enough to 5,000 for comfort.

5. William Primrose, *Walk on the North Side* (Provo, Utah: Brigham Young University Press, 1978), pp. 154–157. Primrose may actually have been thinking of the previous year's recital, for he cites a program containing Chausson's *Poème* and a the Brahms G major Sonata. He also incorrectly gives the date of Elman's death as 1968. But the sentiments are worth quoting.

Chapter Twenty-Four

1. This transcript is taken from a tape of the speech, rather than from Elman's typescript. The differences between the two versions are organizational rather than substantive, although when telling anecdotes involving other performers, Elman chose not to use their names in delivering his talk. He did, however, include them in his notes, and since he told the same tales

in interviews, with the identities included, these were hardly delicate secrets. In such cases, I have added the names of those involved [bracketed] to the text.

2. The Tchaikovsky Competition.

3. Actually, Elman drew this quotation not from the book he mentions, *The Agony of Modern Music*, but from the last chapter of another book by Pleasants, *The Great Singers* (New York: Fireside, 1966, p. 350). Interestingly, Elman approached the quotation in very much the same way he approached musical works. Where he felt it was appropriate, he added or subtracted a few words, although most of the quotation is delivered as written. For instance, in the first sentence Pleasants refers only to the singer; Elman added "or performer." And in the final sentence, Pleasants wrote of a singer having to repeat a section "because of his own or somebody else's mistakes." Possibly feeling sensitive about the idea of an artist's fallibility, Elman deleted "his own or."

APPENDIX 1:

The Mischa Elman Legacy —Papers and Memorabilia

In 1972, Helen Elman endowed the Mischa Elman Chair in Violin at the Manhattan School of Music, in New York, a gesture meant, as she explained it in her letter to the school, "to perpetuate the name of my late and beloved husband, Mischa Elman." Under the terms of the gift, an endowment was established, to be maintained intact in perpetuity, and its income (supplemented by funds from the school's operating budget) is to be used "to maintain The Mischa Elman Chair under the direction of an internationally renowned artist-teacher." Among those who have held the chair since then are Henryk Szeryng, Erica Morini, Jaime Laredo, Ruggiero Ricci, Josef Gingold, and Elmar Oliveira, each of whom has given a series of master classes at the Manhattan School. At the same time, a Mischa Elman Studio was established at the Manhattan School, to which Mrs. Elman has donated her husband's music library, as well as a huge assortment of photographs, testimonials, and recordings—including test pressings of discs that were not commercially issued.

Mrs. Elman also made a substantial gift of her husband's memorabilia to the Boston University Mugar Memorial Library (in 1969, with addenda between 1970 and 1973). Besides a series of organized scrapbooks containing reviews and articles from the mid-1930s through the early 1960s, the collection's 17 boxes are packed with approximately 10,000 newspaper clippings, concert programs, flyers, posters, honorary degrees and citations, photographs, and press releases. There are also more than 1,100 letters to and from Elman, as well his typescripts for nearly two dozen speeches and articles. That collection contains only one recording, a 78rpm disc of the Drdla *Souvenir*, donated to the collection by Harold C. Schonberg.

APPENDIX 2:

The Mischa Elman Legacy
—Recordings

PART ONE: RECORDINGS CURRENTLY AVAILABLE

Elman's career stretched from the cylinder era to the age of the LP, and between his first sessions for the French Pathé label, in 1905, and his final ones for Vanguard, in New York, sixty-one years later, he set down hundreds of performances, representing the works of 105 composers (plus Anonymous, which in Elman's case adds only two to the count). The bulk of these performances were issued on 78rpm discs, and are now unavailable.

In fact, of Elman's RCA Victor recordings, only the four he made with Enrico Caruso are available on domestically produced LP pressings—and those are available only because RCA was intent on issuing its complete Caruso archive. The Elman collaborations appear on two volumes in the set:

The Complete Caruso Volume 11 1913–1914 (RCA ARM1-4047)
Kahn: Ave Maria   [with Percy Kahn]
Massenet: Elégie   [with Percy Kahn]

The Complete Caruso Volume 13 1915–1916 (RCA ARM1-4686)
Denza: Si vous l'aviez compris [with Gaetano Scognamiglio]
Leoncavallo: Les deux serenades   [with Gaetano Scognamiglio]

In the mid-1980s, RCA considered reissuing some of its Elman catalogue, but corporate changeovers may have put those plans on hold. A bright sign, however, is the vigor with which the label is digging into its archives for historical reissues on CD. It may be that some long out-of-print Elman recordings will resurface in this form. Meanwhile, RCA's Japanese affiliate released a five-disc survey of Elman's work in 1980. Entitled *The Art of Mischa Elman* (RCA Japan, RCL-3001-05), this impressive set contains 79 selections recorded between 1906 and 1952:

Schubert:	Moment Musical No. 3	[accompanist unidentified]
Bohm:	Perpetuum Mobile	" "
Barnes:	Swing Song	" "
Wieniawski:	Fantasia on the Garden Scene from Gounod's Faust	" "
Drigo-Auer:	Serenade	" "
Gossec-Elman:	Gavotte	" "
Dittersdorf-Burmester:	German Dance	" "
Haydn-Burmester:	Minuet	[with Percy Kahn]
Hummel-Burmester:	Waltz	" "
Chopin-Sarasate:	Nocturne	" "
Tchaikovsky:	Melodie	" "
Mendelssohn-Burmester:	Canzonetta	" "
Grétry-Franko:	Gavotte	" "
Sammartini-Elman:	Canto Amoroso	" "
Paganini-Vogrich:	Dans le Bois	" "
Monsigny-Franko:	Rigaudon	" "
Brahms-Joachim:	Hungarian Dance No. 7	" "
Haydn-Burmester:	Minuet	[with Walter H. Golde]
Elman:	In a Gondola	" "
Gluck-Wilhelmj:	Melodie from Orfeo	" "
Kreisler:	Rondino on a theme by Beethoven	" "
Kreisler:	Chanson Louis XIII	" "
Weber-Elman:	Country Dance	" "
Sarasate:	Romanza Andaluza	" "
Scarlatti-Bridgewater:	Pastorale	[with Phillip Gordon]
Scarlatti-Burmester:	Capriccio	" "
Rissland:	Valse Caprice	" "
Sarasate:	Caprice Basque	[accompanist unidentified]
Moore-Auer:	The Last Rose of Summer	[with Arthur Loesser]
Brahms-Joachim:	Hungarian Dance No. 17	" "

Lalo:	Andante (from Symphonie Espagnole)	[with Emanuel Balaban]
Anonymous-Elman:	Eili, Eili	" "
Gabriel-Marie:	La Cinquantaine	[with orchestra]
Popper:	Fond Recollections	" "
Hummel:	Waltz in A	[with Joseph Bonime]
Albeniz:	Tango	" "
Bruch:	Kol Nidre	" "
Delibes-Elman:	Passapied	" "
Beethoven-Auer:	Turkish March	" "
Mozart:	Landler	" "
Mozart-Friedberg:	Adagio	" "
Ries:	Gondoliera	" "
Herbert:	A la Valse	" "
Beethoven-Burmester:	Minuet in G	" "
Arensky:	Serenade	" "
Raff:	Cavatina	" "
Elman:	Tango	" "
Massenet:	Méditation, from Thaïs	" "
Schubert-Wilhelmj:	Ave Maria	" "
Handel:	Largo, from Xerxes	[with Herbert Dawson, organ]
Drdla:	Souvenir	[with Raymond Bauman]
Wieniawski-Kreisler:	Caprice Etude	" "
Rachmaninoff-Press:	Vocalise	" "
Dvořák:	Humoresque	" "
Sibelius-Franko:	Valse Triste	" "
Bach-Wilhelmj:	Air on the G String	" "
Cui:	Orientale	[with orchestra]
Beethoven-Elman:	Country Dance	[with Marcel van Gool]
Espejo:	Aires Tziganes	" "
Ysaÿe:	Rêve d'Enfant	" "
Saint-Saëns:	Le Cygne	[with Caroll Hollister]
Schubert-Franko:	Valse Sentimentale	" "
Sarasate:	Zigeunerweisen	" "
Bach:	Prelude in E major	[unaccompanied]
Drigo-Auer:	Serenade	[with Carroll Hollister]
Drdla:	Serenade	" "

Ravel:	Piece en forma de Habanera	[with Carroll Hollister]
Wieniawski:	Legende	" "
Dinicu-Heifetz:	Hora Staccato	[with Vladimir Padwa]
Tchaikovsky:	Sérénade mélancolique	[with Orchestra, Shilkret, cond.]
Wieniawski:	Souvenir de Moscow	[with Vladimir Padwa]
Schubert-Elman:	Standchen	" "
Mendelssohn-Kreisler:	May Breezes	" "
Schumann:	Träumerei	[with Leopold Mittman]
Hubay:	Herje Kati	" "
Gossec-Elman:	Gavotte	[with Wolfgang Rosé]
Tchaikovsky:	Andante cantabile	[with Joseph Seiger]

This well-selected overview conveys something of the variety of Elman's RCA discography, and it includes several of his finest recorded performances. It was preceded,in 1979, by a single disc, called *The Magic String/Mischa Elman* (RCA Japan Gold Seal RVC-1572), a selection of 13 tracks that are also included in the above set.

As the copyrights have lapsed on Elman's earlier recordings, it has become legal for firms other than RCA to issue transfers of his 78rpm discs. Several of these vintage performances have, in recent years, turned up on labels that specialize in historical material. Some of this material is extremely enlightening, and very little of it duplicates the Japanese set. The following contain single Elman recordings, amid other material.

Hulda Lashanska, Soprano 1893–1974 (Club 99 99-99)
    includes:
Schubert: Litanie auf das Fest aller Seelen   [with Hulda Lashanska, Rudolf Serkin, and Emanuel Feuermann]

Great Virtuosi of the Golden Age, Vol.I—Violin (Pearl GEMM 101)
    includes:
Schubert: Ave Maria   [with Percy Kahn]

The following historical issues are devoted entirely to the work of Mischa Elman:

Mischa Elman (Pearl GEMM 270)

Tchaikovsky:	Concerto in D major, Op. 35	[with the London Symphony Orchestra, John Barbirolli, cond.]
Rimsky-Korsakov:	Hymn to the Sun	[accompanist unidentified]
Ascher:	Alice, Where Art Thou?	[with orchestra]
Wieniawski:	Legende	[with Carroll Hollister]
Massenet:	Méditation, from Thaïs	[with Carroll Hollister]
Tchaikovsky:	Melodie	[with Carroll Hollister]
Saint-Saëns:	Le Cygne	[with Carroll Hollister]
Massenet:	Elégie	[with Enrico Caruso and Percy Kahn]

Mischa Elman (Discocorp/Recital Records RR-318)

Tchaikovsky:	Concerto in D major, Op. 35	[as above]
Vivaldi-Nachez:	Concerto in G minor, Op. 12, No. 1	[with New Symphony, L. Collingwood, cond.]
Bach:	Prelude in E major	[unaccompanied]
Beethoven:	Minuet in G	[with Joseph Bonime]

Interview, dated 1947, from a Hollywood Bowl broadcast

Mischa Elman, Violinist (Discocorp/Recital Records RR-453)

Tchaikovsky:	Concerto in D major, Op. 35	[live recording, with Boston Symphony, Paul Paray, cond.]
Bach:	Concerto No. 2 in E major, BWV 1042	[with unidentified orchestra, L. Collingwood, cond.]
Bach:	Prelude in E major from Partita No. 3, BWV 1006	[unaccompanied]

The LP recordings Elman made for Decca/London are all out-of-print, as are four of the seven discs he made for Vanguard. The three Vanguards still available are recital discs, with Joseph Seiger accompanying, and in late 1987, Vanguard began issuing some of its Elman recordings on CD:

Elman Jubilee Record, Celebrating Fifty Years of Violinistic Triumph (Vanguard VSD-2048)

Massenet:	Méditation, from Thaïs
Arensky:	Serenade
Schumann-Hullweck:	Träumerei
Cui:	Orientale
Drigo-Auer:	Valse Bluette
Sarasate:	Zigeunerweisen
Schubert-Wilhelmj:	Ave Maria
Dvořák-Wilhelmj:	Humoresque
Gossec-Elman:	Gavotte
Chopin-Sarasate:	Nocturne
Schumann-Auer:	The Prophet Bird
Beethoven-Burmester:	Minuet in G
Tchaikovsky:	Melodie

[NOTE: Current pressings of this LP do not include the Sarabande by Sulzer, listed on earlier issues.]

Mischa Elman Plays Kreisler Favorites (Vanguard Everyman Classics, SRV 367 SD; also on CD, VBD 367)

Kreisler:	Liebesfreud
Dvořák-Kreisler:	Slavonic Dance No. 2
Kreisler:	Schön Rosmarin
Kreisler:	La Gitana
Kreisler:	Rondino on a Theme of Beethoven
Kreisler:	Caprice Viennois
Tartini-Kreisler:	Variations on a Theme of Corelli
Kreisler:	Preghiera in the style of Martini
Kreisler:	Allegretto in the style of Boccherini
Kreisler:	Sicilienne and Rigaudon in the style of Francoeur
Dvořák-Kreisler:	Slavonic Dance No. 1
Kreisler:	Praeludium and Allegro in the style of Pugnani

[NOTE: Originally issued as *Caprice Viennois*]

The Art of Mischa Elman (Vanguard VSD-71173)

Dvořák-Kreisler:	Slavonic Fantasia
Tchaikovksy-Koutzen:	Russian Dance
Debussy-Roques:	La plus que lente
Gluck-Ries:	Largo
Kroll:	Juanita
Benjamin:	From San Domingo
Smetana:	From My Home
Fauré:	Berceuse

Kreisler: La Precieuse in the style of F. Couperin
Espejo: Aires Tziganes

❖ ❖ ❖ ❖ ❖

PART TWO: THE COMPLETE RECORDINGS OF
MISCHA ELMAN

The following discography lists all of Elman's published commercial recordings, as well as several important unissued ones. It is arranged chronologically, broken down year by year until 1940. Thereafter, the tapering off of his session work, and other factors, indicated divisions in longer stretches, so during the final dozen years of his RCA association, the breaks in the discography reflect his changes of accompanist.

The section devoted to Elman's early recordings on the Pathé, Gramophone and Typewriter and Victor (later RCA) labels—which is to say, the bulk of his recorded legacy—is based principally on the work of Dennis D. Rooney, who has done archival research on the recordings of many of the great violinists of Elman's generation for The Strad. An acknowledgement is also due to James Creighton, whose pioneering *Discopaedia of the Violin* has proven a valuable resource both in the preparation of the discography and in the writing of the biography. Some inaccuracies that have crept into Creighton's tome, however, are corrected here. For instance, the recordings Creighton lists as collaborations between Elman and Rosa Ponselle actually contain violin contributions from one Mischa Violin, a session player. In other cases, discrepancies between the Victor ledgers and Creighton's listings are noted.

The assistance of Ruth Edge, of the Archives of Thorn-EMI, Ltd., England (who provided information about Elman's early G&T and HMV recordings; and John Pfeiffer and Bernadette Moore, of RCA/BMG Records, New York (who provided Dennis Rooney with invaluable help during his research in RCA's archives) is also gratefully acknowledged.

The section on the Victor and RCA material was compiled from information included in Victor's ledgers, which list the daily recording activity for each of the company's studios; and the "blue cards" retained in the RCA library for each disc in the company's catalogue. These include information about matrix and take numbers, recording dates, dates of issue and other data.

For the discographer—and for readers of a discography that extends as far back in the recording era as Elman's does—the early material poses certain listing problems, and requires a more extensive kind of listing than, for instance, an LP recording from the 1960s. Until 1925, recording was accomplished by the acoustic method: the performer played before a large metal horn, which conveyed the sound waves to the cutting stylus that inscribed the beeswax master matrix. The Victor Talking Machine Company assigned a matrix number to each piece of music it recorded—a letter prefix, indicating the diameter of the disc (B for 10-inch, C for 12-inch), followed by a take number denoting each attempt to record a work. Although British (HMV) pressings of Victor matrices reveal these numbers, Victor's pressings usually do not, making visual identification difficult.

This is important because Elman re-recorded certain items several times during the acoustic period, either for musical or technical reasons; and these new recordings were often issued with the same catalogue number as the original. In some cases, Elman remade the work with a different accompanist. And with the introduction of Victor Red Seal discs, in 1923, matters become further complicated, since some of the double faced issues (indicated by catalogue numbers containing –A and –B suffixes) contain new performances, while others couple older ones.

Thus, a listing of works and catalogue numbers does not tell the whole story, since a single catalogue number can be tied to two distinct performances, and therefore matrix and take numbers are given here for all discs issued during the period these subsitutions were common. Several known replacements are indicated in the footnotes.

In 1925, the company began making electrical recordings, which improved the fidelity of the sound (but did not lengthen the recording time, as tape did, a quarter century later). Since all the electrically recorded discs were issued under their own new catalogue numbers (and not as substitutions on older discs), the matrix and take numbers no longer serve an identifying function, and have been eliminated from the entries after 1924.

Through 1924, the first set of numbers given after the composer's names and work titles are the matrix and take numbers. The catalogue numbers in the right hand column are those assigned to the original issues in the United States, with some exceptions, and those without G&T or HMV designations should be assumed to be Victor or RCA Red Seal releases. The earliest G&T and HMV discs, released in Great Britain first, and later in the United States, are listed with both their British and American catalogue numbers. And the handful of cases in which recordings were issued in Great Britain only are indicated by the presence of an HMV number without a Victor equivalent.

Towards the end of the RCA section, when Elman's recordings were issued both on 78rpm discs (and sets of discs) and on LP, we have included the original LP catalogue to the right of the 78rpm numbers. Obviously, several of the LP issues include older catalogue material. Not counting reissues on such RCA multi-artist compilations as "Magic Strings," the earliest of Elman's 78rpm era recordings to be retrospectively issued on early LPs were short selections the violinist recorded with Leopold Mittman between 1940 and 1946 (two years before the LP was invented). It is therefore at that point that we have included a separate column for LP catalogue numbers.

Generally, we have avoided listing RCA's 45rpm issues, but these are included (in the 78rpm column, with a notation) in cases where a recording was issued only in that format.

Pathé Records (Vertical Cut)

1905–1908 (?)
in Paris, with unidentified accompanist:

Arensky (arr. Elman):
    Serenade in G, Op. 30, No. 2   5398; 8073; 8503
Aulin:
    Humoresque   5396; 8072; 8506
Bach:
    Gavotte from Partita No. 3, BWV1006,   5397; 8072; 8505
Drigo (arr. Auer):
    Serenade   5397; 9547
Franck:
    Sonata in A (abridged)   9589/90
Rubinstein (arr. Wilhelmj):
    Melody in F   5395; 8074; 8509

Schubert (arr. Auer):
   Moment musical, f minor, D870/3   5398; 8074; 8502;
                                              K79942

Schubert (arr. Elman):
   Serenade, D957/4   8504

Schumann (arr. Joachim):
   Abendlied, Op. 85, No. 12   5396; 8071; 8507

Schumann (arr. Hullweck):
   Träumerei   8501; K77945

Gramophone & Typewriter / His Master's Voice / Victor / RCA: 1906–1952

Selection	Matrix/ Take	Catalogue Number

1906
in London, with Percy B. Kahn, pianist:

Sinigaglia:
   Capricio all' antica, Op. 25, No. 2;
   Bagatelle, Op. 25, No. 3   8148b   G&T 37943; 47960
                                                 HMV 3-7910

with unidentified accompanist:

Bohm:
   Perpetuum mobile, Op. 184, No. 4   8330-$^1/_2$b   G&T 37942; 47958
                                                 HMV 3-7908;
                                                 Victor 61184

Schubert:
   Moment Musical, D873/3   HMV 3-7908

Bohm:
   Gavotte, Op. 314, No. 6   HMV 3-7916;
                                                     Victor 61184

Wieniawski:
   Souvenir de Moscou, Op. 6   670c   G&T 07904; 047909;
                                                 037900;
                                              Victor 74051

Brüll:
   Scène espagnole, Op. 90, No. 1   724c   G&T 07907; 037904;
                                                 047912; HMV 4420

Tchaikovsky:
   Melodie, Op. 42, No. 3   725c   G&T 07905; 047910
                                                 Victor 74053

Chopin (arr. Sarasate):
    Nocturne in E-flat, Op. 9, No. 2   727c   G&T 07906; 037903;
                                              047911; HMV 4420;
                                            Victor 74052

Drdla:
    Souvenir   8741b   G&T 37911; 47959

Brüll:
    Souvenir   G&T 37954

Wieniawski:
    Fantasia on the Garden Scene
    from Gounod's Faust   8772b   G&T 37912; 37955;
                                              47961; Victor 61182

1907

Saint-Saëns:
    Introduction and Rondo capriccioso   2054f   G&T 07908;
                                              Victor 71038

Barnes:
    Swing Song   6654e   G&T 37957;
                                              HMV 3-7915;
                                            Victor 61183

1908
in London, with Percy B. Kahn, piano:

Dittersdorf (arr. Burmester):
    German Dance; &
    Gossec (arr. Elman): Gavotte   2356f   G&T 07909
                                            Victor 71039

Drigo (arr. Auer):
    Serenade   8877   G&T 37596;
                                            HMV 3-7914;
                                          Victor 61185

1910
in New York, with Percy B. Kahn, piano:

Dvořák:
    Humoresque   C 8799-2   74163 [1]

Tchaikovsky (arr. Elman):
    None But the Lonely Heart   C 8800[-1]   74178

---

[1]   Replaced by C8799-5 (recorded in 1911). Blue card indicates this
       number was "first made #2". Both were replaced by C8799-11
       (w. Bonime, 1919).

Sarasate:
 Caprice Basque   C 8801[-1] 74176
Beethoven:
 Minuet in G   B 8802-4 64121; 607-A
Mozart (arr. Auer):
 Gavotte in G   B 8803[-1] 64140
Wagner (arr. Wilhelmj):
 Prize Song, from Meistersinger C 8810[-1] 74186
Saint-Saëns:
 Introduction and Rondo Capriccioso C 8811[-1] 74165; (6089-A?)
Tchaikovsky:
 Melodie, Op. 42, No. 3   C 8812[-1] 74053
Wieniawski:
 Souvenir de Moscou, Op. 6   C 8814[-1] 74051; 6093-B
Schubert (arr. Elman):
 Serenade, D957/4   C 8798-2 74167
Chopin (arr. Sarasate):
 Nocturne in E-flat, Op. 9, No. 2 C 8813-2 74052; 6099-A
Dittersdorf (arr. Burmester):
 German Dance; &
 Gossec (arr. Elman): Gavotte   C 8820[-1] 74164; 6424-B
Drigo (arr. Auer):
 Serenade   B 8821[-1] 64123
Pente (arr. Elman):
 Les farfadets, Op. 12, No. 2   B 8822[-1] 64128
Haydn (arr. Burmester):
 Minuet in F   B 8823[-1] 64135
Wieniawski:
 Fantasia on the Garden Scene
 from Gounod's Faust   B 8824[-1] 64122

1911

in New York(?), with Percy B. Kahn, piano:

Schubert (arr. Elman):
 Wiegenlied   B 9870 unpublished
           (3 takes)
Kreisler:
 Andantino (Padre Martini); &
 Grétry (arr. Franko): Danse
 en rond (fr. Colinette à la cour) C 9875-1 unpublished

in Camden, New Jersey(?), with Percy B. Kahn, piano:
Kreisler:
 Siciliano (Francoeur)   C 9951-1 74308

Monsigny (arr. Franko):
Rigaudon   B 10406-1   64201; 606-A
Bach (arr. Wilhelmj):
Air on the G String   C 9871-3/M 74292
Mendelssohn (arr. Burmester):
"Capriccietto" (Canzonetta
fr. Quartet in E-flat, Op. 12)   B 9950-2   64204; 605-A
Schumann (arr. Hüllweck):
Träumerei   B 9952-2   64197 [2]
Pergolesi:
Aria tre giorno; &
Kreisler: Schön Rosmarin   C 10407-1   unpublished
Grétry (arr. Franko):
Gavotte; &
Gossek (arr. Burmester): Tambourin   B 10408-1   64198
Dvořák (arr. Elman):
Humoresque   C 8799-5   74163 [3]

1913

in New York, with Enrico Caruso, tenor; Percy B. Kahn, piano:
Kahn:
Ave Maria   C 13004-1   89065; 8007-B
Massenet:
Elégie   C 13005-1   89066; 8007-A

in Camden(?), with Percy B. Kahn, piano:
Raff:
Cavatina, Op. 85, No. 3   C 13183-2   74336; 6093-A
Schubert (arr. Wilhelmj):
Ave Maria   C 13184-2   74339; 6101-A
Massenet (arr. Marsick)
Méditation, from Thaïs   C 13186-2
/M   74361
Hummel (arr. Burmester):
Waltz in E-flat   B 13187-1   64336; 604-B

---

2   Catalogue number assigned to this take, but it is marked "D" in ledger
and was re-recorded in 1919 (with Bonime, piano) and issued with the
same number.
3   This take replaced C8799-2 from 1910.

1914

in Camden(?), with Percy B. Kahn, piano:

Sammartini (arr. Elman):
    Canto amoroso (Andante fr.
    Sonata, Op. 1, No. 4)   C 14680-1   74392; 6092-B
Schumann (arr. Auer):
    Vogel als Prophete   B 14682-1   64438
Brahms (arr. Joachim):
    Hungarian Dance No. 7   B 14683-1   64439; 597-A
Martini (arr. Burmester):
    Minuet   C 14684-1   74394 [4]
Vogrich:
    Dans le bois
    (based on 9th Paganini Caprice)   C 14685-1   74395; 6096-B

1915

in New York, with Enrico Caruso, tenor; Gaetano Scognamiglio, piano:

Denza:
    Si vous l'aviez compris!   C 15682-3   89084; 8008-A
Leoncavallo:
    Les deux sérénades   C 15683-2   89085; 8008-B

with Frances Alda, Soprano; Frank La Forge, piano:

Hollman:
    Chanson d'amour   C 15792-1   88521; 89128
Rabey:
    Dans tes yeux en pleurs   B 15793-1   87216; 87556;
                                         3030-A

Bach-Gounod:
    Ave Maria   C 15794-1   88522; 89129;
                                         8001-A

Braga:
    Angel's Serenade   C 15795-1   88523; 89130;
                                         8001-B

---

4   Blue card in file for this number. Label on reverse has Kahn's name. No
    other take traced. Presumably unissued.

in Camden(?), with Walter H. Golde, piano:

Michiels (arr. Elman):
    Nuit de mai   B   16589   destroyed [5]
Weber (arr. Elman):
    Contretanz in D   B   16591-1   64537; 598-B
Drdla:
    Valse
Gluck (arr. Wilhelmj):
    Mélodie   C   9872-1   74459; 6090-B
Sarasate:
    Romanze andaluza, Op. 22, No. 1   C   16607-3   74455; 6094-B
Haydn (arr. Burmester):
    Minuet in D   B   13188-2   64538; 607-B
Kreisler:
    Rondino   B   16685-3   64547; 611-A
Kreisler:
    Chanson Louis XIII et Pavane   C   13185-2   74340
Saint-Saëns:
    Introduction and Rondo Capriccioso   C   8811-4   74165; 6089-A [6]
Elman:
    In a Gondola (Impromtu)   B   16590-5   64530; 603-B
Wagner (arr. Wilhelmj):
    Prize Song, from Meistersinger   C   8810-4   74186; 6090-A [7]

1917
in Camden(?), with Phillip Gordon, piano:

Scarlatti (arr. Bridgewater):
    Pastorale (Sonata, L413)   B   18960-1   64636; 609-A
Scarlatti (arr. Burmester):
    Capriccio (Sonata, L375)   B   18961-1   64642; 602-B
Thomé:
    Simple aveu, Op. 25   C   18965-1   74515; 6097-A

---

5   Elman made five attempts to record this in 1915. All takes are marked
    "D" and he made no subsequent attempts to record it.
6   This take was intended to replace the earlier one from 1910; however,
    there is confusion as to its ultimate use. Both ledger and blue card list
    Golde as pianist, blue card also has the notation "Replaced 1916", but
    the single- and double-face labels filed with the blue card both list
    Kahn as pianist. At the time of publication, it had not been possible to
    audition the various pressings in search of enlightenment.
7   Replaced Take from 1910, w. Kahn.

Rissland:

Valse caprice, Op. 16	B	18962-3	64643; 604-A

Drdla:

Souvenir	B	18966-1	64644; 599-A

with orchestra, J. Pasternack, cond.:

Cui:

Orientale, Op. 50, No. 9	B	18963-2	64639; 599-B

in Camden(?), with the Elman String Quartet [Adolf Bak, violin; Karl Rissland, viola; Rudolf Nagel, cello]:

Dittersdorf:

Quartet No. 3 in G/Andante	C	19168-1	74525; 6102-A

Haydn:

Quartet in C, Op. 76, No. 3 "Emperor": Theme and Variations	C	19161-1	74516; 6103-A

Mozart:

Quartet, K421/Minuet	B	19170-2	64661; 612-A

Dittersdorf:

Quartet No. 5 in E-flat/Finale	B	19171-1	64671; 612-B

1918

with the Elman String Quartet (as above):

Schubert:

Quartet, D804/Minuet	C	21496-1	74574

Tchaikovsky:

Andante cantabile	C	21497-1	74575; 6103-B

Mozart:

Quartet, K428/Minuet	C	21498-1	74576; 6102-B

Schubert:

Andante con moto (unid.)	C	21499-1	unpublished

1919

in Camden(?), with Joseph Bonime, piano:

Beethoven (arr. Auer):

Turkish March, Op. 113, No. 4	B	22637-2	64915; 598-A

Albéniz (arr. Elman):

Tango in D, Op. 165, No. 2	B	22638-2	64821; 610-B

Rimsky-Korsakov (arr. Franko):

Hymn to the Sun	C	22639-1	74597; 6100-B

Chopin (arr. Wilhelmj):

Nocturne in D-flat, Op. 27, No. 2	C	22640-2	74590; 6099-B

Hummel:

Waltz in A	B	22644-1	64829; 610-A

Drigo:
| Serenade | B | 8821-9 | 64123; 600-B [8] |

Tchaikovsky (arr. Elman)
| None but the lonely heart | C | 8800-4 | 74178; 6091-B [9] |

Sarasate:
| Caprice Basque | C | 8801-3 | 74176; 6094-A [10] |

Bruch:
| Kol Nidre | C | 23443-1 | 74601; 6098-B |

Grieg (arr. Elman):
| Nocturne, Op. 54, No. 4 | C | 23441-4 | 74643; 6092-A |

Mendelssohn (arr. Kreisler):
Serenade (Song w/o Words,
| Op. 67, No. 6) | C | 23442-5 | 74607; 6096-A [11] |

Rubinstein (arr. Elman):
| "The Dew is Sparkling", Op. 72, No. 1 | B | 23435-3 | 64894; 605-B |
| | | | 3030-B |

Saenger:
| Scotch Pastorale, Op. 130, No. 2 | B | 23331-2 | 64884; 609-B |

Tchaikovsky:
| Melodie, Op. 42, No. 3 | C | 8812-3 | 74053; 6091-A [12] |

Massenet (arr. Marsick):
| Méditation, from Thaïs | C | 13186-3 | 74341; 6100-A |

Bach (arr. Wilhelmj):
| Air on the G String | C | 9871-5 | 74292; 6101-B |

Dvořák:
| Humoresque | C | 8799-11 | 74163; 6095-A [13] |

Wieniawski:
Fantasia on Garden Scene
| from Gounod's Faust | B | 8824-6 | 64122; 601-B [14] |

Schumann (arr. Hüllweck):
| Träumerei | B | 9952-7 | 64197; 600-A [15] |

Delibes (arr. Elman):
| Passapied | B | 23437-4 | 64903; 606-B |

---

8   Replaced B8821-1 (with Kahn) from 1910.
9   Replaced C8800-1 (with Kahn) from 1910.
10   Replaced C8801-1 (with Kahn) from 1910.
11   Creighton identifies the selection thus; however, ledger calls it a
     "Cradle Song" and credits Elman as the arranger.
12   Replaced C8812-1 (with Kahn) from 1910.
13   Replaced C8812-2 (1910) and -5 (1911), both with Kahn.
14   Replaced B8824-1 (with Kahn) from 1910.
15   Replaced B9952-2 (with Kahn) from 1911.

1921

in Camden, with Arthur Loesser, piano:

Moore (arr. Auer):			
The Last Rose of Summer	B	24778-2	64958; 608-A
Brahms (arr. Joachim):			
Hungarian Dance No. 17	B	24770-3	64977; 611-B
Lalo:			
Symphonie espagnole / Andante	C	24772-1	74771; 6089-B
Beethoven (arr. Elman):			
Contretanz No. 1 in C	B	23436-5	64968; 597-B

with orchestra, J. Pasternack, cond.:

d'Ambrosio:			
Canzonetta, Op. 6	B	25587-3	66008; 602-A
Popper:			
Wie einst in schönern Tagen,			
Op. 64, No. 3	B	25589-1	66099; 608-B
Ascher (arr. Elman):			
Alice, Where art Thou?	C	25590-3	74724; 6097-B
Gabriel-Marie:			
La cinquantaine	B	25588-6	66073; 603-A

with Arthur Loesser, piano:

Moszkowski (arr. Sarasate):			
Guitarre, Op. 45, No. 2	B	25591	unpublished

with Emmanuel Balaban, piano:

Anonymous (arr. Elman):			
Eili, Eili	C	25654-4	74732; 6098-A
Drdla:			
Serenade	B	25592-5	66048; 601-A

1923

in New York with Joseph Bonime, piano:

Millöcker (arr. Winternitz):			
The Blue Lagoon	B	24771-3	66144; 900-
Mozart:			
Ländler No. 1 in B-flat, K603	B	27691-2	66151; 900-
Schubert (arr. Elman):			
Serenade	C	8798-5	74167; 6095-B [16]

---

16   Replaced Take 2 (with Kahn) from 1910.

Mozart (arr. Friedberg):

Adagio (fr. Sonata, K282)	C	27690-4	74837; 6424-A

Rubinstein (arr. Bonime):

Romance in E-flat Op. 44, No. 1	B	28685-1	66205; 974-A

Tchaikovsky (arr. Auer):

Lenski's Aria (fr. Eugene Onegin)	C	28686	unpublished

Schindler:

Souvenir poétique (paraphrase on Fibich's Poem, Op. 41, No. 14)	B	28688-2	66206; 974-B

1924

in Camden(?), with Joseph Bonime, piano:

Schubert (arr. Franko):

Valse sentimentale	B	29888-3	1034-A

Nardini:

Unspecified sonata movement	C	29889	unpublished

Haydn (arr. Burmester):

Minuet in E-flat	B	30032-1	1060-A

Wagner (arr. Wilhelmj):

Albumblatt in C	C	29887-8	74892; 6457-A

Ries:

Gondoliera, Op. 34, No. 4	C	29890-6	74893; 6457-B

Ravina (arr. Piastro-Borissov):

Valse staccato, Op. 60, No. 3	B	29894-11	1034-B

Sammartini (arr. Elman):

"Canto amoroso" (Andante fr. Sonata, Op. 1, No. 4)	C	14680-2	74392; 6092-B [17]

Raff:

Cavatina, Op. 85, No. 3	C	13183-13	6093-A [18]

Wieniawski:

Souvenir de Moscou, Op. 6	C	8814-10	6093-B [19]

Rode (arr. Elman):

Etude caprice, Op. 22, No. 17	B	30611-1	1060-B

Bach (arr. Winternitz):

Minuet (unsp.)	B	31417	unpublished

Haydn (arr. Hartmann):

Minuet (unsp.)	B	31418	unpublished

Barbella (arr. Nachéz):

Larghetto	C	31419	unpublished

---

17 Replaced Take 1 (with Kahn) from 1914.
18 Replaced Take 2 (with Kahn, piano), from 1913. No single-sided issue.
19 Replaced Take 1 (with Kahn, piano), from 1910. No single-sided issue.

Kopylow (arr. Hartmann):
    To Slumberland, Op. 52, No. 9   B 31420-2   1079-B
Herbert:
    A la valse   B 31421-1   1079-A

Selection	*Catalogue Number*

1925

in Camden, with the Elman String Quartet [Edwin Bachmann, violin; Nicola Moldovan, viola; Horace Britt, cello] [Electrical Recording]:

Mozart:
    Quartet in B-flat, K458 "Hunt"   unpublished

1926

with the Elman String Quartet (L. Bailly replacing Moldovan as violist):

Mozart:
    Quartet in B-flat, K458 "Hunt"   unpublished

with Josef Bonime, piano:

Bonime:
    Danse hebraïque   unpublished
Arensky (arr. Elman):
    Serenade in G, Op. 30, No. 2   1434-B; 10-0018-B
Elman:
    Paraphrase on Deep River   unpublished
Friml (arr. Kramer):
    Au soir   1160-A
Cui (arr. Elman):
    Lettre d'amour, Op. 50, No. 21   1160-B

1927

in Camden, with the Elman String Quartet (1925 personnel):

Haydn:
    Quartet in D minor, Op. 76, No. 2/I   6701-A
Ditto/II   6701-B
Ditto/III   6702-A
Ditto/IV   6702-B
Haydn:
    Quartet in C, Op. 76, No. 3, "Emperor":
    Theme and Variations   6634-B

Tchaikovsky:
    Andante cantabile   6634-A

1928
in Camden, with Raymond Bauman, piano:
Dvořák:
    Humoresque   6836-A
Rachmaninoff (arr. Press):
    Vocalise, Op. 13, No. 14   1364-B
Barbella (arr. Nachéz):
    Larghetto   7654-A
Drdla:
    Souvenir   1354-A
Bach (arr. Wilhelmj):
    Air for the G String   7103-B
Schubert (arr. Elman):
    Serenade   7461-B
Sibelius l(arr. Frank):
    Valse triste   6836-B
Wieniawski (arr. Kreisler):
    Caprice (Etude alla saltarella, Op. 10., No. 5)   1364-A

in New York, with orchestra, Rosario Bourdon, cond.:
Cui:
    Orientale, Op. 50, No. 9   1354-B

1929
in New York, with Marcel van Gool, piano:
Schumann (arr. Hüllweck):
    Träumerei   1482-A

with Josef Bonime, piano:
Schubert (arr. Wilhelmj):
    Ave Maria   7103-A
Albéniz (arr. Elman):
    Tango in D   7195-A
Massenet (arr. Marsick):
    Méditation, from Thaïs   7392-A
Rimsky-Korsakov (arr. Franko):
    Hymn to the Sun   7392-B
Beethoven (arr. Elman):
    Minuet in G   1434-A; 10-0018-A

Gluck (arr. Sgambati):
    Mélodie   7654-B [20]
Raff:
    Cavatina, Op. 85, No. 3   7461-A
Wagner (arr. Wilhelmj):
    Albumblatt in C   7195-B

1930
in New York, with Carroll Hollister, piano:

Tchaikovsky:
    Mélodie, Op. 42, No. 3   HMV DA1143 [21]
Wieniawski:
    Legend, Op. 17   7649-B
Schubert (arr. Franko):
    Valse sentimentale   1482-B
Saint-Saëns:
    Le cygne   1592-A
Wagner (arr. Wilhelmj):
    Prize Song, from Meistersinger   7649-B
Nin:
    Sobre un aire de danza de Pablo Esteve   unpublished

in New York, with orchestra, Nathaniel Shilkret, cond.:

Tchaikovsky:
    Sérénade mélancolique, Op. 26   (Part 1) 7744-A
                                       (Part 2) 7744-B

in London, with Marcel van Gool, piano:

Sarasate:
    Zigeunerweisen   unpublished

1931
in New York, with Carroll Hollister, piano:

Drigo:
    Serenade   1538-A
Sarasate:
    Zigeunerweisen   (Part 1)   7780-A
                        (Part 2)   7780-B
Drdla:
    Serenade   1538-B

---

20 Sgambati credited on ledger as arranger; however, Creighton lists
    Wilhelmj.
21 No U. S. issue.

Handel (arr. Rissland):
    Largo   unpublished
Thomé:
    Simple aveu, Op. 25   HMV DA1232
                                              (no U. S. issue)
Warner:
    Serenade, Op. 20, No. 2   1567-A
Drdla:
    Sehnsucht, Op. 22, No. 8   1567-B

in London, with the New Symphony Orchestra, Lawrence Collingwood, cond.:

Vivaldi (arr. Nachéz):
    Concerto in G minor   7585/6

with Marcel van Gool, piano:

Ysaÿe:
    Rêve d'enfant, Op. 14   7574
Espejo:
    Airs tziganes   7574

1932
in New York, with Carroll Hollister, piano:

Vieuxtemps:
    Ballade et Polonaise, Op. 32   unpublished
Ravel:
    Pièce en forme de habanera   1592-B
Kreisler:
    Scherzo (Dittersdorf)   HMV DA1290
                                              (no U. S. issue)
Haydn (arr. Burmester):
    Capriccietto   HMV DA1290
                                            (no U. S. issue)
Perlman:
    A Birdling Sings (Ghetto Sketches, No. 2)   unpublished
Tchaikovsky (arr. Elman):
    None but the Lonely Heart   HMV DB1854
                                            (no U. S. issue)

in London, with orchestra, John Barbirolli, cond.:

Bach:
    Concerto in E, BWV1042   destroyed
    [Rejected ("records lack musical breadth of tone")]

in London, with unidentified orchestra and conductor:

Cui:
    Orientale, Op. 50, No. 9   unpublished
Scarlatescu:
    Bagatelle   destroyed
    [Rejected ("title not commercial")]

in London, with Herbert Dawson, organ:

Sulzer:
    Sarabande   HMV DB1853
                                   (no U. S. issue)

with orchestra, Lawrence Collingwood, cond.:

Beethoven:
    Romance No. 1 in G., Op. 40   HMV DB1846
                                   (no U. S. issues)

Beethoven:
    Romance No. 2 in F, Op. 50   HMV DB1847
                                   (no U. S. issue)

with Herbert Dawson, organ:

Handel:
    Largo   HMV DB1853
                                   (no U. S. issue)

with orchestra, John Barbirolli, cond.:

Bach:
    Concerto in E, BWV1042   HMV DB1871/2/3
                                   (no U. S. issue)

unaccompanied:

Bach:
    Preludio from Partita in E, BWV1006   HMV DB1873
                                   (no U. S. issue)

1939

in New York, with Hulda Lashanska, soprano; Emmanuel Feuermann, cello; Rudolf Serkin, piano:

Handel:
    Dank sei Dir, Herr (Arioso)   15365-A
Schubert:
    Litanie auf das Fest aller Seelen   15365-B

with Vladimir Padwa, piano:

Bloch:
    Nigun   Part I   11-8575-A
                Part II   11-8575-B
Mendelssohn (arr. Kreisler):
    May Breezes
    (Song without Words, Op. 62, No. 1)   2064-B
Dinicu (arr. Heifetz):
    Hora staccato   2064-A

Selection	Catalogue Numbers:	78rpm	LP

1940–1946

in New York, with Leopold Mittman, piano:

Kreisler:		
Preghiera (Padre Martini)	unpublished	
Ibert (arr. Hoeree):		
Le petit ane blanc	unpublished	
Brahms (arr. Joachim):		
Hungarian Dance No. 4	unpublished	
Tchaikovsky (arr. Koutzen):		
Russian Dance, Op. 40, No. 10	unpublished	
Fauré:		
Sonata No. 1 in A minor, Op. 13	M(DM)859 (set)	

with Leopold Mittman, piano:

Debussy:		
Sonata	M(DM)938 (set)	
Fauré (arr. Elman):		
Après un rêve	(in M(DM)938)	
Massenet (arr. Marsick):		
Méditation, from Thaïs	11-8950-A	LM 83
Dvořák:		
Humoresque	11-8950-B	LM 83
Achron (arr. Auer):		
Hebrew Melody, Op. 33	11-9111-A	
Sibelius:		
Mazurka, Op. 81, no. 4	11-9111-B	
Schumann (arr. Hüllweck*):		
Träumerei	10-1271-A	

*Hüllweck crossed out on ledger sheet w. notation "Saenger, per [?] Mohr's letter 2/14/47"

Grieg (arr. Hartmann):
    Album-leaf, Op. 28, No. 3   10-1271-B
Hubay:
    Hejre Kati, Op. 32, No. 4   11-9423-A
Balakirev (arr. Volpe):
    Oh, come to me   11-9423-B

1947
in Chicago, with the Chicago Symphony Orchestra, Desiré Defauw, cond.:

Mendelssohn:
    Concerto in E minor, Op. 64   M(DM)1196 (set)   LM 5
                                            LM 9024

1947–1951
in New York, with Wolfgang Rosé, piano:

Smetana:
    From My Home / Moderato   12-0241-B
Kreisler:
    Slavonic Fantasia in B minor
    (on themes of Dvořák)   12-0241-A
Mendelssohn (arr. Kreisler):
    May Breezes
    (Song w/o Wds, Op. 62, No. 1   12-0131 (in M1196)
Brahms:
    Sonata No. 3 in D minor, Op. 108   DM1232 (set)   LM 30
Drigo:
    Serenade   10-1491-A   LM 83
        (in DM1328)
Gossec (arr. Elman):
    Gavotte   10-1492-A   LM 83
        (in DM1328)
Cui:
    Orientale, Op. 50, no. 9   10-1491-B   LM 83
        (in DM1328);
        10-3299-A
Drdla:
    Souvenir   10-1493-A   LM 83
        (in DM1328);
        10-3299-B
Beethoven (arr. Burmester):
    Minuet in G   10-1493-B   LM 83
        (in DM1328)

Arensky (arr. Elman):
    Serenade, Op. 30, No. 2   10-1492-B   LM 83
                                      (in DM1328)
Handel:
    Sonata No. 15 in E   LM 1183
Handel:
    Sonata No. 14 in A   LM 1183
Handel:
    Sonata No. 13 in D   LM 1183
Paganini (arr. Elman):
    Caprice No. 24   unpublished
Smetana:
    From My Home / Andantino   HMV DA1942
                                        (no U. S. issue)

1950

in Philadelphia, with the Philadelphia Orchestra as Robin Hood Dell Orchestra, Alexander Hilsberg, cond.:

Wieniawski:
    Concerto No. 2 in D minor, Op. 22   DM1504 (set) LM 53

1951

in New York, with Wolfgang Rosé, piano:

Mozart:
    Sonata in B-flat, K454   LM 1208-A
Paganini (arr. Elman):
    Caprice No. 24   WDM1625
                                        (45 rpm)   LM 1208-B
Elman:
    Tango   49-3658-B
                                        (in WDM1625)
Kaminski:
    Recitative and Dance   unpublished

1952

in New York, with Joseph Seiger, piano

Tchaikovsky and Wieniawski Favorites   LM 1740
(Side 1)   Tchaikovsky:
    1.   (arr. Kreisler): Song without Words, Op. 2, No. 3
    2.   (arr. Wilhelmj): Scherzo, Op. 42, No. 2
    3.   (arr. Kreisler): Andante Cantabile
    4.   (arr. Grunes): Valse sentimentale, Op. 51, No. 6
    5.   (arr. Auer): Waltz from Serenade, Op. 48
    6.   (arr. Elman): None but the Lonely Heart

7.	(arr. Koutzen): Russian Dance, Op. 40, No. 10
(Side 2)	Wieniawski:
1.	Legend, Op. 17
2.	Mazurka in D, Op. 19, No. 12
3.	Mazurka in G minor, Op. 12, No. 2
4.	Mazurka in A minor, Op. 3
5.	Polonaise brillante in D, Op. 4

Brahms:
Sonata No. 2 in A, Op. 100   unpublished

Decca/London: 1953–1958

All performances are with Joseph Seiger, pianist, except where noted.
The catalogue numbers given are those of the American (London) issues and refer to 12-inch LPs. The sole exception is the Bruch Second
Concerto, with Fistoulari, which was issued on a 10-inch disc by Decca
in the United Kingdom, and was never issued in the United States. A
recording of the Mendelssohn Concerto from the same sessions
remains unreleased. All the recordings were made in London, and
were issued only in mono.

Tchaikovsky:
  Concerto in D, Op. 35   LL1073
  [with the London Philharmonic, Sir Adrian Boult, cond.]

Grieg Sonatas: LL1253
  No. 1 in F major, Op. 8
  No. 3 in C minor, Op. 45

Beethoven:
  Concerto in D major, Op. 61 (cadenzas: Elman)   LL1257
  [with the London Philharmonic, Georg Solti, cond.]

Beethoven Sonatas: LL1258
  No. 5 in F major, Op. 25 ("Spring")
  No. 9 in A Major, Op. 47 ("Kreutzer")

Mozart Concertos: LL1271
  No. 4 in D major, K218 (cadenzas: Joachim)
  No. 5 in A major, K219 (cadenzas: Joachim) "Turkish"

Mischa Elman Program   LL1467
  Korngold: Suite from Much Ado about Nothing
  Achron: Hebrew Melody
  Josten: Sonata
  Bloch: Ningun (Improvisation from Baal Shem)

(Concertos)   LL1486
  Bruch: Concerto No. 1 in G minor, Op. 26
  Wieniawski: Concerto No. 2 in D minor, Op. 22
  [with the London Philharmonic, Sir Adrian Boult, cond.]

(Sonatas)   LL1628
  Franck: Sonata in A major
  Fauré: Sonata No. 1 in A major, Op. 13

Mischa Elman Encores   LL1629
  Dvořák-Kreisler:
                Slavonic Fantasia
  Mendelssohn-Kreisler:
                Song Without Words No. 25 in G, Op. 62, No. 1
                (May Breezes)
  Miller: Cubanaise
  Kreisler: Liebeslied
  Elman: Tango
  Espejo: Airs Tziganes
  Sammartini-Elman:
                Canto Amoroso
  Wieniawski: Canson Polonaise
  Benjamin: From Santo Domingo
  Smetana: From My Homeland, No. 2: Vltava

Brahms Sonatas: LL1630
                No. 2 in A major, Op. 100
                No. 3 in D minor, Op. 108

Mischa Elman Recital   LL1631
  Sammartini-Nachez:
                Passacaglia
  Vitali-Charlier: Ciaccona
  Handel: Sonata No. 4 in D major
  Bach: Air on the G String
  Bruch: Concerto No. 2 in D minor   LW5290
  [with the London Symphony Orchestra, Anatole Fistoulari, cond.]
  (British Decca release only)

Vanguard: 1959–1967

Elman's Vanguard concerto recordings were made in Europe in a concentrated set of sessions in 1959, with Vladimir Golschmann conducting the Vienna State Opera Orchestra. The recital albums were recorded in New York, with Joseph Seiger at the piano. The The Vanguard recordings were issued in both mono and stereo; the catalogue numbers listed below are for the stereo issues only.

(Concertos)   VSD-2037
  Khachaturian: Concerto
  Saint-Saëns: Introduction and Rondo Capriccioso, Op. 28

(Concertos)   VSD-2047
  Mendelssohn: Concerto in E minor, Op. 64
  Lalo: Symphonie Espagnole, Op. 21

(Concertos)   VSD-2073
  Bach: Concerto No. 2 in E major, BWV 1042
  Nardini: Concerto in E minor
  Vivaldi: Concerto in G minor, Op. 12, No. 1

Elman Jubilee Record, Celebrating Fifty Years of Violinistic Triumph   VSD-2048
  Massenet: Méditation, from Thaïs
  Arensky: Serenade
  Schumann-Hullweck: Träumerei
  Cui: Orientale
  Drigo-Auer: Valse Bluette
  Sarasate: Zigeunerweisen
  Schubert-Wilhelmj: Ave Maria
  Dvořák-Wilhelmj: Humoresque
  Gossec-Elman: Gavotte
  Chopin-Sarasate: Nocturne
  Schumann-Auer: The Prophet Bird
  Beethoven-Burmester: Minuet in G
  Tchaikovsky: Melodie
  Sulzer: Sarabande

Caprice Viennois   VSD-2084
[reissued as *Mischa Elman Plays Kreisler Favorites,* Vanguard Everyman
Classics SRV 367 SD, and on CD, VBD 367]
  Kreisler: Liebesfreud
  Dvořák-Kreisler: Slavonic Dance No. 2
  Kreisler: Schön Rosmarin

Kreisler:	La Gitana
Kreisler:	Rondino on a Theme of Beethoven
Kreisler:	Caprice Viennois
Tartini-Kreisler:	Variations on a Theme of Corelli
Kreisler:	Preghiera in the style of Martini
Kreisler:	Allegretto in the style of Boccherini
Kreisler:	Sicilienne and Rigaudon in the style of Francoeur
Dvořák-Kreisler:	Slavonic Dance No. 1
Kreisler:	Praeludium and Allegro in the style of Pugnani

Hebraic Melodies   VSD-2137

Bonime:	Danșe Hebraïque
Bloch:	Ningun (Improvisation from Baal Shem)
Perlman:	Dance of the Rebbitzen
Chajes:	The Chassid
Goldfaden:	Raisins and Almonds
Achron:	Hebrew Melody
Elman:	Eili, Eili
Lavry:	Yemenite Wedding
Bruch:	Kol Nidre, Op. 47

The Art of Mischa Elman   VSD-71173

Dvořák-Kreisler:	Slavonic Fantasia
Tchaikovksy-Koutzen:	Russian Dance
Debussy-Roques:	La plus que lente
Gluck-Ries:	Largo
Kroll:	Juanita
Benjamin:	From San Domingo
Smetana:	From My Home
Fauré:	Berceuse
Kreisler:	La Precieuse in the style of F. Couperin
Espejo:	Aires Tziganes

Index